Global Ideologies Surrounding Children's Rights and Social Justice

Icarbord Tshabangu
Leeds Trinity University, UK

A volume in the Advances in Religious and Cultural Studies (ARCS) Book Series

IGI Global
DISSEMINATOR OF KNOWLEDGE

Published in the United States of America by
IGI Global
Information Science Reference (an imprint of IGI Global)
701 E. Chocolate Avenue
Hershey PA, USA 17033
Tel: 717-533-8845
Fax: 717-533-8661
E-mail: cust@igi-global.com
Web site: http://www.igi-global.com

Library of Congress Cataloging-in-Publication Data

Names: Tshabangu, Icarbord, 1968- editor.
Title: Global ideologies surrounding children's rights and social justice / Icarbord Tshabangu, editor.
Description: Hershey : Information Science Reference, [2018]
Identifiers: LCCN 2017006792| ISBN 9781522525783 (hardcover) | ISBN 9781522525790 (ebook)
Subjects: LCSH: Children's rights. | Social justice. | Education--Case studies.
Classification: LCC HQ789 .G586 2017 | DDC 323.3/52--dc23 LC record available at https://lccn.loc.gov/2017006792

This book is published in the IGI Global book series Advances in Religious and Cultural Studies (ARCS) (ISSN: 2475-675X; eISSN: 2475-6768)

British Cataloguing in Publication Data
A Cataloguing in Publication record for this book is available from the British Library.

All work contributed to this book is new, previously-unpublished material. The views expressed in this book are those of the authors, but not necessarily of the publisher.

For electronic access to this publication, please contact: eresources@igi-global.com.

Advances in Religious and Cultural Studies (ARCS) Book Series

Nancy Erbe
California State University-Dominguez Hills, USA

ISSN:2475-675X
EISSN:2475-6768

Mission

In the era of globalization, the diversity of the world and various cultures becomes apparent as cross-cultural interactions turn into a daily occurrence for individuals in all professions. Understanding these differences is necessary in order to promote effective partnerships and interactions between those from different religious and cultural backgrounds.

The **Advances in Religious and Cultural Studies (ARCS)** book series brings together a collection of scholarly publications on topics pertaining to religious beliefs, culture, population studies, and sociology. Books published within this series are ideal for professionals, theorists, researchers, and students seeking the latest research on collective human behavior in terms of religion, social structure, and cultural identity and practice.

Coverage

- Cultural Identity
- Globalization and Culture
- Cults and Religious Movements
- Sociology
- Politics and Religion
- Cross-Cultural Interaction
- Stereotypes and Racism
- Impact of Religion on Society
- Human Rights and Ethics
- Group Behavior

IGI Global is currently accepting manuscripts for publication within this series. To submit a proposal for a volume in this series, please contact our Acquisition Editors at Acquisitions@igi-global.com or visit: http://www.igi-global.com/publish/.

The Advances in Religious and Cultural Studies (ARCS) Book Series (ISSN 2475-675X) is published by IGI Global, 701 E. Chocolate Avenue, Hershey, PA 17033-1240, USA, www.igi-global.com. This series is composed of titles available for purchase individually; each title is edited to be contextually exclusive from any other title within the series. For pricing and ordering information please visit http://www.igi-global.com/book-series/advances-religious-cultural-studies/84269. Postmaster: Send all address changes to above address.

Titles in this Series

For a list of additional titles in this series, please visit: www.igi-global.com/book-series

Interpretation of Visual Arts Across Societies and Political Culture Emerging Research and Opportunities
Mika Markus Merviö (Kibi International University, Japan)
Information Science Reference • copyright 2017 • 110pp • H/C (ISBN: 9781522525547) • US $115.00 (our price)

Family Dynamics and Romantic Relationships in a Changing Society
Nava R. Silton (Marymount Manhattan College, USA)
Information Science Reference • copyright 2017 • 439pp • H/C (ISBN: 9781522524045) • US $215.00 (our price)

Creating a Sustainable Vision of Nonviolence in Schools and Society
Swaranjit Singh (California State University, USA) and Nancy D. Erbe (California State Education Vendor, USA)
Information Science Reference • copyright 2017 • 322pp • H/C (ISBN: 9781522522096) • US $195.00 (our price)

Multiculturalism and the Convergence of Faith and Practical Wisdom in Modern Society
Ana-Maria Pascal (Regent's University London, UK)
Information Science Reference • copyright 2017 • 397pp • H/C (ISBN: 9781522519553) • US $205.00 (our price)

Police Brutality, Racial Profiling, and Discrimination in the Criminal Justice System
Stephen Egharevba (University of Turku, Finland)
Information Science Reference • copyright 2017 • 372pp • H/C (ISBN: 9781522510888) • US $195.00 (our price)

Defending Human Rights and Democracy in the Era of Globalization
Christina Akrivopoulou (Hellenic Open University, Greece)
Information Science Reference • copyright 2017 • 422pp • H/C (ISBN: 9781522507239) • US $180.00 (our price)

Handbook of Research on Emerging Technologies for Architectural and Archaeological Heritage
Alfonso Ippolito (Sapienza University of Rome, Italy)
Information Science Reference • copyright 2017 • 647pp • H/C (ISBN: 9781522506751) • US $255.00 (our price)

Intercultural Relations and Ethnic Conflict in Asia
Swati Jaywant Rao Bute (AMITY University, India)
Information Science Reference • copyright 2017 • 236pp • H/C (ISBN: 9781522505822) • US $150.00 (our price)

IGI Global
DISSEMINATOR OF KNOWLEDGE

701 East Chocolate Avenue, Hershey, PA 17033, USA
Tel: 717-533-8845 x100 • Fax: 717-533-8661
E-Mail: cust@igi-global.com • www.igi-global.com

Table of Contents

Detailed Table of Contents

This study explored the prevalence and causes of child abuses e.g., physical, emotional, and sexual abuse of child domestic workers in Bangladesh. This study used a mixed method approach. Data sources were 849 child domestic workers, 849 house owners, and 15 development practitioners and experts. A household survey was carried out in three different areas in the Dhaka city. The study employed semi-structured interviews, focus group discussions (FGDs), and observation methods. The results showed that the prevalence of child abuses was very high and manifested physically, emotionally, and sexually among the studied child domestic workers. This was noted as a violation of Bangladesh law and of the United Nations Convention on the Rights of the Child (CRC). The findings of this study could be an important guideline to the policy makers, human rights practitioners, and international human and child rights organisations in seeking to alleviate these violations.

Child maltreatment in Zimbabwe is a pervasive and structural phenomenon that requires a grounded analysis to understand its drivers and impact. This chapter is focused on providing extensive literature review of work done focusing on child maltreatment in Zimbabwe. It provides an analysis of emerging patterns of child maltreatment in Zimbabwe, arguing that children are found within multiple and intersecting forms of discrimination. The social determinants outlined in this chapter are not mutually exclusive but rather reinforce each other. This makes the problem of child maltreatment complex and multifarious. Child maltreatment is variously described as any form (physical, emotional or symbolic) of abuse of a child or children. The paper discusses the intersection of various factors that cause child

prospects for most children. This chapter discusses child poverty and social inequalities since these aspects are critical to child development and welfare. An analytic review of World Bank and United Nations agencies data was conducted, consisting of existing surveyed data and literature on contemporary contexts in Sub-Saharan Africa. It was noted how inadequate investment levels; children's voicelessness and a lack of social security safety nets, has negatively impacted children's rights and development. Indications are that child poverty and other social inequalities continue to be experienced in most parts of the continent despite the economic rise in some of these emerging economies.

This chapter discusses social norms which purportedly condone "unpaid child labour" as a way of bringing up children, especially girls, in preparation for early marriage in the Maasai community in Kenya. International organisations such as the International Labour Office (ILO) and United Nations Children's Fund (UNICEF) view "unpaid child labour" as detrimental to children's education and welfare. Yet, in the Maasai culture, it is viewed as a way mothers prepare girls to be responsible married women from an early age. Findings revealed that the young educated Maasai girls and boys who are "agents of change" are actively engaged in sensitising their communities and advocating for the rights of girls, and women. The Chapter recommends that the Government of Kenya, international NGOs and stakeholders work together with agents of change in their communities to create awareness concerning children's rights.

This chapter outlines the results of an original pilot which investigated young British people's usage and opinions of social networking. The underpinning literature outlines psychological and neurological evidence that suggests young people's personalities are both fledgling and fragile, and that consequently, the online environment may be an inappropriate environment in which to engage in social processes that input to identity development due to the persistence, visibility, and spreadability of information that users commit to their profiles. The data gathered largely supported this thesis and additionally indicated that there may be a gender difference in orientation to online activity in early adolescence.

In this chapter, HIV and AIDS education for learners in Catholic schools was interrogated from a social justice perspective. The author advances the argument that the learners' right to access HIV and AIDS education in the school context was superficial in addressing the needs of learners. Hence, depriving them of the much needed knowledge, skills, and attitudes necessary for their survival in the context of HIV and AIDS. Therefore, this call for continued dialogue among different stakeholders in order to enable Catholic Schools play the 'social vaccine' role in the face of HIV and AIDS.

Students with significant emotional-behavioral concerns and mental illness tend to experience poor educational and social outcomes. This chapter describes some of the challenges facing schools that are responsible for educating students with and at-risk for mental health challenges. Although some students encounter numerous risks, thereby increasing the chances of developing mental illness and failing school, there are also protective factors that can be identified and harnessed to counterbalance such risks and promote higher levels of resilience. By examining relationships among factors such as poverty, mental well-being, family engagement, resiliency, and school performance, a school-focused, community-based framework is suggested for responding to and overcoming these challenges. This chapter provides practical guidelines for schools, community agencies, and families to work together to support and engage young people who are at-risk for school failure due to emotional-behavioral concerns and mental health challenges.

Global development discourse around the interplay between social justice and childhood issues are complicated when interpreting these ideas contextually through translocational gender and cultural lenses. This chapter attempted to address some of the following questions: How do international gender and education interventions problematize the transition for Maasai girls as they transition from childhood to adulthood? Can Amartya Sen's 'capability framework, work effectively for African children in Kenya who by their cultural norms become adults before the age of 18? In what ways are the social justice schemes producing disaggregated cultural structures for Maasai Girls? This chapter, therefore examined how Maasai girls' subjectivities are affected by gender and education rights mediation through Amartya Sen's 'capabilities approach' and a human rights framework. The experiences and perspectives of female subjects have seemingly been distorted within feminist and geopolitical rhetoric. Transnational feminism in this work is positioned as a postcolonial project that employs theories of human rights, capabilities, and multiculturalism as lenses in which to interrogate practices of erasures of voice and representation of active participants within the movement, but reconsider what feminist theory can do to move the conversation away from male-centric ideologies.

This chapter aims at developing a critique of the so-called "New Paradigm" of the sociology of childhood, which was developed in British sociological schools between the 1960s and 1980s. The New Paradigm represented a substantial challenge to mainstream sociology of childhood and from this basis, Childhood Studies were capable of producing influential thinking about childhood and practices involving childhood. The main idea of this chapter is that the New Paradigm cannot constitute an adequate theoretical basis for ensuring the fulfilment of children's lives in terms of freedom and social justice. Its central point, that childhood is socially constructed, is not articulated coherently and is internally inconsistent. Italian alternative pedagogical practices are used to provide a concrete backdrop for the theoretical objections raised against the New Paradigm. These alternative critical practices commonly assert that theory cannot be separated from practice and that ideals of social justice for children are based on the struggles of marginalised communities.

This chapter draws on a study which was conducted over a period of one and half years on orphans in Zimbabwe. While this chapter discusses extensive issues around resilience, survival and development of children, the highlights on their wellness are critically engaged with as well. The aim is to provide empirical insights to current and emerging debates on experiences of orphans especially from a developing country's perspective and Zimbabwe in particular. Drawing on the Ubuntu theory and the Wellness theory, the chapter consists of two sections. In section one; the chapter shall conceptualise the notions of Child Resilience, Survival and Development and further explore Ubuntu and Wellness through a theoretical lens. In section two there will be an in-depth discussion on issues around resilience, survival and development of orphans and how these are impacting their wellness.

Foreword

It is hard to imagine when might be a more significant time for us to be concerned about social justice and children's rights on a global scale than the present. Whilst these issues are always of concern, recent global events have given us pause to think much more closely about what we may have taken for granted in terms of political progress globally. Clearly, there are especially heartbreaking concerns about the plight of children amongst our refugee populations, and how their rights to asylum, safety and education are constantly violated as governments and dissident groups play out their disagreements through mass violence and political stalemate.

Recent decisions such as the Brexit vote in the United Kingdom and the election of Donald Trump in the USA, have taken much of the educated public (those who thought there had been global progress towards a more equitable and socially just society) by complete surprise. Such events have in fact highlighted huge chasms between different social and economic groups, and underscore the very real despair of people who have become more marginalised, impoverished and disempowered with the march of global capitalism. What of the dream of social justice, equality, and the demise of poverty?

Children, of course, are the most vulnerable group in this mix, and their experiences will differ greatly depending on their country and current events. Ironically, despite the many world events which threaten children's security and rights, the digital age ostensibly brings with it potential opportunities for children's learning and communication, not seen before. This book attempts to place these different aspects of what affects children's experiences in global context and to weigh up how their rights and social justice is affected in a contemporary context. It, therefore, tackles all the major issues: poverty, abuse, education, and the influence of the digital age. The chapters also cover a range of country contexts, contributing a sound in-depth study of specific issues, with a more transferable set of issues which are of concern to us who are involved with the rights and welfare of children: educators, care workers and professionals, policy makers and researchers. The chapters are written by a range of authors, all specialists in their specific fields, and constitute studies as well as essays and arguments on each of the important topics addressed. I do hope you find it an insightful read, and a stimulation to keep pursuing social justice and rights for children on a global scale.

Janis Fook
Leeds Trinity University, UK

Janis Fook *publishes broadly in social work and professional education, and has a particular interest in social justice and critical perspectives and reflection in higher education. Professor Fook is a social worker by original background and has held Chairs in Australia, Canada, and the UK.*

Preface

In view of liberal democratic advances in the 21st century, also buoyed by technological revolutions affecting most parts of the world, there is a philosophical struggle to reconstruct and understand childhood in ways that mirror the present challenges as well as paint a picture of emerging conceptions in different parts of the world.

Grier (2006) notes that:

The notion that children are passive and subordinate grows out of a twentieth century and western reconstruction of childhood as a time of dependence upon, nurturing from and guidance (control) by adults. It also grows out of an understanding of pre-colonial and pre-capitalistic African societies as rigidly hierarchical, unchanging and without tension or conflict particularly between generations. In both constructions, children are to be seen not heard. (p. 7)

Such a view of children marginalizes them and masks their location and influential role in societies. It silences their voices, sometimes causing them to rebel and pursue whatever action is necessary to emancipate themselves. In their daily struggles, some of them abusive and violent, children have persevered to improve the quality of their lifestyles, wherever they are located. Paternalistic tendencies abound where children are not only physically abused but are also seen as 'citizens to be' and not as 'current active citizens' who can be strategic partners in search for solutions both micro politically in their institutions and macro politically elsewhere.

This book was brought about by a desire to capture both, the philosophical and practical struggles children encounter in different parts of the globe, and shed light on how the conceptions and constructions of childhood could be shifting due to liberal democratic forces. Even though most countries in the world are signatory to the United Nations Declaration of Human Rights Charter, and the United Nations Convention on the Rights of the Child, children continue to be passed over as non-entities even on issues that directly affect them. Under such exploitative and discriminatory institutional arrangements, as shown in some of the chapters, children are directly and indirectly denied their rights in a world that largely perceive them as 'containers and receptacles' only to be filled by guardians, teachers and parents, having no right in shaping various processes and procedures around them.

INSIDE THIS BOOK

The book is organized into 15 chapters under five sections, and the brief descriptions are as follows: Section 1 on Child Abuses consists of Chapters 1-3, and Section 2 on Children's Socio-Economic Rights includes Chapters 4-6, while Chapter 7 is a standalone under Section 3 dealing with Children's Rights and Vulnerabilities in the Digital Age. Section 4 on Childhood and Multi-Dimensional Rights in Education comprise Chapters 8-12, and Section 5 on Understanding and Confronting Social Injustice in Childhood comprise of Chapters 13-15.

Chapter 1 identifies and explores the prevalence and causes of child abuses in Bangladesh. These are recorded as physical, emotional, and sexual abuse of child domestic workers. Drawing from large study samples the results showed that the prevalence of child abuses was very high and manifested physically, emotionally, and sexually among the studied child domestic workers. This was noted as a violation of Bangladesh law and of the United Nations Convention on the Rights of the Child (UNCRC). The findings of this study provide an important guideline for policy makers, human rights practitioners, not just in Bangladesh but in other areas similarly affected.

Chapter 2 provides a comprehensive analysis and grounded understanding of the social determinants of child abuse and maltreatment in Zimbabwe. These social determinants of child abuses are multiple, varied and intertwined. Based on a systematic review of the literature the chapter highlights factors that leave children vulnerable to abuse. It is also noted that various forms of child abuses tend to increase in line with a country's economic downturn. The low status granted to children in most societies makes them the most vulnerable groups of people. They have neither the power nor the means to ensure their protection and realisation of their full growth and potential without the state or parental support. The chapter advances a view that the 'silences of childhood' promoted by cultural and religious practices steeped in patriarchal norms, require systematic revisiting, to find best ways of combating violence against children.

Chapter 3 takes a considered view on child abuse from a human rights perspective. Violence against children is a profound violation of human rights that has far-reaching consequences for children's well-being. The chapter observes that experiences of violence and abuse can lead to lasting physical, mental, and emotional harm, regardless of whether a child is a direct victim or witness. While these chapter focuses on Botswana, it is noted that violence against children cuts across geographic boundaries, culture, race, class, religion, educational and socio-economic backgrounds. This chapter analyzed the complex and multifaceted nature of violence against children in Botswana, noting the types and contexts of violence that children are exposed and the effects these have on children.

Chapter 4 observes that children around the globe are confronted with numerous social welfare issues that adversely affect their wellbeing. These issues differ across countries and regions. The chapter explores childhood social welfare issues in Botswana, illuminating the ideological differences between traditional and more contemporary conceptualizations of childhood. Because children's issues are currently so myriad and complex, this chapter focuses primarily on HIV and AIDS-related orphanhood, alcohol and substance abuse manifesting in traumatic events in the lives of children. The chapter demonstrates, that while several commendable efforts have been undertaken by stakeholders to address social welfare issues in childhood, a lot more still needs to be done to improve the quality of life for most vulnerable children.

Chapter 5 provides a qualitative deconstruction of child poverty in Sub Saharan Africa, highlighting the depth of the crisis and the possible causes. The chapter observes that many children have continually experienced poor attainment levels and dim prospects in life and that child poverty and inequalities in education need address since these are critical to social mobility and national socio-economic growth. The chapter ascertains that child poverty is largely due to inadequate investment levels; corruption; overdependence on foreign aid; lack of access to resources; women marginalization and poor political motives.

Chapter 6 discusses social norms which purportedly condone "unpaid child labour" as a way of bringing up children, especially girls, in preparation for early marriage in the Maasai community in Kenya. international organisations such as the International Labour Office (ILO) and United Nations Children's Fund (UNICEF) view "unpaid child labour" as detrimental to children's education and welfare. The chapter interrogates the Maasai culture, while also noting that the young educated Maasai girls and boys who are "agents of change" that are actively engaged in sensitising their communities and advocating for the rights of children, girls, and women.

Chapter 7 outlines the results of an original pilot which investigated young British people's opinions on the usage of social networking. The underpinning literature outlines psychological and neurological evidence that suggests young people's personalities are both fledgling and fragile, and that consequently, the online environment may be an inappropriate environment, especially for children. This online environment provides for engagement in social processes that input to identity development due to the persistence, visibility, and spreadability of information that users commit to their profiles. Several vulnerabilities are noted.

Chapter 8 focuses on HIV and AIDS education for learners in Catholic schools, and interrogates this arrangement from a social justice perspective. Children in Zambian experience challenges such as living in households where there is AIDS, and that loved ones may have died as a result. Left without parents some children manage households, care for other children, face labour exploitation and defilement, and forced early marriages. The chapter highlights the importance children's rights to adequate AIDS education and free access to valuable information on health care.

Chapter 9 deals with students who have significant emotional-behavioral concerns and mental illness and these students tend to experience poor educational and social outcomes. The chapter describes some of the challenges facing schools, that are responsible for educating students with and/or at-risk of mental health challenges. Although some students encounter numerous risks, thereby increasing the chances of developing mental illness and failing school, there are also protective factors that can be identified and harnessed to counterbalance such risks and promote higher levels of resilience. By examining relationships among factors such as poverty, mental well-being, family engagement, resiliency, and school performance, a school-focused, community-based framework is suggested for responding to and overcoming these challenges.

Chapter 10 discusses generic concepts on global development discourse around the interplay between social justice and childhood issues. These are complicated when interpreting the ideas contextually through translocational gender and cultural lenses. This chapter addresses some of the following questions: How do international gender and education interventions problematize the transition for Maasai girls as they transition from childhood to adulthood? In what ways are the social justice schemes producing disaggregated cultural structures for Maasai Girls? The chapter, therefore examined how Maasai girls' subjectivities are affected by gender and education rights mediation and human rights frameworks.

Chapter 11 presents the notion of 'intelligent agents'. The chapter opens with a broad statement that coins the social justice and inclusion mantra as prominent concepts and lays a foundation by giving a clear background using a South African context where there is a gap between the policy and implementation of social justice and inclusion in mainstream schools.

Chapter 12 explores the socioeconomic status of learners which has implications for research and the provision of mathematics education. Literature has shown that learners from a disadvantaged socioeconomic background begin their education with a gap. Hence, a lot of research advocates for quality early childhood stimulation, which aims to close such gaps. The challenges faced by school provision include; inequities and poor quality education in some schools, which has implications on children's educational rights.

Chapter 13 observes that language and identity are inextricably intertwined. Over the years, countless Hispanic students have been categorized dichotomously in schools in ways that marginalize their language practices and restrict their evolving identities. American public schools often unjustly force Hispanic students to deny who they are, stripping them of the ability to retain their self-claimed identity and linguistic freedom. This common practice in American schools is nothing short of social injustice. This chapter illuminates more deeply an understanding of Hispanic youth's experiences in schools and examines closely through analysis of classroom discourse and interaction the identities and ideologies that come into play in mixed classrooms.

Chapter 14 aims at developing a critique of the so-called 'New Paradigm' of the sociology of childhood, which was developed in British sociological schools between the 1960s and 1980s. The New Paradigm represented a substantial challenge to mainstream sociology of childhood and from this basis, childhood Studies were capable of producing influential thinking about childhood and practices involving childhood. The main idea of this chapter is that the New Paradigm cannot constitute an adequate theoretical basis for ensuring the fulfilment of children's lives in terms of freedom and social justice. The central point is that childhood is socially constructed, is not articulated coherently and internally inconsistent. Italian alternative pedagogical practices are used to provide a concrete backdrop for the theoretical objections raised against the New Paradigm.

Chapter 15 draws on a study which was conducted over a period of one and half years on orphans in Zimbabwe. While this chapter discusses extensive issues around resilience, survival and development of children, the highlights on their wellness are critically engaged with as well. The chapter's aim is to provide empirical insights to current and emerging debates on experiences of orphans especially from a developing country's perspective. Drawing on the Ubuntu theory and the Wellness theory, the chapter conceptualises the notions of Child Resilience, Survival and Development and further explores Ubuntu and Wellness through a theoretical lens and how the wellness of orphans is linked or impacted.

CONCLUSION

The chapters in this book have addressed various issues on children's rights and social justice, with a view to mirror global experiences from different contexts and further bring about deeper understanding of existing trends and challenges in our conceptions of childhood in a dynamic world. Furthermore, the chapters provide in-depth discussions and relevant theoretical understanding from multiple global contexts on social justice and children's rights. This collaborative approach undoubtedly advances the sharing of knowledge in various aspects of childhood, in ways that explore and enhance both theory and practice, particularly for those working with children in different settings. The chapters also provide opportunities for shared solutions, especially in areas of policy development. It is hoped that the issues raised in this book will further inspire more debate and research on the conceptions of childhood and children's rights from a global worldview.

Icarbord Tshabangu
Leeds Trinity University, UK

REFERENCE

Grier, B. C. (2006). *Invisible hands: Child labour and the state in colonial Zimbabwe*. Portsmouth, UK: Heinemann.

Acknowledgment

The editor would like to acknowledge the help of all the people involved in this project and, more specifically, the editorial board members, and the reviewers that took part in the review process. Their valuable contributions helped in the improvement of quality, coherence, and content presentation. Without their support, this book would not have become a reality.

Finally, the editor would like to thank each one of the authors for their tremendous contributions through committing their time and expertise to this book, including some of the authors who also served as referees and their double task is highly appreciated.

Section 1
Child Abuses

Chapter 1
Abuse Among Child Domestic Workers in Bangladesh

M. Rezaul Islam
University of Dhaka, Bangladesh & University of Malaya, Malaysia

ABSTRACT

This study explored the prevalence and causes of child abuses e.g., physical, emotional, and sexual abuse of child domestic workers in Bangladesh. This study used a mixed method approach. Data sources were 849 child domestic workers, 849 house owners, and 15 development practitioners and experts. A household survey was carried out in three different areas in the Dhaka city. The study employed semi-structured interviews, focus group discussions (FGDs), and observation methods. The results showed that the prevalence of child abuses was very high and manifested physically, emotionally, and sexually among the studied child domestic workers. This was noted as a violation of Bangladesh law and of the United Nations Convention on the Rights of the Child (CRC). The findings of this study could be an important guideline to the policy makers, human rights practitioners, and international human and child rights organisations in seeking to alleviate these violations.

INTRODUCTION AND BACKGROUND

Child abuse is a complex social challenge that cannot be understood from a single disciplinary perspective (Davidov et al., 2016). The first recognisable child abuse society was instituted in the late 19th century in North America, but it was a century before the first global rights-based legislation in the form of the United Nations Convention on the Rights of the Child (UNCRC) came into play (Cutland, 2012). According to recent global data, more than one in four children worldwide reported having experienced severe and frequent physical abuse, while child sexual abuse was experienced by nearly one in five females and one in eleven males (UNICEF, 2012). The World Health Organization (2010) states that approximately 20% of women and 5–10% of men report being sexually abused as children, while 25–50% of all children report being physically abused. Child abuse has vast consequences include impaired lifelong physical and mental health, and the social and occupational outcomes can ultimately slow a country's economic and social development. This has profound and damaging consequences during childhood and

DOI: 10.4018/978-1-5225-2578-3.ch001

adolescence and throughout adult life. Children who have experienced abuse or neglect are more likely to have poorer physical and/or mental health outcomes; social difficulties, such as insecure attachments with caregivers and problematic relationships with peers, and as adults later in life; cognitive dysfunction, attributable to the negative impact of excessive stress on brain development; high-risk behaviours, such as drug and alcohol abuse, early sexual activity and resulting teenage parenting; and behavioural problems, including aggression and adult criminality (UNICEF, 2012).

There is neither profound nor recognised statistics about the number of child domestic workers in the world as well as in Bangladesh. According to the International Labour Organization (2016), there are 17.2 million children in paid or unpaid domestic work in the home of a third party or employer in the world. Of these, 11.5 million are in child labour, of which 3.7 million are in hazardous work, of which 21.4% are child domestic workers.; It is noted that 67.1% of all child domestic workers are girls, and 65.1% of all child domestic workers are below the age of 14 years old and 7.4 million aged 5 to 11 years and 3.8 million aged 12 to 14 years. On the other hand, according to the most up to date estimates, over 52 million children in the world are employed as domestic workers. Nearly 44 million of these children are girls (International Labour Organization, 2012, Gamlin et al., 2015). In Bangladesh, there is no recent data on the number of child domestic workers. According to a Baseline Survey (BBS, 2006), there are approximately 400,000 child domestic workers aged 6-17 years old in Bangladesh. There are total 331,000 domestic workers, and the number of child domestic workers are 420,000. Among them, 83% are female, who are mostly child and young in age. On the other hand, the UNICEF (2006) reported that there are 7.4 million people are working in the informal sector, as many as 421 thousand children aged between 6-17 years are working as domestic help, of which around 132,000 are in Dhaka City alone. Child domestic work is a common phenomenon in Bangladesh. Employing children as domestic workers is socially and culturally accepted in Bangladeshi society (Islam, 2013; UNICEF, 2012). Many of these children live and work under conditions that are so extreme, exploitative and abusive that no adults would accept. As child domestic workers belong to the informal labour sector, they are excluded from legal protection, which makes them even more vulnerable (Islam, 2013; Islam, 2010).

A number of international and national policies, conventions, and laws are active to combat domestic child abuse. However, incorporating and implementing the UNCRC and other child protection based legislations on a global scale is not without difficulty and there are many obstacles to fulfilling its principles and monitoring its progress (Cutland, 2012). In addition, domestic work is a predominately female-dominated sector that is poorly regulated and often unprotected by labour law. It is also often embedded within sociocultural structures, which may make it difficult for employers to see themselves as such. Child domestic workers themselves often work long hours; have poor remuneration and little access to social protection. Their isolation and vulnerability as workers is made more complex by their invisibility in private homes and their dependence on the good will of their employers (Islam, 2013). Many, though not all, come from poor households, often in rural communities, where limited access to education and skills development, leave them with few employment opportunities and choices. They are prone to verbal, physical and sexual violence, and the impact of this abuse can leave permanent scars (Flores-Oebanda, 2006). Kane (2004) and Islam (2013) argued that the exploitation of the child domestic workers is extreme and includes trafficking, slavery or practices similar to slavery, or work which by its nature or the circumstances in which it is carried out is hazardous and likely to harm the health, safety or morals of children, then this constitutes the worst form of child domestic labour, and it needs to be tackled as a matter of urgency. This study attempts to explore the prevalence and course of child abuses among the child domestic workers in Bangladesh. To consider the socioeconomic and cultural contexts, and multiple negative impacts on these children, this study has significant value in Bangladesh.

LITERATURE REVIEW: CONCEPTS AND THEORIES

This study underpins two main concepts e.g., child domestic worker and child abuse. The Children Act, 2013 (officially known as *Shishu Ain 2013*) in Bangladesh defines children as less than 18 years old. According to the Bangladesh Bureau of Statistics, child workers are defined as children in the age group of 5–14 years who were found to be working during the survey reference period (Salmon, 2005). In Bangladesh, the official term for 'child labour' is *shishu srom*, particularly relevant to children employed in the official economy, while *kaj* denotes work done by children in the household or the informal economy. To qualify as a worker, children must be *sromik* (workers/labourers) (Haider, 2008). Child domestic work is a general reference to children's work in the domestic work sector in the home of a third party or employer (Islam, 2013; ILO, 2016). This general concept encapsulates both permissible as well as non-permissible situations. According to the International Labour Organization (2016), child domestic labour refers to domestic work undertaken by children under the legal minimum working age, as well as by children under the age of 18 under. Wilson-Oyelaran (1989) considered this kind of child labour as the exploitative child labour that is defined by both or only one of the conditions- i) the work performed by children under 15 years of age interferes with their developmental, health, and educational needs; ii) the child is not remunerated adequately for his/her labor, has no access to his/her remuneration, or no decision-making role in the determination of how the remuneration will be used. Islam (2013) mentioned child domestic workers who belong to the informal labour sector, they are excluded from legal protection, which makes them even more vulnerable. In general, child domestic labour refers to 'situation where children are engaged to perform domestic tasks in the home of a third party or employer that are exploitive' (Islam, 2013).

The concept child abuse remains problematic and this is largely due to the difficulty of making reliable predictions about the 'abusive' potential of actions/experiences. The attribution of meaning, whether of abusive 'intention' in the perpetrator or of 'harm' experienced by the supposed victim, is central to this (Maitra, 1996). Child abuse has different meanings for different cultures (Korbin, 1991; Meinck et al., 2015). Culture has a tremendous impact on child-rearing practices and the value placed on children. Each culture has its own unique norms around this issue (Feng et al., 2005). Many individuals have argued that child abuse refers to physical harm only (Parke and Collner, 1975). Others argue that all forms of child maltreatment (for example, emotional abuse and child labour) constitute child abuse (Alvy, 1975). Gil (1975) argues that any action which impedes a child's development should be considered abuse. This paper showed child domestic workers' abuse in three different categories such as physical, emotional, and sexual. Physical abuse involves inflicting bodily injury through excessive force or forcing a child to engage in a physically harmful activity, such as excessive exercise. Emotional abuse is coercive, demeaning, or overly distant behaviour by a parent or other caretaker that interferes with a child's normal social or psychological development. Sexual abuse includes the inappropriate exposure of a child to sexual acts or materials, the passive use of children as sexual stimuli for adults, and actual sexual contact between children and older people (Wissow, 1995).

Child abuse and its related problems have significant negative impacts on children's body, mind, and their culture. The processes, causes, and possible exploitations of child abuse among child domestic workers are far different than the normal child abuse in the society. A problem for this informal sector is that it is always the adults who make the decisions on the fate of child domestic workers and when the children are in the employers' household, they live under the overall control of the employers. In these circumstances, the children have no opportunity to make their own choice or decision (Save the Children Sweden-Denmark, 2010). Most of them live in their employer's home. They are dependent on the good or bad will of their employer (Islam and Cojocaru, 2016; Islam, 2013). When children are forced to work, they are often denied their rights to education, leisure, and play. They are also exposed to situations that make them vulnerable to trafficking, abuse, violence, and exploitation. Millions of children are reported not to attend school; however, estimates vary (UNICEF, 2012). Another important aspect is that domestic work is a predominately female-dominated sector that is poorly regulated and often unprotected by labour law (Islam, 2013). Varia and Becker (2012), and Islam and Cojocaru (2016) reported that the gaps in legal protection, isolation in private homes, and social norms that have sanctioned exploitation of a 'servant' class have given rise to abuses ranging from endemic labour exploitation, in which workers toil around the clock for little or no pay, to trafficking; domestic servitude and slavery. The Human Rights Watch (2007) has recorded physical violence against domestic workers ranging from slaps to severe beatings using implements such as shoes, belts, sticks, electrical cords, or household tools; knocking heads against walls, and burning skin with irons or chemicals. In some cases, physical abuse is so severe it has led to paralysis, blindness, or even death.

The consequences of child domestic workers are multiple. Gamlin et al., (2015) stated that because child domestic workers are hidden from view, the degree of harm to which they are exposed is not clear. Regulations to protect child domestic workers are extremely difficult to enforce because the workplace is a private dwelling, effectively giving the employer total control over the person in their 'service', consequentially domestic workers are uniquely vulnerable. A number of qualitative studies such as Blagbrough (2008); Jacquemin (2004); Black (2005); Bourdillon (2010); and Gamlin et al., (2015) mentioned that young women and men working in domestic employment are exposed to physical, psychological, verbal and sexual abuse, are 'treated worse than dogs', usually work extremely long hours and feel intensely subordinated to their employer. Davidov et al., (2016), and the UNICEF (2006) and BBS (2006) mentioned that child abuse is composed of multiple foci and is not a singular homogeneous domain. The contextual factors represent the broader social systems that influence parental functioning, including microsystem factors representing the social or cultural forces that contribute to and sustain abuse or neglect. Petersen et al., (2014) found a number of consequences such as the abused children having a disability, parental psychopathology, early childbearing, low socioeconomic status, and social beliefs about discipline and corporal punishment

The UNICEF (2012) conducted a systematic review of research to examine 364 peer-reviewed and grey literature research studies on the prevalence and incidence of child physical abuse, sexual abuse, emotional abuse, neglect, exploitation, witnessing family violence and peer-to-peer violence as well as the consequences of child maltreatment across five categories including: education and employment, mental health, physical health, aggression, violence, and criminality and other consequences in the East Asia and Pacific Region. The Human Rights Watch (2007) conducted another study on exploitation and abuse of girl domestic workers in Guinea and documented how girls as young as 8 years old work up to 18 hours a day as domestic workers, frequently without pay, and are often insulted, beaten and raped by their employers.

A number of studies in Bangladesh investigated the contextual aspects of the child domestic workers. Hossain (2000) found that among 1,000 girl domestic workers in Dhaka, two-thirds were 11-13 years of age. Haider (2008) argued that in Bangladesh, the social perspective perceives children's work with regard to social rather than economic contexts. This approach conceptualises child labour as a problem of social exclusion, leading to work that exploits children. Salmon (2005) found that one-half of all child workers live in a household where all the adults work. He mentioned only 3% of incomes in Bangladesh are earned by children – somewhat lower than the 5% contribution of their mothers. He argued that these figures hide large disparities depending on the level of income of the household and the engagement of children in income-generating work. Bissell (2001) and Delap (2001) argued that in Bangladesh, after bans on child garment labour, many child workers moved into unsafe activities, e.g. domestic service, hawking flowers and candy, begging, brick breaking, and sex work. UNICEF (2010), and Islam (2013) found that social norms and economic realities are widely accepted and very common in Bangladesh. As a result, many families rely on the income generated by their children for survival, so child labour is often highly valued. Additionally, employers often prefer to employ children in Bangladesh as household workers because they are cheaper and considered to be more compliant and obedient than adults. The International Labour Organization (2016) permits the ages 15-17 can take at least 43 hours of economic or domestic work per week, though the application of this rule is violated across the country due to the contextual reality.

The objective and conceptual framework of this study has a strong theoretical base. The studies investigating risk and protective factors for child abuse primarily use Bronfenbrenner's Ecological Model of Human Development (Bardi and Borgognini-Tarli, 2001; Bronfenbrenner, 1979). The ecological model (Belsky, 1980) attempts to fuse the findings of these earlier perspectives to develop a more unified explanation of child mistreatment. Based on Brofenbrenner's (1979) ecology of human development, the model proposes that child abuse and neglect can only be understood if it is analyzed from a perspective which incorporates the previously disparate levels of analysis, namely the individual, the family, the social environment, and the cultural milieu, and also examines the dynamic interactions both between and within each level (Meinck et al., 2015). However, this study has a great relevance with the ecological model. According to this model, the cumulative and counterbalancing effects of risk and protective factors within and across spheres, depending on their severity and strength, may lead to or prevent child abuse (Belsky, 1980; WHO, 2002). Wilson-Oyelaran (1989) mentioned that in ecological theory, certain biological and psychological characteristics when combined with a specific type of behavioural history may influence an individual to abuse or to be abused. This ecological theory offers a valuable outline to observe the risk and protective factors for child abuse among domestic workers in Bangladesh. However, few studies examined such factors within Bangladesh context, and a comprehensive review of risk and protective factors has not been previously conducted. This study explores child domestic workers physical, emotional, and sexual abuses in Bangladesh.

LAWS, POLICIES, AND ARENAS OF CHILD DOMESTIC WORKERS

Bangladesh has several laws regarding children's work in specific sectors. The government has ratified the UNCRC and the ILO Convention on the Worst Forms of Child Labour. The Children Act, 2013 has been enacted for the purpose of implementing the United Nations Convention on the Rights of the Child. The country has the 'Domestic Servants' Registration Ordinance of 1961 that requires domestic servants to register themselves with the police station, but this law does not delineate any rights and privileges for domestic workers nor does it define the obligations of employers. The Bangladesh Labour Act 2006 includes the minimum age for admission to work is 14 years and 18 years for hazardous work provides many regulations related labour. Other laws are also functioning in Bangladesh such as the Employment of Children Act (No. 26 of 1938), (as amended 1974), Factories Act, 1965 (No. 4 of 1965), Factories Rules, 1979, Mines Act, 1923 (No. 4 of 1923), Tea Plantations Labour Ordinance, 1962 (No. 39 of 1962) (as amended), Road Transport Workers Ordinance, 1961 (No. 18 of 1961), Shops and Establishments Act, 1965 (No. 7 of 1965), Children (Pledging of Labour) Act, 1933 (No. 11 of 1933), and Compulsory Primary Education Act, 1990 (education compulsory for children ages 6-10). But the domestic workers are devoid of any formal mechanism for effectively enforcing their rights. Basic education is often a prerequisite for participation in society. Even though primary education, e.g., grades 1 to 5, is free and has been compulsory for children aged 6-10 years since 1993 in Bangladesh, the law is not enforced, and many poor children in Bangladesh are deprived of their right to education. When child participation becomes institutionalised, children are able to participate in forums for exchanging experiences, raising public awareness, and even for policy dialogue. However, there is no forum in Bangladesh for domestic workers.

In the last several years, the government, through the Ministry of Women's and Children's Affairs, together with BSAF (Bangladesh Shishu Adhikar Forum), Save the Children, and UNICEF, has provided lots of supports to the child domestic workers in Bangladesh. The Ministry of Women and Children Affair Bangladesh formulated the National Plan of Action for Children (NPA) (2004-2009) and included child development such as health, food and nutrition, protection, education, and physical environment. The Save the Children has been successful in making the government include children in the policy formulation process. A Child right has also been practised in the formulation of the National Plan of Action against Sexual Abuse and Exploitation of Children including Trafficking. A National Children 's Task Force was established for children to provide input and to monitor the implementation of the plan. Finally, the government adopted National Child Policy 2010, which included different aspects such as preventive and primitive aspects of child health; nutrition for infants and children in the pre-school age along with nutrition for nursing and expectant mothers; maintenance, education and training of orphan and destitute children; facilities for the care of children of working or ailing mothers; and care, education, training and rehabilitation of handicapped children.

Bangladesh joined the ILO in 1972 and ratified several conventions. The Convention No. 138 concerning the minimum age for employment has not yet been ratified. However, Bangladesh ratified the UN Convention on the Rights of the Child in 1989, and Convention No. 182 on the Worst Forms of Child Labour in 2001, demonstrating its commitment to the compliance with child rights and the elimination of hazardous child labour. Other significant conventions ratified by Bangladesh include the ILO Convention No. 29 on Forced Labour and Convention No. 105 on Abolition of Forced Labour. The Convention 182 states that ratifying countries should take immediate action to secure the prohibition and elimination of the worst forms of child labour and determine the hazardous activities by national laws or regulations.

METHODOLOGY

Research Objective

The general objective of this study was to explore the prevalence and course of child abuse (e.g., physical, emotional, and sexual) among the child domestic workers in Bangladesh. The specific objectives were to-

1. Know the prevalence of child abuse among the domestic child workers, and
2. Investigate the course of child abuse among the domestic child workers.

Research Methodology

The study used a mixed method approach consisting of both qualitative and quantitative research. The fundamental rationale behind this mixed method was to combine the strengths of qualitative research with the quantitative research. The overall purpose and central premise of mixed methods are that the use of this combination would provide us with a better understanding of the complex phenomena than either approach alone (Azorin and Cameron, 2010).

Research Method

The present study was based on a household survey. This method is considered as an effective research method which is the most flexible to conduct social research on social phenomena. This method enabled to the researcher(s) to investigate comprehensive and diverse socio-demographic conditions under which people live. Our understanding was that this method would provide the sociocultural factors which influenced behaviour, as well as social issues which are related to the child abuses among the child domestic workers.

Respondents: Sample Design and Study Location

For a household survey, this study used the stratified cluster sampling and selected three thanas from 41 thana in the Dhaka District. Our purpose was to select these thanas based on the three socioeconomic statuses. Accordingly, we categorised all thanas into three e.g., high socioeconomic, middle, and low. Within limited time and funding, three thanas (one from each stratum) were selected from 41 thanas in the Dhaka District through a lottery. These are Dhanmondi (high economical and social status), Mohammadpur (medium) and Mirpur (low). Again the lottery was introduced to select three wards (one from each thana) were selected from three thanas. Thana was considered as the sample unit. The households were considered for data collection that had child domestic worker and left out the households where there were no workers or who did not agree to include in the study willingly. To consider the timeframe, we could collect data from the total 865 households (283 from Dhanmondi, 294 from Mohammadpur, and 288 from Mirpur). Finally, the study considered 849 child domestic workers (equal number 283 from each thana) and 849 household owners (head of the family, both male and female who were present in the households during data collection time). Altogether 1698 respondents were selected for interviewing.

The study considered the children who were 6-18 years of age, and able to provide data for the study. Most of the child domestic workers were between 12-18 years of age, and 14-16 was the highest (32%), followed by 16-18 (29%) and 12-14 (22%). In gender distribution, the higher numbers were female (88%) and only 7% were married. For FGDs, 15 people were selected purposively who were from the different professional background but working on the child labour issue e.g., NGO workers, journalists, academics, human rights workers, government representatives, and members of civil society.

Data Collection Methods and Instruments

The study used a face-to-face interview method, where the interviewers directly communicated with the respondents in accordance with the prepared semi-structured questionnaire. This method enabled to acquire factual information, attitudes, preferences and other information coming out during the conversation with the respondents. This method ensured the quality of the obtained data and increases the response rate. For qualitative data, this study employed focus group discussions (FGDs) to gather insightful opinions and ideas, and the inconsistencies and variation that exists in the particular topic in terms of their beliefs, experiences, and practices. A semi-structured interview schedule was developed to collect quantitative data. In this case, the Likert Scale (5 points) was used to gather information about the opinions of the child domestic workers and owners. An observation method was also employed in which the field enumerators used a checklist to put their opinions on the different conditions of abusing such as physical conditions, physical punishment, conditions of housing and living spaces, etc. as they observed during data collection period. For FGDs, a separate guideline was developed to collect qualitative data from the respondents. The FGD session took one-and-a-half-hour time. One facilitator conducted this session where one note taker took notes.

Data Analysis Techniques: Reliability and Validity Issue

The information and data were cross-checked from the field. Reasonable precautions were taken so that members of the field information collection team remained free from any sort of temptation to gain anything from the respondents. For proper data interpretation and improving the validity of data, we compared the evidence provided by three group of respondents, e.g., child workers, owners, and observers. Data collected through FGDs were properly edited instantly after finishing the FGD session. Information and data collected from primary and secondary sources were compiled and edited properly according to the nature, type, and characteristics of data. All sort of data was scrutinised. Data were analysed based on thematic approach. This approach ensured application of an integrated approach to finding the interacting influence of the variables from different dimensions. The simple statistical tools were used for data analysis.

Ethical Consideration

When an adult researcher interacts with child participants, and especially with marginalised children, the relationship is potentially exploitative because the adult is in a position of more power than the child (Punch, 2001). With this in mind, we tried to establish empowering research relationships with the children (Holt, 2004). In order to prevent risks for the child participants, we did not interview any child without consent from her/his employer (Jensen, 2007). As we mentioned that 88% child domestic workers were female, however, we recruited six female enumerators and one research assistant to get proper access to the respondents. We collected three authorised letters from three Government Departments in Dhaka city e.g., Mayor from Dhaka City Council, local Ward Commissioners, and local thanas.

RESULTS

Types and Frequency of Abuse

The study showed that the domestic children were abused multiple times, such as physically, emotionally, and sexually, and the numbers on different categories were high. The highest 73% of the children were physically abused, followed by 54% emotional, and 17% sexual (Table 1). The highest 52% of the children stated that they were abused regularly, 43% very irregularly, 29% often, and irregularly (Table 2). 95% of the children were abused by the owners and the rest of them were by the other family members (30%) and relatives (1%) (Table 3).

*Table 1. Types of Abuse (%)**

Type of abuse	Dhanmondi	Mohammadpur	Mirpur	Total
Physical	55.42	72.51	91.62	73.27
Mental	78.28	72.51	82.12	54.33
Sexual	20.57	15.16	15.64	16.99

* Multiple answers (total number of child domestic workers were 565)

Table 2. Frequency of Abusing (%)

Abuse	Dhanmondi	Mohammadpur	Mirpur	Total
Very regular	0.57	1.42	2.23	1.41
Regularly	80.57	24.64	55.30	51.68
Often	14.28	52.60	16.20	29.20
Irregular	0.57	21.32	22.34	15.22
Very irregular	4.00	00	6.14	3.18
Total	100	100	100	100

Table 3. Abusers (%)*

Abuser	Dhanmondi	Mohammadpur	Mirpur	Total
Owner	93.1	100	89.94	94.69
Other family members of owner	5.71	27.48	50.83	29.91
Relatives	2.85	3.79	5.02	0.88

* Multiple answers (Total number of child workers 565)

According to the FGDs report, a number of participants mentioned that child domestic workers' abuse especially sexual abuse is higher than the evidence published in the studies. A journalist mentioned that due to the lack of cultural barriers, many children do not report this incidence to the researchers or even to their parents. One human rights worker mentioned that due to financial vulnerability and the lack of knowledge about their rights many child domestic workers could not express their real situation that they faced.

Physical Abuse

All types of respondents mentioned that the physical condition of the child workers was moderate. The area wise variation was not ample. In Dhanmondi area, the highest number of children's physical condition was found 'good' (workers mentioned 88%, owners 82%, and observers 83%) (Table 4). A very few child workers mentioned their health condition 'very good' and 'very bad'. Data showed a significant difference between child workers/observers and owners, where 39% child workers and 42% observers reported the child workers' physical condition was moderate, which was mentioned 70% by the owners.

The child domestic workers were enforced to do a number of hazardous works such as ironing cloth, washing heavy cloth, boiling water, operating motor for pumping water, lifting heavy goods, shopping by crossing the road, etc. It is very visible from the bar diagram (Figure 1) that there is a significant difference between the opinions of the child workers and owners. The child workers mentioned that 39% (328 out of 849) of them had to do various hazardous works every day, whereas only 12% (102) of the owners mentioned that they used the children for such hazardous works. According to the child workers, the highest 32% children washed heavy cloth, 32% had to go shopping by crossing road, 30% boiled

Table 4. Physical Condition of the Workers (%)

Opinions	Condition	Dhanmondi	Mohammadpur	Mirpur	Total
Child workers	Very good	0.70	00	0.35	0.35
	Good	87.63	3.18	22.96	37.92
	Moderate	3.88	64.66	46.99	38.51
	Bad	7.06	32.15	22.61	20.61
	Very bad	0.70	00	7.06	2.59
Owners	Very good	00	00	00	00
	Good	14.13	3.18	17.31	34.27
	Moderate	82.33	86.57	42.40	70.43
	Bad	2.12	10.24	25.44	12.60
	Very bad	1.41	00	14.84	5.41
Observer	Very good	2.12	00	1.06	1.06
	Good	83.03	3.18	20.14	35.45
	Moderate	10.60	64.66	50.88	42.04
	Bad	3.88	32.15	20.49	18.84
	Very bad	0.35	00	7.42	2.59
Total		100	100	100	100

Figure 1. Hazardous Works Done by the Domestic Child Workers (%)

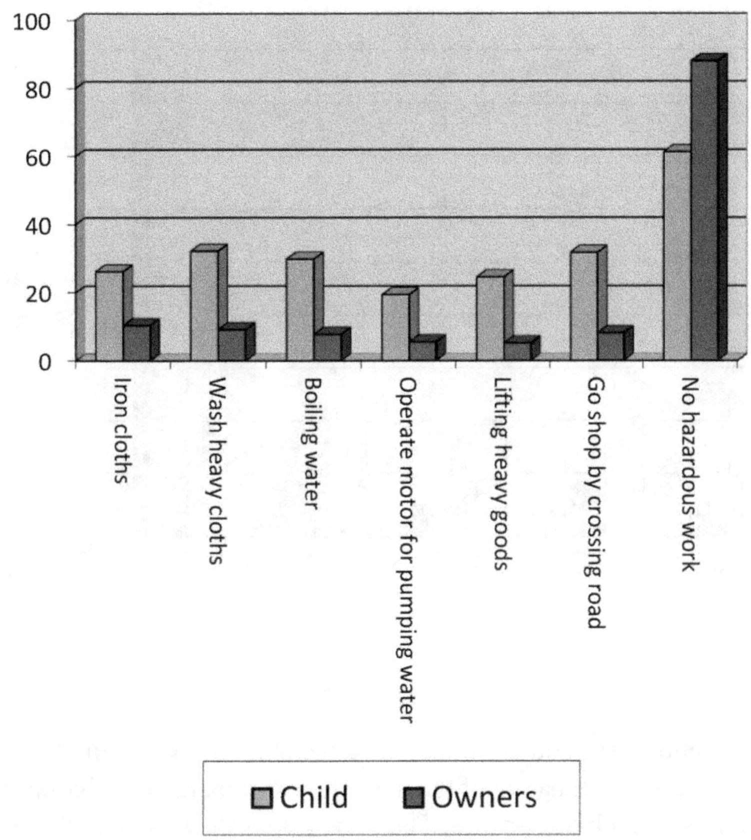

water, 26% ironed cloth, 25% lifted heavy goods, and 19% operated motor for pumping water, where these numbers were 9%, 8%, 5% and 6% respectively among the owners. These numbers were highest 41% boiling water in Mirpur, 31% washing heavy cloth in Dhanmondi, and 34% in Mohammadpur respectively. Data showed that the children had to do some undue works such as body messaging of the owners, shopping, and caring aged people. Sometimes they had to bring the owners' children from the school (Figure 2). There was a significant difference between the opinions of two respondents. 40% of child workers mentioned that they had to do these undue works, where only 8% of the owners agreed with this opinion.

We recorded a number of interesting findings from our FGD report. Every participant in the session mentioned beating and physical assault among the child domestic workers as a common scenario in Bangladesh. One expert informed us that no child in domestic works is safe physically. He expressed that he found this immoral practice even among the human rights workers who enforced the children to do many hazardous and undue works.

Figure 2. Undue Jobs Done by Child Workers (%)

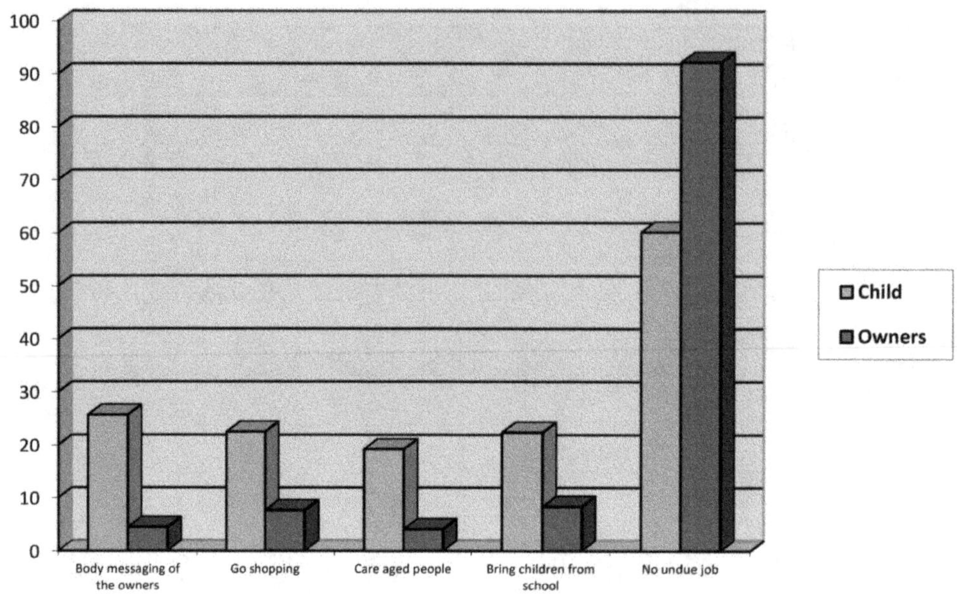

Emotional Abuse

This study considered a number of courses to perceive the child workers' emotional abuse e.g., nature of job contract, the amount of wage, nature of the mental condition, nature of contact with their parents, recreation, living conditions and living spaces. The survey data showed that 79% (not in a table) of the child domestic workers' job was monthly contract basis. A significant number of them (17%) were doing this work just to have false hopes from their owners, which included commitment of their marriage by the owners after certain period of their work, providing better job facilities for them and their family members, providing higher wage in future, and solving their family crises, etc. 80% (not in a table) of children received only Tk. 601-900 (US$4 to US$12) wage per month. This amount is very pitiable to compare the value of money. Around 27% of them received only Tk. 301-600 (US$4 to US$8) per month. Possibly this amount is the lowest wage earner in the country. The highest 64% of the child workers mentioned that their owners did not increase their monthly wage. 67% of the child workers stated that they received only one-time annual leave, and 25% stated that the owners cut-off their wage if they were absent from their work for any reason.

Regarding the mental health condition of the workers, data showed a big variation between the opinions of the child domestic workers and their owners. The highest 69% of the workers mentioned that their mental health condition was moderate followed by 13% bad and 12% good (Table 5). On the other hand, these numbers were 21%, 70% and 5% among the owners.

Data showed that a very few child domestic workers had contact with their parents on very regular and regular basis (Table 6). The highest 80% of the workers could often contact. Watching television was found the only recreational event among the child domestic workers. Data showed that 89% of the children enjoyed this recreation, 18% mentioned playing and 10% had a chance to have outside recreation (Table 7).

Table 5. Mental Condition of the Workers (%)

Opinions	Condition	Dhanmondi	Mohammadpur	Mirpur	Total
Child workers	Very good	0.35	00	00	0.11
	Good	7.06	3.18	26.85	12.36
	Moderate	86.92	86.57	32.15	68.54
	Bad	4.59	10.24	25.08	13.30
	Very bad	1.06	00	15.90	5.65
Owners	Very good	4.24	00	00	1.41
	Good	89.39	80.56	39.57	69.84
	Moderate	3.18	19.43	39.57	20.73
	Bad	1.41	00	12.36	4.59
	Very bad	1.76	00	8.48	3.41

Table 6. Nature of Contact of the Child Domestic Workers With Their Parents (%)

Nature of contact	Dhanmondi	Mohammadpur	Mirpur	Total
Very regular	1.06	2.12	1.76	1.64
Regular	14.84	2.12	3.53	6.83
Often	81.27	80.56	77.73	79.85
Irregular	1.41	8.12	16.60	8.71
Very irregular	1.76	00	00	0.57
Total	100	100	100	100

Table 7. Types of Recreational Facilities (%)*

Types of recreations	Dhanmondi	Mohammdpur	Mirpur	Total
Watching television	95.40	88.33	83.39	89.04
Playing	16.25	21.55	17.66	18.49
Going outside	2.82	4.24	24.02	10.36
No facility	1.41	3.18	6.36	3.65

* Child workers' opinion and multiple answers

The study showed that the domestic child workers lived in different spaces, such as empty places of the house, drawing room, kitchen, veranda, and garage. They also had to live with other family members of the owners, and their parents and husbands. Data showed that on an average 97% of the workers lived at owners' houses and the rest of them by their self-arrangement. Data regarding living spaces obtained from the child workers, observers and owners were likely similar with a little variation. According to the child workers, the highest numbers of them (around 30%) had a separate room for a living (Table 8). The highest numbers of them were enjoying this facility in Dhanmondi. The child workers mentioned this 70%, owners 67%, and observers 75%. Significant numbers of children (25%) lived in the empty places of the house followed by 22% with other family members, and 18% at drawing room.

Table 8. Nature of Living Space (%)

Opinions	Nature of living space	Dhanmondi	Mohammadpur	Mirpur	Total
	Separate room	69.61	18.72	2.82	30.38
	Empty place of the house	18.37	2.47	53.71	24.85
	Drawing room	4.59	24.73	24.73	18.02
	With other family members	4.24	4.24	10.95	21.67
	Kitchen	2.12	2.82	2.47	2.47
	Veranda	00	00	0.35	0.11
	With parents	0.70	00	00	0.23
	With husband	0.35	00	00	0.11
	Others	00	1.41	4.94	2.12
Owners	Separate room	67.49	15.54	2.82	28.62
	Empty place of the house	18.72	3.53	58.30	13.89
	Drawing room	6.00	18.02	21.20	15.07
	With other family members	7.06	58.65	14.48	26.73
	Kitchen	00	3.53	0.35	1.29
	Veranda	00	00	00	00
	With parents	0.70	00	00	0.23
	With husband	00	00	00	00
	Others	00	0.70	2.82	1.17
Observers	Separate room	74.55	18.72	2.12	31.80
	Empty place of the house	14.84	2.47	55.83	24.38
	Drawing room	3.53	24.73	25.44	17.90
	With other family members	5.65	49.82	11.66	22.37
	Kitchen	0.70	2.82	1.76	1.76
	Veranda	00	00	00	00
	With parents	00	00	00	00
	With husband	00	00	00	00
	Others	0.70	1.41	1.41	2.82

Data on living condition showed a significant variation between child domestic workers, owners, and observers. 57% of the observers reported that the living condition of the child domestic workers was moderate which mentioned 49% by the child workers, but this number was only 15% among the owners. On the other hand, 80% of the owners mentioned this living condition was good, where the observers mentioned this 31%, and child workers 41% (Table 9).

The evidence from FGDs showed a number of useful expels about the emotional abuse among the domestic workers. A half of the participants stated us that the emotional condition of the child domestic workers is interrelated with many issues. They argued that the mental condition of the child domestic workers is an ignored matter to the owners. One academic and one NGO worker mentioned that due to

Table 9. Living Condition (%)

Opinions	Condition	Dhanmondi	Mohammadpur	Mirpur	Total
Child workers	Very good	1.41	0.35	0.35	0.70
	Good	87.27	8.48	28.62	41.46
	Moderate	8.48	87.27	52.29	49.35
	Bad	2.12	3.88	15.19	7.06
	Very bad	0.70	00	3.53	1.41
Owners	Very good	3.18	00	0.35	1.17
	Good	92.93	86.21	61.13	80.09
	Moderate	3.88	12.72	27.56	14.72
	Bad	0.35	1.06	7.42	2.94
	Very bad	0.70	00	3.53	1.41
Observers	Very good	00	00	0.35	0.11
	Good	62.54	8.48	21.20	30.74
	Moderate	35.33	87.27	48.76	57.12
	Bad	1.76	4.24	26.50	10.83
	Very bad	0.35	00	3.53	1.29

their financial vulnerability, lack of physical and mental inability, and little age, they are suffered from many mental stresses ordered by their owners. One psychologist told us that due to the lack of education and congenial atmosphere, these children's emotional growth is serious hammered.

DISCUSSION

Based on a mixed method research approach, this paper explored the prevalence and course of child abuse among the child domestic workers in Bangladesh. Results found that the prevalence of child abuses such as physical, emotional, and sexual was high. The overall findings of this study clearly showed that the child abuse among the domestic child workers wrecked the principles and rules of the CRC which sets out the civil, political, economic, social, health and cultural rights of children. The study findings are directly related to CRC's civil, social, health, and cultural rights. Data showed that the child domestic workers were abused in different ways. This result is similar to the study conducted by UNICEF (2012). The study found that that the highest (73%) of the children were physically abused, 54% mentally, and 17% sexually. From our qualitative findings, we would argue that the children's small age and the lack of physical and mental competencies in one hand, and the power relation and the nature of working place on the other, enhanced the higher prevalence of such kind of abuses. This finding is compared with Blagbrough (2008) who mentioned that the workplace is a private dwelling, effectively giving the employer total control over the person in their 'service', where domestic workers are uniquely vulnerable. Blagbrough treated these physical, psychological, verbal and sexual abuses are worse than dogs. We could shoulder that this is a risk factor for 'behavioural problems' (Benvengnú et al., 2005) and this can be prone to an array of psychosocial problems manifest as bedwetting, insomnia, nightmares and depression (Gamlin et al., 2015). Jacquemin (2004), Black (2005), and Blagbrough (2008) mentioned these risks faced by the young child domestic workers working for abusive employers in exploitative conditions akin to slavery.

The study found that the physical and mental conditions of the domestic child workers were moderate, and significant numbers were found bad. The finding is compared with the study conducted by the girls' domestic worker in Guinea by the Human Rights Watch (2007). The study documented how girl domestic workers were working without pay, and are often insulted, beaten and raped by their employers. Our study found that the child domestic workers were enforced to do a number of hazardous works such as ironing cloth, washing heavy cloth, boiling water, operating motor for pumping water, lifting heavy goods, and shopping by crossing the road. The children had to do some undue works such as body messaging of the owners, shopping, care aged people and sometimes they had to bring the owners' children from the school. The findings are similar to a number of studies such as the Save the Children (2010), and the Human Rights Watch (2009).

The study found that most of the child workers job was monthly contract basis, and their monthly salary was extremely low (80% of children received Tk. 601-900 (US$4 to US$12) wage per month, and 27% of them received only Tk. 301-600 (US$4 to US$8) per month), 64% worked without increasing their salary, 67% received only one-time annual leave, and 25% reported to cut-off their wage due to their absence. This finding is similar to the study conducted by the Human Rights Watch (2009) in Indonesia. This study mentioned that almost 90% of the domestic worker in Indonesia had no written contract with their employer, 65% never had a day off and 12% had experienced violence in their workplace. Our study showed that 17% of the children were doing their work just to have false hopes. The similar type of opinions were published by a roundtable organised by the Centre for Services and Information on Disability (CSID) and the Daily Star (2014), Basu (2012), and Lamb (2014).

The mental health condition among the child domestic workers were found poor. 40% of the workers mentioned that their mental health condition was moderate followed by 39% good. This finding is compared with a study conducted in Singapore by Lee (2015). He found that the domestic workers had double the risk to develop mental health problems as compared to the general Singapore population. A very few child domestic workers had contact with very regular and regular basis with their parents. Watching television was found the only recreational event among the child domestic workers. The child workers lived in different spaces, such as empty places of the house, drawing room, kitchen, veranda, and other places such as a garage, etc. Islam, Mahmud, and Rahman (2013) found that 50% of child domestic workers sleep in the drawing room and 27% has a separate room which is located at the empty place of the house.

CONCLUSIONS, POLICY IMPLICATIONS AND RECOMMENDATIONS

This paper reported the findings of the child abuse among the child domestic workers in Bangladesh. Based on three areas in Dhaka city, this paper explored findings on the child domestic workers' physical, mental, and sexual abuses. The prevalence was higher in all three categories of abuses. The physical and mental conditions were found moderate, and significant numbers were bad. They had to involve a number of hazardous works such as ironing cloth, washing heavy cloth, boiling water, operating motor for pumping water, and lifting heavy goods. They had to do some undue jobs such as body messaging of the owners, shopping, and caring aged people. Most of the child domestic workers had no job contract, and their wage was extremely poor. They had to work without any day off and rest. Their contact with their parents and relatives were limited, and television was the only source of their recreation. Their emotional and mental health conditions were found very low, and most of them had no separate room and bed, which seriously impacted on their growth and development. The overall findings clearly indicated that child domestic work in Bangladesh remains highly neglected because of the relatively invisible nature of work. They are far from their families, controlled by their employer, deprived of basic rights and related social services, low working conditions, deprived of protection from physical, mental, and sexual harassments and abuse.

This study had a number of limitations. The study was based on a very small number of sample, and data were collected only from Dhaka city. However, the study findings could not be generalised. But this study reported some important aspects of the domestic child workers' physical, mental and sexual abuses in Bangladesh. The findings have greater policy implications on a number of areas in child welfare. This finding can be considered as important evidence to the policy makers, development practitioners, human rights workers, and NGOs. For greater child wellbeing for the domestic child workers, the Government can rethink a number of legislative and policy documents such as the constitutional rights of the children, Child Act 2013, Bangladesh Labour Act (amended) 2013, and National Children Policy 2011, National Child Labour Elimination Policy 2010, Domestic Worker Protection and Welfare Policy 2010, and Conventions related to labour issues including the United Nations Convention on the Rights of the Child (UNCRC), and ILO Convention No. 182 (Worst forms of Child Labour). Much more research is required to understand the various economic, political, cultural, exploitative, poverty and violence related factors which contribute to the ongoing existence of child abuse among the domestic child workers in Bangladesh.

To consider the findings and discussion, a number of suggestions can be considered to eliminate the abuses among the child domestic workers' in Bangladesh:

- This study suggested a number specific interventions e.g., community-based interventions, social service responses by the government and NGOs, legal and economic supports in order to improve the child abuse situation in Bangladesh.
- A national survey including to identify problems of the domestic workers is an emerging initiative in Bangladesh. The findings clearly identified that the child domestic workers had to do a number of hazardous and undue works, which have adverse negative impacts on their physical and mental development. It is fact that the Government still could not specify such kind of hazardous works appropriately and effectively, which should be bunged up.
- The major causes of the domestic child workers' are related to their parents' economic vulnerability. The government can take a target and family-based projects such as income generation activities. It is noted here that there a number of such kind of projects working in the rural areas. The government can link up those vulnerable parents with these projects.
- Education can be a powerful indicator that can enrich many parts of the vulnerability of the domestic child workers and their parents.
- A child labour policy is considered as an important aspect to facade domestic child labour issue. The Ministry of Women and Children Affairs formulated the National Child Policy 2011, but it does not include many aspects of the domestic child labour.

- The finding of this study confirms that most of the domestic child workers experienced multiple cases of abuse. The existing laws are very week in Bangladesh. It is seen than the numbers of such kind of incidents is much higher than the report and examples of punishment. The Government should be more careful about this.

ACKNOWLEDGMENT

The authors would like to express their sincere thanks to all of the interviewees and survey participants. Special gratitude goes to the Country Director of TDH Netherlands and President and General Secretary of the Bangladesh Shishu Adhikar Forum who helped to facilitate the study.

REFERENCES

Alvy, K. (1975). Preventing child abuse. *The American Psychologist, 30*(9), 921–927. doi:10.1037/0003-066X.30.9.921 PMID:1180422

Bardi, M., & Borgognini-Tarli, S. (2001). A survey on parent-child conflict resolution: Intrafamily violence in Italy. *Child Abuse & Neglect, 25*(6), 839–853. doi:10.1016/S0145-2134(01)00242-3 PMID:11525528

Azorín, J. M., & Cameron, R. (2010). The application of mixed methods in organisational research: A literature review. *Electronic Journal of Business Research Methods, 8*(2), 95–105.

Bangladesh Bureau of Statistics (BBS). (2006). *Report on national child labour survey 2002-2003.* Dhaka: BBS.

Blagbrough, J. (2008). *They respect their animals more voices of child domestic workers.* London: Anti-Slavery International Thomas Clarkson House The Stableyard.

Basu, M. (2012). *The invisible world of domestic work: Report documents abuses.* Retrieved from http://inamerica.blogs.cnn.com/2012/11/27/the-invisible-world-of-domestic-work-report-documents-abuses/comment-page-2/

Belsky, J. (1980). Child maltreatment: An ecological integration. *The American Psychologist, 35*(4), 320–335. doi:10.1037/0003-066X.35.4.320 PMID:7386966

Benvengnú, L. A., Gastal Fassa, A., Augusto Faccini, L., Wegman, D. H., & DallAgnol, M. M. (2005). Work and behavioral problems in children and adolescents. *International Journal of Epidemiology, 34*(6), 1417–1424. doi:10.1093/ije/dyi187 PMID:16144859

Bissell, S. (2001). Young garment workers in Bangladesh: Raising the rights question. *Development, 44*(2), 75–80. doi:10.1057/palgrave.development.1110241

Black, M. (2005). *Child domestic workers: A handbook on good practice in programme interventions.* London: Anti-Slavery International.

Bourdillon, M. (2010). Child domestic workers in Zimbabwe. In Working to be someone: Child focused research and practice with working children (pp. 55–65). London: Jessica Kingsley.

Bronfenbrenner, U. (1979). *The ecology of human development: Experiments by nature and design.* Cambridge, MA: Harvard University Press.

Centre for Services and Information on Disability (CSID) and the Daily Star. (2014). *End domestic child labour*. Retrieved from http://www.thedailystar.net/end-domestic-child-labour-57018

Davidov, J., Sigad, L. I., Lev-Wiesel, R., & Eisikovits, Z. (2016). Cross-disciplinary craftsmanship: The case of child abuse work. *Qualitative Social Work: Research and Practice*. doi:10.1177/1473325016641626

Delap, E. (2001). Economic and cultural forces in the child labour debate: Evidence from urban Bangladesh. *The Journal of Development Studies*, *37*(4), 1–22. doi:10.1080/00220380412331322021

Cutland, M. (2012). Child abuse and its legislation: The global picture. *Archives of Disease in Childhood*, *97*(8), 679–684. doi:10.1136/archdischild-2012-301648 PMID:22563035

Feng, J. Y., Jezewski, M. A., & Hsu, T. W. (2005). The meaning of child abuse for nurses in Taiwan. *Journal of Transcultural Nursing*, *16*(2), 142–149. doi:10.1177/1043659604273551 PMID:15764637

Flores-Oebanda, C. (2006). *Addressing vulnerability and exploitation of child domestic workers: an open challenge to end a hidden shame*. Paper presented at the Expert Group Meeting "Elimination of all forms of discrimination and violence against the girl child", UNICEF Innocenti Research Centre, Florence, Italy.

Gamlin, J., Camacho, A. Z., Ong, M., & Hesketh, T. (2015). Is domestic work the worst form of child labour? The findings of a six-country study of the psychosocial effects of child domestic work. *Childrens Geographies*, *13*(2), 212–225. doi:10.1080/14733285.2013.829660

Gil, D. G. (1975). Unravelling child abuse. *The American Journal of Orthopsychiatry*, *45*(3), 346–356. doi:10.1111/j.1939-0025.1975.tb02545.x PMID:1146967

Haider, M. (2008). Recognising Complexity, Embracing Diversity Working Children in Bangladesh. *South Asia Research*, *28*(1), 49–72. doi:10.1177/026272800702800103

Holt, L. (2004). The voices of children: De-centring empowering research relations. *Childrens Geographies*, *2*(1), 13–27. doi:10.1080/1473328032000168732

Hossain, F. I. (2000). A view of Asia's hapless children: Save child workers. *The Independent*. Retrieved from http://independentbangladesh.com/news/aug/25/25082000pd.htm#1

Human Rights Watch. (2007). *Thousands of Girls Face Abuse as Guinea Domestic Workers*. Guinea, Mali: Human Rights Watch.

Human Rights Watch. (2009). *Workers in the shadows abuse and exploitation of child domestic workers in Indonesia*. Jakarta: Human Rights Watch.

International Labour Organization. (2012). *Effective protection for domestic workers, a guide to designing labour laws*. Geneva: International Labour Organization.

International Labour Organization. (2016). *Child labour and domestic work*. Geneva: International Labour Organization.

Islam, E., Mahmud, K., & Naziza, R. (2014). The situation of Child Domestic Workers in Bangladesh. *Global Journal of Management and Business Research*, *13*(7), 24–34.

Islam, M. R. (2013). Brighter future of child domestic workers in Bangladesh: Government initiatives and challenges. *Elixir International Journal*, *60*, 16498–16503.

Islam, M. R. (2010). *A Child is in the home but imprisoned: a situation of domestic child workers in Dhaka City*. Dhaka: Bangladesh Shishi Adhikar Forum.

Islam, M. R., & Cojocaru, S. (2016). Migrant domestic workers in Asia: Transnational variations and policy concerns. *International Migration (Geneva, Switzerland)*, *54*(1), 48–63. doi:10.1111/imig.12201

Jacquemin, M. Y. (2004). Childrens domestic work in Abidjan, Côte dIvoire The Petites Bonnes have the Floor. *Childhood*, *11*(3), 383–397. doi:10.1177/0907568204044889

Jensen, K. B. (2007). Opportunities for agency and social participation among child domestic workers in Bangladesh. *Children, Youth and Environments*, *17*(1), 148–170.

Kane, J. (2004). *Helping hands or shackled lives? Understanding child domestic labour and responses to it*. Geneva: ILO.

Korbin, J. E. (1991). Cross-cultural perspectives and research directions for the 21st century. *Child Abuse & Neglect*, *15*(Suppl. 1), 67–77. doi:10.1016/0145-2134(91)90010-B PMID:2032129

Lamb, B. (2014). *No justice for diplomatic abuse of domestic workers*. Retrieved from https://traffickingandlabor.wordpress.com/tag/domestic-workers/

Lee, A. (2015). *Foreign domestic workers more likely to develop mental health problems*. Retrieved from http://www.todayonline.com/singapore/foreign-domestic-workers-more-likely-develop-mental-health-problems

Maitra, B. (1996). Child abuse: A universal diagnostic category? The implication of culture in definition and assessment. *The International Journal of Social Psychiatry*, *42*(4), 287–304. doi:10.1177/002076409604200404 PMID:9023610

Meinck, F., Cluver, L. D., Boyes, M. E., & Mhlongo, E. L. (2015). Risk and protective factors for physical and sexual abuse of children and adolescents in Africa a review and implications for practice. *Trauma, Violence & Abuse*, *16*(1), 81–107. doi:10.1177/1524838014523336 PMID:24648489

Parke, R. D., & Collner, C. W. (1975). Child abuse: An interdisciplinary analysis. In M. E. Hetherinton (Ed.), *Review of Child Development Research* (Vol. 5). Chicago: University of Chicago Press.

Petersen, A. C., Joseph, J., & Feit, M. (Eds.). (2014). *New directions in child abuse and neglect research*. National Academies Press.

Punch, S. (2001). Multiple methods and research relations with children in rural Bolivia. In C. Dwyer & M. Limb (Eds.), *Qualitative methodologies for geographers*. London: Arnold.

Salmon, C. (2005). Child labor in Bangladesh are children the last economic resource of the household? *Journal of Developing Societies*, *21*(1-2), 33–54. doi:10.1177/0169796X05053066

Save the Children Sweden-Denmark. (2010). *Living inside room outside law A study on child domestic worker and the role of government and civil society*. Dhaka: Save the Children Sweden-Denmark.

UNICEF. (2006). *Situation analysis of child domestic workers in Dhaka City*. Dhaka: UNICEF Bangladesh.

UNICEF. (2012). *Child maltreatment, prevalence, incidence, and consequences in the East Asia and Pacific Region*. New York: UNICEF.

Varia, N., & Becker, J. (2012). *A landmark victory for domestic workers: New convention establishes first global labor standards for millions of women and girls*. New York: Human Rights Watch.

Wilson-Oyelaran, E. B. (1989). The ecological model and the study of child abuse in Nigeria. *Child Abuse & Neglect, 13*(3), 379–387. doi:10.1016/0145-2134(89)90078-1 PMID:2776046

Wissow, L. S. (1995). Child abuse and neglect. *The New England Journal of Medicine, 332*(21), 1425–1431. doi:10.1056/NEJM199505253322107 PMID:7723800

World Health Organization (WHO). (2010). *Child maltreatment*. Geneva: WHO. Retrieved from http://www.who.int/mediacentre/factsheets/fs150/en/index.html

Chapter 2
Intersectional Analysis of the Social Determinants of Child Maltreatment in Zimbabwe

Manase Kudzai Chiweshe
Chinhoyi University of Technology, Zimbabwe

ABSTRACT

Child maltreatment in Zimbabwe is a pervasive and structural phenomenon that requires a grounded analysis to understand its drivers and impact. This chapter is focused on providing extensive literature review of work done focusing on child maltreatment in Zimbabwe. It provides an analysis of emerging patterns of child maltreatment in Zimbabwe, arguing that children are found within multiple and intersecting forms of discrimination. The social determinants outlined in this chapter are not mutually exclusive but rather reinforce each other. This makes the problem of child maltreatment complex and multifarious. Child maltreatment is variously described as any form (physical, emotional or symbolic) of abuse of a child or children. The paper discusses the intersection of various factors that cause child maltreatment including: Culture, gender norms, religion, poverty, age, social location, class, HIV status, orphanhood, disability, domestic violence, blended families, new media and child carers. Children are the most vulnerable group of people because of their position in society.

INTRODUCTION

Childhood is a period of social, psychological, emotional and physical development. It is thus a crucial stage of development which requires nurturing, support and loving environment. There exists a huge amount of work in the field of anthropology, developmental psychology, medicine, sociology and education which outlines the importance of points to the early years of childhood in the formation of intelligence, personality, and social behaviour. Early childhood is an important foundation for the future as the effects of neglect in these formative years can be cumulative and lasting. This study is thus important because it focuses on violence at this crucial stage in a person's life. In the human life cycle, the early childhood phase: from birth to nine years is considered the most important phase for every human being. Giving

DOI: 10.4018/978-1-5225-2578-3.ch002

children the best start in life means ensuring them good health, proper nutrition, and early learning. Save the Children (2008a) argues that it is important to identify and support "children at risk" early in their lives. If there is early and appropriate treatment and care, this can often reverse the effects of deprivation and support the development of innate potential. Early intervention and provisioning make it possible for children to grow and develop to their full potential, thus reducing the need for remedial services to address stunting; developmental lag and social problems later in life.

NATURE AND SCOPE OF CHILD MALTREATMENT

Maltreatment is often described as violence against children. There is no universal or agreed definition of violence against children. Violence against children is a multi-faceted and often contested concept which describes any act (physical, emotional, symbolic, sexual and spiritual) that brings harm of any kind to a child. The Violence Prevention Alliance initiative describes four categories of interpersonal violence that are included in this study: physical, sexual, psychological and deprivation or neglect. For the purposes of this study, child maltreatment constitutes the following forms of abuse: physical, emotional, sexual and neglect in addition to commercial and/or other exploitation, resulting in actual or potential harm to the child's health, survival, development or dignity in the context of a relationship of responsibility, trust or power (Krug *et al.* 2002).

The work by Childline (civil society organisation working on eradicating violence against children) in all the provinces of Zimbabwe is instructive on the nature and scope of child maltreatment. This section will draw a lot from this work, highlighting the emerging patterns of child maltreatment. Childline (2010) conceptualise child abuse to include physical abuse, emotional abuse, sexual abuse and neglect. Sexual abuse is more prevalent throughout the reported period and statistics from all previous years highlight this. It explains the dominance of academic work and civil society programming on sexual violence. Between January (2012) and October 2012, the Zimbabwe Republic Police (ZRP) recorded that "*2,450 children had been raped countrywide, with neighbours responsible for 41% of the rape cases...rape of juveniles cases increased from 2,883 in 2010 to 3,172 in 2011*" (Dube 2013:3). To further illustrate the pervasiveness of sexual abuse, Makamure (2010) notes that the Family Support Trust Clinic treated 30,000 girls and boys between 2005 and 2009 who were victims of sexual violence.

There is a gendered dimension to child maltreatment in Zimbabwe. In a study of 1,062 females and 1,348 male respondents aged 13-24 years across Zimbabwe, UNICEF and ZimStat (2011: xxi) show that "*among the females and males aged 18-24 years, a third of the females and 9 percent of the males experienced sexual violence before reaching the age of 18 years. For those aged 13-17 years, the victimisation rate for sexual violence was 9 percent and 2 percent for the females and males respectively.*" Girls tend to be overwhelmingly the largest number of survivors of child abuse (especially sexual abuse) for example Childline statistics for 2014 show that between January and October a total of 1,073 cases were reported on the sexual abuse of girls compared to 93 cases involving boys.

Age provides an important prism to analyse the power differentials between perpetrators and survivors of child maltreatment. Birdthislte (2011:1079) notes that: "*Girls and boys less than 12 years most often described vaginal and anal penetration, respectively, by a neighbour or relative at least 10 years older, occurring in their own or the abuser's home. Adolescent girls up to 16 most often described vaginal penetration by their 'boyfriend,' typically up to 10 years older and taking place in his or the girls' own home.*" This shows that in most cases there is a huge age difference between perpetrators and survivors of sexual abuse. Older people have physical, emotional and often economic power over children. They use this power to maltreat and abuse children in vulnerable circumstances. The increased reports of child/early marriages attest to this lack of power amongst children who have very little choice to choose or determine their circumstances. Respondents in a Padare (2014) report argued that it is parents who decided on marriage for young girls. They are cases where parents have declined reporting rape of a child and instead of receiving monetary or cattle compensation from the perpetrator.

Post-2000 Zimbabwe devolved into a socio-economic crisis that had negative consequences for child protection and increased the vulnerability of children. The crisis was characterised by high inflation, high unemployment, food shortages and an almost collapse of the health care system (Chiweshe 2012a). The crisis in Zimbabwe has a longer history but was precipitated by farm occupations by veterans of the liberation struggle and like-minded groups. One of the immediate impacts of the farm occupations was the impact on child protection amongst farm workers who were dependent on white farmers for food, schooling and health care. Children of farm workers suffered after the Fast Track Land Reform as their parents were at times attacked for being perceived to support white farmers. Some workers lost their houses and were left homeless across the country and this negatively impacted on their children (Sachikonye 2004).

The socio-economic crisis was further made worse by Operation *Murambatsvina*/Operation Restore Order which was a government program that occurred in the winter of 2005. What started as an operation to demolish all illegal construction in undesignated areas across the country turned out to be an unusual operation that deteriorated into a humanitarian crisis that saw over 700,000 people being displaced (Action Aid Zimbabwe, 2005). This had a negative impact on children in households who lost their shelter and had to move into shanty towns or live on the banks of the Mukuvisi River in Harare. Such children lost access to shelter, school and suffered from hunger. Typhoid and cholera crisis worsened the situation for many poor people. Zimbabwe experienced a cholera outbreak in August 2008. By 7 December, Oxfam estimated 60,000 cases and a 10% fatality rate by the end of January 2009 (Berger and Thornycroft 2008). Children were among those who lost their lives to cholera. Cholera also kept many children out of school because of fears the disease would spread. Children also lost parents due to the cholera outbreak.

Another dimension of post-2000 Zimbabwe is the increase in child trafficking and unaccompanied children migrating to neighbouring countries (especially South Africa and Botswana). This has provided a new dimension to child protection which Zimbabwe's laws and legal system has not responded to in times. Although there are no exact figures on the number of child migrants, Save the Children (2010) notes that there were 8,631 unaccompanied children deported from South Africa and assisted at Beitbridge Reception and Support Centre during the period July 2006 to January 2009. More children are smuggled in by criminal traffickers for sex labour. From the age distribution of children who accessed the service at the Save the Children Reception Centre, it was evident that 96% of all the children were between the ages of 12 and 17, suggesting that the likelihood of participating in irregular migration increases with the onset of adolescence. It is also noted that children from the ages of 1 to 11 years old (accounting for less than 5% of all children accessing services) are particularly difficult to transport or travel unaccompanied, while conversely, the older age groups are able to travel more readily in the company of their friends (Save the Children Report, 2010).

METHODOLOGY

A systematic review is appropriate in identifying, appraising and synthesising research-based evidence and presenting it in an accessible format (Mulrow 1994). According to the Cochrane Handbook, systematic reviews collate all empirical evidence that fits pre-specified eligibility criteria in order to answer a specific research question. It uses explicit, systematic methods that are selected with a view to minimising bias, thus providing more reliable findings from which conclusions can be drawn and decisions made. Parahoo (2006) suggests that a systematic review should detail the time frame within which the literature was selected, as well as the methods used to evaluate and synthesise findings of the studies in question. In order for the reader to assess the reliability and validity of the review, the reviewer needs to present the precise criteria used to: Formulate the research question; Set inclusion or exclusion criteria; Select and access the literature; Assess the quality of the literature included in the review; Analyse, synthesize and disseminate the findings. Unlike traditional reviews, the purpose of a systematic review is to provide as complete a list as possible of all the published and unpublished studies relating to a particular subject area. While traditional reviews attempt to summarise results of a number of studies, systematic reviews use explicit and rigorous criteria to identify, critically evaluate and synthesise all the literature on a particular topic. The review process used a thematic analysis method to extract or obtain data from published reports. This is a qualitative analytic method for identifying, analysing, interpreting and reporting patterns within data.

FINDINGS AND DISCUSSION

Culture, Patriarchy, and Tradition

Most work covered in this study relate to what are termed harmful cultural practices relating to child maltreatment. These practices refer to 'all behaviour, attitudes and or practices, which negatively affect the fundamental rights of women and girls, such as their right to life, health, dignity, education, and physical integrity'. A Padare report (2014:14) cites a participant who notes that:

In Bindura we identified what are called harmful cultural practices such as parents who marry off daughters under the age of consents; Kuzvarira – which is a practice where parents marry off a child at birth or as a baby in exchange for food or cattle; Chiramu – which is a practice where as a girl, your sister's husband can have certain liberties such as fondling your breast; Nhaka – which is when at the death of a husband a woman is provided with one of the relatives to take over husband duties. All these practices are done without the consent of girls. Their rights are ignored which is why we came up with community commitment charters that promote the community effort to work towards achieving equal rights for girls.

Safaids (2011) outlines another harmful cultural practice in Guruve called *kupisa guva* which is a tradition where after the death of their father, all the girls in the family would be taken to the river for virginity testing. These practices lead to child maltreatment as they infringe on the rights of children. Another practice which is not very common now but still evident is the use of girls to appease vengeful spirits (*kuripa ngozi*) which happens when a person commits murder and to avoid a "*curse on the of-*

fending family, with this family suffering a series of serious setbacks, perhaps even the deaths of some of its own members. In order to appease the avenging spirits, a virgin girl is handed over to the offended family by the family responsible for the harm-doing" (Safaids 2009a:15).

The UN Study on Violence against Children lists *harmful traditional practices* (HTPs) as follows: genital mutilation (including female genital mutilation – cutting of girls' sexual parts and some forms of male circumcision); child sexual abuse, including girls married very young or being forced to marry; honour killings, where men kill girls in the name of family 'honour', for example for having sex outside marriage, or refusing an arranged marriage. In Zimbabwe, Muronda (2009:149) also outlines practices such as *kuputsa or kutengesa* whereby a young child is sold to benefit her family; this could also be referred to as trafficking. All these practices are based on specific traditional and cultural beliefs. The determinants of maltreatment, in this case, are cultural. It is clear that there is a need for a fundamental mental shift from such traditions. Patriarchy is at the root of most harmful practices for both young boys and girls. Patriarchy ultimately is a gendered power system: a network of social, political and economic relationships through which men dominate and control female labour, reproduction, and sexuality as well as define women's status, privileges and rights in a society (Chakona 2012). The term 'patriarch', understood traditionally as 'the father' or 'chief of a clan', captures the dominant position of men in society and the social inequalities that exist between men and women and the gender socialisation of children. Historically, the term patriarchy was used to refer to autocratic rule by the male head of a family. Ferguson (1999) argues that modern historians and sociologists describe a patriarchal society as a society where men hold the positions of power in different institutional spheres: heads of the family unit, leaders of social groups, bosses in the workplace and the elites of government.

One example of patriarchal practices is how males interfere with what females wear; this has led to many cases of abuse on the streets to both girls and women. Nhundu and Shumba (2001) argue that male interference in what women are wearing is a hallmark of Zimbabwean patriarchial societies. There are numerous reports over the years of women being stripped naked by *hwindis* (touts) in Harare for wearing miniskirts. Research undertaken in 2013 by Dube indicates that (61%) of males and (63%) of females found that the way in which a woman dresses could cause a man to rape her. Such statistics paint a worrying picture about attitudes towards dressing as an excuse for sexual assault. The construction of hegemonic masculinities in Zimbabwe centre on men being unable to control their sex drive thus women should dress "properly" as to not provoke them. This leads to the blaming of the child survivors of abuse which in turn normalises sexual violence and its perpetration.

Kambarami (2006) argues that the family is the brewery of patriarchal norms and values. This is an important assertion when focusing on child maltreatment. Conventional wisdom says the family should be the haven for the protection of children yet statistics show that violence experienced by girls and women is in the great majority of the cases, perpetrated by male partners with whom they have an intimate or interdependent relationship with (Mashiri 2013). The family, unfortunately, is the arena where most child maltreatment happens yet parents and close relatives should play an integral role in child protection. Girl Child Network (2005) tracked 20,000 child sex abuse cases from 1998 to 2004 found that the number of incest cases among them ranged from 125 in 1998 to 940 in 2004; in total, 2,930 cases out of the 20,000 involved incest. This shows that biological fathers form a substantial percentage of those that sexually abuse girls. Children in patriarchial societies belong to the father and thus in some way are seen as property. Such thinking provides an excuse by men to sexually abuse their children.

Religion

Religion is a powerful organising force in Zimbabwe. The vast majority of Zimbabweans identify themselves as Christian. Kambarami (2006) notes how Christianity, in particular, is highly patriarchal. Studies have shown how religious ideologies have been used to justify abuse of women and children. According to the Demographic Health Survey (DHS 2010-11), 31% of the girls in Zimbabwe marry before they reach the age of 18 years and about 15% of these girls are married before they reach 15 years. Child marriages are mostly linked to religious beliefs especially among the Johanne Marange Apostolic sect. This is a church commonly known as '*apostolic*' that is believed to constitute approximately 1.2 million members in the country (Sibanda 2011). Chireshe, Chireshe and Mudhovozi (2009) argue that many cases of abuse in Zimbabwe are perpetuated and justified in the name of religion and culture. Participants in a study conducted by Padare (2014) in Zvishavane and Gweru claimed that their religious leaders in the apostolic sects who claim to have dreams from God that they should marry young girls. A member of the church is quoted as saying, "*Men in our church receive their brides from the Holy Spirit through dreams. They then inform the church elders who* will *formalise the marriage. The practice does not normally take age into account and even a 14-year-old can be married off to a man far older than her.*" In Mudzi there were reported cases of four primary children attending apostolic churches that dropped out of school due to pregnancy (Zimbabwe Youth Council 2014). Apart from Christianity, there are other religious beliefs that promote child maltreatment. One example is how some healers' claim that sleeping with a virgin will cure HIV (Safaids 2009). Padare (2014) notes how Zvishavane communities complain about the emergence of fake prophets and healers who are telling people that sleeping with a virgin will cure HIV and AIDS. This is a harmful practice, which has led to many rapes and sexual abuses of women and children.

Poverty

Poverty is an important factor in understanding child maltreatment. Bower (2003) argues that incest and other forms of sexual violence are related to the disempowerment and emasculation of African men that results from unemployment. With Zimbabwe having high levels of formal unemployment, men experience a crisis of masculinity and use abuse as a way of reasserting their lost power. Unemployed men also spend a lot of time at home. In poor areas of Harare, adults living in shacks or two roomed flats with children have no privacy as they share sleeping space with children. The vast majority of work on child maltreatment in Zimbabwe focuses on poor urban and rural communities. Experiences in most African countries show that there are strong linkages between socio-economic status and vulnerability, for example, the poorest 20% of girls ages 10–19 in many countries are those who are also most likely to be out of school, married, and/or forced into non-marital sexual relation. These girls fall into several disadvantaged categories, as age, gender, ethnicity, and family factors combine (Population Council 2009). Children in poor families are found at the intersection of multiple oppressive systems firstly, because of poverty they are unable to access basic services such as health and education. This affects their life chances and impacts on protection from maltreatment. UNICEF (2010:13) states that "*In Zimbabwe, protection [of women and children] is largely influenced by poverty, the negative impact of HIV and AIDS, the deterioration of the welfare and justice systems, violence, exploitation and abuse of children in families and communities.*" The 2010 ZimVac Rural Vulnerability assessment shows that there are around 250,000 rural households in Zimbabwe living in extreme poverty with approximately 700,000 vulnerable children.

Gregson *et al* (2002) found that about 17% of 19-year-old girls in Zimbabwe were infected with HIV, compared with about 3% of boys their age. There are some astounding statistics of HIV and AIDS amongst young women in Africa, for example, an estimated 700,000 new infections occurred among young people aged 15-24 in 2009. These statistics on HIV and AIDS have to be understood within a context in which 42% of girls in Africa get married before turning 18 whilst in places such as Ethiopia and parts of West Africa girls get married as early as aged seven (UNFPA 2005). There are many parents who due to poverty make the girl child engage in sex with rich people so that their monetary needs can be met. Even sometimes without forcing them to engage in sexual activities parents also turn a blind eye to their children's sexual relationships with adults to simply receive financial support (Magwa and Ingwani 2014). As such, it is girls who are married to husbands who are way older than them, that leave young wives vulnerable to HIV as they have less power to negotiate safe sex. In an evaluation of their work, Padare (2014) noted that poverty is believed to be forcing young women and girls into transactional sex as a livelihood option and a lot of intergenerational relationships. The reports note an example of girls as young as 9 or 10 engaging in sex work in Zvishavane and Epworth.

Chiweshe (2012b) argues that girl orphans tend to more vulnerable to adverse reproductive health issues such as HIV, STIs and teenage pregnancies due to earlier and riskier sexual experiences associated with poorer household circumstances and reduced educational opportunities. Loss of family members has emotional consequences that relate to identity and psychological well-being. It is also related to increased malnutrition and reduced opportunity for education. Without adequate care and support, many children are exposed to exploitative child labour and abuse and face increased vulnerability to HIV infection. Families affected by HIV when forced to choose between sending a boy or girl to school; they usually choose boys. This is steeped in patriarchal systems which see girls only as waiting for marriage.

Social Location

When discussing social location it is important to note that there are many children in specific contexts that make them vulnerable to maltreatment. The nature and experiences of child maltreatment are context specific. Below are some specific examples of how social location influences child maltreatment:

1. **Rural vs. Urban Children:** The context and experiences of abuse for rural and urban children tend to be different because of their social location. Whilst in Zimbabwe poverty is widespread, rural children face more challenges than urban children, for example, rural schools are far away and have fewer resources in terms of teachers and learning materials. The demands in terms of chores and labour required in the fields place more burdens on rural youths have no access to electricity to enable them to study in the evenings. For rural girls, one of the biggest problems is that sanitary pads are not readily available. Consequently, some rural girls now use unhygienic means, which further affects their biological system making them susceptible to various infections (Chiweshe 2012b). In discussions with Childline, there was a case of girls being raped whilst watching the fields for baboons during farming seasons in some areas in Zimbabwe. This can also happen when girls do other chores such as collecting water and firewood far away from their homes. Such vulnerabilities are peculiar to rural contexts. Within urban areas, the traditional communal parenting systems have been eroded as the nuclear family becomes more important. This has led to increased stress and

isolation of the family unit from social support structures of the extended family. In such scenarios, child maltreatment tends to be high especially in single parent families and families with working parents.

2. **Children Without Identity Records:** By 2010, 37% of children had birth certificates in Zimbabwe. A FOST baseline survey in 2003 in farm communities found that 43% of all children did not have birth certificates while 74% of orphaned children did not possess birth certificates. A study by Mashumba et al (2004) in Chiredzi and Chipinge shows that the majority of rural children were not in possession of birth certificates. This is mainly due to the distance that rural communities have to travel to urban centres to get the documents. Most parents do not attach any value to registering their children who later become parents in succeeding generations. The documents are important in accessing schooling and other services such as obtaining Zimbabwean citizenship. By legislation, one cannot get a Zimbabwean identity card or passport without a birth certificate, which also affects rural children's access to education and health care. The study also showed that girls are less likely to get registration documents. Children whose parents are of Malawi or Mozambique origin are potentially stateless because they lack Zimbabwean citizenship due to their descent.
3. **Children who are Living on the Street:** Children living on the street face peculiar vulnerabilities because of the lack of protection that a family and parents bring. They are viewed as outcasts and face isolation from basic services that average children receive such as education. Children living on the streets are among the most at-risk populations yet government and civil society programmes have failed to adequately reach these girls. Their plight is worsened by social isolation and stigma associated with children living on the streets. Current strategies, programmes and policies have proved inadequate in responding to this population because there is little documentation of the findings. A report produced by Save the Children Norway and Streets Ahead (2009) states that 25 percent of boys living and working on the streets of Harare are victims of sexual abuse, and only 8 percent of these boys were able to report that the perpetrator had been arrested. Consortium for Street Children was quoted in a newspaper report arguing that children are on the street 'due to unemployment, ravaging effects of the HIV and Aids pandemic, family poverty, persistent droughts, family breakdowns, crime, neglect, physical and sexual abuse some children have found themselves living outside the family environment'. Whilst on the streets the children do not have access to education, food, healthcare and they usually use sex to get food.

Unaccompanied Child Migrants

Since 2005, Save the Children in Zimbabwe has been building literature that provides thick descriptions of the experiences of unaccompanied child migrants. Unaccompanied means that these children are crossing international borders without any adult supervision. Save the Children UK (2007) study shows that the mean age of children migrating unaccompanied and illegally was 14 years but some children as young as seven are migrating alone. From June 2006 to June 2010 the Beitbridge Child Reception Centre assisted 8,408 child migrants, 86% of whom were boys (Save the Children Report 2010). A study conducted by Clacherty for Save the Children (2003) indicates that girls exchange sex for transportation by truckers, are sexually and physically abused by *magumaguma* (guides) at the border crossing points and are abused in their final destinations either by their employers or police. On the other hand, boys are particularly vulnerable to physical abuse and sodomy (Dube 2012). Both boys and girls use different means to cross the borders and they do so either by walking; swimming across the Limpopo River; using trucks or transporters known as *omalaitsha*, or by using trains. Dube (2012) also indicates that the cross-border guides known as *magumaguma* are very dangerous and extort money from the people whom they will be guiding to cross the border. They steal and physically abuse children and can even take their clothing and belongings. According to Reale (2008), girls who migrated from South Africa to other countries reported that they were forced to have sex with the border guards to secure entry while boys were forced to swim across dangerous rivers. Moving across the international borders involves harm and vulnerability to children.

Children Living with HIV

Living with HIV for children is associated with stigma, exclusion, discrimination and various forms of maltreatment. There are 77000 children between the ages of 0 - 14 years are living with HIV. Mavhu *et al* (2013:5) in a study in Harare cites the following from respondents *"...people do not want them around their children once their HIV status is known...These young people are discriminated [against] by caregivers, teachers, and anyone within their vicinity...Young people themselves described how other children from the community avoided them...If you try to get closer to them they will say, ''don't get close to us, you will infect us with AIDS'.*" This is supported by Campbell *et al* (2010) who note the psychological effects of the child to child stigma related to HIV. They found that children in their study made references to the stigmatisation of AIDS-affected children, with other children refusing to play with them, generally keeping their distance and bullying them. HIV status is thus a factor in child maltreatment.

Orphanhood and Child Maltreatment

Fanelli, Musarandega and Chawanda (2007) highlight the need to have orphans participate at all levels in the implementation of the National Action Plan for Orphans and other Vulnerable Children. Currently, children are not fully participating which has a negative impact in that their voices have often been ignored in policy making. This lack of voice in policy is a critical factor in the understanding maltreatment of children. Nyamukapa *et al* (2010) note that orphaned children are often affected by trauma, being out-of-school, being cared for by a non-parent, inadequate care, child labour, physical abuse, and stigma and discrimination. This is supported by Akwara *et al* (2010) who argue that orphanhood leads to decreased school attendance and earlier sexual debut. Birdthistle *et al* (2011) further provide evidence that there is a link between orphanhood, increased sexual abuse, and vulnerability to HIV and AIDS. A UNICEF and ZimStat study (2011) found that 30 percent of double orphaned females aged 13-17 years reported experiences of childhood sexual violence compared to 15 percent of females who were not orphaned. Garutsa (2012) indicates that children orphaned and made vulnerable by AIDS are often seen as amongst the most common vulnerable social groups in Zimbabwe. They experience social and economic difficulties that include psycho-social distress, grief, stigma, discrimination, and isolation, and economic deprivation, loss of educational opportunity, burdensome domestic responsibilities, and fear for their own future. (Government of Zimbabwe and UNICEF 2005). Safaids (2009b) outlines that OVC in urban settings and poor communities are 30% less likely to attend school than other children. Of those children not attending school, 90% cited a lack of funds as the main reason for their non-attendance.

Disability

The term 'children' is often used to describe a homogenous group yet youths are differentiated in multiple ways. Youths living with disabilities face specific vulnerabilities because of their conditions. Choruma (2006) argues that there are still many disabled children not attending school in Zimbabwe. In her study, a third of the respondents did not attend schooling because family members deemed them as being incapable of learning. Padare (2014:20) cites a disabled youth in Zvishavane who said that:

...Among the disabled, there are different types such as amputees, deaf, blind and intellectually challenged (IC). Organisations hesitate to deal with IC youths because they say they are difficult to deal with...yet they need counselling also. When you compare disabled girls and able-bodied girls you see that they are getting pregnant sooner...Deaf girls have left aside because most counsellors and trainers cannot use sign language. There is no brail material for the blind youths.

This also affects secondary schooling where there is a continued lack of teachers for various forms of disability (Choruma 2006). Maltreatment of disabled children draws from the stigma associated with a disability which often brings shame to families. This has led to many disabled children being locked away and failing to access education services.

Domestic Violence

Mangwa and Ingwani (2014) argue that there is a direct link between domestic violence and abuse of children. They cite a respondent in their study who notes that '*When for example parents are in a domestic dispute the husband can vent his anger on children who at times will be against what the father will be doing and will sexually abuse them. Sometimes when for instance, a mother due to domestic violence leaves the home the father can take this opportunity to sexually abuse children who will be left in his custody*' (Mangwa and Ingwani 2014:159). Maruta (2011) argues that children are usually innocent victims of domestic violence in multiple ways. Firstly child violence impairs a parent's ability to care and nurture for children. Secondly, male abusers often beat the children when abusing the mother. The abuse on the mother can also have far-reaching psychological effects on children. Children whose mothers are abused sometimes suffer at the hands of their mothers as well. A 2009 UNFPA/UNICEF/IOM study, in Harare, Mberengwa, Mudzi and Mutare highlighted that young girl, orphans and unaccompanied minors (especially girls), women in female-headed households, both married and unmarried women, and young boys are most at risk of gender-based violence. The battering of the mother is often associated with sexual abuse of her child and mothers who are themselves abused do not feel able to protect their children from sexual abuse; yet, if they leave, these mothers expose their children to further abuse in their absence (Khatlane undated).

Power Differential within Schools

Gudyanda (2014) outlines how within the school setting teachers use their power to abuse students. The study highlights how both male and female students are sexually, physically and emotionally abused by their teachers or people in authority within the school environment. Teachers often take advantage of pupils' ignorance on what constitutes abuse and thus get away with abusing children (Tshabalala and Khosa 2014; Shumba 2001). According to a Plan International report (2009), 13 percent of girls report being sexually harassed by teachers and/or fellow pupils. Of these, 7 percent report having been forced into sex at least once. This shows that the school environment if not properly monitored can lead to rampant maltreatment of children. Table 1 below shows that sexual intercourse was the most rampant form of abuse reported in schools. According to the Girl Child Network, more than 700 rape cases of girls aged 5 to 16 were reported in 2005 (with 93% of victims being girls).

Shumba (2008) in a study in Masvingo indicates how emotional abuse is rampant within the schooling system. The study highlights how the majority of teachers engage in various forms of abuse such as name calling, verbal aggression, labelling and derogatory language. In most instances, verbal abuse is linked to sexual abuse outlined above. This affects girl students more than boys as schools are sites of sexual violence for girls (Leach and Machakanja 2000). The practice of abuse within the school system has to a large extent become institutionalised. Practices such as corporal punishment or using students to do personal chores by teachers are seen as common practices which are not questioned. Corporal punishment is viewed by most parents as cultural and acceptable.

Reconstituted and Stepfamilies' Phenomenon

Studies show that step mothers and fathers are part of the problem in child maltreatment. For example, Mangwa and Ingwani (2014) cite press reports to show that in Zimbabwe the issue of stepfathers sexually abusing step children is prevalent. Simukai Child Protection, a local nongovernmental organisation note that stepmothers are one of the major reasons leading to children living on the streets. In a participatory study with children in informal settlements in Harare, McIvor (2001:42) heard children note that:

We are physically and mentally abused by our stepmothers. They always accuse us of something we have not done. If anything is missing at home, we are always blamed. Some of us girls are given men, whom we do not want. If the men we are given become broke, our stepmothers usually look for another man with money. Some children are abused by stepfathers, while their mothers are away.

Living with a step parent can thus be a risk factor to child maltreatment. This is not to say all step parents are abusive. Rather reports and studies are showing that there is a high likelihood that children living with stepparents will suffer some form of maltreatment.

Table 1. Abuse in schools (Parliament of Zimbabwe 2006)

Nature of Abuse	Number of Cases	Percentage (%)
Sexual intercourse	139	65.5
Love letter	55	26
Fondling, kissing and hugging etc	23	10.9
Rape or attempted rape	4	1.9
Showed Pornographic material	1	0.5
Total	**212**	**100**

Conflict and Macro-Political Environment

Post-2000 Zimbabwe has undergone violent elections periods in which many human rights abuses were perpetrated on men, women, and children. These abuses include beatings, loss of limbs, rape, murder and burning of buttocks. According to Research Advocate Unit and Zimbabwe Doctors for Human Rights (2010), high numbers of rapes happened in public in the eyes of the family and children. This has left a lot of trauma on the survivors and their families. Macro political context has a direct influence on child protection. Child abuse tends to be higher in conflict situations where institutions of public order have lost control.

Survivors as Abusers

Ritcher et al (2013) in a three-country study (including Zimbabwe) conclude that there is 'significant associations between childhood abuse and the range of adult risk behaviours examined. We confirm associations between childhood abuse and adult sexual risk behaviour, and especially notable are rates of childhood abuse among African men, including sexual abuse, as well as high rates of recent forced sex and partner violence among men.' Children who have been abused thus tend to become abusers when they grow up. The trauma of abuse often has negative mental consequences for survivors that require mental health.

New Media and Cyber-Based Child Abuse

There is a lack of studies focusing on the role social media and information technology in the maltreatment of children in Zimbabwe. Various organisations working with girls in Zimbabwe argue the increase in sexual videos on phones amongst youths with detrimental psychological effects on girls. Mangwa and Ingwani (2014) in their study provide an analysis of how the internet, television, social networking sites, cell phones, and video games can expose children to sexual abuse. There is still, however, a gap in research and knowledge of how new media impacts on child maltreatment in Zimbabwe. The increased usage and uptake of these technologies by young people makes it imperative to have research around the possible negative impacts on child protection. Increasingly young people will be spending most of their time online yet child researchers in Zimbabwe have not taken the initiative to understand how children experience this space.

Child Carers

In Zimbabwe children caring for ailing parents especially those affected by the HIV and AIDS pandemic face multiple vulnerabilities. A report by Save the Children (2010) showed that child carers often suffer emotional stress because of the demands of caring and watching sick parents and relatives. For an example, the report notes how children are forced to bath parents of the opposite sex. Child carers face multiple caring roles for the sick parent/s and also their siblings. This includes economic responsibilities for the family which leads to various abuses through child labour and often sex work. The 2011 ZimStats Child Labour Survey shows that 290,684 children aged 15-17 years and 314,173 between 5-14 years are engaged in economic activities. A 2014 report by Zimbabwe Youth Council shows how because of poverty and orphanhood, children are involved in risky livelihood activities that include prostitution, gold panning and border jumping.

Age of Children and Inadequate Legal Protection

Children occupy the lowest rungs of the status hierarchy in many areas of Africa, including Zimbabwe. This is especially true for girls, who may be treated as outsiders because they will ultimately belong to another family upon marriage. Statistics from Childline for 2014 show that the most affected group in terms of sexual and physical abuse is young girls between 13 -15 years of age. There were 447 reported cases for 13 -15-year-old girls compared to 171 for 16-17 yrs and 78 for 0-6-year-olds. Age also matters in terms of ability to speak and report abuse. Young babies that are abused cannot talk or report the abuse.

There are studies that elaborate the problems within the criminal justice system which compromise its ability to provide effective remedies to victims of child sexual abuse. Many people claim that the prison terms are not deterrent enough with reports of perpetrators getting as low as three months depending on the nature of the case and available evidence. WAG and Padare's (2014) documentation report highlights how people in Nkayi, Chivhu and Hurungwe have little faith in the legal system which makes it difficult for many survivors of abuse to report. The report highlights how the police in these districts are finding it difficult to cover all the areas due to transport shortages. Zimbabwe introduced Victim Friendly Units because of a realisation that the criminal justice system was insensitive to survivors of abuse. The problems have continued however with most people having little faith in the system given that it '...emphasises the rights of the accused at the expense of protecting the child victims of sexual abuse' (Mutandwa 2012:21). Mutandwa (2012) provides substantial cases on how victims are sidelined from sentencing and how this alienates people from the criminal justice system. Without deterrents and protection from legal institutions, perpetrators of abuse will continue with no fear of repercussions of their actions.

RECOMMENDATIONS

- **Challenging Structural Determinants of Child Maltreatment:** Patriarchy remains the bedrock of harmful cultural practices yet there are very few organisations involved in questioning and challenging this institution. Whilst advocacy and other activities are good there is need to challenge cultural norms and values that are detrimental to children.
- **Further Reforms to Make the Justice System Survivor Friendly:** Research has shown that most survivors of abuse have lost confidence in the justice system. The process of conviction is long and often perpetrators get bail, which makes it problematic for survivors. The criminal justice system respects the rights of the accused more than the survivor because of the principle of presumed innocence until found guilty.
- **Increased Participation of Children:** Most organisations are attempting to increase the participation of children in their programmes. Whilst children differ with age and maturity there is scope to include all ages in programming by promoting children's views, wishes, hopes, and thoughts. National processes and institutions should include child representatives.

- **Improve Legal Literacy and Enhance Referral Pathways to Reporting Abuse:** There is a need to increase legal aid services for the majority of women and children who have little knowledge about their rights and obligation. Laws and policies need to be cascaded to the grassroots so that they help child abuse survivors.
- **Increased Training and Capacity Building:** Most local organisations have gaps in their capacity especially related to research and documentation. There is a need for more training even within government departments to allow for documentation and follow-up.
- **Longer Projects With Long-Term Goals of Changing Community Norms:** Most programmes are short term with specific goals and targets. Funding organisations usually focus quantifiable outcomes yet certain elements of combating child maltreatment such as changing cultural norms take years and are not easily quantifiable. Changing attitudes and perceptions takes time and concerted effort yet the nature of funding limits this type of work.
- **Facilitate the One-Stop Shops:** There is a need to facilitate the population of one-stop shops that provide survivor friendly services. The one-stop shops should have a medical and legal clinic as well as law enforcement in a single setting. The one-stop shops will use a multi-disciplinary approach to integrating medical and psychological services with legal management.

CONCLUSION

The chapter has highlighted the determinants and social drivers of child maltreatment in Zimbabwe. It used an extensive review of the literature to highlight the complex and intersecting nature of factors that leave children vulnerable to various forms of abuse. The literature review exercise focused on academic studies and project reports published in various formats. Various factors including culture, gender, religion, age and social location were discussed in detail to understand how and why child maltreatment is difficult to combat in Zimbabwe. The major focus of the paper was not to provide solutions or recommendations but rather to unpack and analyse the contextual drivers of child maltreatment. The research concluded that child maltreatment is a factor of multiple reinforcing and intersecting factors.

REFERENCES

ActionAid. (2005). *A Study on the Impact of—Operation Murambatsvina/Restore Order in 26 Wards of Harare High-Density Housing Areas. ActionAid International in Collaboration with Combined Harare Residents Association*. CHRA.

Akwara, P., Noubary, B., Lim Ah Ken, P., Johnson, K., Yates, R., Winfrey, W., & Luo, C. et al. (2010). Who is the Vulnerable Child? Using Survey Data to Identify Children at Risk in the Era of HIV and AIDS. *AIDS Care*, *22*(9), 1066–1085. doi:10.1080/09540121.2010.498878 PMID:20824560

Berger, S., & Thornycroft, P. (2008). *Zimbabwe's Cholera Victims Ten Times More Likely To Die*. London: Telegraph (UK). Retrieved December 8, 2008, from, http://www.telegraph.co.uk/news/worldnews/africaandindianocean/zimbabwe/3660739/Zimbabwes-cholera-victims-ten-times-more-likely-to-die.html

Birdthistle, I. J., Sian, F., Mwanasa, S., Auxillia, N., Gwiza, E., & Glynn, J. R. (2011). Child Sexual Abuse and Links to HIV and Orphanhood in Urban Zimbabwe. *Journal of Epidemiology and Community Health*, *65*(12), 1075–1082. doi:10.1136/jech.2009.094359 PMID:20628080

Bower, C. (2003). The Relationship between Child Abuse and Poverty. *Agenda (Durban, South Africa)*, *56*, 84–85.

Campbell, C., Skovdal, M., Mupambireyi, Z., & Gregson, S. (2010). Exploring Childrens Stigmatisation of AIDS-Affected Children in Zimbabwe through Drawings and Stories. *Social Science & Medicine*, *71*(5), 975–985. doi:10.1016/j.socscimed.2010.05.028 PMID:20591546

Chakona, L. (2012). *The Impact of the Fast Track Land Reform Programme on Women in Goromonzi District, Zimbabwe* (MA Thesis). Rhodes University.

Child Line. (2010). *An Analysis of Child Abuse Cases Reported to Child Line Zimbabwe in the Period December 31st, 2008 to January 1st, 2010*. Child Line Zimbabwe.

Chireshe, R., Chireshe, E., & Mudhovozi, P. (2009). Child Abuse: Psychosocial and Religious Intervention Strategies in Zimbabwe. *Journal of Psychology in Africa*, *19*(2), 261–263.

Chiweshe, M. K. (2012a). *Farm Level Institutions in Emergent Communities in post-Fast Track Zimbabwe: Case of Mazowe District* (Unpublished PhD thesis). Rhodes University, South Africa.

Chiweshe, M. K. (2012b). *For Girls Only: Intersection of Age, Gender, Class and Race as a Source of Vulnerability for Adolescent Girls in Africa*. Addressing Inequalities: The Heart of the Post-2015 Development Agenda and the Future We Want for All, Global Thematic Consultation, UN. Retrieved May 3, 2015, from http://www.comminit.com/clickthru/58f0013972b7e97878b16db0b99c345a?node=9301387

Choruma, T. (2006). *The Forgotten Tribe: People with Disabilities in Zimbabwe*. Progression Report.

Clacherty, G. (2003). *Poverty made this decision for me: Children in Musina: Their Experiences and Needs*. Save the Children UK.

Dube, R. (2012). *Investigation into the experiences of undocumented child migrants from Zimbabwe to South Africa: A case study of experiences of irregular child migrants from Mberengwa* (Unpublished Masters Thesis). Women's University in Africa, Zimbabwe.

Dube, R. (2013). *She probably asked for it!" A Preliminary Study into Zimbabwean Societal Perceptions of Rape*. Harare: Research and Advocacy Unit.

Fanelli, C. W., Musarandega, R., & Chawanda, L. (2007). Child Participation in Zimbabwe's National Action Plan for Orphans and Other Vulnerable Children: Progress, Challenges, and Possibilities. *Children, Youth and Environments*, *17*, 122–145.

Ferguson, K. E. (1999). Patriarchy. In H. Tierney (Ed.), *Women's Studies Encyclopaedia*. Greenwood Publishing.

Girl Child Network. (2005). *Gravity of Girl Child Sexual Abuse in Zimbabwe: "Towards Creating a Culture of Prevention," 6– 7*. Retrieved October 13, 2015, from, http://www.kubatana.net/docs/sexual/gcn_sexual_abuse_zim_050517.pdf

Government of Zimbabwe. (2005). *Zimbabwe National Strategic Plan for the Education of Girls, Orphans, and other Vulnerable Children 2005-2010*. Author.

Government of Zimbabwe & UNICEF. (2005). *Survey on Orphans and Other Vulnerable Children in Rural and Urban High Density Zimbabwe 2004/2005*. Harare: UNICEF.

Gregson, S., Garnett, G. P., Nyamukapa, C. A., Hallet, T. B., Lewis, J. J. C., Mason, P. R., & Anderson, R. M. et al. (2002). HIV Decline Associated with Bahavior Change in Eastern Zimbabwe. *Science*, *311*(5761), 664–666. doi:10.1126/science.1121054 PMID:16456081

Gudyanga, E. (2014). Emerging Issues on Child Abuse: Voices of Student Teachers. *Education Journal*, *3*, 146–152.

Kambarami, M. (2006). *Femininity, Sexuality and Culture: Patriarchy and Female Subordination in Zimbabwe. In Understanding Human Sexuality Seminar Series*. Africa Regional Sexuality Resource Centre.

Khatlane, R. (n.d.). *Domestic Violence: How it Contributes to Sexual Exploitation of Children*. The National Consultative Conference against the Sexual Exploitation of Children.

Krug, E. G., Dahlberg, L. L., Mercy, J. A., Zwi, A. B., & Lozano, R. L. (2002). *World Report on Violence and Health*. Geneva: World Health Organization.

Leach, F., & Machakanja, P. (2000). *Preliminary Investigation of the Abuse of Girls in Zimbabwean Junior Secondary Schools*. Education Research Paper 39, DFID.

Magwa, S., & Ingwani, V. (2014). Exploring Sexual Abuse of School Children in Families: A Case Study of Masvingo District, Zimbabwe. *The International Journal of Humanities & Social Studies*, *2*(9), 156–161.

Makamure, E. (2010). *The Efficacy of the Family Support Trust, (FST) Post Rape Counselling for girl children aged 3 to 12 years in Harare Zimbabwe (Masters in Women's Law). Southern and Eastern African Regional Centre for Women's Law (SEARCWL)*, University of Zimbabwe.

Maruta, S. (2011). *Understanding the Impact of Domestic Violence on the Work or Organizations and Institutions in Ruwa*. Southern Institute of Peace Building and Development.

Mashiri, L. (2013). Conceptualisation of Gender Based Violence in Zimbabwe. *International Journal of Humanities and Social Science*, *3*(15), 94–103.

Mashumba, S., Musa, A., Mupeta, B., & Kinsani, M. (2004). *A Situation Analysis Study; reducing community Vulnerability to HIV/AIDS in Chipinge and Chiredzi Program Areas*. Harare: Plan Zimbabwe.

Mavhu, W., Berwick, J., Chirawu, P., Makamba, M., Copas, A., Dirawo, J., & Cowan, F. M. et al. (2013). Enhancing Psychosocial Support for HIV Positive Adolescents in Harare, Zimbabwe. *PLoS ONE*, *8*(7), e70254. doi:10.1371/journal.pone.0070254 PMID:23894625

McIvor, C. (2001). Do Not Look Down On Us. *Child Researchers Investigate Informal Settlements in Zimbabwe*, *42*, 3–4.

Mulrow, D. C. (1994). Rationale for Systematic reviews. *British Journal of Medicine*, *309*(6954), 597–599. doi:10.1136/bmj.309.6954.597 PMID:8086953

Muronda, Y. (2009). *Social Security And The National Orphan Care Policy In Zimbabwe: Challenges From The Child Headed Household*. Academic Press.

Mutandwa, C. (2012). *How Can Criminal Justice Work Constructively With Shona Justice to Provide Effective Remedies to Child Sexual Abuse Victims?* The Danish Institute for Human Rights.

Nhundu, T., & Shumba, A. (2001). The Nature and Frequency of Reported Cases of Teacher Perpetrated Child Sexual Abuse in Rural Primary Schools in Zimbabwe. *Child Abuse & Neglect*, *25*, 1517–1534.

Nyamukapa, C. A., Gregson, S., Wambe, M., Mushore, P., Lopman, B., Mupambireyi, Z., & Jukes, M. C. H. et al. (2010). Causes and Consequences of Psychological Distress among Orphans in Eastern Zimbabwe. *AIDS Care*, *22*(8), 988–996. doi:10.1080/09540121003615061 PMID:20552465

Padare. (2014). *Walking in our Daughter's Shoes Evaluation Report*. Harare: Padare.

Parahoo, K. (2006). Nursing Research – Principles, Process and Issues (2nd ed.). Houndsmill, UK: Palgrave.

Parliament of Zimbabwe. (2006). *Fact Sheet: Child Abuse in the Education Sector*. Harare: Parliament of Zimbabwe Research Department.

Plan Zimbabwe. (2009). *Research Report on Child Abuse in Schools: A Baseline Study for the Learn Without Fear Campaign*. Harare: Plan International.

Population Council. (2009). *Adolescent Girls Programming and Capacity-Building Workshop*. Retrieved July 7, 2012, from, http://www.popcouncil.org/pdfs/PGY09_AdolWkshopNairobi08.pdf

Protocol on the Multi-Sectoral Management of Sexual Abuse and Violence in Zimbabwe. (2012). Zim Resources.

Reale, D. (2008). *Away from Home. Protecting and Supporting Children on the Move*. London: Save the Children.

Research and Advocacy Unit and Zimbabwe Association of Doctors for Human Rights. (2010). *No Hiding Place: Politically Motivated Rape of Women in Zimbabwe*. Retrieved May 1 2015, from, http://lexglobal.org/files/POLITICAL%20RAPE%20REPORT.pdf

Richter, L. (2013). Reported Physical and Sexual Abuse in Childhood and Adult HIV Risk Behaviour in Three African Countries: Findings from Project Accept (HPTN-043). *AIDS and Behavior*. doi:10.1007/s10461-013-0439-7 PMID:23474641

Sachikonye, L. (2004). Land Reform and Farm Workers. In D. Harold-Barry (Ed.), *Zimbabwe: The Past is the Future*. Harare: Weaver Press.

Safaids. (2009a). *Zimbabwean stories of "Best Practice" in Mitigating the HIV Crisis through a Cultural and Gender Perspective*. Harare: Safaids.

Safaids. (2009b). *Children to the Fore!: An Easy-to-Use Training Handbook That Promotes Child Rights And Cultural Issues in the Face of HIV in Southern Africa*. Harare: Safaids.

Safaids. (2011). *Best Practices on Challenging Gender Dynamics in Cultural Context*. Harare: Safaids.

Save the Children. (2007). *Children Crossing Borders*. Johannesburg: Save the Children UK.

Save the Children. (2008a). *Our Broken Dream: Child Migration in Southern Africa*. Johannesburg: Save the Children UK.

Save the Children. (2008b). *Save the Children Expands Assistance to Children Hurt by Zimbabwe Hunger Crisis*. Save the Children Organisation. Retrieved May 3 2015, from, http://www.savethechildren.org/newsroom/2008/zimbabwe-hungercrisis.html?print=t

Save the Children. (2010). *Child Carers: Child Led Research with Children who are Carers*. Pretoria: Save the Children Southern Africa.

Save the Children Norway, Childline and Streets Ahead. (2009). *The Nature and Prevalence of Violence and Sexual Abuse among Boys Living and Working on the Streets of Harare*. Harare: Childline.

Save the Children UK. (2007). *Children Crossing Borders: Report on Unaccompanied Minors who have Travelled to South Africa*. Johannesburg: Save the Children UK.

Shumba, A. (2001). 'Who Guards the Guards in Schools?' A Study of Reported Cases of Child Abuse by Teachers in Zimbabwean Secondary Schools Sex Education. *Sexuality, Society and Learning*, *1*(1), 77–86.

Shumba, A. (2008). Emotional Abuse in the Classroom. *Journal of Emotional Abuse*, *4*(3-4), 139–149. doi:10.1300/J135v04n03_09

Sibanda, M. (2011). *Married too Soon: Child Marriage in Zimbabwe*. Retrieved June 3 2015, from, http://www.researchandadvocacyunit.org/index.php?view=download&alias=294-child-marriages-in-zimbabwe-printers-version-final&category_slug=womens-programme-1&option=com_docman&Itemid=115

Together for Girls: Sexual Violence Fact Sheet. (2012). Retrieved May 1 2015, from, http://www.togetherforgirls.org/docs/Together%20for%20Girls%20Sexual%20Violence%20Fact%20Sheet%20July%20 2012.pdf

Tshabalala, T., & Khosa, M. T. (2014). Awareness of Various Forms of Child Abuse: Pupils' Attributions – A Case Study of Gomadoda Cluster. *Asian Journal of Social Sciences and Management Studies*, *1*(1), 23–28.

UNFPA. (2005). *Child Marriage Factsheet: State of World Population*. New York: UNFPA.

UNICEF. (2008). *Economic Meltdown Worsens Child Abuse in Zimbabwe*. Harare: UNICEF.

UNICEF. (2010). *Status of Women's and Children's Rights in Zimbabwe, 2005 – 2010: A Call for Reducing Disparities and Improving Equity*. Retrieved September 11 2015, from, http://reliefweb.int/sites/reliefweb.int/files/resources/ADAAAF5498C9072485257857007l7288-Full_Report.pdf

UNICEF & Zimbabwe National Statistics Agency. (2011). *National Baseline Survey on Life Experiences of Adolescents Report*. Harare: ZimStat.

Zimbabwe National Statistics Agency. (2011). *Child Labour Survey*. Harare: ZimStat.

Zimbabwe National Statistics Agency (ZIMSTAT) & ICF International. (2012). *Zimbabwe Demographic and Health Survey 2010-11*. Calverton, MD: ZIMSTAT and ICF International Inc.

Zimbabwe Youth Council. (2014). *Harmful Cultural and Social Practices Affecting Children: Our Collective Responsibility*. Harare: ZYC.

ADDITIONAL READING

1.2.1 The need for systematic reviews. (n.d.). Retrieved from http://handbook.cochrane.org/chapter_1/1_2_1_the_need_for_systematic_reviews.htm

Chifamba, M. (2013, June 12). Sexual abuse rife on the streets. Retrieved from https://www.newsday.co.zw/2013/06/12/sexual-abuse-rife-on-the-streets/

Child sexual abuse victims locked up in psychological prisons. (2014, June 21). Retrieved from https://www.newsday.co.zw/2014/06/21/child-sexual-abuse-victims-locked-psychological-prisons/

Marsh, M., Kenny, E., & Miquel, J. (n.d.). Joint UNICEF, UNFPA & IOM Gender-Based Violence Field Mission Zimbabwe: May 2009. Retrieved from http://cpwg.net/wp-content/uploads/sites/2/2011/09/Joint-UNICEF-UNFPA-IOM-GBV-Mission-Zimbabwe-%E2%80%93-May-2009-.pdf

Phiri, G. (n.d.). War of words at miniskirt march. Retrieved October 5, 2014, from http://www.dailynews.co.zw/articles/2014/10/05/war-of-words-at-miniskirt-march

Promotion and Protection of the Rights of Children. (2006, August 29). Retrieved from http://www.unicef.org/violencestudy/reports/SG_violencestudy_en.pdf

Protocol to the African Charter on Human and Peoples' Rights on the Rights of Women in Africa. (n.d.). Retrieved from http://www.achpr.org/instruments/women-protocol/

Violence Prevention Alliance. (2017). Retrieved from http://www.who.int/violenceprevention/en/

Zimbabwe. (2015). Retrieved from http://www.unaids.org/en/regionscountries/countries/zimbabwe

Chapter 3
Violence Against Children in Botswana:
Reality, Challenges, and the Way Forward

Odireleng Mildred Jankey
University of Botswana, Botswana

Tapologo Maundeni
University of Botswana, Botswana

ABSTRACT

Violence against children is a profound violation of human rights that has far-reaching consequences for children's well-being. Experiences of violence can lead to lasting physical, mental, and emotional harm, regardless of whether a child is a direct victim or witness. Violence against children cuts across geographic boundaries, culture, race, class, religion, educational and socio-economic backgrounds. Yet, it is under- researched in the context of developing countries such as Botswana. Most research on interpersonal violence in developing countries has been conducted on women. This chapter analyses the complex and multifaceted issue of violence against children (VaC) in Botswana. It discusses the types and contexts of violence that children are exposed to; the effects of violence on children; the risk factors for VaC; and the existing approaches to addressing the issue. The chapter uses documents as source materials. It concludes by charting the way forward for research, practice, and policy.

INTRODUCTION

Violence against children is a disturbing and widespread phenomenon the world over. It is a profound violation of human rights with devastating and long-term consequences for those affected. It is a societal and global concern because it blocks opportunities for growth and development. Experiences of violence can lead to long-lasting physical, mental, and emotional harm, whether a child is a direct victim or a witness. Children who have experienced violence are more likely to suffer attachment problems, anxiety, conduct disorders, cognitive and academic problems, and to display delinquent behaviour.

DOI: 10.4018/978-1-5225-2578-3.ch003

For decades, violence against children has been of interest to different professionals such as nurses, social workers, paediatricians, and lawyers, and to public officers and the public. Despite widespread interest in the phenomenon across different fields of study in Botswana existing literature is scarce and the dynamics are insufficiently understood and discussed. Furthermore, incidence and prevalence rates throughout the country are unknown. However, the scanty literature and insights from the field demonstrate that the numbers of children who experience violence cannot be ignored. Violence against children spans geographic boundaries, culture, race, class, religion, and educational, and socio-economic background (Khan, Kapoor, & Cooraswamy, 2000). The image that Botswana has created in the local, regional and international arena is that of child-centeredness and this has been realised through the ratification of regional and international protocols. However, this attractive image is contradicted by negative aspects of children's lives which include poverty, HIV and AIDS, malnutrition, exploitation, and violence.

Violence against children is a global epidemic that requires a multifaceted response. What differs within countries are trends and patterns of violence (UNICEF, 2000). In many societies and communities, the family is an institution wherein children are nurtured, and seek love, safety, shelter, and security. While this should be the norm, practice evidence indicates that it is the same institution that children suffer the worst forms of violence (UNICEF, 2000). Given that violence against children frequently occurs in the home, it is frequently tolerated and met with a culture of silence, especially where the perpetrators are other family members. In Botswana, if such violence is brought to the attention of the state and law enforcement agencies, reports may be met with passivity as violence is tolerated within the patriarchal family structure (Mookodi, 2004; Maundeni, 2002). Violence suffered by children in the country is growing at an alarming rate. Despite scanty literature on the subject, media reports and concerns of community leaders, faith-based organisations, and government and nongovernmental organisations have created a public outcry to protect children from violence. For example, in May 2016, #IShallNotForget campaign drew attention to the issue. This movement came about as a result of an area councillor impregnating a 17-year-old student. Activists and the public engaged in awareness raising about sexual abuse and the inconsistencies in policies that are meant to protect children.

Botswana society could be said to be a child centred society when considering the international protocols ratified by the country such as the UN Convention on the Rights of the Child in 1989 and the UN Declaration on the Elimination of Violence Against Women in 1993. Other programs include free childhood immunisation, infant feeding, orphan care, and prevention of mother-to-child transmission of HIV (PMTCT) (Chopra, & Rollins, 2008). This seemingly child centred approach is contradicted by violence suffered by children in homes, schools, child and health care facilities. Such experiences block their opportunity for growth and development and threaten the realisation of their innate human potential (Caspi, McClay, Moffitt, Mill, Martin, Craig, 2002). In recent decades, there have been concerns among different professionals such as social workers, paediatricians, lawyers, and psychologists as well as the public about violence suffered by children. Yet, despite this and the results of studies conducted worldwide, violence against children is still insufficiently understood. Real incidents and prevalence rates throughout Botswana are not known and relatively little research has been conducted in this regard. However, anecdotal evidence from the field and media reports indicate that children do experience violence in their lives.

BACKGROUND

In Botswana, most of the violence committed against children is underreported. Police reports have indicated that 27% of sexual violence cases concerned children (Police Report on the Study of Rape in Botswana, 1999). Thus, the real numbers of children who are sexually abused and exploited are not known. The World Health Organization (WHO) estimates that 25% of girls and 8% of boys have been victims of sexual violence in their lives and thus the Botswana estimates of 27% are even higher than the universal average. A survey conducted among 560 students in North West Botswana found that 67% of the children experienced unwanted touching, pressure for dates, and sexual harassment and 25% reported that sexual violence was a regular occurrence in their lives. Different police stations in Botswana have raised concern over sexual offences against children, especially young girls, including defilement, rape, indecent assault, and incest. What is disconcerting is that many cases go unreported since the perpetrators are family members. Police statistics reveal that most sexual offenders are known to the victims. These perpetrators include brothers, fathers, uncles, and cousins, friends of the family, babysitters, and neighbours (Police Report on the Study of Rape in Botswana, 1999). Though there are no reliable statistics on violence against children in Botswana, the prevalence is believed to be higher than what is currently reported. Botswana as a country has been struggling with a high incidence of HIV and AIDS. There are traditional and cultural practices such as the belief that having sexual intercourse with a child is a cure for HIV and AIDS. This traditional belief puts children (especially the girl child) at risk of being sexually violated (Heald, 2006). Perpetration of sexual violence is mostly by men in Botswana. Cases of sexual violation of school children by women are very rare. Evidence from police records shows that children are afraid to report such cases, and parents who should be protecting them may remain silent if the abuse is perpetrated by a spouse, family member or a person in a position of authority. The stigma attached to sexual violence in a patriarchal society like Botswana may further put children at risk, where family honour is placed before a child's' safety and wellbeing (Heald, 2006).

Furthermore, In Botswana, there is cultural acceptance of violence. It is traditionally accepted for adults to administer corporal punishment on their children if they misbehave. The Botswana culture does not view children as right holders; they are expected to be subservient to their parents. Cultural practices that perpetuate the subordination of children increase their vulnerability and open them to abuse and exploitation (Mogwe, 1988, UNICEF, 2011).

IMPACT OF VIOLENCE AGAINST CHILDREN: A GLOBAL PERSPECTIVE

There are similarities in the effects on children who experience violence but it would be erroneous to assume that the impact is similar for all children (Holt, Buckley, & Whelan, 2008). Empirical data indicate the short and long-term implications for children who experience violence (McGee, 2000; Saunders, 2003). Reviewed literature reveals gender differences for boys and girls regarding the nature and extent of the presenting problems. Studies show that boys exhibit externalised problems such as hostility and aggression, while girls exhibit internalised problems such as depression and somatic complaints (Martin, 2002). Boys' externalising behaviours are linked to exposure to high levels of violence while girls' internalising behaviours are a result of higher levels of self-blame (Kerig, 1996; McIntosh, 2003).

Children who have experienced violence may exhibit trauma-related symptoms. They may be more aggressive, fearful, depressed, and suffer from anxiety, and post-traumatic stress disorder where they display symptoms of bedwetting and nightmares compared to children who have not experienced or witnessed violence in their lives (Graham-Bermann & Seng, 2005). In addition, these children, (more often than their counterparts) may be at risk for allergies, asthma, headaches, and influenza. The impact of violence on children may appear to diminish with time when they are no longer exposed to such violence. However, it may continue into adulthood. Children who experience violence are more likely to batter their partners and abuse their own children in the future (Strauss, Gelles, & Smith, 1990)

THEORETICAL ANALYSIS OF VIOLENCE AGAINST CHILDREN

This chapter uses the ecological systems theory (Bronfenbrenner, 1979) to explain and understand VaC within the Botswana context. This theory focuses on the developing individual, their environment, and evolving interactions (Cicchetti & Lynch, 1993). The theory emphasises that environmental factors play a critical role in development in a variety of ways. Bronfenbrenner (1979) discusses five levels of the ecological systems, namely microsystems, messosystems, exosystems, macro systems, and chronosystem. The microsystem is the direct environment that includes a child's family, relatives, friends, classmates, teachers, neighbours and any person that have a direct social interaction with a child. A child can experience violence because of interacting directly with any of the persons in this system. The second is the mesosystem which focuses on the interconnections between the microsystems. For example, a child's family experience may be related to their school experience. A child experiencing violence at home may also be a target of bullying in the school environment. Following the mesosystem is the exosystem which entails links between a social setting in which an individual does not have an active role and the individual's immediate context (Bronfenbrenner, 2004). For example, when a parent is a target of a looming job retrenchment, the resultant distress might make them angrier, impatient, irritable, and abusive towards their children for making material demands or wasting available resources. The fourth system is the macro system which is a culture in which an individual live. This may include socioeconomic status, poverty, and ethnicity. For example, a child who is raised in an inner-city environment where communities are struggling with violence and crime would more likely experience violence in such a culture. The last system is the chronosystem which entails transitions and shifts in one's lifespan. For example, a mother experiencing physical violence as a major transition in her life is not the only one affected but the negative effects violence will also affect her children. Research indicates that children who witness violence are more likely to be violent to their partners (Belsky, 1980).

METHODOLOGY

The study for this chapter used the documentary research method. The documents reviewed and analysed included government publications such as Acts of Parliaments, reports of commissions of inquiry, ministerial and departmental reports (Mogalakwe, 2006); and private documents from civil society organisations, non- governmental organisations and international organisations. Documentary sources also included legal and policy frameworks, international conventions, and scholarly papers on violence against children. These documents were subjected to Scott's quality control criteria for handling documentary sources which include checking documents for authenticity, credibility, and meaning (Scott, 1990).

CHILDREN EXPERIENCES OF VIOLENCE IN BOTSWANA

In Botswana, children experience different types of violence, and this could be context specific. In schools and the home environment, evidence shows that children, especially girls, experience sexual and physical violence at the hands of males, be it male students, teachers or uncles, stepfathers, stepbrothers at home and in the community (USAID, 2003; Wible, 2004). Evidence from Botswana supports the ecological systems theory because children are experiencing violence in the micro system from male students, teachers, uncles, stepfathers, and brothers; who have direct social interaction with children (Azar, 1991). Sexual abuse and harassment of girls occur where males demand sexual favours in return for good grades in class or money and gifts in exchange for sex. Evidence of physical and sexual violence is indicated by a 2.4% drop-out rate, where girls (3.25) accounted for higher rates than boys (1.6%) (Chilisa, 2002). In addition, the author contends that pregnancy was a major cause of girls dropping out in Botswana schools. While physical and sexual violence at home and in school is generally affecting girls, it should also be noted that young boys also have this predicament, although it is less common (Rossetti, 2001). The mesosystem is evident here, where young girls who experience physical and sexual violence at home also experience violence in schools.

Corporal punishment in schools is another form of violence suffered by children who may sustain serious injury in this regard. It may also result in truancy and, in the worst scenario, withdrawal from school. As argued by Tafa (2002), canning is not only administered by teachers but also by sundry others such as students, untrained teachers, student teachers, night watchmen, and porters. Canes may be used to monitor students during the study, feeding, punctuality and at the assembly. Canning students is so embedded in the school system in Botswana that parents are sometimes summoned to school to cane their children for misbehaviour (Tafa, 2002). While there are clear regulations about caning by the Ministry of Education (MOE), many schools are in violation of such regulations (Tafa, 2002).

Other types of violence that children in Botswana experience in settings such as homes and other public places) include neglect, abandonment and baby dumping. Infanticide, baby-dumping, and abandonment of children have attracted much attention in the press and child welfare agencies throughout the country over the past several years (Modie-Moroka, 2011). Some of the exo-systemic explanations for the above scenario include unemployment, mine closure and massive job loss, poverty; substance abuse, as well as psychopathology such as depression.

RISK FACTORS FOR VIOLENCE AGAINST CHILDREN

Abuse of Women

Studies indicate that some children in Botswana have experienced violence through witnessing and being hurt by domestic violence (Jankey, 2013). Studies reviewed by Edlesson (1999) show a 50% overlap between domestic violence and child maltreatment. Children may be deliberately or accidentally injured through domestic violence incidents. Research also shows that older children may run the risk of being hurt in an attempt to stop a violent situation between their parents (Edleson, Mbilinyi, Beeman & Hagemeister, 2003). Research studies have clearly linked violence against children with wife abuse, where clinical studies indicate that 40 to 70% of men who abuse their intimate partners also abuse their children (Tajima, 2000). In Botswana, this risk factor has been clearly demonstrated by Jankey (2009) in the study of intimate femicide where the author indicates that, because of violence between intimate lovers, children experience the violence together with their mothers and, in a worst-case scenario; are killed together with their mothers, supporting the exosystem where children are collaterally harmed or killed as result of circumstance beyond their control. In support of this argument, Holden & Ritchie (1991) contend that 50% of women who were battered in the United States of America reported that their partners spanked the children at least once a week. In addition, research in Botswana has focused on gender-based violence against the girl child and neglecting those of the boy child (Maundeni, and Mookodi, 2004).

Parental Characteristics

Straus (1994) identifies the age of a parent as a risk factor in violence against children. Younger mothers are more likely to use violence against their children than older mothers. Parents who had witnessed or experienced violence when they were children are more likely to perpetrate violence against their own children (Merrill, Hervig & Milner, 1996). A parent's physical and mental health is of critical importance. Research indicates that battered women are more likely to be violent to their children because of stress in the lives. Stress has also been identified as having negative consequences for parenting (McCauley, Kern, Kolodner, Dill, Schroeder, DeChant & Bass, 1997). The macro system is evident in this situation given that where children are raised in a culture of violence; they are more likely to experience violence themselves. Use and abuse of alcohol have been linked as a risk factor to violence against children (Widom, & Hiller-Sturmhofel, 2001). In Botswana, studies show a significant relationship between alcohol use among the adult population, exposing children to violence and abuse (Phorano, Nthomang, & Ntseane, 2005).

Child Characteristics

There are certain child characteristics like gender and physical disabilities that have been linked to violence against children. In Botswana for example, girls are particularly vulnerable to sexual violence. Botswana has been hit by the HIV and AIDS epidemic, where many adults died and left children as orphans. Some orphaned children, especially girls, become heads of families and sometimes engage in risky sexual behaviours to earn a living for the family (Phorano, Nthomang, & Ntseane, 2005). Furthermore, these orphaned girls, due to lack of parental guidance, may be enticed by sexual predators who lure them with gifts in exchange for sex. Boys particularly are at increased risk of violence in the home, especially where there is an occurrence of spousal abuse in the home (Ross, 1996). Furthermore, the rates of violence increase with a child's age (Straus, 1994). Children living with physical disabilities are also at increased risk of violence and abuse (Goldson, 1998). Children who are especially vulnerable are those children with behavioural problems like child aggression (O'Keefe, 1995).

Family Characteristics

Marital conflict, as argued by Straus (1994), increases the risk of violence in the home. There is overwhelming evidence from the literature to suggest that the structure and socioeconomic status of the family may be linked to children's safety in the home environment, where family poverty is associated with increased rates of child abuse and violence (Crittenden, 1999; Berger, 2005). This argument is supported by the ecological system theory, where child's culture (macro system) could predict the violence that they may suffer. For example, though Botswana has a rapidly growing economy, there is still unequal distribution of resources given the country's patriarchal nature. The distribution of resources favours men although women bear the brunt of care for children, the elderly, and persons living with disabilities. Many female-headed households in Botswana are affected by poverty (Mookodi, 2004). While poverty does not cause violence against children, it may expose girls to choices that put them at risk of sexual exploitation.

VIOLENCE PERPETUATED BY CHILDREN

While there is evidence that children experience violence from the family, school, and the community, they also experience violence that is perpetuated by their peers (Due & Holstein, 2008). From the microsystem context, children's peers are considered part of the interpersonal relationships and part of the immediate surroundings that a child interacts with. Violence perpetrated by children on other children is mainly evident in the school environment, where children spend most of their day. While all children are vulnerable to violence in schools, their vulnerability is varied in terms of sexuality, gender, stigmatised illness such as HIV and AIDS and disability (Jones, Moore, Villar-Marquez, & Broadbent, 2008). Both boys and girls in Botswana bully each other in schools, but the level of violence perpetrated by boys is higher. Generally, boys in schools carry out sexual harassment and violence against girls. In addition, children also direct violence to other children who do not conform to heterosexual behaviour or conventional appearance codes. Furthermore, children living with disabilities and stigmatised illnesses such as HIV and AIDS are bullied and discriminated against by their peers (Due & Holstein, 2008; Jones, Moore, Villar-Marquez, & Broadbent, 2008).

VIOLENCE AS A HEALTH ISSUE

On October 3, 1996, the World Health Organization declared violence as a public concern, and the first World Report on Violence and Health by WHO was released the same year where violence against children was spelt out as a major health issue the world over (Berger, 2005). Victims of violence, including children, are at risk of both psychological and behavioural problems. Where children are exposed to violence through physical, sexual or emotional abuse and neglect, they are susceptible to risky behaviours and mental health disorders such as smoking, obesity, high-risk sexual behaviour, anxiety, and depression (Graham-Bermann & Seng, 2005). The latter health concerns for children could also be related to major health issues such as heart disease, cancer, suicide, and sexually transmitted diseases (Strauss, Gelles, & Smith, 1990).

EFFECTS OF MEDIA ON CHILDREN'S WELLBEING

Many studies have shown the effect on the aggression of violent media programmes (Anderson & Bushman, 2002). From meta-analysis studies conducted, researchers have identified four critical effects of violent entertainment, be it video games or television for children. The identified effects include the aggressor effect, the victim effect, the bystander effect, and the appetite effect (Donnerstein, Slaby, & Eron, 1994). The aggressor effect states that children who are exposed to a great deal of violent media entertainment display meaner and more aggressive and violent behaviours. The victim effect is whereby children exposed to violent entrainment see the world as a scarier place and are more likely to exhibit self-protective behaviours such as carrying guns and knives to school. The appetite effect is where children who watch violent entertainment will have greater desire to see more of such entertainment. The bystander effect is whereby children who are exposed to a lot of violent entertainment will be desensitised, and less likely to be sympathetic to victims of, violence (Gentile & Anderson, 2003). Meta-analysis studies show that playing violent video games increases a person's physiological arousal, where there is an increase in heart rate and blood pressure (Lynch, 1994). Furthermore, Lynch (1994) argues that the physiological effects may be serious for children who may already be displaying aggressive behaviours. In addition, Gentile and Anderson (1994) contend that watching and participating in violent online entertainment increases aggressive cognitions, emotions, and behaviours and decreases prosocial behaviours.

In a country that is undergoing rapid socio-economic and cultural changes like Botswana, a television is no longer a luxury household item but standard in many households. Furthermore, in most middle-class homes, children have access to video games. One needs to point out that, despite the many effects of violent entertainment for children in Botswana, there have been no systematic studies on this subject. This means that the country is relying on studies abroad, which may not be culturally and content specific to the Botswana situation.

VIOLENCE AND CHILD DEVELOPMENT

Violence against children poses a significant challenge to children's wellbeing. Children who have experienced violence in their lives are exposed to a host of risk factors that may impede their normal development (Hildyard, & Wolfe, 2002). While studies have indicated, adolescent problems related to violence, there has been an erroneous assumption that very young children are not affected (Osofsky, 1995). In early infant and toddler development, there has been a clear association between infant exposure to violence and post-traumatic stress disorder (Drell, Siegel, & Gaensbauer, 1993, Zeanah 1994). For school-going children witnessing and exposed to violence, notable changes have been observed in the increases in anxiety and sleep disturbances (Parsons, 1994). These children often have intrusive thoughts and are unable to play freely and explore their own environment (Osofsky, 1995). The trauma associated with violence interferes with the normal development of trust and autonomy in a child (Parsons, 1993). In addition, these children may regress after having made developmental achievements such as language and toileting (Osofsky, 1995).

LEGAL AND POLICY FRAMEWORK ON CHILDREN AND VIOLENCE

Botswana has several approaches that are aimed at addressing VaC, but due to space limitations, this section will highlight only a few. These approaches form part of the child's macro system. Child protection in Botswana is a mandate of the Ministry of Local Government and Rural Development and the coordination and programming of children's' issues are the responsibility of the Department of Social protection (DSP) within the Ministry. In an effort to implement its mandate, the National Children's council was formed which comprises representatives of central and local government, NGOs, the University of Botswana and relevant civil society organisations. The council seeks to coordinate legal and policy issues and provisions in the best interest of the children of Botswana. The mission of the National Children's council includes ensuring consistency in the application of all legislation related to children and their human rights.

At an international level, Botswana has ratified the Convention on the Rights of the Child and the African Charter on the Rights and Welfare of the Child. Both these instruments provide standards regarding the rights that every child should enjoy. The two instruments focus mainly on child survival, development, protection, and participation.

At a national level, all programmes guiding the protection of children are found in various documents, such as the National Development Plan and Millennium Development Goals. There are legal instruments such as the Constitution of Botswana, the Penal Code, and the Children's Act that are aimed at protecting children.

In domestic legislation, the Constitution of Botswana provides for the protection of 'all persons', but makes no specific reference to children. Section 2 of the constitution enshrines the protection of all fundamental rights without discrimination (Botswana constitution). This clause of the constitution is liberally interpreted by the courts of Botswana to protect all vulnerable groups including children. The Children's Act of 2009 provides that the best interests of the child should be a guiding principle in decisions involving children. Criminal acts against children such as incest, defilement, rape, and indecent assault are regulated by the Penal Code.

Gaps

Though the Government of Botswana has made significant efforts to comply with international standards to ensure that children's rights are observed, these efforts have fallen short of protecting the rights and freedoms of all children. The main reason for this is the lack of coordination and a comprehensive legal framework to protect young people. In addition, there are inadequate systems to support children and their families. Furthermore, there are contradictions in legal instruments, such as the Penal Code and the Children's Act. The Penal Code identifies defilement as applicable to the age of 16 years while the Children's Act defines a child as a person under the age of 18. The lack of consistency among legal instruments creates challenges regarding child protection instruments.

There is a research gap in understanding violence against children in Botswana. The magnitude and scope of the problem is not clear to policy makers and practitioners. Given this background, if policies and interventions are not research based, then such programmes and interventions may not provide the intended outcomes for children. In addition, there is a research gap in Botswana that provides linkages between violence against children and domestic violence. It would be important to understand each type of violence, so as to design comprehensive policies and prevention programmes that are holistic by their very nature.

Currently, the Botswana public health system is overwhelmed by the HIV and AIDS epidemic, overstretching government's public health resources. While it is generally expected that current health care services could decrease the severity of disabilities and physical and psychological effects in children injured in violent acts, the country is challenged by a shortage of emergency response and trauma systems that are vital in violence prevention and its management.

Men have been identified in most studies as perpetrators of violence against children, but there is no intervention strategy that addresses this dimension. In this chapter, schools have also been identified as prospective violent environments for school-going children. In Botswana, there are no specific initiatives in schools that discourage and inhibit violence against children.

RECOMMENDATIONS

Policy

There is a need for coordination between laws that govern violence against children, to ensure that these laws do not have unintended consequences for children experiencing violence. The recommendation is for family courts, and child and domestic violence agencies to work closely together. At the policy level, the government of Botswana should review its policy on canning as it is related to the curbing of violence in schools.

Practice

At the practice level, an appropriate referral system between school, agencies, police, social workers, and health workers should be developed to assist children in violent homes and situations. A proper referral system would assist in early detection of children in need of prompt medical and mental health services. Anecdotal evidence indicates that violence against children is prevalent in schools, necessitating the introduction of relevant prevention programmes.

Since there is a clear connection between violence against children and domestic violence, agencies that deal with children should be trained to recognise signs of domestic abuse and respond in an appropriate manner.

Research

In Botswana and elsewhere in Africa, the magnitude and causes of violence against children are not adequately understood. There is a need for Botswana to concentrate on efforts to improve research in this field to be enabled to calculate, its human, social, and financial costs. Resources to prevent violence against children should be improved as a matter of urgency calling for stakeholders from government, nongovernmental and, faith-based organisations, and the public to coordinate their efforts in violence prevention programmes.

Evidence shows that violence prevention works, for example, in the USA, banning of guns reduced school-based violence. Public health specialists should be committed to using scientific methods of research to help prevent violence against children in Botswana. In addition, this calls for government and other entities to allocate funds to undertake such research if better outcomes for children are to be realised.

CONCLUSION

Violence against children in Botswana is a cause for concern and this has been raised by the government, civil society, politicians and the public. The implications for children can be devastating given that the consequences may be long lasting. The violence experienced by children in Botswana is context specific; for example, girls are more affected by sexual violence than boys. Although the government has ratified international protocols and introduced domestic legislation to regulate violence against children, there are still gaps that the country needs to address to protect young people. For example, the inconsistencies in the legal framework, the lack of coordination of programmes and projects, and a dearth of research and data to inform programmes are some of the issues that the government may have to address to protect the children of Botswana.

REFERENCES

Abbie. A., Olson, A. A., & van Brederode, T. M. (2001, April). *The effects of violent video game habits on adolescent aggressive attitudes and behaviours*. Academic Press.

Azar, S. T. (1991). Models of Child Abuse A Metatheoretical Analysis. *Criminal Justice and Behavior*, *18*(1), 30–46. doi:10.1177/0093854891018001004

Beeld, A. R. (2011). Corporal punishment still in schools. *News 24 Archives*. Retrieved 13 November 2016, from http://www.news24.com

Berger, L. M. (2005). Income, family characteristics, and physical violence toward children. *Child Abuse & Neglect*, *29*(2), 107–133. doi:10.1016/j.chiabu.2004.02.006 PMID:15734178

Bronfenbrenner, U. (Ed.). (2004). The bioecological theory of human development. In U. Bronfenbrenner, (Ed.), Making human beings human: Bioecological perspectives on human development (pp. 3-15). Thousand Oaks, CA: Sage.

Buckner, J. C., Bearslee, W. R., & Bassuk, E. L. (2004). Exposure to violence and low-income childrens mental health: Direct, moderated, and mediated relations. *The American Journal of Orthopsychiatry*, *74*(4), 413–423. doi:10.1037/0002-9432.74.4.413 PMID:15554803

Caspi, A., McClay, J., Moffitt, T. E., Mill, J., Martin, J., Craig, I. W., & Poulton, R. (2002). Role of genotype in the cycle of violence in maltreated children. *Science*, *297*(5582), 851–854. doi:10.1126/science.1072290 PMID:12161658

Chilisa, B. (2002). National policies on pregnancy in education systems in Sub-Saharan Africa: The case of Botswana. *Gender and Education*, *14*(1), 21–35. doi:10.1080/09540250120098852

Chopra, M., & Rollins, N. (2008). Infant feeding in the time of HIV: Rapid assessment of infant feeding policy and programmes in four African countries scaling up prevention of mother to child transmission programmes. *Archives of Disease in Childhood, 93*(4), 288–291. doi:10.1136/adc.2006.096321 PMID:17686796

Cicchetti, D., & Lynch, M. (1993). Toward an ecological/transactional model of community Violence and child maltreatment: Consequences for childrens development. *Psychiatry, 56*(1), 96–118. doi:10.1080/00332747.1993.11024624 PMID:8488217

Crittenden, P. M. (1999). In H. Dubowitz (Ed.), *Neglected children: Research, practice, and policy* (pp. 47–68). Thousand Oaks, CA: Sage. doi:10.4135/9781452225586.n3

Donnerstein, E., Slaby, R. G., & Eron, L. D. (1994). The mass media and youth aggression. In L. D. Eron, J. H. Gentry, & P. Schlegel (Eds.), *Reason to hope: A psychosocial perspective on violence and youth* (pp. 219–250). Washington, DC: American Psychological Association. doi:10.1037/10164-010

Due, P., & Holstein, B. E. (2008). Bullying victimization among 13 to 15 year old school children: Results from two comparative studies in 66 countries and regions. *International Journal of Adolescent Medicine and Health, 20*(2), 209–222. doi:10.1515/IJAMH.2008.20.2.209 PMID:18714557

Edleson, J. L. (1999). Childrens witnessing of adult domestic violence. *Journal of Interpersonal Violence, 14*(8), 839–870. doi:10.1177/088626099014008004

Edleson, J. L., Mbilinyi, L. F., Beeman, S. K., & Hageemeister, A. K. (2003). How children are involved in adult domestic violence: Results from a four city telephone survey. *Journal of Interpersonal Violence, 18*(1), 18–32. doi:10.1177/0886260502238538

Goldson, E. (1998). Children with disabilities and child maltreatment. *Child Abuse & Neglect, 22*, 663–667. PMID:9693844

Graham-Bermann, S. A., & Seng, J. (2005). Violence exposure and traumatic stress symptoms as additional predictors of health problems in high-risk children. *The Journal of Pediatrics, 146*(3), 349–354. doi:10.1016/j.jpeds.2004.10.065 PMID:15756218

Heald, S. (2006). Abstain or die: The development of HIV/AIDS policy in Botswana. *Journal of Biosocial Science, 38*(01), 29–41. doi:10.1017/S0021932005000933 PMID:16266444

Hildyard, K. L., & Wolfe, D. A. (2002). Child neglect: Developmental issues and Outcomes. *Child Abuse & Neglect, 26*(6), 679–695. doi:10.1016/S0145-2134(02)00341-1 PMID:12201162

Holden, G. W., & Ritchie, K. L. (1991). Linking extreme marital discord, child rearing, and child behavior problems: Evidence from battered women. *Child Development, 62*(2), 311–327. doi:10.2307/1131005 PMID:2055124

Holt, S., Buckley, H., & Whelan, S. (2008). The impact of exposure to domestic violence on children and young people: A review of the literature. *Journal of Family Violence, 13*(4), 345–363.

Jankey, O. M. (2013). Children, the forgotten victims of passion killings in Media reporting in Botswana between 2009 and 2013. In Thari ya Bana: Reflections on Children in Botswana 2013. Gaborone: UNICEF Press.

Jones, N., Moore, K., Villar-Marquez, E., & Broadbent, E. (2008). Painful lessons: The politics of preventing sexual violence and bullying at school. London: Overseas Development Institute (ODI).

Kerig, P. K. (1996). Assessing the links between marital conflict and child development: The conflicts and problem-solving scales. *Journal of Family Psychology*, *10*(4), 454–473. doi:10.1037/0893-3200.10.4.454

Khan, M., Kapoor, S., & Cooraswamy, R. (2000). Domestic violence against women and girls. *Innocenti Digest*, *6*, 1–30.

Lynch, P. J. (1994). Type A behavior, hostility, and cardiovascular function at rest and after playing video games in teenagers. *Psychosomatic Medicine*, *2*(56), 152–152.

Lynch, P. J. (1999). Hostility, Type A behavior, and stress hormones at rest and after playing violent video games in teenagers. *Psychosomatic Medicine*, *61*(1), 113. doi:10.1097/00006842-199901000-00157

Lyons-Ruth, K., & Jacobvitz, D. (1999). Attachment disorganization: Unresolved loss, relational violence, and lapses in behavioral and attentional strategies. *Psychosomatic Medicine*, *56*, 152.

Martin, S. G. (2002). Children exposed to domestic violence: Psychological considerations for health care practitioners. *Holistic Nursing Practice*, *16*(3), 7–15. doi:10.1097/00004650-200204000-00005 PMID:11913229

Maundeni, T. (2002). Wife Abuse Among a Sample of Divorced Women in Botswana A Research Note. *Violence Against Women*, *8*(2), 257–274. doi:10.1177/10778010222183035

Maundeni, T., & Mookodi, G. (2009). *Socio-cultural factors that place males at risk of HIV infection in Botswana: Implications for sexual and reproductive health strategies*. Academic Press.

Maundeni, T., Osei-Hwedie, B., McCauley, J., Kern, D. E., Kolodner, K., Dill, L., & Bass, E. B. et al. (1997). Clinical characteristics of women with a history of childhood abuse: Unhealed wounds. *Journal of the American Medical Association*, *277*(17), 1362–1368.

McIntosh, J. E. (2003). Children living with domestic violence: Research foundations for early intervention. *Journal of Family Studies*, *9*(2), 219–234. doi:10.5172/jfs.9.2.219

Merrill, L. L., Hervig, L. K., & Milner, J. S. (1996). Childhood parenting experiences, intimate partner conflict resolution, and adult risk for child physical abuse. *Child Abuse & Neglect*, *20*(11), 1049–1065. doi:10.1016/0145-2134(96)00094-4 PMID:8958455

Modie-Moroka. (2011). Infanticide, baby-dumping and abandonment in Botswana: implications for research, policy, and practice. In Thari ya Bana: Reflections on Children in Botswana 2013. Gaborone: UNICEF and University of Botswana.

Mogalakwe, M. (2006). The Use of Documentary Research Methods in Social Research. *African Sociological Review*, *10*(1), 221–230.

Mogwe, A. (1988). *A Go Itewa Ke Monna wa Gago ke Botshelo? A Preliminary Investigation into Battered Women in Botswana* (MPhil Dissertation). University of Cape Town.

Mookodi, G. (2004). Male violence against women in Botswana: A discussion of gendered uncertainties in a rapidly changing environment. *African Sociological Review/Revue Africaine de Sociologie, 8*(1), 118-138.

Mukamaambo, E., & Ntseane, P. (Eds.), *Male involvement in sexual and reproductive health: Prevention of violence and HIV and AIDS in Botswana.* Cape Town: Made Plain Communications.

OKeefe, M. (1995). Predictors of child abuse in marital violent families. *Journal of Interpersonal Violence, 10*(1), 3–25. doi:10.1177/088626095010001001

Osofsky, J. D. (1995). The effect of exposure to violence on young children. *The American Psychologist, 50*(9), 782–788. doi:10.1037/0003-066X.50.9.782 PMID:7574189

Parsons, E. R. (1994). Inner city children of trauma: Urban violence traumatic stress response syndrome (U-VTS) and therapists' responses. In J. Wilson & J. Lindy (Eds.), *Counter transference in the treatment of post-traumatic stress disorder* (pp. 151–178). New York: Guilford.

Phorano, O., Nthomang, K., & Ntseane, D. (2005). Alcohol abuse, gender-based violence and HIV/AIDS in Botswana: establishing the link based on empirical evidence. *SAHARA-J: Journal of Social Aspects of HIV/AIDS, 2*(1), 188-202.

Ross, S. (1996). Risk of physical abuse to children of spouse abusing parents. *Child Abuse & Neglect, 20*(7), 589–598. doi:10.1016/0145-2134(96)00046-4 PMID:8832115

Rossetti, S. (2001). *Children in School: A Safe Place?* Gaborone, Botswana: UNESCO.

Saunders, B. E. (2003). Understanding children exposed to violence: Towards an integration of overlapping fields. *Journal of Interpersonal Violence, 18*(4), 356–376. doi:10.1177/0886260502250840

Scott, J. (1990). *A Matter of Record, Documentary Sources in Social Research.* Cambridge, UK: Polity Press.

Strauss, Gelles, & Smith. (1990). Physical Violence in American Families. New Brunswick, NJ: Transaction Publishers.

Tafa, E. M. (2002). Corporal punishment: The brutal face of Botswanas authoritarian schools. *Educational Review, 54*(1), 17–26. doi:10.1080/00131910120110848

Tajima, E. A. (2000). The relative importance of wife abuse as a risk factor for violence against children. *Child Abuse & Neglect, 24*(11), 1383–1398. doi:10.1016/S0145-2134(00)00194-0 PMID:11128172

UNICEF. (2011). *The situation analysis of children and their families in Botswana.* Botswana: UNICEF.

USAID. (2003). *Unsafe schools: A literature review of school-related gender-based violence in developing countries.* Washington, DC: Wellesley Centers for Research on Women & DTS/USAID.

Wible, B. (2004). *Making Schools Safe for Girls: Combating Gender-based Violence in Benin.* Washington, DC: US Academy for Educational Development.

Widom, C. S., & Hiller-Sturmhofel, S. (2001). Alcohol abuse as a risk factor for and consequence of child abuse. *Alcohol Research & Health, 25*(1), 52–52. PMID:11496967

KEY TERMS AND DEFINITIONS

Aggression: Feelings of anger which may result in some violent behaviour.

Child: A child is minor or any person below the age of 18.

Child Abuse: When an adult does something or does not do something which may result in a child being harmed or put at risk of harm. Child abuse could be physical, sexual or emotional.

Corporal Punishment: It is a form of physical punishment intended to cause pain and discomfort to a child in response to undesired behaviour.

Ecological Systems Theory: It is a developmental theory that assumes that as people develop, they experience different environments throughout their lifespan and these may influence behaviour.

Gender-Based Violence: It is a serious violation of human rights and a form of discrimination against women.

Violence Against Children: It is a violation of children's rights. This violence encompasses all forms of physical violence, mental violence, injury and abuse, neglect and maltreatment and exploitation.

Section 2

Children's Socio–Economic Rights

Chapter 4
Social Welfare Issues in Childhood:
The Botswana Experience

Tapologo Maundeni
University of Botswana, Botswana

Odireleng Mildred Jankey
University of Botswana, Botswana

Lisa Lopez Levers
Duquesne University, USA

ABSTRACT

Children around the globe are confronted with numerous social welfare issues that adversely affect their wellbeing. These issues differ across countries and regions. This chapter explores childhood social welfare issues in Botswana, illuminating the ideological differences between traditional and more contemporary conceptualizations of childhood. Because children's issues are currently so complex, this chapter focuses primarily on HIV and AIDS-related orphanhood, alcohol and substance abuse, and traumatic events in the lives of the children. Problems in the lives of children in Botswana are identified, related opportunities are discussed, and recommendations made. The chapter demonstrates, among other things, that a number of commendable efforts (at practice, policy, and research levels) have been undertaken by stakeholders to address social welfare issues in childhood: however, a lot more still needs to be done to improve the quality of life among Botswana's most vulnerable children. Therefore, the chapter concludes by highlighting recommendations for research, practice, and policy.

INTRODUCTION

Children in Botswana, like their counterparts in many countries, are confronted with a number of social welfare issues. The issues are so diverse and multifaceted that they cannot be analysed adequately in one chapter. Therefore, this chapter focuses on HIV and AIDS-related orphanhood, substance abuse, and

DOI: 10.4018/978-1-5225-2578-3.ch004

traumatic events in the lives of the children in Botswana. The primary focus is on orphanhood because many parents have died in Botswana, especially related to the HIV and AIDS pandemic, leaving behind orphans of tender age who still need care and support. It is not unusual for a child in Botswana to lose one or more caregivers, after losing parents, as this is the extent of the pandemic in the southern region of Africa. Existing literature shows that although some orphans exhibit resilience and are able to cope adequately with the parental loss (Ginsburg, 2014, 2015), there are many who face enormous challenges that can adversely affect their well-being (e.g., Doyle & Perlman, 2012; Perlman & Doyle, 2012). Consequently, the Government and other stakeholders have put in place various programmes to address the complex and multifaceted needs and challenges of orphans. Despite these programmes, there are still many orphans who do not derive maximum benefit from such programmes; hence, there is a need for improvement to ensure that orphans' wellbeing is adequately addressed.

The interconnected areas of trauma and substance abuse are selected as second and third areas of focus here, because orphaned children in Botswana are exposed to such high levels of trauma (Malinga & Ntshwarang, 2011), and because alcohol and substance abuse by children and young people is a huge problem in Botswana (UNICEF, 2012). However, approaches, programmes, and strategies to mitigate the problem are not comprehensive, and existing services tend to be fragmented. Consequently, the unique challenges faced by traumatised children and youth who abuse alcohol and substances are not adequately addressed.

The purpose of this chapter is threefold: First, it highlights some of the factors that are associated with the above three social welfare issues in Botswana; second, it assesses existing strategies (both formal and informal) that are meant to address the issues, as well as challenges in service delivery; and, third, the chapter highlights several recommendations that could go a long way to ensuring that the above-mentioned social welfare issues confronting children are either prevented or adequately addressed. The structure of this chapter is organised around these aims and provides a description of the methodology and theoretical framework used here for examining the lives of orphans in Botswana. These issues are explicated in the following major sections of the chapter: (1) brief contextual information about child social welfare issues internationally, regionally and nationally; (2) childhood issues in Botswana, (3) solutions and recommendations, and (4) future research directions regarding childhood issues in Botswana. These four sections are followed by a summary of the most salient points of the chapter as well as conclusions.

CONTEXTUAL BACKGROUND

Brief background information about child social welfare globally, regionally and nationally is crucial in order for readers to appreciate some of the issues discussed in this chapter. Concern about child welfare issues at an internationally level started in the 19th century as a result of observations that some children's rights (particularly the rights of those who were victims of world war II) were violated. Consequently, the UN fund for urgency for the children was created in 1947, which became UNICEF. At its inception, UNICEF focused on assisting (in the areas of education, health, and access to water and food) largely European child victims of WW2, but later, its mandate was extended to the whole world (Children's Rights History, n.d.). Between 1947 and 1989, there were various developments that were meant to address child welfare issues at an international level. In 1989, the convention on the rights of the child was adopted and later ratified by almost all countries (except two). The CRC is a comprehensive human rights instrument that covers all aspects of children's lives and their development into adulthood.

It contains political, civil, economic, social and cultural rights, including *inter alia*, the right to be protected from all forms of discrimination. The support and enthusiasm with which the Convention has been received could be taken as an indication that children's rights are respected and promoted around the world. However, this is not always the case, particularly given the diverse social, economic, political and cultural environments which prevail in different countries of the world. Given such diversity, there are country-specific and regional differences in the nature and magnitude of the problems encountered in the implementation of the CRC.

At a regional level, the African Charter on the Rights and Welfare of the Child (ACRWC) was adopted by the Organization of African Unity (OAU) in 1990. This charter was formulated because the member states of the AU believed that the CRC omitted socio-cultural and economic realities that are unique to Africa. The charter emphasises the need to include African cultural values and experiences when dealing with the rights of the child (African Charter on the Rights and Welfare of the Child, 2016).

At a national level, Botswana formulated a children's act in 1981. Later on (in 1989), the country domesticated the requirements of the CRC in 2009 through its children's act. One of the authors was a member of a multi-professional team that spearheaded the above-mentioned process. She vividly recalls how some of the clauses were met with resistance from some communities largely due to communities' beliefs that such proposals clashed with cultural practices and beliefs. This resistance has also been noted in existing literature. Insights from Kgotla meetings facilitated by the Botswana National Council in recent years revealed the resistance to issues and approaches that are viewed as clashing with culture. These issues include children's rights as well as gender equality and women's empowerment. Participants associated children's and women's rights movements with children's antisocial behaviour. One of them asserted:

The reason why children in Botswana today disrespect their fathers is because mothers have a tendency to team up with children to oppose their fathers who seek to exert authority. Mothers say they and their children have rights so when fathers try to discipline children, the mothers tell them that the fathers are violating their rights...and so fathers are powerless. It looks like fathers don't have rights...only mothers and children have rights. Maundeni and Jacques (2012: 78)

Botswana is a completely landlocked country in the centre of southern Africa. It shares borders with Namibia to the west, Zambia to the northeast, Zimbabwe to the east, and South Africa to the south. The total population in 2001 was approximately 1,680 863 million. The census also disclosed that 737,241 of the population, which translated to 43.37%, comprised children. Of this number:

- 15% were below the age of 5,
- 13% between 5 and 9,
- 55% were under the age of 10,
- 11% between 10 and 14,
- 17% fell between 15 and 17, and
- 12% between 15 and 19 (UNICEF, 2009).

The percentage of population aged between 0 and 19 is 48.6 (CSO, 2002). This is a significant number. Much national attention and concern on child welfare issues have been generated in Botswana since independence in 1966. However, it was only until 1981, that the government of Botswana passed an Act on Children. Children are a very important resource for any country and their well-being is crucial for sustained development. As such societies must do their best to ensure that children's rights are promoted, respected, protected, respected and fulfilled. The government has shown commitment to promoting child's rights through numerous ways. These include the establishment of local programs and laws that aim to promote the well-being of children[1] as well as the ratification of the CRC.

Efforts on child social welfare issues cannot be complete without reference to issues of gender in the socialisation of children. Botswana, like many countries, is a patriarchal society, characterised by cultural norms, beliefs, and practices that perpetuate gender inequalities. It is worth noting that progress has been made in modifying and eliminating laws that traditionally discriminated against females, however, in reality, there are still practices and beliefs that promote gender inequality. For example, boys and girls are socialised differently with more emphasis on the need for girls to perform roles that are traditionally meant for females and vice-versa. (Maundeni, 2015). This to some extent has resulted in more girls than boys pursuing professionals that are associated with their feminine roles such as nursing, social work, and others while most of their male counterparts go into professionals that are associated with masculine roles. In addition, Setswana language[2] has proverbs that cast women in a negative light such as '*ga di nke ke etelelwa ke manamagadi pele, di ka wela selomo – Banna ke baeteledipele ka tholego'.* This literally translates to 'A team of oxen is never led by females, otherwise, the oxen will fall into a ditch – men are natural leaders'. Proverbs like this encourage females to be submissive and weaken their self-esteem and confidence (Datla, et al, 1998).

School-based statistics show that Botswana has made and sustained significant progress towards universal access to basic education for boys and girls (Chilisa, Maundeni, and Tabulawa, Un-dated; Republic of Botswana and United Nations, 2010). However, more girls than boys continue to drop out of school, largely due to pregnancy. In comparison, almost zero boys drop out of school because of pregnancy related reasons. It has been noted that a significant number of girls are impregnated by older men and that in a few cases where a boy is involved in a pregnancy, parents negotiated to let the boy continue school. Although there is now a policy to enable girls to re-enter the school system following pregnancy, some of them do not go back due to fear of ridicule, intimidation, social branding and harassment by the school community (Chilisa, 2002). The pregnancy policy has been reviewed to allow the girl to continue schooling for as long as she is comfortable and to return to school 6 months after the baby is born to a school of her choice. These issues are important, as, without a sustainable pool of qualified women, it will be almost impossible to improve the gender balance throughout and at the top in the long term. It is an example of how gender equality in the PA is impacted by many social issues beyond its immediate domain.

Although the government and its partners have made progress in the area of gender equality, there remain challenges to be overcome. One of them is that Botswana operates under a dual legal system: Common Law and Customary Law. The amendments made in the Common Law in line with international instruments/conventions have no effect on the administration of justice under the Customary Law. Consequently, while certain practices have been abolished under Common Law, their application continues under the Customary Law. The endorsement of this dual legal system continues to disadvantage women.

Botswana is an upper-middle-income country located in the southern region of Africa. With a population of a little over 2.1 million, Botswana is the 48th largest country in the world, about the size of France. Botswana is a landlocked country, bordered by Namibia to the west and north, Zimbabwe to the east, and the Republic of South Africa to the south. The country has a young population structure. In 1991, for example, 43.6% of the population was between the ages of 0 and 14 years (Lesetedi and Ngcongco, 1995). The section below offers information about the methodology and theoretical framework used for the examination of childhood in Botswana.

Understanding Key Concepts

This section provides definitions of a few key concepts that are used in this chapter. One of them is children. One of such concepts is a child. The word 'child' is defined differently by various laws in Botswana. For instance, the Botswana Children's Act of 2009 defines a child as a person below the age of 18 years old, the Adoption Act as a person below the age of 19, while the Employment Act defines a child as a person under the age of 15. The variations in the definition/s of a child in the context of Botswana need to be attended to.

The second key concept that needs to be clarified is the family. The family in Botswana is continuously undergoing a transformation as a result of the economic, socio-cultural and technological changes that are happening globally. Changes in marriage patterns, increased divorce rates, death, health including HIV/AIDS and other diseases, urbanisation, unemployment, and poverty, are all impacting the structure and functions of the family and its members. The family structure has moved from largely being extended during the colonial era to the nuclear family of today. Change is slower though among rural families than those in urban areas. Family composition: it is not unusual to find grandparents, the spouses, their children, children's cousins, and their children's children living under one roof. In rural areas, some families still produce their own food, while in urban areas more families have become consumption agencies. Child-headed families are on the increase due to loss of parents through mostly HIV/AIDS and other related health concerns. Family members react differently to these stressful events and sometimes they are known to react violently. Paradoxically, members still look up to the same family for support in times of need.

METHODOLOGY

Documentary research and translational research strategies have been used to review, analyse, and interpret the social welfare issues discussed in this chapter. Documentary research method refers to the analysis of documents or other written records that contain information about the subject being studied (e.g., Ahmed, 2010; Kridel, 2016; Mogalakwe, 2006). A review of documents (both published and unpublished, academic and grey literature) that focus on social welfare issues confronting children in Botswana, including relevant cultural factors, have been conducted. Reviewed documents have included key national legal and policy frameworks, reports on relevant international conventions, as well as scholarly papers and information relating to social welfare issues in childhood. In addition, national and international databases have been accessed and reviewed for supportive data. An American Educational Review Association (AERA) online article described documentary research as both archival inquiry and aesthetic interpretation (Kridel, 2016).

Interpreting from the existing interdisciplinary literature related to orphaned, traumatized, and substance-abusing children, and as an extension of the documentary research described above, we have used translational research (e.g., Breckler, 2006; Dingfelder, 2005; Zerhouni, 2005) as a compatible strategy for distilling and articulating information about the topic and making recommendations for related best practices. The practice of translational research is a relatively recent inclusion in the medical and health-related literatures that is viewed as having newly emerging applications in the behavioural and social sciences (e.g., Dingfelder, 2005) and has been regarded as a major priority by entities such as the American Psychological Association and the National Institutes of Health (APA and NIH, cited in Dingfelder).

THEORETICAL FRAMEWORK

This chapter utilises Bronfenbrenner's (1979, 2001, 2004; Bronfenbrenner & Ceci, 1994) Ecological Systems Theory, which in his later years, he renamed as Bioecological Theory of Development. The theory is relevant to explaining and understanding social welfare issues faced by children and families within the environment that they exist, as well as existing programmes and strategies to address the issues. The model identifies the five following environmental systems that influence the individual within personal and cultural contexts: Microsystem, mesosystem, exosystem, macro system, and chronosystem (see Figure 1).

Bronfenbrenner's (1979) theory of human development positions the individual and his or her personal attributes within a microsystem that is affected by and transacts with multiple environmental systems. These systems interact with one another and with the individual, postulating reciprocal influences between the individual and the environment. From proximal to increasingly more distal influences, environmental factors influence the person in age- and stage-salient ways. This progression from

Figure 1. Bronfenbrenner's Bioecological Theory
Source: Santrock, J.W. (2007). Child Development (11th ed.). NY: McGraw-Hill Companies, Inc.

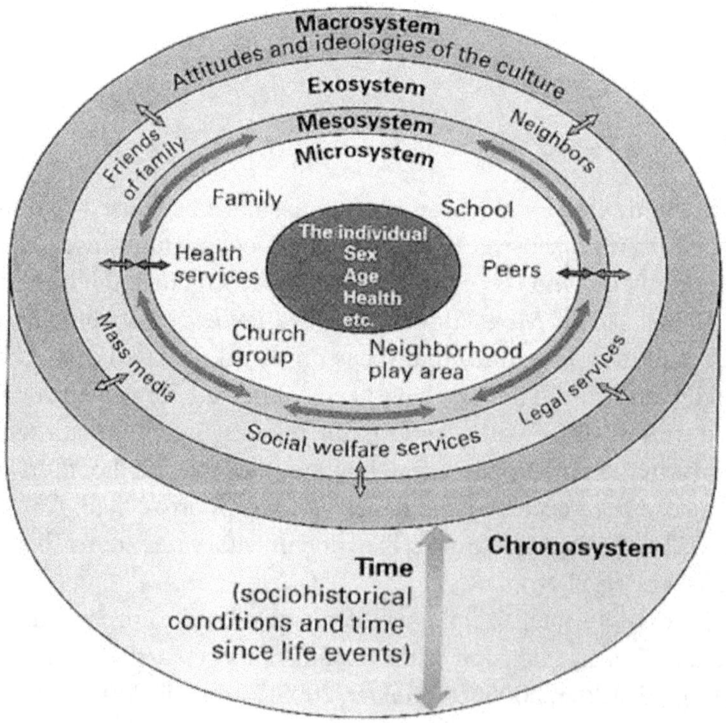

proximal to distal social influences moves from ontogenic (individual) development to microsystemic (immediate family environment), to exosystemic (community and neighbourhood), to macrosystemic (broad cultural values and beliefs) transactions; the model also accounts for events in the personal and socio-historical passage of time. Continual transactions within the multiple environments, or ecology, determine the risk or protective factors present in the individual's ecology.

Of relevance to the current discussion of children who have been orphaned in Botswana, Bronfenbrenner (1992) posits that the child is the centre of five environmental layers of the ecological systems theory, and the child is influenced by experiences related to each of the five systems. The most central influential system on the child, among all the five systems, is the microsystem, which includes the home and the school, in which the child has most of his or her direct interactions (Bronfenbrenner, 1992). The next layer in Bronfenbrenner's ecological systems theory is the mesosystem. The mesosystem comprises the linkages and processes taking place in two or more settings containing the developing person. The third is the exosystem layer, which is comprised of influences that still directly affect the individual but are more distal than in the microsystem, for example, extended family, the media, and social welfare systems. Next is the macro system, which Bronfenbrenner explains as a pattern that links the micro, meso, and exosystem characteristics, with particular reference to the belief systems, knowledge, customs, and life course options that are embedded in the broader cultural systems. Finally, is the chronosystem, which encompasses the dimension of time as it relates to a child's environments and refers to both personal and socio-historical instances. Bronfenbrenner deduced that elements within this system can be either external, such as the timing of a parent's death, or internal, such as the physiological changes that occur with the ageing of a child.

Application of the Theory to Issues Discussed in This Chapter

The ecological systems theory is considered suitable for analysing social welfare issues in childhood, partly because it argues that in order to understand human development, one must consider the entire ecological system in which growth occurs. For instance, experiences of orphanhood and related challenges depend, among other things, on family and community-related factors. For example, orphans who experience traumatic circumstances such as drastic declines in their standard of living, as well as abuse and discrimination following parental death, are more likely to be more traumatised than their counterparts who are not exposed to such high-risk circumstances.

Bronfenbrenner has defined human development, within the context of his bioecological model, as the "...phenomenon of continuity and change in the biopsychological characteristics of human beings both as individuals and as groups. The phenomenon extends over the life course across successive generations and through historical time, both past and present" (Bronfenbrenner 2004, p. 3). Continuity and change formulate integral properties of the model. One important characteristic of Bronfenbrenner's model, for the purpose of this chapter, is the rich framework that it can provide for clinicians and social welfare workers in assessing risks and protective factors in the lives of orphans. The framework further assists in constructing interventions that can minimise or eliminate risks, mediate risks, foster or enhance current protective factors, or create new protective factors; this provides the powerful potential for creative applications, both theoretically and clinically (Lynch & Levers, 2007).

This theory views individuals as active participants in their environments, capable of change and adaptation as well as incorporating the concept of client self-determination. Therefore, despite children's experiences of trauma, some of them are resilient and manage to thrive in the face of adversity. The theory also recognises that multiple approaches are necessary to bring about change. It is against this background that existing strategies to address social welfare issues in childhood are explored in this chapter.

CHILDHOOD ISSUES IN BOTSWANA

This chapter focuses on the profound ideological changes that the theoretical conceptualization of childhood has undergone, approximately, over the last five or six decades. The discussion juxtaposes traditional and more contemporary visions of the construct of childhood, thereby illuminating differences. Like all other countries, Botswana has both deficits and assets. While a full description of these is beyond the scope of this chapter, the major issues, controversies, problems, and opportunities related to existing and emerging conceptions of childhood are described briefly in the subsections below.

Problems Affecting Children in Botswana

The contemporary social landscape in Botswana includes an array of problem areas that have a widespread impact on the populace. Those that most affect the lives of orphans include HIV and AIDS, substance abuse, the status of children, and income disparity, just to mention but a few.

Continuing Impact of HIV and AIDS

Botswana, like many African countries, has been hard hit by the HIV and AIDS scourge. Malinga and Ntshwarang (2011) have emphasised the extreme susceptibility of orphans and other vulnerable children (OVC), those left without parents or in need of care. HIV and AIDS has affected many people, irrespective of social background. Some people have died leaving behind children of tender ages, others are still terminally ill, while some are unemployed. The existence of orphans is not peculiar to contemporary Botswana society, it also prevailed in traditional societies. What has changed is the volume of children who need care, the circumstances that result in children becoming orphans, and the resources available for their care.

In traditional African communities (prior to industrialisation and urbanisation), societies were based on a subsistence economy, characterised by the self-sufficient joint family organisation (Foster, and Williamson, 2000). Several family members who were related to one another by blood, marriage or adoption lived together in the same compound or in the same part of the village, and as such, the needs of family members (e.g., food, shelter, clothing and emotional support) were provided for by the extended family as a whole. When situations such as parental death occurred, orphaned children were absorbed into their kinship group or self-sufficient joint family organisation. In other words, they were taken care of by their kinsmen in the same way as before parental loss (Ministry of Local Government, 2008); this was a naturally occurring protective factor in the ecologies of the children and the communities in which they lived.

The traditional system described above has been transformed by the process of social change (Bigombe & Khadiagala, n.d.). A major change was the disintegration of the system of residence, where members of the same family group do not always live close together in the same household, ward, or village. Some family members now work outside their own villages or even outside the country and are beyond the reach of senior family members who may want to enforce obligations of support. Globalisation and urbanisation have amplified such trends. Furthermore, the high cost of living and limited accommodation facilities in towns may restrict the extent to which people can help others. Related social forces, like poverty and unemployment, serve as mechanisms that ultimately have a negative influence on the lives of vulnerable children. These disintegrative aspects of modernization constitute risk factors for the children, their families, and the communities in which they live.

Child advocates for children's social welfare have been somewhat successful in establishing basic services for children at risk. However, although Botswana has made progress in addressing the OVC situation, policy barriers remain (Feranil, Herstad, Jallow, & Mbuya-Brown, 2010). Graça Machel commented in a keynote speech at the conclusion of the 2004 CIVICUS World Assembly, held in Gaborone, the capital city of Botswana, that the failure of many human services throughout Africa is the extensive fragmentation. It is this very fragmentation that serves as the most ubiquitous barrier to orphans and other vulnerable children having their needs met in Botswana.

Alcohol and Substance Abuse

Alcohol and substance abuse amongst young people continue to be a huge problem in Botswana (Thula, 2015). The use and abuse of alcohol and drugs have serious implications for the wellbeing of children and young people by affecting their educational, physical, emotional, social, and spiritual wellbeing). The stigma associated with addiction compromises the ability of children and young people to seek interventions. Factors associated with young people's engagement in alcohol and drugs include poor parenting skills and negative peer pressure. Although alcohol and substance abuse are rampant and escalating among young people in Botswana, existing programmes to address these problems are inadequate. Examples of such programmes include the PACT programme, BOSASNet, and specific services offered by guidance and counselling teachers. The PACT programme operates from some secondary schools. This programme is unisex and voluntary, therefore most boys do not feel comfortable to participate in it; moreover, the programme is not offered in all schools. BOSASNet is a non-governmental organisation which was formed to provide substance abuse education, prevention, and rehabilitation services to the general public. It operates an outpatient counselling rehabilitation centre in Gaborone, which opened in September 2010. BOSASNet offices are found in the capital city (Gaborone) only; however, the organisation extends its services to people outside Gaborone. BOSASNET's ability to reach out to all young people affected by substances is limited by a shortage of resources (Manyanda, 2015).

Status of Children

The status of children in Botswana is a point of some social contention in the nation. Botswana is a signatory to the *UN Convention on the Rights of the Child* (UN, 1989). Moreover, the country's Children's Act was reviewed in 2009 to reflect the requirements of the CRC. However, children's rights continue to be violated by some people. This is so partly because of lack of societal awareness of children's rights as well as discrepancies between culture and children's rights. By and large, society has not fully embraced the concept of children's rights; instead, it has shown resistance. Most people believe that the children's rights movement is a stumbling block to the way they raise their children (Maundeni, 2010). In many on-going radio shows, where child welfare professionals are invited to participate in various media programmes to sensitise the public about children's rights, numerous callers repeatedly point out that children do not have rights. Some have expressed their sentiments in very explicit and strong terms, thus: "My children are my property"; "Our government has signed documents without understanding their implications"; "I brought my children into this world, and no one is going to tell me how to raise them or tell me that they have rights"; "The reason why our children are uncontrollable is that they are told that they have rights." The traditional culture of Botswana supports a patriarchal and hierarchical view of children. For this reason, children remain vulnerable to exploitation by perpetrators. This is linked to the issue of early childhood trauma as well as trauma experienced across the lifespan.

In tandem with the status of children, the issue of education is relevant to this discussion. Although literacy among youth is high, and primary schooling is free, the development of early education has not been as progressive. Relatively few professionals in the country have been trained in early childhood education, development, or intervention. There are relatively few trained helping professionals who have had much (if any) specialised training in traumatology, let alone training on the effects of trauma and bereavement on childhood development. While indigenous knowledge and traditional practices offer much to parents in the way of cultural childrearing tenets, such trans-generational wisdom cannot begin to anticipate the current problems associated with the pandemic's effects on children. A further complexity resides in the reality that few professionals in the country have been trained to design and implement the level of cross-sectoral/interdisciplinary community-based systems that is required to address a problem of the magnitude of the current situation.

The Early Childhood Care and Education (ECCE) Policy was released in Botswana in 2001. A review of the recent status of ECCE programs was conducted, and the research findings suggested some important gaps between policy and practice (Bose, 2008). More recently, Maundeni (2013) pointed out that little attention has been paid to early childhood education in Botswana. Finally, Maunganidze and Tsamaase (2014) have observed fragmentation in the delivery of early childhood education in Botswana and noted the "absence of national framework guiding the structure and content of early childhood curriculum and instruction" (p. 6). The argument can be made that without an adequate early educational foundation, the talents of the most vulnerable children may be left untapped. Having said that, it is comforting to note that in 2015, the government started to pilot the ECCE programmes in some of its primary schools.

Income Disparity

The countries in the southern region of Africa have the highest incidence rates of HIV/AIDS in the world, and Botswana continues to have one of the highest prevalence rates (Kaiser Family Foundation, 2015). The HIV and AIDS pandemic has affected Botswana's economic and social structures in multi-faceted ways. One significant outcome of a pandemic in which so many adults of childbearing age have died is the number of orphaned children who have been left behind, many to live in poverty. Some have become street children, and many are forced to live in deleterious circumstances where they are sexually abused or otherwise exploited; these are highly vulnerable children who are also at risk of contracting HIV and AIDS and thus perpetuating the pandemic.

The issue of child abuse, especially of sexual abuse, remains "silenced" in Botswana. Some of the factors that lead to the concealment of sexual abuse among children and adolescents include cultural factors and social status of the perpetrators (Seloilwe, & Thupayagale-Tshweneagae, 2009). The silence surrounding child sexual abuse contributes to the problems associated with orphanhood, as well as to constituting a separate or independent set of problems.

Although Botswana is an upper middle-income country, there is a huge income gap between the smaller, more affluent stratum of society and the larger, poorer stratum (Jefferis & Kelly, 1999). Many children are living in poverty in Botswana. The poverty experienced in many developing countries affects women and children more than any other groups. Poverty among children is intertwined with that of women; therefore, the rising concentration of poverty among female-headed households in developing countries in particular compounds children's poverty. The government of Botswana has in place several programmes that aim to alleviate poverty among households. One such programme is the orphan care programme. The service aims to respond to the immediate needs of orphans with food, clothing, education, shelter, protection, and other necessary care). The programme has universal coverage, with eligibility open to all Batswana children, under the age of 18, who do not have parents and lack access to basic necessities of life, including food, clothing, toiletry, and shelter (Ministry of Local Government, (2008). Benefits include a food basket, school fees, clothing, other educational costs, and psychosocial support. Although the provision of psychosocial support is crucial to orphans, in reality, more often than not, orphans are provided with material assistance, and minimal attention is paid to emotional needs, like grief counselling. Psychosocial support (PSS) tends to be small-scale and provided by nongovernmental organisations (NGOs). Shortage of human resources in the local authorities also accounts for the relative neglect of psychosocial support to orphans (Seboni, Maundeni, & Rapinyana, 2015).

Despite noble initiatives, a significant number of children in Botswana still live in poverty-stricken environments. Poverty places children at a greater risk of, among other things, sexual exploitation, child prostitution, and poor school performance. Consequently, children are deprived of major human rights. Because many orphaned children have lost large portions of extended family before losing parents, they often experience economic hardships. This has far reaching implications for their welfare.

It is estimated that there are over 12 million children in Africa who have been orphaned due to AIDS, with perhaps as many as 85,000 orphans reported in Botswana (governmental figures estimate 42,000 *registered* orphans; however, other child-concerned entities estimate the number of registered *and* unregistered orphans who have lost *at least one* biological parent as approximately 85,000—either way, in a population of about 1.5 million, the number is extremely large). In addition, children are orphaned for a variety of reasons, with a high number of children losing parents in automobile accidents, for example.

Areas of Opportunity for Children in Botswana

Botswana has several opportunities, unlike many other African countries, that are conducive for combatting and addressing social welfare problems facing children; however, the country is still confronted with problems in the area of child welfare. Therefore, there is still a lot that needs to be done to address such problems. When social welfare issues in childhood are not adequately addressed, this has far-reaching consequences for children's well-being across the lifespan, both in the short and long term (Felitti, Vincent, Anda, Robert, Nordenberg, Williamson, & James, 1998).

One of Botswana's primary opportunities is that since attaining independence in 1966, the country has never experienced a civil war or the civil strife that has characterised the political turf in many African countries. Therefore, the peace and stability that prevails in the country provide a conducive environment for addressing and combatting social welfare issues in childhood. Wars tend to disrupt the entire fabric of social, economic and community relations, creating a fragmented and disempowered society, an environment that violates children's rights (Higson-Smith & Killian, 2000).

Another opportunity evident in Botswana's case is that for many years, the country's economy has been doing relatively well. Since Independence, Botswana has made considerable progress economically as well as in the provision of social services. At independence, the country was so poor that it could not even meet its recurrent budget obligations; hence, both recurrent and development budgets depended heavily on foreign aid. The discovery of minerals in the late 1960s and early 1970s, combined with good economic management and democratic governance, contributed significantly to the country's economic growth, such that by the mid-1990s, Botswana was designated a middle-income country by the World Bank (Kapunda & Moffat, 2010).

SOLUTIONS AND RECOMMENDATIONS

This chapter has analysed three of the numerous social welfare issues that children experience in Botswana. These experiences have far-reaching consequences for the wellbeing of children. The HIV and AIDS pandemic has had profound negative effects on the situation of many children in Botswana, particularly orphans. HIV and AIDS, trauma, and alcohol and substance abuse have affected the developmental trajectories of children in Botswana, and the nation needs to identify strategic ways to move forward in addressing these problems.

Orphaned children who are without sufficient adult support in their lives are highly vulnerable to child maltreatment and other forms of abuse. According to a recent United Nations Children's Fund report (UNICEF, 2012, p. 16), "The key drivers of the [HIV and AIDS] epidemic are gender-based violence, intergenerational sex, multiple concurrent partners and substance abuse." The egregious effects of sexual assault and incest on children have been well-documented (e.g., Choate, 2012; Doyle & Perlman, 2012; Levers, 2012; Maundeni & Levers, 2006; McCoyd, Walter, & Levers, 2012; Maundeni, Levers, & Jacques, 2008; Perlman & Doyle, 2012).

The following recommendations are made for practice/programming to address some of the complex issues analysed in this chapter. First, strategies for addressing the child-related social problems of HIV and AIDS, trauma, and alcohol and substance abuse need to use formal (state and private) and informal (community and family) mechanisms. Trauma-informed care is a strategy that should be infused across a larger integrative health care system. Following Felitti et al.'s (1998) innovative work on adverse childhood experiences, Botswana's children who are at highest risk should be assessed for trauma. Parallel with this, and also following the Felitti et al. work, a culturally appropriate ACE study should be conducted among adults to evaluate the magnitude of the problems related to adverse childhood problems. According to the original ACE studies, early childhood trauma significantly affects the health of affected individuals across the lifespan; those with higher ACE scores die earlier. Such results suggest the need for a more integrated system of health care. In integrative health care, behavioural health care services are blended into the health care delivery system, along with biomedical care. Additionally, behavioural work with children should revolve around promoting resilience and hardiness.

Second, there is a need for residential rehabilitation centres for children and young people who abuse drugs. A related point is that educational institutions should intensify efforts to sensitise children about alcohol and drugs. Such efforts should use participatory methods to involve children as active agents in the sensitization programmes. Tertiary educational institutions should prepare preservice professionals, like teachers and other social service providers, to deal with childhood alcohol and drug abuse. Third, professionals offering psychosocial services to children need to understand the effects of trauma and receive preservice education related to the trauma. Fourth, efforts to sensitise society at large about children's rights are crucial in light of the fact that most people in the country have not embraced the concept of children's rights. Fifth, parenting programmes need to be mounted to empower parents and guardians with knowledge and skills on parenting. This recommendation is vital, taking into account that minimal efforts have been taken to teach parenting skills, and yet some of the welfare problems that children experience (e.g., drug abuse) result from poor parenting skills. Finally, programmes aimed at preventing the three social welfare problems discussed in this chapter need to be intensified.

FUTURE RESEARCH DIRECTIONS

While the reality of childhood has changed dramatically over the last half century, much of Tswana society clings to traditional constructs of childhood. One example is the taboo about discussing death or even illness with children. For the most part, a parent's death or a child's illness would not be discussed with a particular child. This cultural silence on sensitive issues has been noted by Thamuku and Daniel (2013), who asserted that it reflects persistent taboos concerning adults talking to children about death, sex, and related issues. From her study entitled, *Hidden Wounds: Orphanhood, Expediency and Cultural Silence in Botswana*, Daniel (2005) found that children in Botswana are traditionally excluded from funerals and may not even be told about the death of their parent. One of the authors of this chapter led a focus group with caregivers of HIV-positive children at a major paediatric facility in Botswana. Many of the caregivers argued against explaining to a young child that a parent had died, even though the child was no longer with the parent; many also argued that the child should not be told about his or her status, even though the child would be expected to take ARV's, at home and at school. Alternatively, some of the other caregivers argued that the culture needs to change to accommodate contemporary needs, like effectively dealing with HIV and AIDS, and that children need to be brought into the conversation in age-appropriate ways. Malema (2006) explored this important issue in terms of culturally appropriate ways to have a positive impact on this traditional taboo.

Issues analysed in this chapter do not only have implications for practice, they also have implications for research. First, more qualitative research is necessary in order to understand the phenomena associated with changing conceptualizations of childhood in Botswana. Second, there is a need for a situational analysis of social welfare problems affecting children in the country. The one that was conducted in 2008 focused only on OVC and the findings are outdated. A situational analysis, framed by a bio-ecological perspective, could identify the risk and protective factors associated with children's lived experiences. The identification of risk and protective factors could, in turn, inform program development and service provision by highlighting ways to mitigate children's environments, especially in terms of extinguishing or diminishing risk factors and creating new or enhancing existing protective factors. Third, there is a need for research on interventions (both formal and informal) targeting children and adolescents following bereavement, as well as on interventions targeting children who have experienced various traumatic circumstances. Such research should focus on issues like the nature and mechanisms of targeted interventions, the challenges inherent in the interventions, and the effectiveness of the interventions, just to mention but a few. This recommendation is made in light of the fact that most strategies that are used in the informal arena are not documented; therefore, there is a dearth of literature on such issues. Finally, the psychosocial effects of trauma need to be explored among children and adults. People's experiences of traumatic events tend to be silenced in traditional culture. Investigations replicating the ACE Study would enhance understandings of the effects and implications of early childhood trauma and inform policy decisions, program development, and service delivery.

When conducting research and collecting the above-mentioned information, researchers must ensure that they design their studies in a manner that will allow them to get both the positives and the negatives, that is, both best practices and areas that need improvements. Moreover, they not only should collect data from urban areas (as has been the case with many researchers who operate under resource constraints), but they should target all areas (i.e., urban, rural, as well as remote). In addition, the voices of children should be of paramount importance throughout the research process, because the lived experiences of children in Botswana need to be better understood.

As was emphasised in the most recently available UNICEF Annual Report (UNICEF, 2015), attention to evidence-based policy development is of paramount importance. Therefore, more evidence-based research is necessary so that informed policy development in Botswana can enlighten child welfare-related practice.

CONCLUSION

The most salient points regarding childhood social welfare issues relate to the changing conceptualization of childhood over the last half century. Traditional concepts of and attitudes about childhood prevail, even in the face of contemporary realities that have increased risks for children along with the need for social safety nets. HIV and AIDS-related orphanhood, substance, and alcohol abuse, and trauma continue to confront children; therefore, there is a need to address these issues at prevention, curative, and support levels, as a matter of urgency.

REFERENCES

Ahmed, J. U. (2010, Spring). Documentary research method: New dimensions. *Indus Journal of Management & Social Sciences, 4*(1), 1-14. Retrieved from https://www.academia.edu/4900830/Documentary_Research_Method_New_Dimensions

Bose, K. (2008). Gaps and remedies of early childhood care and education (ECCE) programs of Botswana. *Educational Research and Reviews, 3*(3), 77-82. Retrieved from http://www.academicjournals.org/article/article1379585818_Kabita.pdf

Breckler, S. J. (2006). Psychology is translational science. *Science Directions, 37*(6), 22. Retrieved from http://www.apa.org/monitor/jun06/sd.aspx

Bigombe, B., & Khadiagala, G. M. (n.d.). *Major trends affecting families in sub-Saharan Africa.* Retrieved from http://www.un.org/esa/socdev/family/Publications/mtbigombe.pdf

Bronfenbrenner, U. (1979). *The ecology of human development: Experiments by nature and design.* Cambridge, MA: Harvard University Press.

Bronfenbrenner, U. (2001). The bioecological theory of human development. In N. J. Smelser & P. B. Baltes (Eds.), *International encyclopaedia of the social and behavioral sciences* (Vol. 10, pp. 6963–6970). New York: Elsevier. doi:10.1016/B0-08-043076-7/00359-4

Bronfenbrenner, U. (Ed.). (2004). The bioecological theory of human development. In U. Bronfenbrenner (Ed.), Making human beings human: Bioecological perspectives on human development (pp. 3-15). Thousand Oaks, CA: Sage.

Bronfenbrenner, U., & Ceci, S. J. (1994). Nature-nurture reconceptualized in developmental perspective: A bioecological model. *Psychological Review, 101*(4), 568–586. doi:10.1037/0033-295X.101.4.568 PMID:7984707

Choate, L. H. (2012). Sexual trauma: An ecological approach to conceptualization and treatment. In L. L. Levers (Ed.), *Trauma counseling: Theories and interventions* (pp. 116–131). New York: Springer.

Daniel, M. (2005). Hidden wounds: Orphanhood, expediency and cultural silence in Botswana (PhD thesis). Norwich, UK: School of Development Studies, University of East Anglia. Retrieved from http://hdl.handle.net/1956/3294

Dingfelder, S. D. (2005, April). Fresh funding for translational research. *Monitor on Psychology, 36*(4), 66. Retrieved from http://www.apa.org/monitor/apr05/funding.html

Doyle, A., & Perlman, S. (2012). Trauma experienced in adolescence. In L. L. Levers (Ed.), *Trauma counseling: Theories and interventions* (pp. 146–160). New York: Springer.

Felitti, M. D., Vincent, J., Anda, M. D., Robert, F., Nordenberg, M. D., Williamson, M. S., & James, S. et al. (1998). Relationship of childhood abuse and household dysfunction to many of the leading causes of death in adults: The Adverse Childhood Experiences (ACE) Study. *American Journal of Preventive Medicine, 14*(4), 245–258. doi:10.1016/S0749-3797(98)00017-8 PMID:9635069

Feranil, I., Herstad, B., Jallow, W., & Mbuya-Brown, R. (2010). *Assessing Implementation of Botswana's Program for Orphans and Vulnerable Children.* Washington, DC: Futures Group, Health Policy Initiative, Task Order 1, for USAID. Retrieved from http://www.healthpolicyinitiative.com/Publications/Documents/1265_1_PIBA_Botswana_FINAL_acc.pdf

Foster, G., & Williamson, J. (2000). A review of current literature of the impact of HIV/AIDS on children in sub-Saharan Africa. *AIDS (London, England), 14*(suppl. 3), S275–S284. PMID:11086871

Ginsburg, K. R. (2014). *Building resilience in children and teens: Giving kids roots and wings* (3rd ed.). Washington, DC: American Academy of Pediatrics.

Ginsburg, K. R. (2015). *Raising kids to thrive: Balancing love with expectations and protection with trust.* Washington, DC: American Academy.

Higson-Smith, C., & Killian, B. J. (2000). Caring for Children in Fragmented Communities. In D. Donald, A. Dawes, & J. Louw (Eds.), *Addressing Childhood Adversity* (pp. 202–224). Cape Town: David Philip.

Jefferis, K. R., & Kelly, T. F. (1999). Botswana: Poverty Amid Plenty. *Oxford Development Studies, 27*(2), 211–231. doi:10.1080/13600819908424174

Kapunda, S. M., & Moffat, B. D. (2010). *Corruption Control, Economic Growth and Poverty Reduction in SADC: The Case of Botswana and Tanzania.* Paper Presented at the SAUSSC Conference, Mafikeng.

Kaiser Family Foundation. (2015). *The global HIV/AIDS epidemic*. Retrieved from http://kff.org/global-health-policy/fact-sheet/the-global-hivaids-epidemic/

Kridel, C. (2016). *An introduction to documentary research*. American Educational Research Association Website. Retrieved from http://www.aera.net/SIG013/ResearchConnections/IntroductiontoDocumentaryResearch/tabid/15485/Default.aspx

Lesetedi, G., & Ngcongco, N. (1995). A demographic and socio-economic profile of women and men in Botswana: A review of summary indicators of population composition and distribution, mortality, migration and economic ability. In 1991 Population and housing census dissemination seminar, (pp. 176-188). Gaborone, Botswana: Central Statistics Office.

Levers, L. L. (2012). An introduction to counseling survivors of trauma: Beginning to understand the context of trauma. In L. L. Levers (Ed.), *Trauma counseling: Theories and interventions* (pp. 1–22). New York: Springer.

Lynch, M. F., & Levers, L. L. (2007). Ecological-transactional and motivational perspectives in counseling. In J. Gregoire & C. Jungers (Eds.), *Counselor's companion: Handbook for professional helpers* (pp. 586–605). New York: Earlbaum.

Malema, N. (2006). *Challenges and adjustment strategies facing caregivers of children living with HIV in Gaborone: Implications for counselling* (Unpublished Master's Thesis). University of Botswana, Gaborone, Botswana.

Malinga, T., & Ntshwarang, P. N. (2011). Alternative care for children in Botswana: A reality or idealism? *Social Work and Society: International Online Journal, 2*(9). Retrieved from http://www.socwork.net/sws/article/view/277/593

Maundeni, T. (2013). Early childhood care and education in Botswana: A necessity that is accessible to few children. *Creative Education, 4*(7A), 54-59. Retrieved from http://file.scirp.org/pdf/CE_2013071710353641.pdf

Maundeni, T. (2010). Challenges Faced in the Implementation of Provisions of the United Nations Convention on the Rights of the Child (CRC) in Botswana. *Journal of Social Development in Africa, 25*(1), 59–84. doi:10.4314/jsda.v25i1.54279

Maundeni, T., & Levers, L. L. (2006). Concerns about child subject research in Botswana: A call for establishing structures and guidelines that protect children. *African Sociological Review, 9*(2), 153–167. doi:10.4314/asr.v9i2.23265

Maundeni, T., Levers, L. L., & Jacques, G. (Eds.). (2008). *Changing family systems: A global perspective*. Gaborone, Botswana: Bay Publishers.

Maunganidze, L., & Tsamaase, M. (2014). Early childhood education in Botswana: A case of fragmented "fits". *International Education Studies, 7*(5), 1-7. Retrieved from http://files.eric.ed.gov/fulltext/EJ1069296.pdf

Manyanda, K. (2015). *Rehabilitation of Youths with Alcohol and Substance Use Disorders: Experiences from BOSASNET.* Paper presented at the Africa and middle east congress on addiction, Gaborone, Botswana.

McCoyd, J. L. M., Walter, C. A., & Levers, L. L. (2012). Issues of loss and grief. In L. L. Levers (Ed.), *Trauma counseling: Theories and interventions* (pp. 77–97). New York: Springer.

Ministry of Local Government. (2008). *National situational analysis on orphans and vulnerable children in Botswana*. Gaborone: Ministry of Local Government.

Mogalakwe, M. (2006). The Use of Documentary Research Methods in Social Research. *African Sociological Review*, *10*(1), 221–230.

Perlman, S., & Doyle, A. (2012). Trauma experienced in early childhood. In L. L. Levers (Ed.), *Trauma counseling: Theories and interventions* (pp. 132–145). New York: Springer.

Seboni, N., Maundeni, T., & Rapinyana, O. (2015). An Analysis of Responses to Orphaned and Vulnerable Children (OVC) in Botswana. In M. Lombe (Ed.), *Children and AIDS*. Ashgate Publishing Ltd.

Seloilwe, E. S., & Thupayagale-Tshweneagae, G. (2009). Sexual Abuse and Violence Among Adolescent Girls in Botswana: A Mental Health Perspective. *Issues in Mental Health Nursing*, *30*(7), 456–459. doi:10.1080/01612840903039367 PMID:19544130

Thamuku, M., & Daniel, M. (2013). Exploring responses to transformative group therapy for orphaned children in the context of mass orphaning in Botswana. *Death Studies*, *37*(5), 413–447. doi:10.1080/07481187.2012.654594 PMID:24517564

Thula, M. (2015). *Rehabilitation of youths who abuse drugs and substances: Lessons from Sbrana Hospital*. Paper presented at the Africa and middle east congress on addiction, Gaborone, Botswana.

United Nations Children's Fund. (2011). *UNICEF Botswana: Annual report 2011*. Retrieved from http://www.unicef.org/botswana/BCO__Annual_Report_2011.pdf

United Nations Children's Fund. (2012). *UNICEF Botswana: Annual report 2011*. Gaborone, Botswana: Author. Retrieved from http://www.unicef.org/botswana/BCO__Annual_Report_2011.pdf

United Nations Children's Fund. (n.d.). *UNICEF Botswana: Annual report 2015*. Retrieved from http://www.unicef.org/about/annualreport/files/Botswana_2015_COAR.pdf

United Nations Human Rights Office of the High Commissioner. (1989, November). *Convention on the rights of the child*. Retrieved from http://www.ohchr.org/EN/ProfessionalInterest/Pages/CRC.aspx

Zerhouni, E. A. (2005). US biomedical research: Basic, translational, and clinical sciences. *Journal of the American Medical Association*, *294*(11), 1352–1358. doi:10.1001/jama.294.11.1352 PMID:16174693

ENDNOTES

1 Some of these measures will be highlighted later in this chapter.

2 The mother-tongue of the majority of people in Botswana.

Chapter 5
Child Poverty and Social Inequalities in Africa:
A Social Justice Perspective

Icarbord Tshabangu
Leeds Trinity University, UK

ABSTRACT

Africa has continually faced challenges in providing public services for its vast populations culminating in wider inequality gaps and rising levels of child poverty. Consequently, child poverty has led to dim prospects for most children. This chapter discusses child poverty and social inequalities since these aspects are critical to child development and welfare. An analytic review of World Bank and United Nations agencies data was conducted, consisting of existing surveyed data and literature on contemporary contexts in Sub-Saharan Africa. It was noted how inadequate investment levels; children's voicelessness and a lack of social security safety nets, has negatively impacted children's rights and development. Indications are that child poverty and other social inequalities continue to be experienced in most parts of the continent despite the economic rise in some of these emerging economies.

INTRODUCTION

This chapter draws part of its analysis and findings from the author's previous broader study on educational inequalities in Africa. It is noted that while extreme poverty has fallen globally over the last 30 years, from about 40% to under 20%, most African countries have barely extricated themselves from the yoke of poverty. Sub-Saharan Africa still records over 40% of people living in abject poverty and most of these are children (World Bank, 2014). Sub-Saharan Africa continues to record higher levels of poverty; unchecked corruption, the higher incidence of disease, poor infrastructure, poor economic growth, fluctuating and unstable democracies that are prone to conflict and civil war (World Bank 2014; Moyo, 2010; Salih, 2001). These sad and unfavourable descriptions shared by most Africa countries are closely tied to various manifestations, but primarily child poverty and social inequalities. Over 600 million children live in Africa, with at least 40-50 per cent of children in most African countries living

DOI: 10.4018/978-1-5225-2578-3.ch005

below the poverty line (World Bank, 2014). It is noted that in sub-Saharan Africa alone, 247 million children are deprived of their basic rights as enshrined in the United Nations Convention on the Rights of the Child (UNCRC). Key among such forms of deprivation include lack of access to water, food, healthcare, shelter, and education. From the 30 sub-Saharan countries, UNICEF estimates that two-thirds of children tend to suffer from two or more of the deprivations stated above (Garcia, 2015).

One of the major reasons for focusing on child poverty and social inequalities is because these are a social justice and human rights issue. The Universal Declaration of Human Rights, 1948 Article 1, states that 'All human beings are born free and equal in dignity and rights.' This means that those degraded by poverty tend to have less or no rights as citizens in their countries. They have less dignity and less equality and freedom. The United Nations Convention on the rights of the child provides for child protection from poverty (article 26). The Convention, which almost all African governments have ratified, considers children to be people under the age of 18. It is also often stated that children are the future of every nation and that a nation's future strength and posterity can largely be measured and guaranteed with quality investment in its children. Part of the reason why Africa has perpetually faced the scourge of underdevelopment could be due to low levels of investment and lack of social security for her children (World Bank, 2014). Africa has 81 per 1000 under 5 mortality rates, which is seven times that of Europe (WHO, 2015). Most of these avoidable deaths are due to child poverty; inequalities and low-level investment on child welfare. Africa continues to have a disproportionate concentration of poverty among children compared to adults. The Status of Poverty Report showed that both rural and urban children were more likely to be poor than adults (World Bank 2014). There is, therefore, compelling rationale to seek to understand better the state of child poverty in Africa. It is noted that Africa may not turn a corner in its quest for success and economic development if there is no political will to uphold children's rights and economic welfare. Poverty in Africa will mostly likely continue to rise unless the benefits of economic development reach its people through the establishment of social security and safety nets, especially for children.

Definitions of Poverty

Child poverty is a multidimensional phenomenon and needs to be measured and understood in many ways (UNICEF 2016). In basic terms, poverty refers to general scarcity and a state of material lack. Child poverty is not just about lack of money. UNESCO 2015 defines absolute poverty and destitution as a lack of means necessary to meet basic needs. For children, these may include food, clothing, healthcare and shelter. There is also relative poverty. Sabates (2008), defines this as varying from country to country and occurring when people do not enjoy a certain minimum level of living standards compared to the rest of their population. In most parts of Africa, especially the rural areas, governments have been slow in providing basic needs, leading to soaring levels of deprivation, compared to the urban areas. This has been due in part to government's lack of political will, lack of resources, tax avoidance, poor policy implementation, corruption and the mass exodus of healthcare and educational professionals to cities or other greener pastures. Child poverty and deprivation therefore tends to be experienced differently in urban and rural areas by comparison, but is more likely to be severe in rural areas due to low levels of investment and infrastructure. UNICEF (2016)'s approaches to child poverty both from a monetary and non-monetary perspective, involve moving many children out of monetary poverty and simultaneously ensuring they are not hungry or malnourished.

BACKGROUND

Perpetual poverty levels in Africa cannot be fully appreciated without the understanding of colonial; post-colonial and neo-colonialism that have visited the continent. When the industrial powers of Europe colonised Africa in the 19th century they produced a capitalist economy with similarities to their own countries. Africa was intended to serve two purposes: firstly, to provide a potential market and secondly to be a source of raw materials (Mbah and Igariwey, 2001). In the process, Africa was turned from a pre-colonial, self-sufficient communal agricultural economy to one compelled to embrace interdependence with other economies. Gradually the society was stratified and modelled after capitalism – mostly, state capitalism, which tended to manifest in excessive greed and corruption among the government elite.

The dawn of independence in most African countries heralded systems that modelled socialist ideologies such as „Humanism" in Zambia, "Harambee" in Kenya, "Education with Production" in Zimbabwe and "Ujamaa" in Tanzania. But as Mbah and Igariwey (2001) would argue, either way, state socialism like state capitalism is fatalistically doomed, particularly due to over-centralisation of state apparatus and lack of democratic spaces; leading to unaccountable governance and corruption. In postcolonial Africa, most countries moved from being biggest exporters of agricultural and mineral products to being biggest importers, thereby further weakening their economies. Most of these economic failures have impacted heavily on child poverty and social inequalities. It is noted that most African leaders failed to analyse imperialism in relation to the African context and hence most of Africa found herself faced with neo-colonialism. Furthermore, the leaders' radical rhetoric was not matched by actual performance, and therefore counter-productive (Babu, 1981). State capitalism found allies in the new African leaders especially through corruption and greed (Lacey, 1970; Rodney, 1981; Mbah and Igariwey, 2001; Babu, 1981). Some multinational corporations who are also steeped in exploitative greed have found allies among some elites in Africa, engaging in underhand deals that tend to deprive some countries of their natural wealth and economic growth.

As part of the global vision, the eight Millennium Development Goals (MDGs) sought to half extreme poverty rates by 2015. These global obligations, agreed upon by all countries, including the world's leading development institutions, such as the World bank, have in the recent past motivated most countries to address the levels of poverty in their constituents, with some notable improvements (Global Monitoring Report, 2015). Despite successes made in reducing poverty, progress has been reported as uneven, and needing more work. It is recorded that 900 million people in 2012 were living on less than \$1.90 a day based on the updated international poverty line and 700 million in 2015 (Global Monitoring Report, 2015). Extreme poverty remains unacceptably high and much of it is concentrated in Sub-Saharan Africa. Just as Our Africa (2015) observed, poverty is sometimes more about how society shares the money out than how much money there is overall. They note that some African countries are very poor, but others are wealthier, often from oil and mineral resources, yet with extreme inequalities among their citizens. It is hoped that the momentum gained towards poverty reduction, especially child poverty, will be maintained and improved upon, post-2015 development agenda, through closer collaboration between the United Nations, the national governments, civil society and other global agencies.

METHODOLOGY

The study conducted an analytic review of existing survey data and literature on contemporary contexts in Africa, focusing on children's experiences of poverty and how this impacted their welfare. Several World Bank and United Nations agencies data were used to establish a qualitative understanding of child poverty and social inequalities and how these have negatively impacted childhood development. There was also an analytical review of unpublished sources of data and use of observation accounts from Sub-Saharan Africa to provide a triangulated approach in the data reviewed. In using World Bank and the United Nations data the study has been able to establish better understanding on child poverty and social inequalities in Africa and to propose plausible solutions.

CAUSES OF POVERTY

At a theoretical level, child poverty is caused by deprivation which is a lack of material conditions and services. However, there are two signifiers to child poverty. These are *exclusion* and *vulnerability*. Exclusion often occurs because of unjust processes through which children's dignity, voice, and rights are denied (Green, 2006; Rank, Yoon & Herschl, 2003). In this study, there was evidence to suggest that most children in Africa are not accorded their rights as enshrined in the UNCRC. As children grow, so does their capacity to make decisions. However, children in most parts of Africa are often seen but not heard and this takes place both in the home and in the classroom (Harber, 1995). In some cases, children are just unacknowledged 'invisible hands' that help drive the economy (Grier, 2006). This means that while some children may provide labour, both at home and in the community, they have no voice in decision-making processes or on issues that directly affect their well-being, which violates article 12 of UNCRC. The second one is a vulnerability. This is an inability of society to cope with existing or probable threats to children in their environment (Green, 2006; Rank, Yoon & Herschl, 2003). It is noted that there are weak social security laws in Africa that protect children, and children are often left to the whims of adults who control all resources, sometimes abusively. It is not uncommon to find traditional and paternalistic communities in Africa that deny children their rights. This may include marrying girls off at a tender age; failure by the state to protect through social security schemes or to prosecute abuses on children. In several urban areas, children resort to begging and sleeping on the streets due to lack or ineffective social security laws that compel the state to protect children. Oftentimes such a sacred task of national significance is relegated to external donor organisations, which raises moral questions on some state governance. This moral dilemma is discussed further under the subtitle 'Over-reliance on external donor funding'. It is noted therefore that household poverty, which tends to impact heavily on children, can occur through personal failings, that is, poor individual character traits and habits which make a family vulnerable to poverty. Secondly, through structural failings, that is, social and economic structures that are ineffective at state level. Thirdly, poverty may occur due to cultural characteristics, that is, maintaining a national mindset which often leads to the impoverishing of many citizens, mostly children (Green, 2006; Rank, Yoon & Herschl, 2003).

Causes of Child Poverty in Africa

While globalisation and interconnectedness have brought prosperity in some parts of the world, Africa has not generally benefited from global decisions, policies and practices, since these are wholly influenced, by the rich and powerful countries and their transnational corporations in line with their national interests. Faced with such enormous external economic influences, poor and powerless African governments have been unable to bargain better trade deals for their people. Consequently, globalisation has therefore witnessed, a few getting wealthy while the majority especially children in Africa, struggle. While other regions of the world such as North Africa and South East Asia have recorded 81% and 84% reduction in extreme poverty, respectively, Sub-Saharan Africa only registered 28%, a stark contrast. Falk (2007) urges Africa to shift away from global integration and to return to the "developmental state" to focus on internal links and raising domestic funds, which include, increased tax rates, improved tax collection, better use of remittances from workers abroad, and control of foreign outflows. He concludes that these measures would significantly reduce African countries' dependence on foreign aid and MF loans.

Rowntree's (1901), findings on general causes of poverty gives us some understanding of how children in Africa often become poor. With endemic diseases, such as HIV/AIDS, malaria and tuberculosis in Africa it is not uncommon that most children are robbed of the family's breadwinner/ wage earner quite early in life. Accidents, long-term illness have also been known to incapacitate some wage earners leaving children in abject poverty, since most of these workers may not have comprehensive insurance schemes to cover such eventualities. Most countries have high levels of unemployment meaning that parents may be out of work and that there is generally chronic irregularity of work in the employment sector (ILO, 2016). Traditionally most African families are large or extended, which may strain the meagre resources available to the household. While the largeness of a family may be an advantage in agrarian and mostly rural Africa, rural-urban migration and urbanisation of life in general renders this notion questionable. Low wages have also been a factor contributing to child poverty and inequality. In some cases, this has driven up child labour and abuse.

In some parts of Africa, access to land and ownership of land has been declining due to rising populations and related environmental issues (Hanmer et al, 1996; Holden & Otsuka, 2014), In southern and parts of Eastern Africa, there continues to be unequal access to land and contestations on land thereby discouraging potential local and external investors who may help drive these economies. It is noted that in some paternalistic communities, women often have no access to land or rights to land ownership since they are statutorily perceived to be minors (Mnisi,1998; Hanmer et al, 1996; Holden & Otsuka, 2014). Furthermore, in the urban areas, most women tend to be in the informal sector which often hampers their ability to access credit from financial institutions. Seeing that most women in Africa are often left to fend for their children, particularly in the rural areas, where a husband has died or left, such paternalistic traditions and laws thus only help to impoverish children.

CHILDHOOD AND POVERTY

Children tend to understand poverty as a deeply physical, emotional and social experience and this experience is felt acutely and minutely from an early age. For most children, it is more about the experience than about resources.

For both adults and children, poverty can be a source of stigma and shame. It is noted that some individuals are more affected than others, and people cope in different ways. Poverty-related stigma and shame may be particularly difficult for children, who have less life experience and fewer emotional resources to draw upon than adults (Howard and Millard, 1997). Childhood is a tender period where children's sensitivities to the physical, mental, emotional and social are quite strong. Their growth and development often make them more vulnerable when exposed to poverty and degradation. While adults may be resilient putting into use their accumulated experiences, children may be lacking and therefore susceptible to negative long-term impact arising from poverty and social injustice. Coletta et al, (1996) also observed that for younger children, malnutrition at an early age can adversely impair a child's physical development thus impacting their mental capacities and the ability to learn at school. Half the number of children who die under the age of 5 in Africa is attributed to malnutrition (WHO, 2015). Such large numbers of children dying at an early age is indicative of their vulnerability, and a demonstration of inequalities and the failure by adults or the state to protect. Coletta et al (1996) further note that girls who are undernourished are more likely to give birth to undernourished infants who in turn face a higher rate of mortality. Children who face such deprivation and lack of opportunities often become trapped in the cycle of poverty.

UNDERSTANDING CHILD POVERTY IN AFRICA

It is noted that in Africa there is a higher concentration of poverty among children than adults. Such disproportionate concentration of poverty among children is also unique in comparison to other regions of the world (World Bank, 2014). While adults may have means and abilities to combat poverty, most children are heavily dependent and powerless. In Africa where poverty indices are much higher, children turn to bear the brunt of such deprivation with long lasting consequences on social mobility. In countries where there has been poor governance, disasters, war and famine children have been the worst affected by such impoverishing forces, in some cases leading to abusive child labour. It is, therefore, important to understand that child poverty is separate from adults' poverty and efforts to measure it independently may help establish better understanding and suitable policy solutions for most children.

Understanding child poverty in Africa may entail measuring it at micro levels, as opposed to macro level or sub-regional levels, or using incomes as a benchmark. As stated earlier, Africa consists of different countries with varying economic capacities and leadership ethos. While for example, the state of children's welfare in South Africa may appear much stronger compared to South Sudan, there are some pockets of abject child poverty in South Africa that might be overlooked if policymakers neglected child individuality; the intra-household dynamics and variations between rural districts, towns, cities and regions. There is evidence and general acceptance that children in rural Africa are often exposed to higher levels of deprivation and poverty compared to their urban counterparts (World Bank, 2012). In countries with low rates of urbanisation such as Tanzania and Uganda, the levels of child poverty in rural areas are generally more profound than in countries such as South Africa where most men and women trek to the cities in search of work, leaving children with relatives. Rural-urban migration in search of work has in some cases undermined social cohesion and child safety culminating in poor child welfare.

The increasing numbers of people settling in the cities in most countries have over the years put pressure on urban services and employment availability, thereby leading to increased child poverty in the cities (Rebelo, 1999), culminating in street children; child prostitutes; trafficking and child criminality. While the macro levels of seeking to understand child poverty may be useful, particularly using children's ability to access health and welfare support, Harper & Marcus (2002) propose a child-centred focus which measures and seeks to understand child poverty from the following perspectives;

- Inadequate household livelihood resources and capacity;
- Inadequate social cohesion and capital for child protection, nurturance and development; and
- Inadequate opportunities for human development, such as health and welfare support.

Such a comprehensive approach to measuring and understanding child poverty will undoubtedly provide a broader but more focused definition of child poverty, which is more likely to help generate solutions for a continent largely seen as steeped in poverty.

POVERTY ISSUES IMPACTING CHILDREN

The Human Rights Perspectives

It is critical to acknowledge that child poverty, particularly in Africa is largely due to children's powerlessness and exclusion from decisions that directly affect them. In almost all societies, children are perceived as a dependent lot and in most cases, structurally powerless. In the larger African context, where paternalistic ideologies concerning childhood are still profound (Indabawa, 1997; Ncube, 1998; Harber, 1999), democratic participation in most fora by the young often faces resistance in some subcultures. In schools, teachers often exercise unquestioned authority over children (Harber, 1995), thereby nurturing a culture of docility and exclusion from active participation in violation of children's rights as enshrined in the UNCRC Article 12.1. Generally, millions of people in Africa have fallen into poverty without a democratic voice, and the ability to hold their governments to account (Rivera-Batiz, 1999). Cornwall, (1998) further observed that while girls have generally been excluded in decisions that affect them, more boys also share in this powerlessness and voicelessness. It is observed that despite widespread political rhetoric that 'children are the future' most governments' budget allocations, especially on health and child welfare, do not reflect this mantra and the effects of child poverty tend to continue unabated. It is difficult to imagine effective eradication of child poverty and social inequalities where children's rights continue to be partially observed and where there are minimal investments by ministries and non-governmental organisations that deal directly with children's welfare issues.

Over Reliance on External Donor Funding: Dead Aid

Due to higher levels of poverty, Africa has over the years been labelled the 'basket case' of the world. Consequently, the western world has continually funded various programmes in different countries, in some cases influencing policies in strategic areas including poverty alleviation. However, Moyo (2010) has argued against western aid in Africa citing three main strands that need consideration if Africa is to eradicate poverty. First, it is a complaint about how the West is patronising Africans through aid and secondly, how aid has harmed Africa particularly in view of unfair international trade practices that tend to disadvantage Africa, coupled with political immorality that is contented with over-reliance on external aid, especially on efforts towards poverty eradication. An entrepreneurial alternative is then proposed which is likely to chart a better path for Africa leading to economic independence and poverty reduction.

During colonial, rule aid was used as a form of control and influence over colonial empires. The British Colonial Development and Welfare Act of 1940, for example, was a paternalistic tool, meant, as per the coloniser, for "peoples not yet able to stand by themselves." While the former empirical powers like France and Britain have dropped some of the racist innuendos associated with development aid in Africa today, authoritarian paternalism is merely denied in name but implemented in practice (Easterly, 2009). Health Poverty Action (2015) co-authored by a range of other civil society organisations, concluded that inflows through development aid to Africa were negligible compared to illicit outflows from Africa to the Western governments and their transnational corporations by an annual net loss of US$ 58.2 billion to Africa.

On the international stage, it is observed that rarely do African politicians get involved in proffering strategic solutions on poverty reduction but the west, through its megaphone diplomacy and through its pop stars like Bob Geldof and movie stars like Angelina Jolie (who supposedly represent Africa's poor) tends to set the agenda on fighting poverty. This moral vacuum and a lack of ethical leadership indicate that child poverty reduction has been left to persons outside Africa. Such abdication of responsibility on the part of African leaders can only be retrogressive to many other efforts made (Moyo, 2010). The western countries' child welfare policy and practice have had a pervasive influence on conceptions about child poverty in Africa and on development policy more generally (MacPherson & Midgely, 1987). Such failures to fully appreciate child poverty dynamics in Africa has often led to the misidentification of vulnerable groups and to overly focus exclusively on health and education provision. Despite these conflictual views, the rich countries may need to continue helping African countries in areas such as technology, infrastructural development and ensuring a fair trading system.

Child Labour: The Invisible Hands

Our appreciation of child poverty and social inequalities in Africa may not be complete if we didn't touch on child labour, which is a long-standing feature spanning the pre-colonial to the postcolonial era (Tyrell and Jurgens, 1983; Summers, 2002; Grier, 2006). Traditionally, child labour may have motivated polygamy to ensure more children in the homestead, who will, in turn, provide labour. In the modern economies of Africa, large households are generally more likely to be poor than smaller households, and therefore a likely cause of higher levels of child poverty. In some instances, large families can be a means of coping with poverty, rather than a cause of it, especially in rural agrarian settings (Hanmer et al, 1996).

The International Labour Organisation (ILO) describes worst forms of child labour as slavery, debt, bondage, prostitution, pornography, forced recruitment of children for use in armed conflict, use of children in drug trafficking and other illicit activities, and all other work likely to be harmful or hazardous to the health, safety or morals of children under 18 years (Work in Freedom, 2016). Compared to other world regions, Africa has the largest number of child labour at around 59 million children aged between of 5 and 17, with some classed as working under hazardous conditions (ILO, 2016). It is recorded that one in 5 children in Africa is employed against their will in stone quarries, farms, and mines (ILO, 2016). While several efforts are needful to combat child labour it is sadly noted that most of it arise due to higher levels of poverty and desperation. Despite notable decline on child labour at the global level, from 246 million in 2000 to168 million, Sub-Saharan Africa continues to be the region with the highest concentrations of child labour with more than one in five children in child labour, and with a higher ten percentage point in hazardous work (ILO, 2016).

Grier (2006: 8) observes that:

To be sure, no one familiar with African economies and societies is oblivious to the tremendous amount of labour that children contribute to peasant farming household maintenance, childcare and the informal economy.

Despite playing a significant role in these African economies, and in some schools where there is student labour, children are largely ignored and unwelcome in decision-making processes. In contemporary Africa, some children still work at some homesteads and have their wages paid to their parents. The rise in capitalistic interactions both during colonialism and the post-colonial era, both at home and within the employment sector, has in some cases witnessed depraved child labour practices in some countries, with some children forfeiting their rights.

Gender and Child Poverty

Since the 1980s, the levels of girl-child enrolment in Africa, across most mainstream sectors of education have reflected rapid improvement in terms of equity and access. However, this has not translated to the realisation of women senior leaders or politicians who may be more sensitive and appreciative of child poverty and welfare issues. In some communities, both urban and rural girls are more likely to be asked to drop out of school in preference of boys, since traditionally, boys are perceived to have a greater potential of supporting the family in the long-term, whereas girls are married off to live under their husbands' control. It is not uncommon in most traditional communities that girls are sometimes married off quite early to raise funds through the bride price and therefore address poverty-related challenges in the home (Narayan and Nyamwaya, 1996).

While we may not simplistically conflate child poverty and that of women, it is noted that there is a strong relationship between women's state of well-being and child poverty, especially for infants and young dependent children. The advance of women's rights in Africa or lack thereof is inextricably linked to child poverty challenges. Evidence suggests that women tend to prioritise children's welfare compared to men, and are therefore more likely to devote resources to child welfare and poverty relief (World Bank, 1998).

Poor Investments and the Economy

George (1990) observed that debt is an efficient tool, which ensures access to other peoples' raw materials and infrastructure on the cheapest possible terms. She noted that most countries in Africa must compete for shrinking export markets and thus can manage only to export a limited range of products because of Western countries protectionism. Exporters from developing countries such as Africa find that their exporters' income is reduced to a bare minimum while the Western nations enjoy huge savings. It is noted that many developing nations are in debt and poverty partly due to the policies of international institutions such as the International Monetary Fund (IMF) and the World Bank. Programmes such as the Structural Adjustment Policies (SAPs) have been heavily criticised in Africa, for many years, since they are perceived as causing poverty and deprivation, as opposed to claims made to the contrary by richer nations, the IMF and the World Bank.

It is argued that Structural Adjustment Policies (SAPs) have been imposed to ensure debt repayment and economic restructuring and growth. As part of continuing aid and ensuring competitive debt repayment plans, poor countries are coerced to cut spending on basic but primary services such as health, education, child welfare and development thereby lowering the standards of living for the people. Despite public protests in countries such as Tunisia, Zimbabwe and several others against IMF's induced economic hardships and high unemployment rates, the IMF has maintained the status quo on the implementation of austerity measures (Global Research).

Garcia (2015) noted that social protection programmes in countries have a long-lasting benefit for many families and children living in poverty and yet only one-third of the world's poor are covered. He argues that for countries to end child poverty, they must ensure that children are protected from risks and vulnerabilities. Like in most parts of the world the urban middle class in Africa is driving economic expansion and growth. However, there is a traditional lack or weaker health schemes or national health insurance programs that cater for this group. Many workers and people in general have no access to health insurance and when sickness strikes, there are usually out-of-pocket and often lose their jobs or source of livelihood. This consequently cripples the family support system upon which children depend, and damages economic growth.

The World Bank's African Development Indicators of 2007 showed that on average, African countries were experiencing economic growth of 5.4 percent per year, which was significant enough to spare efforts towards poverty reduction. However, the global economic downturn of 2008, and reduced competitiveness on global markets, coupled with poor infrastructure, has held Africa back. There is still need for more investment to raise standards of living, especially aimed at child poverty alleviation.

Conflict and Poverty

Thirty-eight percent of the world's refugees are in Africa due to war, conflict and rampant human rights abuses. There have been numerous wars waged in Africa in the last three decades with devastating short and long-term consequences on children such as lack of access to education, health and welfare; separation from family; child-headed households; child soldiers and street children; child prostitution, forced marriages and sexual abuse. In the mid-1990s Africa had as many soldiers as teachers (Morgan, 1995), and those numbers have not reduced in some countries. The devastation caused by conflict has often left behind dilapidated public infrastructure such as schools and hospitals which are often vital for child development and welfare. This often culminates in cases of malnutrition; polluted water supplies and mushrooming of various diseases which often attack children due to their vulnerability. It is noted that almost all the African countries with the highest child mortality rates have experienced conflict in recent years (World Bank, 2014).

SOLUTIONS AND RECOMMENDATIONS

In line with UNICEF (2016), approaches to child welfare, there is need to continue working on improving child poverty profiles in Sub-Saharan countries as part of addressing equity concerns. This may mean helping countries to adopt rigorous measures in identifying poverty across both monetary and non-monetary approaches. Low-income countries with higher incidence of child poverty, need to commit to child poverty reduction, which means recognising, prioritising, and building effective response mechanisms.

The rampant inequalities in most parts of Sub-Saharan Africa calls for policy approaches that will boost shared prosperity as part of child poverty address. There is a need for complementary policies that favour economic growth as a means of raising living standards for the poor. Such policies should also seek to increase investment and ensure infrastructural development especially in rural Africa where most populations live.

Due to unfair trade practices against low-income countries, there is a need for Western countries to revisit some of their protectionist trade arrangements and to have oversight of their transnational corporations who may engage in exploitative practices such as child labour and other malpractice including tax avoidance. Sub-Saharan countries will also need to invest more in human capital since a country's economic growth and development is tied to the investment made on its people. Investing in human development should also entail providing competitive social security schemes for the workers and means-tested schemes for the poor. Such social security measures will indirectly benefit children who might be trapped in poverty. Multiple economic strategies that help increase state revenues are needful and will ensure that basic needs such as children's welfare, and other economic freedoms are met (Global Issues, 2015). Strategies for debt relief should be enhanced since, in some countries, half the share of GDP is devoted to servicing debt. The cancellation of debt for some countries, in the recent past, has reduced debt burden from 3.9% in 2000 to 1.4% in 2011 (Prizzon and Mustapha, 2014). This has allowed increased spending on health and education as part of child poverty reduction.

Recommendations

- To effectively address child poverty there is need to measure and report it at the national level, as opposed to relying on external measures.
- There should be a change of the discussion on child poverty in Africa in ways that redefine the issues and further allows African policy makers to take initiative rather than heavily depend on foreign aid.
- Concerted efforts should be made such that the nature of the policy dialogue is appropriately contextualised to influence budgetary measures in a child-centered approach rather than political led.
- There needs to be a change in paternalistic cultures, thus allowing for the empowerment of children and various civic society interest groups in decision-making, to help minimise discrimination, exclusion, and inequalities.

- The empowerment of women and the refining of gender laws should be central to the efforts meant to eradicate child poverty in Africa.
- Sub-Saharan nations need to work with a coalition of partners, focusing on ending child poverty as part of the Sustainable Development Goals (SDGs).
- There is need to effectively identify and understand multiple natures of child poverty and how countries can better measure these as part of the SDGs.

CONCLUSION

This chapter has explored multidimensional aspects related to child poverty in Africa, based on various indices from international agencies. While there have been solid improvements on poverty reduction in some parts of the world, children in Sub-Saharan Africa have only experienced negligible progress. The literature and data indices point to a need for African countries to revisit their measures and responses to child poverty; address the unfair trade practices and excessive foreign influences; deal decisively with malpractice and corruption; improve revenue streams and invest in infrastructure and human capital. At the national level, there is also need to address human rights disparities and the violation of children economic and social rights as enshrined in United Nations Convention on the Rights of the Child. Confronting these rights violations and abuses will help narrow the gaps in ways that lead to improved child health and welfare. Policymakers in Africa would do well to assume enhanced responsibility on child poverty alleviation rather than abdicate to international donors. That entails exerting ownership and relying less on external data gathering but creating useful locally informed estimates on child poverty and further establishing child disparities by wealth, gender, regions and ethnic groupings based on in-country national statistics. It may be critical to also analyse characteristics and causes of child poverty relying more on qualitative methods to appreciate child poverty and social inequities in depth. In every society, the children are perceived as the future. While child poverty and deprivation remains unaddressed in an effective way, it is improbable to conceive Africa's restoration of dignity and competitiveness on the world stage.

REFERENCES

Africa, O. (2016). *State of children.* Retrieved October 13, 2016, from: http://www.our-africa.org/state-of-children

Ake, C. (1996). *Democracy and development in Africa.* Washington, DC: Brookings Institution.

Babu, A. M. (1981). *African socialism or socialist Africa?* Harare: Zimbabwe Publishing House.

Coletta, N. J., Balachander, J., & Liang, X. (1996). *The Condition of Young Children in Sub-Saharan Africa. The convergence of health, nutrition and early education.* World Bank Technical Paper 326, Africa Technical Department Series. World Bank.

Falk, R. (2007). *World Economy and Development.* Retrieved October 13, 2016, from https://www.globalpolicy.org/component/content/article/211/44646.html

Garcia, A. F. (2015). *7 facts about child poverty you should know*. UNICEF Connect. Retrieved June 14, 2016, from https://blogs.unicef.org/blog/7-facts-about-child-poverty-you-should-know/

George, S. (1990). *A Fate Worse Than Debt*. New York: Grove Weidenfeld.

Global Monitoring Report. (2015). *Development Goals in an Era of Demographic Change*. Retrieved December 12, 2016, from www.worldbank.org/gmr

Grier, B. C. (2006). *Invisible Hands: Child labour and the State in Colonial Zimbabwe*. Portsmouth: Heinemann.

Hanmer, L., Pyatt, G., White, H., & Pouw, N. (1996). *Poverty in Sub-Saharan Africa. What can we learn from the World Bank's Poverty Assessments*. The Hague: Institute of Social Studies.

Harber, C. (1995). *Developing Democratic Education*. Derby: Education Now Books.

Harber, C. (1999). *Voices for Democracy: a North – South Dialogue on Education for Sustainable Democracy*. Derby: Education Now Books.

Harper, C., & Marcus, R. (2002). *Child poverty in Africa*. London: The Save the Children Fund.

Health Poverty Action. (2015). *Africa's billion dollar losses*. Retrieved October 13, 2016, from https://www.healthpovertyaction.org/speaking-out/honest-accounts/

Holden, S., & Otsuka, K. (2014). The roles of land tenure reforms and land markets in the context of population growth and land use intensification in Africa. *Food Policy*, *48*, 88–97. doi:10.1016/j.foodpol.2014.03.005

Howard and Millard. (1997). *Hunger and Shame: Child Malnutrition and Poverty of Mount Kilimanjaro*. London: Routledge.

ILO. (2016). *Child labour in Africa*. Retrieved January 13, 2017, from http://ilo.org/ipec/Regionsandcountries/Africa/lang--en/index.htm-title=IPEC-Africa-accessdate=17

Indabawa, A. S. (1997). Pupil's autonomy, cultural hegemony and education for democracy in an African society. In D. Bridges (Ed.), *Education, autonomy and democratic citizenship: Philosophy in a changing world*. London: Routledge.

Issues, G. (2015). *Causes of Poverty*. Retrieved October 13, 2016, from www.globalissues.org

Lacey, L. A. (1970). *The life of W.E. B. Du Bois. Cheer the Lonesome Traveller*. New York: The Dial Press.

MacPherson, S., & Midgely, J. (1987). *Comparative Social Policy and the Third World: Studies in International Social Policy and Welfare*. London: Palgrave Macmillan.

Mbah, S., & Igariwey, I. E. (2001). *African Anarchism: The History of a Movement*. Tucson, AZ: Sharp Press.

Moyo, D. (2010). *Dead Aid: Why aid is not working and how there is another way for Africa*. London: Penguin.

Narayan, D., & Nyamwaya, D. (1996). *Learning from the poor: A participatory poverty assessment in Kenya. Environment Department working papers; no. 34. Participation series. Social Development papers; no. SDP 14*. Washington, DC: World Bank.

Ncube, W. (Ed.). (1998). Law, culture, tradition and children's rights in eastern and southern Africa. Aldershot, UK: Ashgate.

Prizzon, A., & Mustapha, S. (2014). *Debt sustainability in HIPCs in a new age of choice*. Retrieved October 13, 2016, from: https://www.odi.org/publications/8476-debt-sustainability-hipcs-new-age-choice

Rank, M. R., Hong-Sik, Y., & Hirschl, T. A. (2003). American Poverty as a Structural Failing: Evidence and Arguments. *Journal of Sociology and Social Welfare*, *30*(4), 3–29.

Rivera-Batiz, F. L. (1999). *Democracy, governance and economic growth: Theory and evidence*. New York: Columbia University.

Rodney, W. (1981). *How Europe Underdeveloped Africa*. New York: Howard University Press.

Rowntree, S. (1901). *Poverty: A Study of Town Life*. London: Macmillan.

Sabates, R. (2008). The Impact of Lifelong Learning on Poverty Reduction. IFLL Public Value Paper 1. Latimer Trend.

Salih, M. M. A. (2001). *African Democracies and African Politics*. New York: Pluto Press.

Summers, C. (2002). *Colonial Lessons: African's education in Southern Rhodesia, 1918-1940*. Cape Town: David Phillip Publishers.

Tyrell, P., & Jurgens, B. (1983). *African Heritage*. London: Macmillan Press.

UNESCO. (2015). *Poverty*. Retrieved October 13, 2016, from: http://www.unesco.org

UNICEF. (2016). *Child poverty and social protection*. Retrieved October 13, 2016, from: https://www.unicef.org/socialpolicy/index_childpoverty.html

WHO. (2015). *Global Health Observatory (GHO) data: Under-five mortality*. Retrieved October 13, 2016, from: http://www.who.int/gho/child_health/mortality/mortality_under_five_text/en/

Work in Freedom. (2016). *Child Labour in Africa*. Retrieved January 13, 2017, from: http://www.ilo.org/wcmsp5/groups/public/---ed_norm/---declaration/documents/publication/wcms_decl_fs_37_en.pdf

World Bank. (1998). *Status Report on Poverty. Gender, Growth and Poverty Reduction in Sub-Saharan Africa, discussion draft for SPA*. World Bank.

World Bank. (2014). *Sub-Saharan Africa: Poverty headcount ratio*. Washington, DC: World Bank.

Chapter 6
Social Norms or Child Labour?
The Case of the Maasai Community in Kenya

Josephine Munthali
Child Support Project, UK

ABSTRACT

This chapter discusses social norms which purportedly condone "unpaid child labour" as a way of bringing up children, especially girls, in preparation for early marriage in the Maasai community in Kenya. International organisations such as the International Labour Office (ILO) and United Nations Children's Fund (UNICEF) view "unpaid child labour" as detrimental to children's education and welfare. Yet, in the Maasai culture, it is viewed as a way mothers prepare girls to be responsible married women from an early age. Findings revealed that the young educated Maasai girls and boys who are "agents of change" are actively engaged in sensitising their communities and advocating for the rights of girls, and women. The Chapter recommends that the Government of Kenya, international NGOs and stakeholders work together with agents of change in their communities to create awareness concerning children's rights.

INTRODUCTION

This chapter focuses on the issue of unpaid child labour (traditional work) in which young children, especially girls, engage from a very young age. UNICEF (2016) suggests that children across the world are becoming agents of change and participating in rights campaigns. For instance, child labourers in Bangladesh have joined the Global March against child labour. Among the *Maasai,* the agents of change are committed and willing to do what is best for the *Maasai* children. Their life stories narrate their experiences of growing up in *Maasai* communities. Yet they overcame hardships and some actually fled their homes to rescue centres so as to pursue their education. Agents of change are therefore perceived as best suited to creating awareness on children's rights, which could change communities' attitudes towards young girls. UNESCO rightly asserts that children and young people need a political mechanism through which they can debate important issues such as child labour (UNESCO, 2016). Moreover, UNICEF supports communities in developing countries such as those in Africa in changing their cultural

DOI: 10.4018/978-1-5225-2578-3.ch006

acceptance of child labour, while supporting strategies and programmes to provide alternative income to families, access to nurseries, quality education, and protective services.

This chapter discusses social norms which traditionally require mothers to prepare girls for early marriages and to be responsible women from an early age. Children are not aware of their rights as they are meant to believe that the upbringing is culturally accepted and is a way of life for the *Maasai*. Most of these children engage in activities which are globally viewed as "unpaid child labour" as discussed broadly in this Chapter. Discourse shows that unpaid child labour activities which are mainly done at household level affect children's education, especially that of the girl child.

Social norms and activities which are culturally accepted continue to be in constant competition with Government policies. For instance, whilst the *Maasai* communities concentrate on "culture education", the Government of Kenya has enacted the Basic Education Act, 2013, which requires all school going children to be in school. Furthermore, the policy has put in place tough measures to deal with parents who engage children in activities which keep them out of school. This Chapter shows that agents of change view "unpaid child labour" as a factor affecting children's education and leads to early marriages. The question is: how can communities such as the *Maasai* change their predominant beliefs and practices and embrace children's rights as proposed internationally and adopted by the Government? It is noted that it is often difficult to change people's beliefs and their way of life. In fact, historically even the colonists and missionaries failed in changing communities' beliefs and practices (Munthali, 2001).

The objective of the Chapter is to impart knowledge and encourage debate on competing ideologies of predominant social norms versus global and national policies such as child labour; and the importance of engaging communities in participatory approaches to creating a platform for dialogue and consensus. The Chapter will contribute to deeper understanding of childhood conceptions and children's rights in the *Maasai* community. This should benefit students, professionals, and researchers working especially in education and child welfare.

BACKGROUND

As Edmonds (2007) states, any researcher who discuss child labour issues should start by defining the term "child labour". The definition needs to be unpacked as UNICEF and the International Labour Office (ILO) rightly point out that there is work that children do to help their families in ways that are neither harmful nor exploitative. This work usually entails helping parents around the home. It involves activities such as preparing tea, washing up dishes, house cleaning, washing clothes and shopping just to mention a few. However, defining whether an activity is harmful to a child's health and development is a challenge, because whether an activity is harmful depends on what the child would be doing in the absence of work (Edmonds, 2007). It is noted that these activities differ in western countries and vary in African countries. For instance, in addition to activities already mentioned, young children in Africa, especially in sub-Sahara countries and those living in rural areas, walk long distances to fetch water and firewood, wake up early in the morning to clean their homesteads, cook meals for families, look after siblings and engage in agricultural related activities. These activities are normally done by girls before and after the school day. Whilst in western countries the activities children engage in homes are just helping parents, in some communities in Africa it is part and parcel of "culture education" which prepares girls and boys for their future roles. Such activities are traditional demands and are acceptable by most communities in Africa. According to the ILO/IPU Handbook for Parliamentarians (2008), as quoted by

Ottolini (2012), popular perceptions, local customs and traditions play an important part in justifying child labour in the belief that work is good for the character-building and skill development of children.

Understanding Child Labour

Activities which are done at the household level are deemed by UNICEF and the ILO as "unpaid child labour". This is supported by Edmonds (2007) who found that a few researchers also define child labour by adding domestic work at household level in both rural and urban areas. Ololtuaa's (2012) study in Mbita district in Kenya revealed that children heard the phrase "child labour" and understood it to mean overworking them, and any type of work that denied them the opportunity to go to school and employed them under the age of 18 years. Furthermore, head-teachers explained that child labour means domestic chores for children at the expense of schooling. It is estimated by UNICEF and the ILO that 120 million children, some below the age of 14, and a further 30 million children in this age group who are mostly girls perform "unpaid household chores" within their own families. According to UNICEF there are estimated 15.5 million child domestic workers worldwide. The report of the UN Special Envoy for Global Education (Brown, 2011) notes that the number of child labourers in sub-Saharan Africa could rise by around 15 million over the next decade, reaching 65 million by 2020. Edmond's study on UNICEF's Multiple Indicator Cluster Surveys (MICS) Project from 2000-2001 in 34 countries found out that children work more hours per week in domestic work than market work. These children, who are mostly girls, are often hardly visible and face many hazards. The International Labour Organisation rightly argues that the term child labour fits well as it is defined as work that children should not do, because they are too young to work or the work is dangerous or unsuitable for children. Whether or not particular forms of "work" can be called "child labour" depends on the child's age, the type and hours of work performed and the conditions under which it is performed, as set out in the ILO Conventions.

Broader Experiences of Child Labour

Discussions on child labour issues in Kenya vary because of the diversity of the ethnic groups. Kenya is a multi-ethnic state in the Great Lakes region of East Africa. The country consists of eight Provinces. The two official languages are English and Swahili. Peri-urban and rural dwellers are less multilingual with many in rural areas speaking only their ethnic languages. At the beginning of 2016, the population of Kenya was 46,661,552. The number of young people under 15 years old was 19,693,508 (9,919,313 males and 9,774,195 females). It is estimated that approximately 2 million children are working in various sectors including domestic work and agricultural activities (Ololtuaa, 2012).

According to 2015 statistics, 25.6 percent of the population lived in urban areas and the rest in rural areas. Nilotes are the second largest group of peoples. These include the *Maasai* who are mostly herdsmen. The *Maasai* are a small community located in the Southern region of the Great Rift Valley (Rift Valley Province) in both Southern Kenya and North Central Tanzania. They are mainly found in Kajiado, Narok, and Transmara districts in the Western part of Kenya and Namanga (on the Tanzanian border). The population of the *Maasai* in Kenya varies from 350,000 to 453,000.

Maasai children live in very remote areas and yet they walk long distances to fetch firewood and water before and after school among other chores. According to Munthali, (2001), most girls in African countries such as Malawi wake up as early as 4 am in the morning to engage in household chores in order not to miss school. By the time they go to school they are tired and lack concentration in class

(Munthali, 2001). Moreover, such activities rob children of their childhood and can be physically harmful and affect mental development.

According to Dayıoğlu (2013), a few unpaid household services are treated within the United Nations System of National Accounts production boundary and are therefore considered economic work. Fetching water and collecting firewood for household use are therefore considered economic work since they fall under the production of goods. In addition, a study conducted by French (2010) found out that household chores appear to be more harmful to children than labour market jobs, through their impact on education, life satisfaction, and health. Furthermore, girls who bear the brunt of household chores and childcare, which continue even after they enter the workforce, appear to suffer more extensive, adverse consequences than boys. Many children are only being exploited and often being denied education and basic health care by their families and communities (UNICEF, 2016). It is vital to note that like other African countries especially in sub-Saharan Africa, the Government of Kenya introduced Free Primary Education in 2003 and Free Day Secondary Education in 2008 respectively with the intention of providing education to children, especially from poor rural households.

Several factors cause children to engage in paid and unpaid child labour. These include poverty, orphanage, HIV/AIDS, culture and tradition, decent work opportunities for adults and adolescents, migration, and emergencies. Discourse on child labour usually concentrates on other forms of child labour. Yet as UNICEF notes, children are hidden from sight and beyond the reach of the law. Girls' domestic work (both paid and unpaid) is the most invisible of all. Edmonds (2007) states that in countries such as Kenya, Tanzania, and Zambia private households are large employers of child domestic workers. Brown's (2011) report noted that in countries as diverse as Indonesia, Morocco, India and Nigeria, it is not uncommon for young girls to be working more than 12 hours a day for less than the minimum wage. Many of these girls are facing acute risks. One survey in Bangladesh found that almost 70 percent of girls involved in domestic service experienced physical abuse and systematic beatings. UNICEF's MICS Project in 34 countries found out that domestic work has a higher prevalence in rural areas than urban areas although the difference was small (68 percent in rural areas compared to 61 percent in urban). This is partly due to cultural perceptions of child labour among communities, particularly in rural areas.

Munthali (2001)'s study revealed that in many communities in Africa it is culturally accepted for girls to start engaging in activities mainly referred to as "traditional work" and household chores from the age as young as 4 years old as they learn from their mothers. Indigenous leaders who are custodians of culture condone such activities as its part of the package of bringing up children with the cultural values of their communities. Ottolini (2012) argues that while international policies offer the blanket generalisation of "commercial agriculture" as "hazardous child labour", the community looks at it as an ordinary activity which has been part of children's duties for a long time, as they are traditionally requested to work on the family farm. Malawi Chief Kaomba's (2013) paper which was presented at a conference on "the role of community leaders and impact of culture in eliminating child labour", argued that children need to learn skills that will assist them in the future. Furthermore, male children are supposed to learn skills that are considered appropriate for males while girls learn skills so that they can effectively manage their womanhood especially when they get married.

The International Labour Organisation and Indigenous Traditions

The International Labour Organisation noted that the indigenous leaders in the Philippines, Kenya and Guatemala make a clear distinction between traditional child work adapted to the age and the learning needs of the child, and exploitative forms of child labour. While traditional child work was seen as essential for the transmission of knowledge and skills and for ensuring the continuity of their distinct indigenous identity, exploitative child labour was perceived as a symptom of and an aggravating factor in the continuous marginalisation of indigenous communities. However, debates on whether traditional child work is classified, as actually being child labour, need to be unpacked. It is not surprising that during the ILO's consultations in Kenya, participants stressed that not all cultural practices are harmful but that there is a need to "unpack culture" and identify the negative practices and traditions that contribute to child labour. Okoy and Tanyi's (2009) study in Nigeria noted that many parents do not see traditional work as child labour especially mothers, who see this as a training ground for their daughters as future mothers.

Many indigenous peoples consider their children as invaluable wealth and at the same time treat them as the collective children of the clan and tribe, and not just as children of an individual family. In the Philippines, for instance, children are seen as the connecting thread to the future of the family as well as the clan. Therefore, it is a collective responsibility to protect, nurture and train the children in their traditional knowledge, culture, socio-economic systems and values and ensure the continuation of their distinct indigenous identity as ILO notes. International Labour Organization Article 8 of Convention No. 169 clearly states that collective rights to culture and custom should not infringe upon core human rights. Consequently, "culture" or "tradition", whether used by governments or communities, does not legitimise child labour, gender discrimination, unequal access to education services or any other violations of individual human rights. If some indigenous communities and parents defend traditional work as culturally appropriate and yet it affects children's right, for instance, in education, then it is important to confront such traditional activities and properly classify them as child labour.

As the ILO points out, becoming a good pastoralist like the *Maasai*, hunter-gatherer, and a well-balanced indigenous individual requires something different from, and complementary to, formal education. Light child work is often part of this. During the ILO consultations, people at the community level in Kenya were little aware of the problems related to child labour and some of the local organisations felt that they would be at loggerheads with their members if they raised the issue. As already mentioned this chapter provides some views of young people who were brought up in *Maasai* communities and adhered to cultural demands. They are now agents of change who are advocating and sensitising communities to change some practices which affect the welfare of children, particularly girls. The next section discusses the concept of child labour in Kenya.

DEBATES ON MAASAI'S "SOCIAL NORMS" OR "CHILD LABOUR"

The Concept of Child Labour in Kenya

According to Ottolini (2012), child labour is a recent concept in the East Africa region, mostly derived from the international legal framework on children rights, ratified and adopted by Kenya through local legislation. This was confirmed during ILO consultations undertaken in 2005 with indigenous representatives in the Philippines, Kenya, and Guatemala. The ILO noted that discussion about child labour among indigenous peoples is relatively new and in many indigenous communities, the concept is not yet well understood. Nevertheless, child labour has existed in Kenya since the pre-independence days, when children were sent by their parents to work in farms and homes of white settlers to earn money to pay taxes for their household (Ottolini, 2012). Muriithi (2010) notes that colonial policies such as land alienation, hut tax, and forced labour created an environment where children were forced into child labour. Furthermore, household chores, as well as herding or agriculture work, were also part of children duties and responsibility in line with the traditional understanding of child developmental stages (Ottolini, 2012).

To understand the issues of child labour in Kenya this chapter focused on collecting views of the young people who advocate for children's rights. This can be seen through essays written by the young Kenyan women and men who are referred to by their initials. For instance, KT's description of child labourers includes domestic workers who engage in work such as cooking, fetching firewood, cleaning, child minding and running errands. These domestic workers mostly travel to cities and they are paid minimal wages. This is supported by the ILO by suggesting that indigenous child labour still prevails in rural areas but is also on the increase in urban areas; children of female-headed households and orphans are the most vulnerable; Edmonds' study on UNICEF's MICS project revealed that countries with the highest prevalence of work outside the household also have the highest prevalence of work inside the household. For instance, Sierra Leone has the highest rate of work outside the household, and the second highest rate of work inside the household. Niger is second with 43 percent of children working outside the household, while it has the fifth highest rate of market work inside the household (Edmonds, 2007).

On the other hand, VM illustrates the situation of boys of tender age who wake up very early in the morning to work as "*shamba*" farm boys all day long without breakfast and food. After heavy work, they are forced to do more work late afternoon before they retire to bed. Other activities in which young children engage include loading and unloading goods from a vehicle, mowing or slashing grass on a compound, transferring goods from one place to another by means of pushing carts which are often heavily loaded, and travel far destinations. They also look after grazing cattle or any other kind of livestock, just to mention a few. Some young children work in construction sites carrying sand, water, bricks and digging foundations and in companies where they load or offload goods from vehicles. These children work hard but they are paid poorly.

Another essay by AM states that there are many forms of child labour. For instance, whereby parents force children to engage in work before going to school; another form by which parents command children to concentrate more on manual work than school work. He further mentions that child labour activities, including unpaid child labour, result from lack of parents caring for the rights of their children. Based on these essays one can see that young people presume "traditional work" and other forms of work in which children engage are "child labour". These examples of child labour activities are not unique to Kenya but take place in other developing countries especially in Africa and Asia. Edmonds (2007) outlines detailed analysis of child labour related activities in UNICEF's MICS project in 34 countries and Okoye & Tanyi (2009) study in Nigeria. Unpaid child labour activities which are hidden also dominate discussions and debates in research articles.

Perspectives From The Maasai Traditions

As already mentioned, in some African countries the *Maasai* communities bring up their children keeping in mind their future roles as wives and husbands. Girls who are often expected to marry into the family of their husband are trained in household chores in order to be good housewives (Smits and Jong, (2013); Munthali, (2001 and Ololtuaa (2012). According to one, Kenyan's essay notes; parents think that it is a way of bringing up children in order to become responsible adults. In this connection, Bingham (2012) states that the *Maasai* culture and tradition tend to keep particularly girls at home. Bingham further quotes Phillips and Bhavnagri (2002) who said that "girls are expected to help their mothers in drawing water, hewing and fetching firewood, and plastering houses" (p.7). Moreover, they are often caretakers for younger siblings and provide labour in the fields (Bingham, 2012). This is supported by Brown's (2011) report which notes that agriculture is by far the largest sector employing children, with unpaid family work dominating. For instance, In West Africa, an estimated two million children are involved in cultivating cocoa, while some 400,000 children are working on India's cotton seed farms.

Edmonds (2007) quotes Globalmarch, (2001) and Suda, (2001) by noting that exploitation of domestic child workers is also rampant in Kenya, though local research is unable to provide reliable data on its magnitude because it is largely invisible due to the privacy of the domestic sector, the ineffectiveness of legislation and law enforcement, cultural values and perceptions as well as lack of public awareness. In addition, children's work as domestic servants is not reported being generally regarded as a normal process of child upbringing and many families and employers expect children to work and contribute to their families' income. Accordingly, domestic work is among the least regulated of all occupations. Working in the privacy of individual homes, child, and adult domestic workers are often invisible to the outside world and thus particularly vulnerable to violence, exploitation, and abuse. Most domestic child workers live in with their employers and work full time under difficult and deprived circumstances lacking adequate care and protection and being vulnerable to physical and emotional violence, economic exploitation and sexual and verbal abuse.

Brown's (2011) report suggested that some 60 million children are involved, the majority being in sub-Saharan Africa. Moreover, young girls who should be in school are collecting water and firewood or caring for siblings. Discourse on the relation between child labour and education suggests that all forms of child labour whether paid or unpaid, interfere with children's participation in education. Ololtuaa's (2012) study in Mbita District in Kenya found that girls were quite often involved in domestic chores that eventually affected school attendance. Despite education being free in most developing countries including Kenya child labour either denies children's access to or hinders their effective participation in education by causing drop-out and absenteeism.

Bingham's study which concentrated on the *Maasai* girl-child revealed that *Maasai* men look at girls as a way out of poverty. By selling them through forced early marriages, they can acquire cows, educate their boys, and get food. These assumptions appear to be in line with Ololtuaa, (2012); Munthali, (2001) and Smit's, (2013) studies which found that parents may find investing in educating their daughters not worthwhile as there are no direct returns for the family. Therefore, an important part of the child's economic contribution to the family might be through not attending school if direct and indirect schooling costs are high (Edmonds, 2007).

There are many factors which cause children to work or engage in unpaid child labour. Researchers suggest that poverty is the main contributory factor (Brown, 2011); (Edmonds, 2007); (Munthali, 2001); (Ololtuaa, 2012) and (Muriithi, 2010). Many countries in Africa including Kenya as already discussed have introduced free primary education. However, there are direct and indirect costs which parents, especially in rural areas, cannot afford. Edmonds (2007) rightly argues that "an important part of the child's economic contribution to the family might be through not attending school if direct and indirect schooling costs are high". Studies reveal that working children economically contribute to poor families. Edmonds quotes Psacharopoulos' (1997) observations that Bolivian children aged 13 amount to 13 percent of total household income on average. Moreover, Menon et al (2005) estimated that children contribute roughly 11 percent of the value of total agriculture production in Nepal.

UNICEF MICS countries (Ethiopia and Nepal) reveal that child labour is prevalent in poor economies. On the other hand, it is interesting to note Edmonds study on UNICEF MICS countries which reveal that researchers that compare poor households to rich households find mixed evidence of a link between poverty and child labour. This was evident in Zimbabwe, Ghana, Nepal, Peru and Bolivia. Edmonds (2007) cited how "comparative studies which implemented the same empirical approach in multiple countries by researchers illustrated how varied the cross-sectional relationships between economic status and child labour can be such as Bhalotra and Heady (Pakistan and Ghana, 2003), Ersado (Nepal, Peru, and Zimbabwe, 2005), Maitra and Ray (Peru, Pakistan, and Ghana, 2002), Psacharopoulos (Bolivia and Venezuela, 1997), and Ray (Pakistan and Peru, 2000) illustrate how varied the cross-sectional relationship between economic status and child labour can be. Edmonds rightly suggests that the problem is that poor households differ from rich in many ways when conducting studies of the link between economic status and child labour. For instance, Munthali's (2001) findings revealed that children in Malawi work in fields during the rainy season and children stop after the harvest. As a result, attendance trends differ in schools for children from poor households.

Edmonds (2007) quoted Beegle et al (2006) which tracked children in Tanzania over a three-year period and revealed the same trend. As Brown (2011) notes while household poverty is the primary driver of child labour, other forces are also at play. The ILO estimates that around 5.7 million children are forced into employment through bonded labour and some 1.2 million children are trafficked each year for forced labour. Children in conflict-affected countries face many challenges. Many are forced into child labour by poverty and the absence of educational opportunities. Others are forcibly recruited into armed militia or workforces used to exploit natural resources.

As already discussed in this chapter other factors are related to cultural beliefs and social norms. There are also myths in certain ethnic groups in Africa including Kenya about educated women. Webbink et al. (2013) quote Bequele and Boyden (1988) who states that the established female role in certain countries dictates that women will not fit into traditional roles if they become educated. Moreover, belief in some nations that educated females will not get married or have children. Therefore, many families raise daughters solely to take over the household duties in order release the mother for paid labour. Such cultural practices restrict the education of females and promote child employment (Webbink et al., 2013). A young Kenyan man who wrote an essay on child labour in Kenya argued that lack of knowledge also contributes to child labour in communities such as the *Maasai* who do not value education. They believe that to educate a child, especially a girl child is a waste of time. Nevertheless, Kenya like other countries has enacted policies to promote children's rights.

The Labour Law

The law under the Employment Act, 2007, and the Children Act, defines a child in Kenya as a person below the age of 18 years. The Employment Act, Part VII provides for protection of children including protection from the worst forms of child labour. Section 56 prohibits employing a child below 13 years in any form of work. It is vital to note that the *Maasai* young girls engage in household chores at the very early age of 3 to 5 as already discussed. The Act allows employment of children from the ages of 13 to16 years for light work and defines those of 16 to 18 as employable. Again *Maasai* young girls engage in activities which may not be classified as light, for instance, walking long distances to fetch water and firewood before and after school. In this connection, it appears the *Maasai* communities are not aware of this policy or simply ignore it. Nevertheless, the Act does not clearly define the parameters of this employment. It does not define light work and does not provide protection for children in such employment, but leaves it to the discretion of the minister.

It is noted that despite policies and laws on child labour issues, unpaid child labour which has consequences on children has not been documented and featured in the Act. Yet the study shows that indeed unpaid child labour which is condoned by many communities especially the *Maasai* affects education and leads to early marriages. The Children Act, No. 8 of 2001, Section 10, provides that every child shall be protected from economic exploitation, any work that interferes with his/her education, or is harmful to the child's health or physical, mental, spiritual, moral or social development and recruitment to militia in armed conflicts, and where armed conflict occurs.

Article 30 (1), of the Kenya Constitution (2010) prohibits slavery and servitude. In addition, it states that a person shall not be required to perform forced labour (2). The Constitution clearly outlines basic education to be free and compulsory and children to protected from abuse, neglect, harmful cultural practices and hazardous or exploitative labour (Article 53 1 (b) & 1 (d) and forced labour (Article 30 & 2). Article 21 (c) states that the state and all public officers have a duty to address the needs of vulnerable groups within society including children and youth, and members of particular ethnic or cultural communities. Having examined child labour issues in Kenya, the next section explores the question of whether the social norms of engaging the *Maasai* young children in traditional work should be classified as "unpaid child labour".

METHODOLOGY

The study explored the question of whether the *Maasai*'s perceived "social norms" which prepares children, especially the girl-child, for early marriage be classified as "unpaid child labour". To answer such a question, it was imperative to interview and collect life stories and essays of young women and men who have become agents of change in addressing social norms which continue to affect children's education and welfare. The young people were brought up in *Maasai* communities in Kajiado, Southern Region of Kenya.

Qualitative methodology was used in this study to secure life stories and opinions of the agents of change. Empirical tools included semi-structured questionnaires, focus group discussions and interviews with the key informants. Semi-structured questionnaires were circulated to respondents and focus groups discussions took place in a community hall in Kajiado. English was used in questionnaires and in focus groups discussions. It is observed and interacted with the *Maasai* communities at a *Maasai* homestead to learn more of the *Maasai* way of life and with teachers at a school and rescue centre. The *Maasai* language "*Maa*" was used in interactions at the homestead with help from change agents as interpreters. It was observed that women, in particular, were very frightened to engage in interactions as they feared their husbands would beat them up. Therefore, the interactions were very limited. However, a young married *Maasai* girl provided crucial information.

Interviews were conducted on a cross-section of the *Maasai* people (mostly working class) who gave first-hand information about the *Maasai's* cultural practices and norms which affect boys and in particular girls. The major contributors for this Chapter were 25 (14 females and 11 males) young people who provided crucial information on their experiences of growing up in a *Maasai* environment and engagement in traditional work. Five *Maasai* female teachers at a secondary school and rescue centres narrated challenges women face and the upbringing of girls. Professional *Maasai* women and men provided more insights on the life of the *Maasai* and gave feedback to the findings.

FINDINGS

The findings provide an overview of and insight into the upbringing of the *Maasai* children, paying attention to girls' activities. This section concentrates on the life stories and experiences of the agents of change. Discussions include how the activities robbed their childhood and to some extent their education. To understand the issue of unpaid child labour for *Maasai* children it is vital to understand how they are perceived culturally. As Bingham (2011) points out:

The Maasai are a tight-knit community. They see themselves as collectivists rather than individualists. They are defined by their family, community, and property. Those who have grown up in the same village, surrounded by the same family and friends show the least amount of self-awareness. Their goal is to live in harmony with others while practising the same cultural and social lifestyle that their ancestors have for hundreds of years (Bingham, 2011).

For years the *Maasai* communities have viewed boys and girls differently regarding their roles and responsibilities. Ottolini's (2012) analysis on how children and communities look at child labour in Nyanza in Kenya revealed dominant cultural perspectives on children's roles and responsibilities which are in disagreement with local and international legislation. Ottolini's findings indicate that child labour is part of the family existing conditions rather than an external issue out of their reach. Therefore, child labour issues for girls and boys come in different forms. The ILO argues that child labour affects boys and girls differently because of widespread gender discrimination including indigenous cultural practices. Girls in the rural areas are less likely to go to school and many migrate instead to urban areas to work as domestic servants. It is important to note that in developing countries girls start engaging in domestic work in households while very young before some girls eventually move to urban areas. On the other hand, boys have higher participation rates in market work than girls and lower participation rates in domestic work. For example, UNICEF's MICS Project in 34 countries found that girls are 18 percent more likely to be involved in domestic work and nearly 30 percent less likely to participate in paid market work (Edmonds 2007).

According to these narrative experiences, boys and girls are treated the same before the age of six years old. During this period, children are taught to respect elders and ancestors, always listen to them and respect their parents' decisions without questioning. This is supported by Bingham who notes that the *Maasai* communities dictate who their children are and what they can become (Bingham (2011). At this point in life parents and elders have total control of their lives. *Maasai* leaders who are custodians of culture ensure that cultural beliefs are observed and respected. This is typical of African countries where children cannot argue or question parents on practices which are detrimental to their welfare. Moreover, at a young age, they are not aware of their rights. This is exactly the mandate of agents of change who sensitise young people and communities about children's rights. As Ottolini (2012) rightly argues, the findings of the study in Nyanza in Kenya raise a concern on child rights awareness among working children and within communities starting with the right to education and health. This was due to the fact that some child respondents confirmed their willingness to be allowed to work in particular house chores and domestic labour. Meanwhile, while 40 percent of children indicated the preferred starting age for work to be 10-14 age bracket, 56.1 percent of community leaders gave a broader indication of (5-15 years).

All respondents (100% of agents of change) agreed that fathers view girls as property to be given for marriage whilst boys are prepared to inherit property and land. Therefore, roles for girls dramatically change to prepare them for early marriages. These assumptions are perceived in other African countries as noted by Okoye & Tanyi (2009) and Bingham (2011). During discussions and observations at a homestead, it is evident that girls concentrate their activities on domestic work, agriculture and helping mothers during construction of the *Maasai* home while boys concentrate mostly in agriculture and the land. Seven male respondents documented their experiences and here is an expert of one of the agents of change:

I am a Maasai man and first born in the family of 4. I was born and brought up in the Maasai culture in the heart of the Maasai land. As a Maasai boy, I grew up in the deep culture of the Maasai community. At the age of 5 years, I looked after calves and lambs around the compound until the age of 8 years when I joined a pre-school in my locality which was almost 10kms from home. During weekends and holidays, I helped my parents to look after goats and cattle (A male agent of change).

As we drove to the *Maasa*i land, young boys who were expected to be in school looked after cattle. Moreover, discussions with the 3 *Maasai* women teachers at the rescue centre revealed that girls continue to engage in household activities at home; walking long distances to fetch water among other chores including construction of the *Maasai* houses. This was confirmed by a young married woman who narrated that:

Women and girls construct houses as it is said that all work involving the home is to be done by women and men are to go look for food and do other things outside the home. Men, therefore, do not do anything in the home: they say their work is outside the home. Men have no idea how the houses are constructed. I went to train the custodians of culture in one of the Maasai areas and they told me they have no idea how the houses are constructed as it is not their responsibility (Maasai Woman).

Ottolini's study suggested that in Kenya like other African countries child labour may be so deeply ingrained in local customs and habits that neither the parents nor the children themselves realise that it is against their interests and illegal. Besides, education is often not perceived by children or their parents to be a viable alternative to working (Ottolini, 2012).

As already mentioned, we were particularly interested to hear life stories of "agents of change", particularly 14 young women who narrated their upbringing and childhood years. The experiences of the activities they engaged while young were similar. One young woman remembered childhood years as being very tough for young girls in the *Maasai* community. Young children woke up early in the morning and walked for seven kilometres to fetch clean water from a water point near Kilimanjaro Mountain. This was normal for many *Maasai* young girls, she narrated. Below is an excerpt from her life story:

Ottolini's study in Nyanza in Kenya found similar results of girls engaging in traditional work at five years old. Working children at this age can have negative effects on education as they usually work before and after school with no time for parental guidance. The same trends in female respondents' questionnaires were noted. Young girls' tasks increase as they grow older and progress towards puberty and early marriages. Such activities and lifestyle force children to miss schooling and poor attendance and may end by them dropping out of school altogether. Okoye & Tanyi (2009) suggests that there have been various proposals by scholars as to what constitute a critical threshold for the child. Examples are cited of Syed, Mirza, Sultana and Ram (1991) and Krone (2005) who consider 20 weekly hours of work as a critical threshold beyond which the child's education starts being significantly affected. From discussions and feedback from respondents, it was clear that the *Maasai* girls engage in unpaid labour for more than 20 hours a week including walking long distances to fetch water. Moreover, the activities increase further when they marry at an early age. Bingham's (2011) study on the *Maasai* girl child found out that oppressive cultural traditions are still practised in their tribe. Girls as young as 12 years of age are expected to get married soon after their initiation ceremonies.

The study revealed that it is common for a teenage *Maasai* girl to become the second or third wife of an older man who is over 60 years of age. Bingham's study noted similar findings. Many girls who are forced to marry older men with many wives become breadwinners and have to find the means of fending for their families. Okoye & Tanyi (2009) cite the following researchers (Zapata, 2006; Pacis, 2003); Canagarajah and Coulombe, (1997) whose study revealed that scholars regard child domestic service as one of the occupations that can cause serious psychological and social adjustment problems. Children in this occupation are especially vulnerable to particular types of abuse. For example, they are victims of verbal and sexual abuse, beatings or punishment by starvation. According to the Government of Kenya Employment Act, some young girls are still at the age which prohibits from carrying out activities not classified as "light"."

The *Maasai* Girls' Education Fund notes that early marriage is the most often cited reason that *Maasai* girls drop out of school. Marriages take place after circumcision, where usually girls between the ages of 11-13, are taught a rite of passage into womanhood that accompanies puberty and early marriages. Bingham quotes Ma and Schoeneman's findings which state that the *Maasai* women stay closer to home and have fewer opportunities to attend school (Bingham, 2011). Responses from respondents confirm these views when asked about communities' attitudes towards girls' education.

Ottolini (2012) rightly argues that for many families, even if schooling is "free", it is perceived as a cost for the foregone income of a school going child. Besides, the education provided is frequently of poor quality, and/or perceived by parents and children as irrelevant to local needs and conditions. Poor quality of education systems, particularly in countries in Africa, has been reported by Education for All Global Monitoring report (2013/14) as affecting the achievement of Education for All. A young man who wrote an essay on child labour in Kenya mentioned that in most communities' children have been denied their rights to education. Some parents don't consider education as something important. As Ololtuaa (2012) notes, children provide a substantial amount of labour that is used at the household level; these activities often take precedence over school because parents perceive the chores to be more important than schooling. Despite the provision of free primary education in developing countries, ILO mentions that "Education for all" cannot be achieved while child labour exists. Education for All 2015 National Review of Kenya indicates some of the factors which have hindered the attainment of the targets. These include negative cultural practices that affect girls, in particular, such as early marriage and child labour.

During discussions, all agents of change were adamant about the need to change attitudes or beliefs which continue to affect children including child labour whether paid or unpaid. Bhargava (2009) noted that many parents do not see this as child labour especially mothers who see this as a training ground for their daughters as future mothers. On the other hand, findings in Nigeria by Okoye & Tanyi (2009) revealed that educated mothers viewed household chores as child labour. Therefore, education is a key to changing social norms which affect children's welfare. Ottolini (2012) points out that, since families are a major player in child labour exploitation and child labour is part of local communities' existing conditions, its elimination needs an integrated approach to influence community changes in values and attitudes by addressing the cultural understanding of children's rights, roles, and responsibilities.

During focus group discussions with agents of change it was evident that the challenge remains on changing attitudes of communities such as the *Maasai* which are deeply rooted in their beliefs. The young *Maasai* people who have become agents of change are creating awareness to change attitudes affecting particularly young girls and women. Will agents of change identify challenges affecting the welfare of children and young people in their communities and come up with solutions to their problems? Apparently, the agents of change believe their approach is best and will be sustainable.

SOLUTIONS AND RECOMMENDATIONS

This study has shown that what the *Maasai* communities perceive as "social norms" of preparing children, especially girls, for their future roles is actually deemed as "unpaid child labour" which steals children's childhood and their education (among other factors). The *Maasai* Education Fund reports that more than 70% and 90% of *Maasai* men and women, respectively, will never receive any formal education. They will never learn to read or write or speak a language other than their native "*Maa*". In addition, eight out of 10, *Maasai* children will not complete primary education. During research, it was evident that the question of how challenges affecting children can be addressed depends on the *Maasai* themselves. First of all, it is very difficult to change people's endowed beliefs and attitudes which have been practised for a long time. Secondly, social norms are difficult to break because they form a strong identity to communities who believe in them.

As already mentioned, the dynamic *Maasai* young people who have become agents of change in their own communities participated in this study. Their mandate is to create awareness and change attitudes towards issues which affect children including traditional work which basically is unpaid child labour. Parents, especially fathers, have been targeted because they are the decision makers of the family. The group believes that communities need empowerment through education to realise that some of the traditions should be abolished. Communities listen because they are role models but on another hand, the group admits that changing communities' attitudes is difficult as a result of predominant cultural practices.

There is a need for more research and government engagement with other agencies and stakeholders in addressing social norms such as unpaid child labour which are detrimental to children's rights and welfare. The ILO rightly argues that raising awareness about child labour and its factors as well as a firm commitment to support communities in identifying the problems and appropriate steps from their perspective can generate both community support and relevant responses. It is, therefore, critical to analyse the causes and drivers of child labour whether paid or unpaid and perspectives firmly situate the analysis of causes and drivers of child labour and to unpack key issues emerging from the indigenous peoples. Solving the child labour challenge involves understanding it as a symptom reflecting wider collective problems and working with communities to identify collective solutions. Agents of change should, therefore, use participatory approaches in engaging the *Maasai* communities in identifying their problems and coming up with the solutions to problems.

Participatory approaches work very well as all stakeholders including women and men, boys and girls and custodians of culture are encouraged to participate in discussions through a facilitator. It is vital that discussions should not be dominated by any individual or group, or by a single point of view. Unless the *Maasai* themselves identify problems it will be difficult for anybody to convince them to change behaviours which they have adopted from their ancestors. Therefore, the agents of change are best positioned to facilitate such discussions with support from the government and other players.

FUTURE RESEARCH DIRECTIONS

The International Labour Office notes that child labour among indigenous peoples has until recently received little attention from governments and international institutions as well as from indigenous peoples themselves. It remains an invisible issue and there exist no comprehensive data on the magnitude of the problem or on the conditions and types of work in which indigenous children are engaged. There is a need for research to be centred on exploring Government policies on children's rights and unpaid child labour activities as discussed in this chapter. In addition, future research should follow up agents of change to assess if communities' attitudes are changing towards social norms which affect children's welfare. Research should also involve all stakeholders, especially at the local level to address social norms among the *Maasai* and develop strategies in achieving long-term solutions. The Government, non-governmental agencies, and other stakeholders must work together in supporting agents of change.

CONCLUSION

This Chapter has explored the question of whether the social norms which the *Maasai* communities condone of engaging girl children in traditional work, can be classified as unpaid child labour activities. Researchers on child labour reveal that poverty is a major contributory factor. However, this study concentrated on an aspect of traditional practice which condones child labour activities. Based on discussions in this chapter, traditional work is perceived as child labour since it has far-reaching consequences on young children. The Chapter has explored definitions of child labour and unpaid child labour. Furthermore, it has discussed child labour issues (paid and unpaid) at the global level, national and local level in Kenya. It is seen that actually girls who engage in unpaid child labour are invisible and it is this group which engages much in activities which affect their childhood development, welfare, and education. Discussions reveal that the Government of Kenya has enacted policies on child labour. Yet children start engaging in traditional work from the age three to five in *Maasai* communities. Moreover, girls as young as 10 to 13 years are forced into an early marriage which further puts them into risks of continuing engaging in paid and unpaid child labour work. Therefore, it is vital to review Government's policies to identify loopholes.

The study has revealed that it is difficult to change communities' attitudes which have been passed on for generations. However, there is hope since the *Maasai* agents of change believe that they can help change communities' attitudes. It remains to be seen if their approach produces result since the *Maasai* communities perceive these change agents as role models. Discourse in this study has revealed that participatory approaches can be employed by the agents of change. Moreover, as Chief Kaomba (2013) of Malawi rightly suggests: "the fight against child labour requires combined effort of all local leaders and other stakeholders which include religious leaders, political leaders, community-based organizations, area development committees, village development committees, chiefs, child labour committees, parents, teachers, school committees and other stakeholders". Further work with communities is needed to unpack the root causes of child labour and to come up with solutions in achieving long term results.

This study has contributed to the knowledge about how predominant social norms can overlook children's rights, beliefs, and practices. It gives ground for more research to be conducted on this subject to contribute to the knowledge of how to promote children's rights amid social norms which are always competing especially with Government's policies. A young Kenyan man who contributed to the essays on child labour, mentions that another way of eradicating child labour is by forming a forum which will protect and safeguard the rights of children. It is therefore vital to initiate debates on "unpaid child labour" and involve the *Maasai* young people, women, leaders and custodians of culture as part of participatory approaches to achieving the intended goals of social justice. Such dialogue must be based on the recognition of the individual as well as collective rights of the indigenous Maasai children.

REFERENCES

Bhargava, D. (2009). *Child labour-a hindrance in development.* Retrieved 8 November 2016 from http://www.countercurrents.org/bhargava090709.htm

Bingham, K. S. (2011). *Helpleness to Hope: Cultural Transformations for the Maasai Girl-Child* (Unpublished doctoral dissertation). Liberty University. Retrieved 21 May 2016 from http://digitalcommons.liberty.edu/cgi/viewcontent.cgi?article=1490&context=doctoral

Brown, G. (2012). *Child Labour & Educational Disadvantage – Breaking the Link, Building Opportunity. A Review by Gordon Brown.* London: The Office of the UN Special Envoy for Global Education.

Dayıoğlu, M. (2013). *Impact of unpaid household services on the measurement of child labour. MICS Methodological papers. Paper No. 2, Statistics and Monitoring Section, Division of Policy and Strategy.* Ankara, Turkey: Department of Economics, Middle East Technical University.

Edmonds Eric, V. (2007). *Child Labour.* NBER Working Paper Series. Working Paper 12926. National Bureau of Economic Research. Retrieved 8 November 2016 from http://www.nber.org/papers/w12926

French, L. (2010), Pamplin. Research. Child Labour. More complex than you think. *College of Business Magazine.* Retrieved 20 June 2016 from http://www.magazine.pamplin.vt.edu/spring10/childlabor.html

Global Education Partnership. Kenya. (n.d.). *Essays on child labour in Kenya written by young people.* Retrieved 21 May 2016 from http://www.iearn.org.au/clp/archive/write30.htm

International Labour Organisation. (n.d.a). *What is Child Labour?* Retrieved 6 April 2016 from http://www.ilo.org/ipec/facts/lang--en/index.htm

International Labour Organisation. (n.d.b). *Child Labour and Education for All.* Retrieved 21 May 2016 from http://www.ilo.org/ipec/Action/Education/ChildlabourandEducationforAll/lang--en/index.html

Kaomba. (2013). *Role of Community Leaders and Impact of Culture in Eliminating Child Labour.* Retrieved 19 October 2016 http://www.eclt.org/wp-content/uploads/2013/07/Role_of_Community_Leaders_and_Impact_of_Culture_in_Eliminating_Child_Labour.pdf

Maasai Girls Education Fund. (n.d.). *The Life of the Maasai Woman.* Retrieved on 9 August 2016 from http://Maasaigirlseducation.org/the-need/the-life-of-a-Maasai-woman

Munthali, J. (2001). *Education for All. Problems and Possibilities of Girls' schooling in Malawi* (Unpublished PhD Thesis). Edinburgh University

Muriithi, A. G. (2010). Education for All and Child Labour in Kenya: A conflict of capabilities?. *Procedia: Social and Behavioral Sciences, 2*(2), 4613–4621. doi:10.1016/j.sbspro.2010.03.739

Okoye, U. O., & Tanyi, P. L. (n.d.). Perception of Child Labour in South Eastern Nigeria: A Study of Onitsha Metropolis. *International Journal of Research in Arts and Social Sciences, 1*, 425-440. Retrieved 25 October 2016 from http://academicexcellencesociety.com/perception_of_child_labour_in_south_eastern_nigeria.pdf

Ololtuaa Lekakeny John. (2012). *Effect of Child Labour on Access and Retention of Primary School Pupils in Mbita District, Homa Bay County*. Kenyatta University.

Ottolini, D. (2012). *Unearthing the Invisible. Worst forms of Child Labour in Nairobi and Nyanza Provinces. A Baseline Survey Analytical Report.* Nairobi, Kenya: CESVI.

Republic of Kenya. (2001). *Kenya: Children's Act 8 of 2001.* Retrieved 21 May 2016 from http://www.chr.up.ac.za/undp/domestic/docs/legislation_03.pdf

Republic of Kenya. (2007). *Kenya Employment Act, 2007.* Retrieved on 4th August 2016 from http://www.lawnotes.in/Kenya_Employment_Act,_2007

Republic of Kenya. (2010). *Laws of Kenya. The Constitution of Kenya.* National Council for Law Reporting.

Republic of Kenya. (2014). *Education for All. The 2015 National Review.* Ministry of Education, Science and Technology.

Siddiqi, F., & Patrinos, H. A. (1995). *Child Labour: Issues, Causes and Interventions.* World Bank.

UNESCO. (2013/14). *Education for All: Global monitoring report.* UNESCO.

UNICEF. (2016). *The State of the World's Children 2016.* Retrieved April 6, 2016, from http://www.unicef.org/protection/57929_child_labour.html

UNICEF. (n.d.). *Basic education and gender equality. Child Labour and Exploitation.* Retrieved 21 May 2016 from http://www.unicef.org/education/index_focus_exploitation.html

United Nations. (n.d.). *Child labour. Overview. What is Child Labour?* Retrieved April 6, 2016, from http://www.un.org/en/globalissues/briefingpapers/childlabour/

United Nations Resources for Speakers on Global Issues. (n.d.). *Child Labour. International Conventions of Child Labour.* Retrieved 21 May 2016 from http://www.un.org/en/globalissues/briefingpapers/childlabour/intlconvs.shtml

Webbink, E., Smits, J. & de Jong, E. (2013). Social Indicators Research. *International and Interdisciplinary Journal for Quality-of-Life Measurement, 110*(2), 819-836. doi:10.1007/s11205-011-9960-0

KEY TERMS AND DEFINITIONS

Agents of Change: Young men and women speaking on behalf of children on issues which affect their wellbeing and education in their own communities.

Child Labour: Work in which children under the age of 18 engage with minimal wages, depriving them of their childhood and interfering with their education.

Children's Rights: Human rights for children, for instance, the right to education and protection from all forms of child abuse.

Culture Education: Informal education which is imparted by any ethnic group to children based on cultural practices and beliefs.

Cultural Practices: Norms in behaviours in ethnic groups and communities. These norms are passed through generations.

Early Marriages: Marriages from the age of 10 to 18.

Girlchild: A girl aged below the age of 14.

Unpaid Child Labour: Work carried out by young children aged from 5 – 14 years of age mainly at a household level without pay.

Section 3

Children's Rights and Vulnerabilities in the Digital Age

Chapter 7
Deconstructing the Social Network:
Balancing Young People's Rights and Vulnerabilities Within the Online Omopticon

Pam Jarvis
Leeds Trinity University, UK

ABSTRACT

This chapter outlines the results of an original pilot which investigated young British people's usage and opinions of social networking. The underpinning literature outlines psychological and neurological evidence that suggests young people's personalities are both fledgling and fragile, and that consequently, the online environment may be an inappropriate environment in which to engage in social processes that input to identity development due to the persistence, visibility, and spreadability of information that users commit to their profiles. The data gathered largely supported this thesis and additionally indicated that there may be a gender difference in orientation to online activity in early adolescence.

INTRODUCTION

Over the past decade, children's lives in rich western nations have changed in many ways. This chapter will focus on one of the most profound changes, the advent of social networking- websites designed to facilitate ongoing online 'conversations'- and consequent impacts upon the socialisation of young people between twelve and eighteen. The issues that arise from social networking for children and for adults are inevitably similar, but it is proposed that the effects upon children are more profound, due to developmental vulnerability. It should be noted that the First iPhone was released in 2006, the same year as Facebook became generally available to anyone over thirteen. It took some time for both of these innovations to become 'mainstream' in the western cultural milieu, hence those who fully inhabited a

DOI: 10.4018/978-1-5225-2578-3.ch007

socially-networked culture during adolescence are now only just moving into adulthood; as such the effects of a socially networked adolescence will not be fully revealed for some years to come.

The United Nations are already discussing 'the right of all individuals to seek, receive and impart information and ideas of all kinds through the Internet' (United Nations 2011: online) and have come to the tentative conclusion that complete restriction would be a transgression against article 19 of the International Covenant on Civil and Political Rights (1976), the right to freedom of expression. With respect to the UK, Wagner (2012: online) comments 'the current position of UK courts rightly makes it very difficult indeed for the state to ban completely a citizen's use of the internet, however, strong the justification'. Where this level of conversation currently exists relating to adult rights to engage in the online environment, it is likely that related debates about children and young people, focusing on their similarities and differences to adults will inevitably follow, although what the schedule and content of such a debate might be is as yet uncertain. For example, while tobacco smoking gradually became widespread in the UK between the 17th and 18th century, legislation banning its use by children and young people due to its harmful and addictive properties was not enacted until 1908 (ASH 2016: online).

Additionally, there is no general agreement as yet that social networking *is* harmful or addictive.

Whether social networking addiction exists is debatable depending upon the definition of addiction used, but there is clearly emerging evidence that a minority of social network users experience addiction-like symptoms as a consequence of their excessive use. Griffiths (2013, online)

What is clear is that social networking was designed to be used by adults, but has been taken up enthusiastically by young people whose social development processes are still ongoing. As such, the likelihood is that social networking activities are 'reshaping youthful practices of communication, identity and relationship management' (Livingston et al 2013:303).

Attitudes towards social networking vary between researchers of the phenomenon, particularly those who focus on young people. Turkel (2011:295) views the issues raised by networked lives as inevitably problematic: 'we have invented inspiring and enhancing technologies, and yet we have allowed them to diminish us'. Boyd (2014:11) takes a more neutral position, that social networking offers 'new opportunities and challenges' which are not inherently problematic, while Harris (2014:214) takes a more philosophical approach: 'the revolution is complete and the next one is coming. The question is: how do we make human these new worlds?'

This chapter will consider a research project in which young people discussed their engagement with social networking, and their reflections upon the part that it plays in their day-to-day lives.

BACKGROUND

As reflected in the phenomenon in which research is in its very early stages, researchers' orientations vary. Boyd (2014) takes the position that on the whole, social networking creates new opportunities for young people alongside some underlying challenges. She proposes that young people's enthusiastic uptake of social media has been generated by a society in which they have constricted opportunities to connect with each other in the physical world, due to heightened parental concern relating to environmental danger and consequent adult direction of children and young people's leisure time, leaving little time for reflection, socialisation and relaxation. She reports that many of her research participants commented that their parents organised the vast majority of their leisure time and that consequently, 'social media has become a place... to connect, gossip and hang out' (Boyd 2014:91). Wider issues relating to adult "colonisation" of children's lives is discussed at length in Jarvis et al (2014). However, while teenagers may see online socialisation as a means of escape, paradoxically, the online environment actually extends the potential for surveillance: 'being in a networked public- unlike gathering with friends in a public park- often makes interactions more visible' (Boyd 2014:57).

Therefore, one of the key points to consider in respect of teenage socialisation moving so rapidly online is the nature of the metaphorical glass box in which they find themselves. Harris (2014:14) reflects 'as we embrace technology's gifts, we usually fail to consider what they ask from us in return', and what is demanded in this situation is the exposure of highly personal information within a public environment. Schurgin O'Keeffe et al (2011:802) comment 'one of the biggest threats to young people on social media sites is their digital footprint and future reputations', reflecting on troubling statistics that indicate 20% of young people have posted nude or semi-nude photographs of themselves on the internet. Five years later, this problem seems to have grown to even more worrying proportions. The British teachers' union, the National Association of Schoolmasters Union of Women Teachers (NASUWT) recently undertook a survey which found that 50% of teachers responding were aware of at least one case of peer 'sexting' amongst their pupils, including cases involving children as young as 7 and 11 (NASUWT 2016). Children and young people are nowadays routinely warned by parents and teachers to carefully consider the very public arena of the internet before posting material, so why would they act in such a fashion? To effectively consider this question, we need to deconstruct the biopsychological nature of the adolescent brain.

Recent advances in biopsychology have clearly indicated that neuronally, human beings remain in their developmental period until their mid-20s, with a great deal of neuronal development occurring during the early adolescent period. This involves a burst of pruning and connection amongst neurones in the pre-frontal context, in areas that mediate inhibition, planning, and attention, all of which are socio-cognitive skills that underpin the sophisticated ways in which adults interact with other people. The ways in which neuronal connections are made during this process are heavily dependent upon experiences encountered, a routine process within the development of primates, human beings in particular, which has been termed 'Nature via Nurture' (Ridley 2003).

Neuroimaging and behavioural studies in humans, and neuroanatomical and behavioural studies in animals have demonstrated that the social brain and social cognition undergo a profound period of development in adolescence... the social environment during adolescence has a profound impact on life course trajectories. (Blakemore and Mills 2014:201)

Vulnerability and Risk

Blakemore and Mills (2014) suggest that adolescents are, in this respect, highly socially vulnerable, in some ways more so than they were during earlier stages of development, citing empirical evidence that suggests when adolescents find themselves in socially complex situations, they are more likely to make risky decisions than younger children. These researchers conclude 'what is sometimes seen as the problem with adolescents- risk taking, poor impulse control, self-consciousness... is actually reflective of brain changes that provide an excellent opportunity for education and social development' (2014: 201).

This social vulnerability in the adolescent brain is also found in the specially-appropriate biology of all mammalian species. For example, while human beings cannot ethically be experimentally deprived of social contact, such studies have been carried out with young rats, with the result that they became more likely to engage in addictive behaviour which later socialisation cannot remedy (Blakemore and Mills 2014). Studies in this area are currently in the early stages, but there are growing indications that what human adolescents are doing during this final stage of development is building self-awareness in order to better integrate their own self-judgements with peer evaluation. In order to do this, they have to 'play' with their identities both alone and in interaction with each other, which leads them to become hypersensitive to the opinions of others, whilst at the same time taking social risks that they would not consider during the earlier and later stages of their lives. Dumontheil (2016) explains that the paradox of adolescent insensitivity to others mixed with hypersensitivity to criticism is rooted in a centring upon the self during this life-stage, which heightens concerns about peer criticism and hence leads to the greater likelihood that the young person will take risks in order to fit in with/ impress peers. Wolf et al (2015:43) call this the 'audience effect', demonstrating through empirical research that the presence of a peer impacted far more heavily upon the performance of adolescents carrying out reasoning tasks than was the case for adults.

Blakemore and Mills propose that enhanced self-focus and heightened concern about the judgments of peers facilitates the process by which young people eventually emerge into adulthood 'equipped to navigate the social complexities of their community' (2014:189). In the human social environment, this crucially includes 'the ability to attribute and manipulate mental states in the self and others' (Dumontheil 2015:118). Guyer et al (2016:76) comment that adolescence is a period of both vulnerability and opportunity 'hinged on the power of the effective systems to influence behaviour'. In essence then, 'Youth is principally about becoming' (Kelly 2001:30).

However, the glass box of the internet is a risky environment in which to undertake such personal and social experimentation.

A large part of this generation's social and emotional development is occurring while on the internet and on cell phones. Because of their limited capacity for self-regulation and susceptibility to peer pressure, children and adolescents are at some risk as they navigate and experiment with social media. (Shurgin O'Keeffe and Clarke Pearson 2011:800)

The core risk is, as Galvan (2014) pinpoints, the characteristics required to seize independence from adult control are, in the 'identity experiment' stage, the key factor that draws adolescents into behaviour that becomes harmful, especially to themselves. 'The characteristics that distinguish adolescents offline also shape their online activities' (Davis et al 2012:1527). However, a major difference between 'real life' and online activities is that online activities leave a trail of evidence that is widely publicly available and cannot be erased. Harris (2014:51) cites the case of Amanda Todd, a 15-year-old Canadian girl who was blackmailed into uploading nude pictures of herself and subsequently committed suicide in response to the deluge of peer censure and teasing that followed. Even moving schools did not curtail this, as her new contacts very quickly accessed the digital footprint created by her previous activities. Her mother Carol commented: 'she realised the error in her actions, but that error couldn't be erased'. Ringrose et al (2013) articulate the online minefield that teenage girls have to negotiate in a socially networked society, illustrating the catch 22 situations of being teased as timid and babyish if they do not engage in the sexually risky behaviour, but facing moral condemnation and "slut shaming" when they do.

Privacy and Independence

The whole concept of online privacy is hugely complicated by the practices of social networking sites, which frequently change the rules relating to privacy settings. This is largely a ploy to create more efficient ways to collate individuals' personal information in order to generate huge amounts of income through the facilitation of targeted marketing for commercial sponsors. The result is that novice social networkers find that creating privacy settings is not necessarily straightforward, most particularly on the currently most popular social networking service, Facebook, which frequently makes changes in this respect. Boyd (2014:60) reflects that 'controlling a social situation [online] is neither easy nor obvious' and proposes that this has been consciously manipulated by social media oligarchs: 'Facebook's founder Mark Zuckerberg and Google chairman Eric Schmidt... argue that social norms around privacy have changed in order to justify their own business decisions regarding user privacy' (2014:56).

Boyd identifies four overarching features of social networking that may be viewed as either benefits or drawbacks, depending upon the purposes of the user:

- Persistence- durability of content.
- Visibility- the potential audience.
- Spreadability- the ease with which content is shared.
- Searchability- the ability to find content. Boyd (2014:11)

All of these features have the potential to disrupt the processes of identity formation for socially naive young people in a highly neuronally sensitive period of development.

As a psychoanalyst, Turkel (2011) focuses on the problem of adolescent teenage identity creation in a highly public environment, drawing upon the theories of the iconic psychoanalytic identity theorist Erik Erikson, who emphatically proposed that adolescence should be a period in which young people should be able to play with their identities without enduring consequence. She raises grave concerns about the lack of ability for the current generation of young people to accomplish this, in a society in which 'Facebook feels like "home" but you know that it puts you in a public square with a surveillance camera turned on' (Turkel 2011:243). This image invokes the Foucaultian concept of the 'Panopticon', a type of prison in which the prisoner is constantly aware that s/he is visible to the guards at all times (Focault 1979). Turkel (2011) did indeed find that many of her research participants were fully aware of their visibility, but were willing to sacrifice this for the sake of connectivity:

Even if her worst fears of surveillance by high school administrators and local police were true, she would not take action. She cannot imagine life without Facebook... As long as Facebook and Google are seen as necessities, if they demand information, young people know they will supply it. They don't know what else to do. (Turkel 2011:254-255)

Turkel gives the example of one of her participants who experienced an intense "double bind" relationship with her BlackBerry, in the sense that she felt stressed when she left it at home because she might miss an urgent message, but equally stressed by the constant stream of messages arriving when it was present.

The indication that such relentless connectivity is potentially addictive to a species that has evolved to rely so heavily upon its capacity for social interaction is also of concern. Boyd (2014:80) comments ''most teens aren't addicted to social media; if anything, they are addicted to one another'. The most powerful reinforcement for such a highly social creature is a signal that others are seeking contact, raising levels of dopamine and oxytocin within the physical brain (Ritvo 2012). Human responses to message notification sounds from networked devices resemble animal responses within operant conditioning contingencies (McMahon 2015).

Rayner (2012) proposes that the surveillance experienced by today's young people goes far beyond the panopticon prisoner and guard relationship envisioned by Foucault, into what could be termed an "omopticon" where all users of a social network surveil *each other*: 'There are no guards and no prisoners in Facebook's virtual Panopticon. We are both guards and prisoners, watching and implicitly judging one another as we share content' (Rayner 2011: online). This opens up the situation for further Foucaultian analysis in that the internet can be constructed as a key management tool for a society in which people are not only subject to surveillance by an Orwellian state but have been additionally induced to surveil each other: 'Power is everywhere' and 'comes from everywhere' (Foucault 1998:63), and indeed, the omnipresent internet environment is an ideal medium for such a process.

In this way, the human right to access the internet becomes a paradox, in which we are drawn by our human social instincts into an arena in which what we share can become the instrument of our social enslavement, most particularly for those who enter at an age where they are not yet neuronally or socially mature enough to competently judge what should be shared and what should not. Boyd raises the issue of the socially sterile "real life" environment of "caged" post-industrial teenagers, which can drive them into a poorly judged sense of liberation within online socialisation: 'teens find social media appealing because it allows them access to their friends and provides an opportunity to be a part of a broader public world while still situated physically in their bedrooms'(2014:201).

The emergent question that we have to address is whether social networking may be tantamount to "omopticon enslavement". This is an issue that affects both young people and adults, but due to immature social skills, young people may be far more vulnerable; their fragile, "under construction" identities are not yet robust enough to cope with such complex social demands. Boyd (2014) summarises the overall situation, proposing that young people are growing up within 'an environment in which contexts are networked and collapsed, audiences are invisible and anything they say or do can easily be taken out of context... whilst under constant surveillance and without a firm grasp of who they are' (2014:53). Turkel (2011:186) agrees: 'while none of these conflicts about self-presentation is new to adolescence... what is new is living them out in public, sharing every mistake and false step.' Young people thus find their fledgling identity experiments 'on show' in an omnipresent forum in which there is no escape from ongoing public evaluation, raising the inherent danger that for adolescents, social networking may be experienced as a process of 'breaking a butterfly upon a wheel' (Pope 1735, online).

Social Networking, Vulnerabilities and Independence

The deluge of information that arrives through social networking on mobile devices is an additional, formidable challenge for a species which evolved to pay concentrated attention (Levitin 2015), and again, this is of particular concern for those who are in the psychologically vulnerable stage of constructing the intricate neuronal architecture that underpins a relatively stable self-concept and competent prediction of potential responses from others. The 'always on' nature of interaction in a networked world tends to reduce the depth and complexity of individual interaction, resulting in a self-protection process Turkel refers to as 'emotional dumbing down' (2011:6) which encourages people not only to become less empathic due to the invisibility of "grey" areas in other peoples' behaviours and responses but also to create simplified "edited" selves through their profiles. In this way, human interaction is deprived of its nuances, which, added to the volume of messages received, results in people becoming 'so busy with many shallow communications we lack time for deep conversation' (Turkel 2011:207). 'It's the impulse to hold more of the world in our arms that leaves us holding more of reality at arm's length.... a child's cell phone keeps her in constant touch with her friends but trains her to think of text messaging as a soulful communication' (Harris 2014:100).

Such simplification of human interaction, in which cues such as smiles, frowns, and tone of voice are entirely absent also has the tendency to create discord and misunderstanding, which emerges from the process that psychologists have termed "deindividuation". This occurs when traditional conventions of social engagement are absent due to the lack of real life signalling such as facial expression and "body language", and has been extensively researched by psychologists studying driver "road rage" behaviour (Gardiner 2015: online).

Turkel additionally points out that young people are not only "tethered" constantly to one another through social networking, but also to their parents, with the result that 'the tethered child does not have the experience of being alone with only him or herself to count on' (2011:173). In this sense then, the increasing independence of the adolescent becomes to a great extent an illusion, as s/he is equipped with a mobile device upon which support and direction from parents and friends is available in all situations, including those in which previous generations would have had only the self to depend upon; for example getting lost on unfamiliar streets or dealing with a difficult interaction with a stranger. 'Feeling a bit stranded used to be considered a part of adolescence, and one that developed inner resources. Now it is something that the network makes it possible to bypass' (Turkel 2011:243).

Additionally, while previous generations formed ephemeral friendships during the adolescent period which waxed and waned as an inevitable consequence of growing up and moving on, social networking provides an environment in which if nothing is actively done to cut such ties (the Facebook action referred to as 'unfriending', which can have socially awkward implications), young people remain forever tethered to the Facebook pages of people who are no longer part of their everyday lives, and with whom they may have less and less in common.

Turkel's (2011) participants vividly described the problem of being unable to leave the person that they were in adolescence behind. Comments included:

- "I feel that my childhood has been stolen by the internet"
- "It's like somebody is about to find a horrible secret that I didn't know I left someplace"
- "For the first time, people will stay your friends. It makes it harder to let go of your life and move on"
- "It used to be good that people could leave their high school friends behind and take on new identities"

Turkel (2011:259-260) concludes: 'we see a first generation going through adolescence knowing that every misstep, all the awkward gestures of their youth are being frozen in a computer's memory... This is the anxiety of always... the persistence of people and data'.

There are therefore some significant experiential differences between the up-and-coming first 'social networked' generation and that of previous generations. Today's young adults were the first to construct their identities within a glass box in which their every false start and error was potentially on the show to friends, parents, and teachers, and to everyone they might meet in the future, including potential life-partners and employers. They had to cope with a frenetic pace of online communication that frequently fragmented and truncated the resulting messages. Their movement towards personal independence was also impacted by the ongoing surveillance of those to whom they were tethered through social networks, including potentially directive adults such as parents. Through these processes, which 'crowd the world into our small lives' Harris (2014:.20), the development of a somewhat "tethered" identity may be inevitable. This creates a disjuncture between adolescence experienced largely within a contemporary online environment and the adolescence that was experienced in wholly conventional environments in the past. It can be suggested that such major cultural change has, in effect, created Adolescence 2.0.

In conclusion, young people meet many social paradoxes in these early days of social networking. Social networks open up the world to them but eventually constrain them through relentless information collection and collation, which leads to the creation of online identities that can never be erased. Social networking allows young people a previously unimaginable breadth of interaction opportunities, but because the nature of the connection is within an environment which is 'always on', such interactions tend to lack in depth and substance; there is evidence that while social networking increases the quantity of interaction, it reduces quality. There is clearly a huge amount of research yet to be carried out in this area with respect to the effect of social networking upon human society in general; however an immediate area of concern is its effects upon young people in terms of the fragility and tentativeness of an identity "under construction"; a fundamental developmental process within the teenage years. This is the arena in which this pilot project was placed, using a small sample of participants to further explore some of the issues identified within the existing literature and to scope their responses in order to frame a more extensive piece of research.

MAIN FOCUS

This project was designed to address a gap in the literature; what young people between 11 and 15 construct as 'fun' in a world which has recently experienced a great opening up of opportunities to both play and socially connect online (Jarvis et al 2014). The methodology used was that of a questionnaire with a mixture of open and closed questions, followed a few weeks later by a focus group which used eighteen-year-old students in the same school. The school in question was an English state comprehensive school serving a small town at the edge of the Yorkshire Dales. The questionnaire-based research was undertaken by a Personal, Social, and Health Education teacher in his routine teaching practice with students in Year 7 (aged 11-12), Year 8 (aged 12-13) and Year 10 (aged 14-15), and the focus group was conducted by the same teacher and the lead researcher with a small sample of eighteen-year-old Year 13 students within the same school.

English state schools are routinely provided by the Department for Education online advice document *Cyber-bullying: Advice for Head Teachers and School Staff* (DFE 2014), which contains periodically updated links to online advisory documents from bodies such as the UK Council for Child Internet Safety, for example *Sexting in Schools* (2016) and *Online Safety in Schools and Colleges* (2016). The school safeguarding policy (which cannot be referenced here due to the ethical requirement for anonymity) identifies sexting and cyber-bullying as two of a range of issues in its 'safeguarding related' section, commenting that staff should be vigilant and report any concerns to the school safeguarding co-ordinator.

Ethical protocols were followed which meant that permissions for participation in this research project had to be received from the Head Teacher, the young person him/ herself and the young person's parent or guardian. While the questionnaire did not collect the name of the participant, it did require a report of the participant's age in years and months and form designation ('forms' are cohorts to which English pupils are allocated for registration). This meant that they could be identified with a small amount of subsequent investigation if this was considered necessary for safeguarding purposes: if the investigators judged that what was written on the form indicated that the participant and/or another person were at risk of physical or moral harm. Participants were informed that protocols relating to anonymity and confidentiality must be disapplied in such circumstances, and the relevant information would be passed to the school safeguarding co-ordinator. In the event, no such information was reported. The Head Teacher gave permission for the research to go ahead within the school in general, but although all students invited to participate consented to fill out the questionnaire for the purposes of the research, only the questionnaires completed by students whose parents had given permission for the young person to take part in the research could be passed to the lead researcher for analysis. This created an insoluble ethical problem, in that the teacher found that while the children were uniformly eager to have their voices heard within the research, some were nevertheless quashed by the lack of formal parental permission.

Final participant numbers were weighted towards girls in an approximately two-thirds/ one –third gender split and towards children in Y7 with a smaller sample of Y8s and an even smaller sample of Y10s.

Given that the lack of parental permission (overwhelmingly on the basis of omission rather than deliberate refusal) had the effect of 'silencing' some of these voices from the initial sample, when it came to sourcing participants for the focus group stage of the research, instead of drawing from the same participant pool, young people in their last year at the school who were already eighteen were asked to

Table 1. Sample Demography

Gender	Year	Totals	% of whole sample
Boy	7	11	15
	8	10	14
	10	4	6
Girl	7	27	38
	8	13	18
	10	7	10

take part. This meant that they were able to sign their own participation permission documents, and it was then entirely up to them whether their data went forward into the analysis; none subsequently withdrew.

QUESTIONNAIRE-BASED FINDINGS (YEARS 7, 8 AND 10)

The overall statistics suggested that all participants generally agreed that they spent a lot of time on their networked smartphones (68%), within an interesting pattern of data. This sample of young people was increasingly likely to agree with this statement as they grew older. The Y7 and 8 data were similar at 64% and 60% respectively, but Y10 was much higher at 91%. When the statistics are split between boys and girls, boys showed a gradual increase in time spent on their networked smartphones as they grew older. Girls showed a slight *decrease* in usage at Y8 compared to Y7, but a much higher reported usage at Y10, where 100% of participants agreed with the statement.

When asked if 'Life would be much more fun if we didn't have mobile phones' (note that 'mobile phone' is the colloquial British term for what is termed a 'cell phone' in the US, and most commonly

Figure 1. Time Spent on Social Media

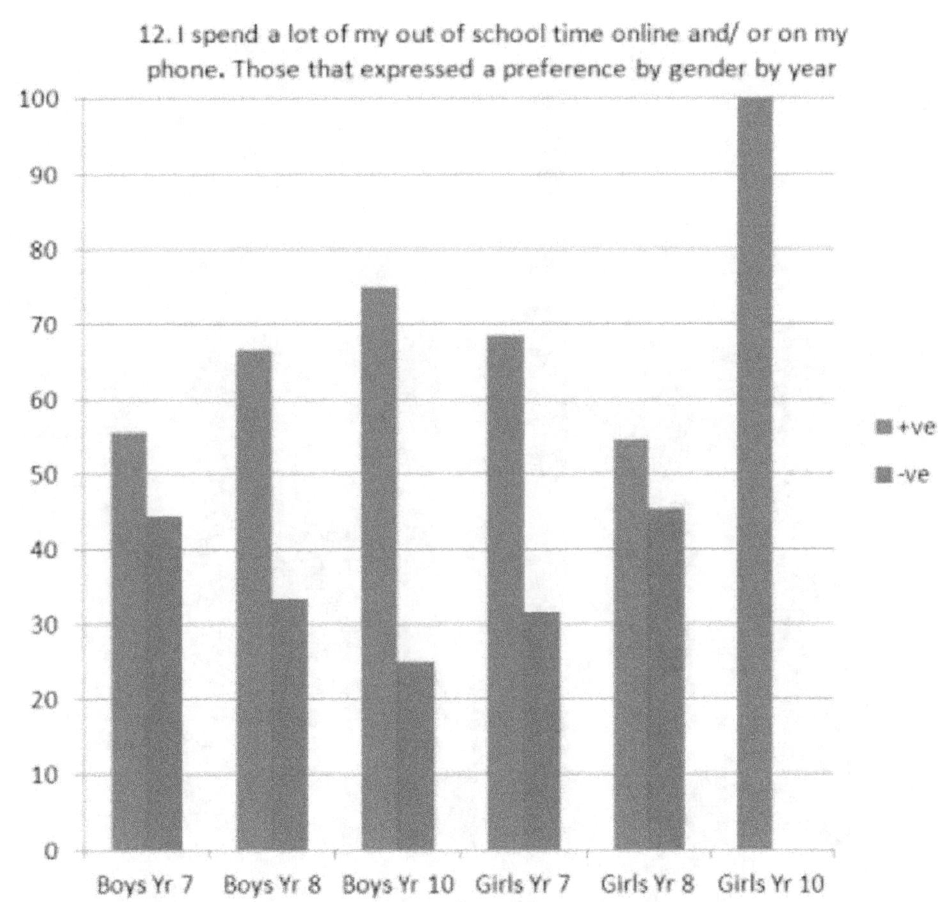

describes a networked smartphone) boys and girls in Y7 were quite similar in their response with 71% of boys disagreeing with this statement and 79% of girls. However, the older boys got, the more they disagreed with this statement- 86% in Y8 and 100% in Y10, while the older girls got, the more they *agreed* with it; 56% of girls in Y8 and 75% in Y10. This indicates that from the age of 13, the *majority* of the female sample agreed that their lives would be more fun without mobile phones and this increased to two-thirds of the Y10 female sample. This statistic also needs to be considered alongside a further indication that Y10 girls reported higher usage of their phones than the younger female participants. This is a conflicting finding; that while girls seem to use their phones more as they grow older, they develop a less positive attitude towards them, reflecting Turkel's (2011) participant who described a "double bind" relationship with her BlackBerry.

The finding that older girls' relationship with their phones is extremely ambivalent follows through into the qualitative data to some extent. There were several questions which asked participants to finish a sentence; for example, one question asked 'if adults wanted us to have more fun they would....'

Several participants gave similar answers, one being the idea that young people should be sent outside or told to engage in play/ fun activity in real life. Such an answer was given by the following percentage of the sample:

Figure 2. Would Life be More Fun Without Mobile Phones?

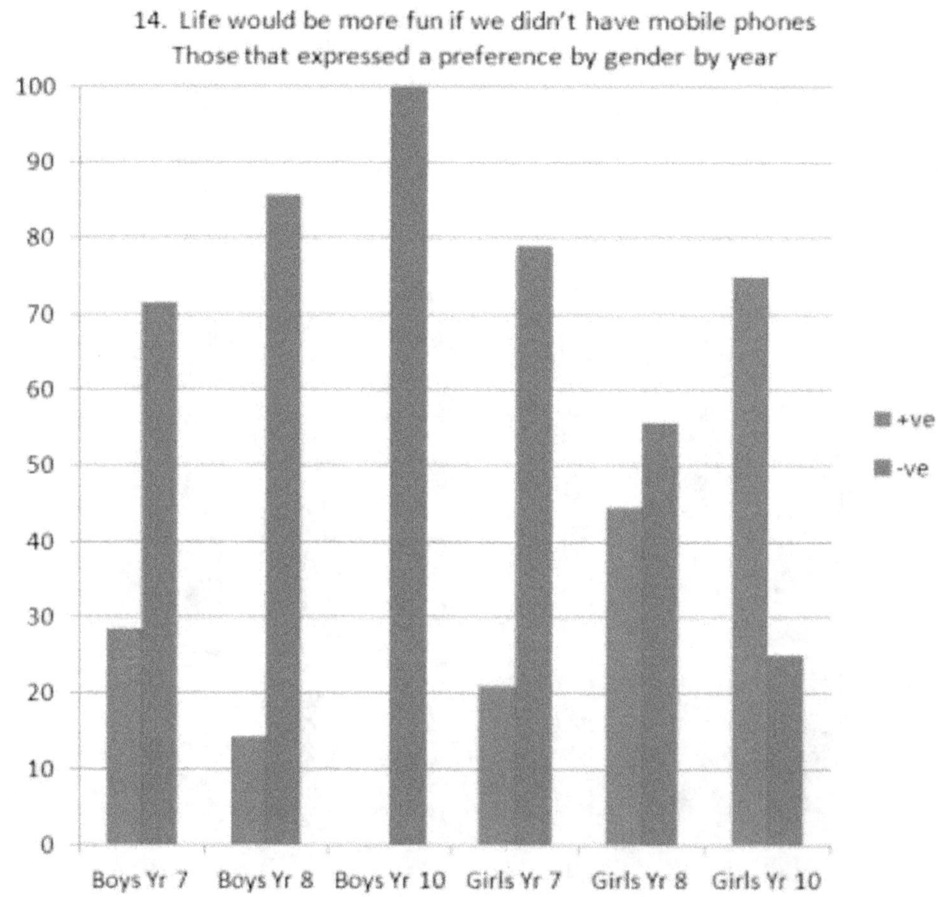

Table 2. Percentage of Sample Proposing 'Send Us Outside/ Tell Us to Play in Real Life'

	Girls	Boys
Year 7	29%	36%
Year 8	54%	40%
Year 10	57%	0%

This again indicates that while there is little difference between Y7 and 8 boys, and Y10 boys have become more positive towards their phones, Y10 girls become less positive towards their phones as they grow older, and that there is a large drop in positivity between Y7 and Y8 which is the period in which most girls enter early adolescence (aged 12/13). When added to the finding that there is a slightly reported decrease in phone usage by girls between Y7 and Y8, followed by a huge surge in usage at Y10, the pattern of findings becomes intriguing, although the small size of the sample means that no firm conclusions can be drawn. However, the effect could be usefully followed up in more extensive research.

When the participants were asked to identify the main problems with networked smartphones, their answers fell into several categories, one relating to people spending too much time on phones, with the term 'addicted' and 'addictive' mentioned by several participants. There were several references to the potential for cyber-bullying by peers, and others to the problem of not being able to discern other people's reactions online leading to misunderstandings, reflecting issues raised in the literature. A related point made was that people are inclined to be braver in terms of saying things online, which some participants saw as a problem and others as an advantage.

Y7 Girl: *'People get addicted [to their phones] and never, ever want to lose them and some people can't last a day without them'*
Y7 Girl: *'A lot of people go on their phones rather than going outside, people aren't really social anymore'.*
Y10 boy: *'It is too easy to say things that could be mean or hurtful towards other people [on phones or online]'.*
Y7 Girl: *'You can't connect and see things like their facial expressions'.*
Y7 Girl: *'When you are face-to-face they can change the tone of voice to say that they are joking'.*
Y7 Boy: *'Face to face, you'll probably be more scared'.*
Y8 Girl: *'You don't get shy [online] and it's easier to talk to people about something important and emotional'.*
Y10 Girl: *'You're more confident over the phone'.*
Y10 Boy: *'I can say a whole lot more when on my phone'.*

The benefits of networked smartphones were seen by participants as their instant connectivity to friends and relatives, particularly those far away, and photo-sharing apps such as Instagram and Snapchat. Facebook was also mentioned, but far less. One Y10 boy cast doubt on the value of such instant connectivity on a continual basis: 'there are no breaks in communications, you are always accessible', while conversely, a Y10 girl took the alternative perspective proposing that one of the most fun things about networked smartphones was 'being able to talk to friends 24-7 on social media'. However, another Y10 girl commented that it was 'more lonely online, no banter, less human interaction'.

The participants showed a considerable amount of deep reflection about their online activities that is not wholly mirrored in the existing literature, for example:

Y7 Boy: *'When I feel I go on a game too much, I delete it'*
Y8 Girl: *'[Online activity] can disturb your sleeping patterns'*
Y10 Boy: *'[Networked smart phones] give people a fear of missing out on things if they don't have it'.*
Y7 Girl: *'[When you interact with people online] you can't hold their hand or give them a hug or give them some sweets'.*
Y7 Boy: *'When online I always feel as if they are different people to when I talk to them in real life'.*

All groups apart from Y7 girls mentioned the problem of people deceiving them online:

Y7 Boy: *'You can't see facial expressions, so you don't know if they are lying'*
Y8 Girl: *'[You don't know who people are online, so] they could be horrible'*

The Y10 girls also mentioned having to beware of 'paedophiles' and 'weirdos' online. One 'and finally' comment in the section of the questionnaire which asked for 'any other thoughts' seemed, to sum up, the most general underlying orientation to networked smartphone interaction: *'phones aren't all fun... we only go on them to see what other people are doing or just to talk to them if we can't go and see them in person'*. This clearly mirrors several dominant findings within the existing literature, most poignantly Boyd's point about young people being 'addicted to each other' (2014: 80).

FOCUS GROUP-BASED FINDINGS (YEAR 13)

The focus group consisted of seven eighteen-year-olds, four girls, and three boys. The researchers present were their male sociology/ Personal, Social and Health education teacher and the female lead researcher. Despite being in a minority, the boys tended to 'hold the floor' throughout the discussion. The group was asked to focus on how they had used social media throughout the secondary school years, but by and large, they focused on their current activities. All had a Facebook page, however, they began by describing their activity on the more recent pictorially-based social networking Snapchat app:

A male participant commented:

It's like, for instance, more personal compared to Facebook... With Snapchat you put up photos, images or videos that last for a certain amount of time, and you can send it to people and caption it, like this is me having dinner... send it to your friend you've got on Snapchat and they can send you a picture back, and the whole idea lasts for a certain amount of time, it's about 10 seconds. You send it, they open it and it goes no further unless they screenshot it..... Like that way, it doesn't sound like an attractive thing, does it... like you want to spend your time doing, but you just do it.

A female participant responded: '*When you say it out loud when you have to explain it, it sounds like the most narcissistic thing.*'

The group went on to consider that despite the purposely ephemeral nature of Snapchat, it could still have lasting consequences:

You get all these random people that you would go round adding on Snapchat... you are basically talking to whoever this person is and you don't know them personally, but they have given out their name and you've added them...They give out their name on Snapchat, people search their name, add them and then they can start talking to them, sending pictures to them.

This triggered further reflection between the group on the implications of online interaction, after which a participant commented '*it probably is [dangerous] if you're younger and you don't understand internet safety*'. A female participant agreed:

I [recently] went back and changed all my privacy settings [on Facebook] because I never, ever checked them... basically, I had none on at all and it only occurred to me recently that I have had this account since I was 15 or so and that just all of this stuff was there... I just assumed that the default setting would be "only your friends can see this stuff" but it's not, it's like friends of friends and that sort of thing.

The participants' attitudes to 'friends' on Facebook varied, with one participant claiming 1500 Facebook friends, after which the group discussed various orientations to the ways in which they 'friended' people, some admitting to adding people that they met casually whilst out shopping or at a party. One female jokingly participant commented '*like... I met you the other night but... if you don't know their name, how have they managed to find you... they might practically stalk you to add you on, that's social media*'. A male participant replied '*It's that mentality, though like you'll meet someone, you'll add them on Facebook, like you'll go to a party and you'll meet someone you'll like "oh, I'll add you on Facebook" like you're best friends now*'.

The group reflected upon the amount of time that they spent on the internet, not only on social media but on sites such as youtube, watching videos as a way of '*procrastinating*', often with respect to study, and that this was very 'addictive'; that it was in a way like being '*taken over*'. They did however greatly value the ability to stay in touch with distant friends and family through Facebook, citing discussions with cousins in America and Australia, one commenting that on reflection he felt that this was '*the only positive thing*' about Facebook.

The group were concerned about the amount of freedom they perceived that younger children had when it came to social networking, and discussed the associated dangers, in particular with relation to a recent high profile murder of a fourteen-year-old who had met his psychiatrically disturbed murderer through playing a socially networked game on the internet (BBC 2015). There was a debate about whether younger children's access to the internet should be limited, with a female participant proposing:

Every time a new piece of technology comes out, like people panic and think the influence it is going to have on young kids, and you know, it's fine! People say like "when I was younger, I didn't have an iPad, and you know I had much more fun", well, you probably didn't, you had a different type of fun. You don't see the appeal of sitting and playing Angry Birds for like three hours or whatever, but for kids, that's brilliant.

A male participant countered:

Half of Year 7 have got Facebook; half of Year 5 in primary school, they've all got Facebook...and they could be doing anything.... if you are an adult, and you have kids, I would say sometimes you generally have to make the decision for them. If you've got a kid in Year 6 and everyone is getting Facebook, you can't stop them... getting Facebook and lying about their age.

A female participant concluded:

I think education is more important than completely limiting... if you want to say to them, well, you're not allowed to use this at all, you know, as soon as they came of age they would just use it... they still wouldn't understand why it was dangerous and stuff. But if you said to them, well you need to do all this to make sure you're safe, and never have anyone you don't know and make sure your privacy settings are up to date, I think that would be more valuable for the rest of their life.

This was generally agreed by the group; however, the final reflection from one of the male participants was *'you can't trust others... sometimes we can't even trust ourselves to follow the rules. You think, this doesn't happen to me, it happens to other people'.*

ISSUES, CONTROVERSIES, PROBLEMS

In general, this pilot study confirmed many of the issues and controversies raised within the literature. One new issue that it raised was a gender difference that within this small sample at least, seemed to arise in early adolescence, with both genders becoming more attached to their networked smartphones as they grow older, but girls becoming increasingly ambivalent about them, depending on them more, but liking them less. Why this might be could be would be very usefully followed up in further research, and might reveal multiple issues that emerge for young women when interacting online, both with people they know and people that they are meeting online. There has been a recent concern raised about the sharply increasing rates of anxiety amongst young women between 2006 and 2016 (Wise 2016) and there is a possibility that social networking may be a contributing factor.

This may relate to gender styles in which relationships are negotiated, both with regard to 'romantic' relationships and friendships. Differing styles of male and female competition identified in younger children, in that boys are more inclined to physically confront one another, while girls more typically engage in relationship sabotage (Jarvis 2006) may be a productive theoretical starting point. Jones et al (2013:64) found that cyber-bullying was more likely to occur between girls, commenting 'females tend to predominate in verbal and relational types of aggression and the social networking platforms are clearly more suited to such exchanges than physical aggression and intimidation'. Underwood et al (2012) found that girls sent far more texts to each other than were exchanged between boys, although their investigation did not elicit the content of such communications. Davis (2012) found that boys were more likely to engage in instrumental exchanges between themselves, discussing practical, concrete-world topics while girls were more likely to discuss feelings, disclosing personal information to other girls. It would certainly, therefore, appear that the visibility, persistence and spreadability elements of social networking might more effectively serve female styles of relationship sabotage.

This pilot study also found that particularly amongst the younger sample, online gaming was far more popular with boys than with girls. It is possible that, in this way, male styles of interaction are more positively served in the internet environment than female styles given that in online gaming, physical fighting is undertaken by avatars, muting instead of heightening the capacity for damage. This suggestion is of course, highly speculative and would need to be far more extensively explored in further research. Olson (2010) found that many young online gamers reported psychological benefits resulting from their activities:

Informal discussions with young adult game players suggest that some use survival and horror games to process fear, playing the game over and over (from different character perspectives, as the game allows) until the frightening content has been mastered..... Compared with other media such as books, films, and radio, electronic games appear to have an unusually expansive appeal and serve a surprising number of emotional, social, and intellectual needs. Olson 2010:185

More general issues raised within the literature and further illustrated by the pilot research, such as the distortions, fragmentation and displacement that are experienced within human interaction when it is undertaken in the 'removed' environment of social networking will take many years to fully investigate. Marwick (2012:378) comments that one of the key effects of social media is to 'collapse social contexts and social roles' which she proposes allows users to 'strategically reveal, disclose and conceal personal information to create connections with others and tend social boundaries'. The problem for young people is that they have not yet built the social sophistication to engage competently with such complexity, and enter the social networking maze at a stage of development in which they are unready to cope with its demands, and this, in turn, has the potential to impact upon their subsequent developmental processes. Both Boyd (2014) and Turkel (2011) discuss the simplification and collapsing of social 'players' within online networking interaction, raising the consequent potential for undermining social relationships amongst socially vulnerable adolescents.

Van Dijck (2013:213) points out that social media can provide 'the very tools for shaping identities', however, it could be counter-argued that young people have not yet developed the neuronal or social capacity to competently manage such tools, and therefore, introducing them to a social networking environment designed for adults is akin to allowing a group of toddlers to run amok in a workspace equipped with sharp tools and blowtorches. McMahon (2015:728) comments that psychologists will need to develop a new concept of 'cyber-psychology' in order to engage in this 'new research frontier'. One point that is clear in this area of research is that it will provide many formidable challenges for investigators, for at least a generation to come.

SOLUTIONS AND RECOMMENDATIONS

There are no immediate solutions to any of the issues raised within this chapter. Social networking is such a new phenomenon, researchers are only just defining the key questions; answers will take a long time to emerge. Viner proposes that there are many deep and troubling issues connected to social networking in general that are only just beginning to appear:

Confusing battles between opposing forces: between truth and falsehood, fact and rumour, kindness and cruelty; between the few and the many, the connected and the alienated; between the open platform of the web as its architects envisioned it and the gated enclosures of Facebook and other social networks; between an informed public and a misguided mob.(Viner 2016, online)

Spies et al (2014) propose that the positive and negative aspects of social networking for adolescents mirror each other, in that whilst the online environment provides a space for trying out new identities, it also entices young people to make unhealthy comparisons between themselves and others, and while it can be a forum for practising social skills, there is always the potential for instant, damagingly hostile feedback, which creates a permanent record that others may subsequently access. And while young people may be able to tap into a huge pool of potential friends in the online environment, they may also be tempted to over-disclose to people they barely know.

Perhaps, as the young participants of my pilot study suggested, that while the intricacies of these complex issues are slowly unravelled by years of painstaking research, contemporary adults could act more decisively to better protect young people from full engagement within such a maelstrom during one of the most highly neuronal and psychologically vulnerable stages of development. While policy makers have become focused upon the human right to *access* contemporary technology, they have not considered how that technology may *impact* upon people, in particular, those in a vulnerable stage of development. In 2014, disseminating the findings of a literature review on the topic of disappearing play opportunities for children in "real life", I commented, in collaboration with my co-writers, that we should focus on creating policies that take into account how human beings, particularly those in different developmental stages actually function in the neurobiological and psychological sense (Jarvis et al 2014:64). This observation seems equally salient with respect to the consideration of how we might mediate children's online activity in terms of more carefully balancing participation rights with developmental vulnerabilities.

However, we also need to consider whether, if we restrict children from the online environment but at the same time do nothing to actively create more time and space for them to engage in "real life" association, they may be in grave danger of never having sufficient freedom for fully independent interaction with peers. A restricted online profile, created under close adult surveillance is not a viable experience in the production of a fully functioning human being. It is imperative that young people are not placed in a situation that never allows them the freedom to construct a deep multi-faceted, human identity, restricted by circumstance to experience the self and others only through adult directed activities and shallow, sterile online profiles. In such a situation 'the years of identity construction are recast in terms of profile production' (Turkel 2011:182). From this perspective, it is clear that increasing adult control in the online environment without the provision of suitable 'real world' opportunities for unstructured, independent peer interaction might exacerbate an already problematic situation impacting upon western adolescents, who may be economically privileged but, through socialising principally through online modes of communication, appear to be experiencing an as yet undefined level of social and emotional impoverishment.

FUTURE RESEARCH DIRECTIONS

Future research directions in this arena at the macro level are obviously myriad. In terms of a more 'micro' approach, the findings of the pilot study suggest a possible difference between the online vulnerabilities of boys and girls, and this would be a useful project that could be effectively scoped and pursued. Twenty years ago, Mary Pipher wrote a book called 'Reviving Ophelia' which, by exploring the mental health issue of 'Ophelia Syndrome' suggested that modern western media was creating a beauty-obsessed "girl-poisoning" culture. She suggested that this had increased incidences of sexual violence, and created a society in which girls were measured against impossible standards, creating a deluge of depression, suicide attempts and eating disorders.

[Girls] are coming of age in a... dangerous, sexualized and media-saturated culture. They face incredible pressures to be beautiful and sophisticated... which means using chemicals and being sexual... [this] limits girls' development, truncates their wholeness and leaves many of them traumatized. (Pipher 1996:12)

It is possible that over the past decade, social media, via facilitation of negative styles of female interaction, has acted to further magnify this effect, and this would be a useful focus from which to begin unravelling the effects of social networking upon fragile, fledgeling "under construction" teenage identities.

CONCLUSION

The literature suggests that young people who carry out a large percentage of the socialisation necessary to underpin the formation of their adult identity in an online environment are vulnerable to a range of issues created by the persistence, visibility, and spreadability of the profiles that they create. It is proposed that young people need space to play with their identities in arenas more suited to a developmental stage in which preferences and opinions may be ephemeral, and alliances and friendships may be fleeting. Additionally, such an arena should not create permanent records of teenage errors and indiscretions. The data gathered in the pilot study outlined within this chapter largely supported this viewpoint, and additionally raised an original question relating to a potential gender difference, generating data that suggested the online environment may be more hostile to girls' modes of development in early adolescence than to boys'. Further research to explore this topic was suggested. The young research participants additionally suggested that adults should pay more focused attention to ensuring that children are protected from developmentally inappropriate online environments. A good starting point in this respect lies within a discussion of the neurological and psychological evidence relating to human development, mapping this against what may be appropriate and inappropriate online environments for children and young people with regard to differing levels of maturation. Article 36 of the United Nations Convention on the Rights of the Child states: 'children should be protected from any activity that... could harm their welfare and development' (UNICEF 1989 online). However, policy makers also need to be mindful of children and young people's rights under Article 13 (freedom of expression), Article 15 (free association) and Article 17 (accessing information). At the beginning of the 21st century, we have only just begun to consider how human rights to access the online environment might be more effectively aligned with young people's rights to protection from harm within environments which are potentially unsuitable for their neuronal and psychological stage of development.

REFERENCES

ASH. (2016). *Key Dates in the History of Anti-Tobacco Campaigning*. Available at: http://www.ash.org.uk/files/documents/ASH_741.pdf

BBC. (2015). *Breck Bednar murder: How Lewis Daynes manipulated his victim*. Available at: http://www.bbc.co.uk/news/uk-england-essex-30730807

Blakemore, S., & Mills, K. (2014). Is Adolescence a Sensitive Period for Sociocultural Processing? *Annual Review of Psychology*, *65*(1), 187–207. doi:10.1146/annurev-psych-010213-115202 PMID:24016274

Boyd, D. (2014). *It's Complicated: The social lives of networked teens*. New Haven, CT: Yale.

Davis, K. (2012). Friendship 2.0: Adolescents experiences of belonging and self-disclosure online. *Journal of Adolescence*, *35*(6), 1527–1536. doi:10.1016/j.adolescence.2012.02.013 PMID:22475444

DFE. (2014). *Cyber-bullying: Advice for Head Teachers and School Staff.* Available at: https://www.gov.uk/government/uploads/system/uploads/attachment_data/file/374850/Cyberbullying_Advice_for_Headteachers_and_School_Staff_121114.pdf

Dumontheil, I. (2015). Development of the Social Brain during Adolescence. *Psycologia Eucativa*, *21*(2), 117–124. doi:10.1016/j.pse.2015.08.001

Dumontheil, I. (2016). Adolescent Brain Development. *Current Opinion in Behavioural Sciences*, *10*(39), 39–44. doi:10.1016/j.cobeha.2016.04.012

Foucault, M. (1979). *Discipline and punish: The birth of the prison*. New York: Vintage Books.

Foucault, M. (1998). *The History of Sexuality: The Will to Knowledge*. London: Penguin.

Galvan, A. (2014). Insights about adolescent behaviour: Plasticity and policy from neuroscience research. *Neuron*, *83*(2), 262–265. doi:10.1016/j.neuron.2014.06.027 PMID:25033176

Gardiner, B. (2015). *My Way on the Highway: why driving makes jerks of us all.* Available at: http://www.slate.com/articles/health_and_science/science/2015/05/the_psychology_of_road_rage_driving_makes_you_angry_anonymous_and_emotionally.html

Griffiths, M. (2013). Social Networking Addiction: Emerging Themes and Issues. *Journal of Addiction Research & Therapy, 4*, 118. Available at http://www.omicsonline.org/social-networking-addiction-emerging-themes-and-issues-2155-6105.1000e118.php?aid=22152

Guyer, A., Silk, J., & Nelson, E. (2016). The Neurobiology of the Emotional Adolescent. *Neuroscience Bio-Behaviour Review*, *70*, 74–85. doi:10.1016/j.neubiorev.2016.07.037 PMID:27506384

Harris, M. (2014). *The End of Absence: Reclaiming what we've lost in a world of constant connection*. New York: Penguin.

Jarvis, P. (2006). Rough and Tumble Play: Lessons in Life. *Evolutionary Psychology*, *4*(1), 330–346. doi:10.1177/147470490600400128

Jarvis, P., Newman, S., & Swiniarski, L. (2014). On becoming social: The importance of collaborative free play in childhood. *International Journal of Play.*, *3*(1), 53–68. doi:10.1080/21594937.2013.863440

Jones, L., Mitchell, K., & Finkellar, D. (2013). Online Harassment in Context: Trends from three youth internet surveys. *Psychology of Violence*, *3*, 53–69. doi:10.1037/a0030309

Kelly, P. (2001). Youth at risk: Processes of individualisation and responsibilisation in the risk society. *Discourse (Abingdon)*, *22*(1), 23–33. doi:10.1080/01596300120039731

Levitin, D. (2005). *The Organized Mind: How to better structure our time in the age of social media and constant distraction.* LSE Blog, British Politics, and Policy. Available at: http://blogs.lse.ac.uk/politicsandpolicy/the-organized-mind-how-to-better-structure-our-time-in-the-age-of-social-media-and-constant-distraction/

Livingstone, S., Olafsson, K., & Staksrud, E. (2013). Risky Social Networking Practices among underage users: Lessons for evidence-based policy. *Journal of Computer-Mediated Communication*, *18*(3), 303–320. doi:10.1111/jcc4.12012

Marwick, A. (2012). The Public Domain: Surveillance in everyday life. *Surveillance & Society*, *9*(4), 378–393.

McMahon, C. (2015). Why do we 'like' Social Media? *The Psychologist*, *28*(9), 724–728.

NASUWT. (2016). *Social Media Abuse Endemic in Schools.* Available at: https://www.nasuwt.org.uk/article-listing/social-media-abuse-endemic-in-schools-.html

Olson, C. (2010). Childrens Motivations for Video Game Play in the Context of Normal Development. *Review of General Psychology*, *13*(2), 180–187. doi:10.1037/a0018984

Pipher, M. (1996). *Reviving Ophelia.* London: Vermillion.

Pope, A. (1735). *Epistle to Dr. Arbuthnot.* Available at: https://www.poetryfoundation.org/resources/learning/core-poems/detail/44895

Rayner, T. (2012). Foucault and social media: life in a virtual panopticon. *Philosophy For Change.* Available at: https://philosophyforchange.wordpress.com/2012/06/21/foucault-and-social-media-life-in-a-virtual-panopticon/

Ridley, M. (2003). *Nature via Nurture: Genes, experience, and what makes us human.* New York, NY: HarperCollins.

Ringrose, J., Harvey, L., Gill, R., & Livingstone, S. (2013). Teen Girls, Sexual Double Standards and Sexting: Gendered value in digital image exchange. *Feminist Theory*, *14*(3), 305–323. doi:10.1177/1464700113499853

Ritvo, E. (2012). Facebook and your Brain. *Psychology Today.* Available at: https://www.psychologytoday.com/blog/vitality/201205/facebook-and-your-brain

Shurgin OKeeffe, G., & Clarke Pearson, K. (2011). Clinical Report- The Impact of Social Media on Children, Adolescents and Families. *Paediatrics*, *127*(4), 800–804. doi:10.1542/peds.2011-0054

Spies Shapiro, L., & Margolin, G. (2014). Growing up Wired: Social networking sites and adolescent psychosocial development. *Clinical and Family Psychology Review*, *17*(1), 1–18. doi:10.1007/s10567-013-0135-1 PMID:23645343

Turkel, S. (2011). *Alone Together: Why we expect more from technology and less from each other*. New York: Basic Books.

UK Council for Child Internet Safety. (2016). *Online Safety in Schools and Colleges*. Available at: https://www.gov.uk/government/uploads/system/uploads/attachment_data/file/562876/Guidance_for_School_Governors_-_Question_list.pdf

UK Council for Child Internet Safety. (2016). *Sexting in Schools*. Available at: https://www.gov.uk/government/uploads/system/uploads/attachment_data/file/551575/6.2439_KG_NCA_Sexting_in_Schools_WEB__1_.PDF

Underwood, M., Rosen, L., More, D., Erenreich, S., & Gentsch, J. (2012). The Blackberry Project: Capturing the messaging of adolescent text. *Developmental Psychology*, *48*(2), 295–302. doi:10.1037/a0025914 PMID:22004337

UNICEF. (1989). *A Summary of the United Nations Convention on the Rights of the Child*. Available at: http://www.unicef.org/crc/files/Rights_overview.pdf

United Nations. (1976). *International Covenant on Civil and Political Rights*. Available at: http://www.ohchr.org/en/professionalinterest/pages/ccpr.aspx

United Nations. (2011). *Report of the Special Rapporteur on the promotion and protection of the right to freedom of opinion and expression*. Available at: http://www2.ohchr.org/english/bodies/hrcouncil/docs/17session/A.HRC.17.27_en.pdfAccessed

van Dijck, J. (2013). You have one identity: Performing the self on Facebook and Linked-in. *Media Culture & Society*, *35*(2), 199–215. doi:10.1177/0163443712468605

Viner, K. (2016). How Technology Disrupted the Truth. *The Guardian Long Read*. Available at: https://www.theguardian.com/media/2016/jul/12/how-technology-disrupted-the-truth

Wagner, A. (2012). Is Internet Access a Human Right? *UK Human Rights Blog*. Available at: https://ukhumanrightsblog.com/2012/01/11/is-internet-access-a-human-right/

Wise, J. (2016). Anxiety in teenage girls rises sharply between 2006 and 2016. *BMJ (Clinical Research Ed.)*, *354*, 4649.

Wolf, L., Bazargan, N., Kilford, E., Dumontheil, I., & Blakemore, S. J. (2015). The audience effect in adolescence depends on whos looking over your shoulder. *Journal of Adolescence*, *43*, 5–14. doi:10.1016/j.adolescence.2015.05.003 PMID:26043167

KEY TERMS AND DEFINITIONS

Adolescence 2.0: Web 1.0 was the original version of the internet which carried only static words and pictures, and through which only asynchronous typed communication was possible. Web 2.0 is the version of the internet that appeared in the early 21st century, which carries moving images and the possibility for synchronous communication via video link (e.g., iPhone 'Facetime'). This has greatly changed the arena for adolescent communication, hence 'Adolescence 2.0'.

Digital Footprint: The information that is present on the internet about a particular individual. Once submitted to a website, it is usually impossible to completely erase, as it will exist across multiple servers.

Games/ Gaming: Some social networking sites are set up as games, in which a user adopts a fantasy identity in keeping with the conventions of the game (for example soldiers in war games, or space travellers in science fiction games). Where these characters are moving images (as is usually the case in Web 2.0) these are termed 'avatars'. Researchers studying adolescents and social networking generally find that games are more popular with boys than girls. Many can be played through Play Station and X-Box consoles.

Identity Formation: It is generally accepted amongst psychologists that adolescence is a time during which human beings become highly focused on developing an 'identity', which involves a set of choices, some more conscious than others, about the type of person one wishes to become. Prominent theories include the mid-twentieth century psychoanalytic theory of Erik Erikson and the more recent, empirically based neurological theory piloted by Sarah-Jane Blakemore.

Mobile Phone: The British term for a phone that works via radio transmitter rather than a landline. The more common American English term is 'cell phone'. The term mobile phone is most commonly used in everyday British English to refer to a networked smartphone; that is a phone which can receive information via voice, text, pictorial and video formats. Early mobile phones were limited to voice and text.

'Ophelia' Syndrome: This is a psychological condition, principally affecting young females. It is based on Shakespeare's character in the play *Hamlet.* What it refers to is defining the self only in terms of other people's opinions; a form of objectifying the self. It impacts negatively upon mental health due to the individual's belief that she only has worth if the responses of other people indicate that she does. Psychologists propose that, in the modern world where a huge range of media expound ideal female appearance that this is frequently a fixation for those expressing the syndrome.

Panopticon/ Omopticon: The Panopticon is a prison imagined by the French Sociologist Michel Foucault, where all prisoners are constantly surveilled by guards, through technological means. Rayner (2012) proposes that social media has gone beyond Foucault's imagination to an 'omopticon' where all users of a social media site are able to surveil all others- in this sense all users are both prisoners and guards.

Sexting: The sending of explicit pictures, most usually of the self, over the internet with the intention to sexually arouse.

Social Media: Websites designed to facilitate ongoing online communication between people, which includes both synchronous and asynchronous message, and the posting of pictures and videos. Early examples include Facebook and MySpace; there are now many such sites, for example, What's App, which is principally designed for mobile/ cell phones, and Instagram, which is designed principally for picture sharing.

United Nations Convention on the Rights of the Child (UNCRC): The UNCRC is a set of articles created by the United Nations which stipulate a set of rights for children- people between birth and eighteen- that signatory nations pledge to provide. Most of the nations of the world have signed the convention, with the notable exception of the United States.

Section 4

Childhood and Multi-Dimensional Rights in Education

Chapter 8
HIV Education for Learners in Zambian Catholic Schools:
A Social Justice Perspective

Joseph Chita
The University of Zambia, Zambia

ABSTRACT

In this chapter, HIV and AIDS education for learners in Catholic schools was interrogated from a social justice perspective. The author advances the argument that the learners' right to access HIV and AIDS education in the school context was superficial in addressing the needs of learners. Hence, depriving them of the much needed knowledge, skills, and attitudes necessary for their survival in the context of HIV and AIDS. Therefore, this call for continued dialogue among different stakeholders in order to enable Catholic Schools play the 'social vaccine' role in the face of HIV and AIDS.

INTRODUCTION

This chapter interrogates the theme of HIV education in Catholic secondary schools in Zambia in the context of children's right to access information and social justice. In the advent of HIV and AIDS, the Ministry of Education (MoE) now Ministry of General Education and other sister ministries in the country embraced different strategies to mitigate the effects of HIV and AIDS in the country. In education, policies were formulated to guide the implementation of HIV and AIDS programmes in schools and other learning institutions. Different stakeholders in the schools were to benefit from the HIV and AIDS policy differently. Of interest in this chapter are the learners, whose right to access HIV information is at stake due to different factors (teacher inadequacies, lack of learning materials, cultural taboos among others) at play. This is despite the stress by some scholars that education is a social vaccine in the shadow of HIV and AIDS.

In order to explore what the catholic schools were teaching learners on HIV and AIDS, and how they were teaching, the author interviewed the school administrators, teachers, and learners or pupils. In addition, group discussions were held with learners and document reviews conducted on the phenomena of

DOI: 10.4018/978-1-5225-2578-3.ch008

interest. The data collected was analysed to answer the research question, why and how HIV education for learners in catholic schools was a social justice issue?

The author argues that learners' access to comprehensive HIV education in the context of the school is a social justice issue, given that schools are social vaccines. More so, the catholic schools should strive to foster social justice especially that they have long been associated with being the mirror of social justice in the society. However, these schools are challenged by the recommended comprehensive and targeted HIV education, thus compromising the reputation of fostering fairness, equity, and preparation of change agents (learners) in the context of HIV and AIDS.

In the following sections the author contexualises the phenomena by highlighting the background to the inquiry (brief history of Zambia, HIV and AIDS in Zambia, Education provision, Catholic education and the of philosophy of social justice in the milieu of HIV and AIDS).

BACKGROUND

Brief History of Zambia

Zambia is a landlocked country with eight neighbouring countries sharing its boundaries. The country measures about 752, 612 square kilometers translating into 2.5% of Africa. Zambia got its independence from Britain in 1964. The country has ten administrative provinces with more than 72 districts (CSO, et al, 2007, p.1). The population by mid 2016 was projected at 15,933,883 of which 7,884,009 constitute males and 8,049,874 female. Health is a priority due to the high disease burden in Zambia, which is compounded by high prevalence of HIV, high poverty levels, and poor macroeconomic situation (CSO, 2016, p.2 & 4).

HIV and AIDS in Zambia

Zambia, like many sub-Saharan countries, has been adversely affected by the HIV and AIDS pandemic (CSO, et al, 2007, p.5). Historical accounts reported the first AIDS case in Zambia in 1984. Government through different ministries put up plans and strategies to combat the national HIV and AIDS epidemic. Knowledge of HIV and AIDS is universal in Zambia. Almost all of women and men aged 15-49 have heard of HIV and AIDS. However, only 36% of women and 39% of men have what can be considered comprehensive knowledge about the modes of transmission and prevention. *Comprehensive knowledge is defined as knowing that consistent use of condoms during sexual intercourse and having just one uninfected faithful partner can reduce the chances of getting the AIDS virus, knowing that a healthy-looking person can have HIV, and rejecting the two most common local misconceptions about HIV transmission (that the AIDS virus can be transmitted by mosquito bites and that a person can become infected by sharing food with someone who has the AIDS virus),* CSO, et al, 2007, p.7;CSO, et al, 2014, p.199.

According to 'the 2011-2015 National HIV and AIDS Strategic Framework,' launched in 2010, ... *four national priorities for tackling the epidemic [were emphasized]... the first priority [was] to accelerate and intensify prevention in order to reduce annual rates of new HIV infections...* (CSO, et al, 2014, p.6). According to the same report, *the proportion of women and men with knowledge of HIV prevention methods increases with age, with youth aged 15-19 having the lowest level of knowledge* (CSO et al, 2014, p.198), in addition, the same groups was reported having the lowest HIV prevalence rates (NAC, 2015, p. 9). The preceding findings justified the integration of HIV education in the school with the hope of increasing the knowledge of HIV prevention methods and to maintain or reduce further the HIV prevalence rates.

However, these strategies were not without their own challenges, the National AIDS Council in Zambia was cognizance of obstacle to prevention services, which included *fragmented nature of the interventions and efforts... duplication of efforts ... leading to inefficient use of limited resources. Similarly, HIV prevention messages are not often harmonized to ensure that clear and non-conflicting messages are disseminated to community members including young people* (NAC, 2015, p. 32). The situation was not any different from the undertakings in the Catholic schools, where fragmented teaching was evident. With the HIV and AIDS situation in Zambia outlined in brief, it is important to locate the HIV and AIDS education discourse in the education system.

Education System in Zambia

A three-tier system of education is identical with the formal education in Zambia. The first 7 years are spent at primary level followed by 2 years of junior secondary school, and 3 years of senior secondary school. After completing 12 years of schooling, one may choose to further his or her education by either going to university for 4 to 7 years, depending on the field of study, and obtain a degree, or by attending a vocational or technical institute for a 2 to 3 year certificate or diploma course. The participants (learners) falls in the second tier system of education – secondary education, which caters for those in the age bracket 14-18 years, (CSO, et al, 2007, p.15 & 19).

Catholic Church and Schooling in Zambia

Since inception of the Catholic missionary activities in Zambia at the turn of the 19th Century, the church has been involved in the provision of education. Catholic presence in education has been acknowledged by different scholars (Snelson, 1974, Mwanakatwe, 1968, Kelly 1991, Carmody, 2004) among others. As Carmody (2007) observed, the Catholic Church has contributed immensely to Zambia's education.

According to a 'Pastoral Letter' from the Catholic Bishops of Zambia on Education, ZEC (2004:2) reported that *up to 1973 the Church owned and managed over 700 Primary Schools. At present the Catholic Church owns and manages: 40 High Schools, 32 of which are Grant-Aided, 34 Grant Aided Basic Schools, 8 Grant Aided Special Schools, 2 Grant Aided Teachers' College of Education and 2 Grant Aided Institutions under Technical Education and Vocational and Entrepreneurship Training Authority...'*

At the core of Catholic education are the following values, children's right to education and social justice. For the latter, the Church's position holds that their education will *foster the integral development of the whole person [especially for]... the generation that faces an unpredictable world* (ZEC, 2004: 5). This position differentiate the Catholic schools from other schools that *sacrifices the dimension of values to the acquisition of facts and skills... [the latter] measure the value of the person in terms of examinations passed or the position one holds in society'* (Ibid).

For the Catholic schools, *education should seek to awaken the students' sense of responsibility for their own lives, the lives of others and for their environment. It should help them understand their capacity to act in changing the situation and to refuse to 'take refuge in supposed impossibility of changing the world'* (ZEC, 2004:7). This position underlines the value of justice, embedded in the school ethos and curriculum. Beyond the ideal Catholic schooling, is the challenge of HIV and AIDS, which has confronted education provision in the country. Therefore, what has been the Catholic education's response to HIV and AIDS in Zambia?

The Catholic Schools and the Challenge of HIV and AIDS

The recognition of the role of the school in the fight against HIV and AIDS by the Catholic Church and the Ministry of Education has been supported by research findings and scholarship in the field. According to Kelly, integrated HIV and AIDS and sexual education into the school curriculum offers *good quality sexual health and HIV/AIDS education [which] is needed in order to equip young people with the information which they rarely get from their parents or senior family members, ... This education should go beyond the biological facts to include many aspects of behaviour and ultimately of attitudes and values* (Kelly, 2000, p.9).

This role of the schools in the shadow of HIV and AIDS is also linked to the universal right to education (Article 26 of the UN Declaration of Human Rights), *the right to education includes the right to the knowledge and skills needed for HIV prevention. Such a right can only be exercised if the school curriculum deals effectively with sexual health and HIV/AIDS prevention and care* (Kelly, 2000, p.9).

The Church has taken cognizance of the challenge of HIV and AIDS, because the effects of HIV and AIDS have been felt in the schools they run and communities they serve. In response to this encounter, the Church directed its teachers in Catholic run schools to *teach pupils the facts about HIV and AIDS. It is imperative as educators, that they teach the beauty and dignity of human sexuality. Christian morality and sound medicine all now agree that the only appropriate conduct is abstinence before marriage and fidelity within marriage* (ZEC, 2004, p.14). This was to complement government's (MoE) effort in stream lining HIV and AIDS education in the school curriculum.

Both the Catholic Church and the government (MoE) identified education as a key determinant of one's future in terms of lifestyle and societal status an individual accrue during and after schooling. This was supported by studies that have shown that *educational attainment has a strong effect on health behaviours and attitudes*, (CSO, et al, 2007, p.15.). In the age of HIV and AIDS, society needs health behaviours and health attitudes to life of the future generation. In line with research findings, the Ministry of Education through its policy document guided that *the curriculum for each school should include an education programme in the area of sexuality and interpersonal relationship appropriate to the age and development of its pupils* (MoE, 1996, p.77). The position of the Church and government, relates to the notion of education as a *social vaccine*, as reflected upon in the following paragraph.

HIV Education as a Social Vaccine

In the absence of HIV and AIDS vaccine and cure, there was consensus that education was the only alternative, thus the notion 'education as a social vaccine' (World Bank, 2002; Kelly & Bain, 2005; UNESCO, 2007; MoE, 2008). As such, the Ministry of Education in partnership with other stakeholders in Zambia embraced the integration of HIV education in the school curriculum along side the introduction of HIV prevention programmes. With HIV education in the school curriculum, it was assumed that young people would be equipped *with knowledge about HIV and AIDS and skills essential for HIV prevention. It was envisaged that, with increased information, knowledge and awareness, educated young people's behaviour will change faster in terms of delaying their sexual debut, reducing the number of partners, increasing condom use, and any other action that may lessen the risk of infection* (Chikwanda, 2015, p.62).

According to Breidlid (2015, p.12), *research seems to show that students have knowledge about the pandemic…* however he also noted that some *students are less able to relate this knowledge to their own situation by, for example, effecting behaviour change, [thus the question, does] the classroom provide the necessary tools or skills and the necessary language and is the teacher and the teaching materials authoritative enough to achieve the goal of HIV and AIDS education.*

This chapter therefore focused on Catholic schools in order to explore learners' rights to access information through HIV education in the context of social justice. Of the Catholic schools which were studied, only two constitute a reference point and therefore the findings in this chapter are not for purposes of generalisations as is the situation in case studies (Creswell, 2007).

Two Catholic schools were under study. One girls' secondary school privately run by the Catholic Church and the second was a grant-aided school for boys. Both girls and boys participated in the research and they constituted those from grade 11 and 12, in the age group of 15 – 19 years old. It was assumed that those in the two grades mentioned had enough stay in the school to be able to reflect on their experiences of HIV education in the school curriculum. Moreover, they were the end users of the content and learning activities in schools.

In addition, teachers as facilitators of learning and implementers of the curriculum were interviewed to explore what they taught and how they taught it in class. School administrators were also engaged to establish their positions on policies that related to HIV Education in the school.

LEARNERS' RIGHT TO ACCESS HIV EDUCATION IN THE CATHOLIC SCHOOLS

The study established that there was HIV education in Catholic schools that was embedded in the school curriculum and co - curricular activities. However, the kind of HIV education that was taught to the learners was basic and largely selective. For example, the teaching on HIV education consisted of definitions, modes of transmission and prevention messages, which largely was centred on Abstinence and Faithfulness to one partner. The format of presenting prevention messages coincided with the expectation of Church, but constitute basic information sharing without detailed or comprehensive discussion of alternative options available like condom use for those that are sexually active.

Strategies of Teaching HIV Education

The teaching howbeit selective was achieved through different strategies. These included the use of adages or slogans such as *virgin power, virgin pride, abstinence ili che* (translated 'Abstinence is good') eta cetera. Poems, role-play, or drama were used too. Posters with catchy prevention messages were displayed on notice boards assuming that passerby would read. This mode of delivery constituted the official discourse on HIV and AIDS as illustrated by Munachonga in her findings that, *the prominent message during assembly from the school management was that of abstinence as a preventive measure from HIV infection as well as pregnancy… it was evident that an abstinence discourse was prominent, but was not discussed in details… on how to abstain, and as a result they do not have the necessary skills they needed to uphold abstinence (2015, p.88).*

HIV education in the Catholic schools was accounted for in numerous ways, which could not be detached from cultural factors as well as Catholic teachings. Culturally, the idea that children and elders cannot converse about sexuality outside the initiation schools and parents reluctance to have children talked to by a stranger were the main reasons for the selective teaching of HIV education. More so, the teachers were not comfortable to talk about issues of sexuality and HIV, this was so because of their positionalities – cultural factors – taboo and having experienced HIV and AIDS in their own capacity and at family level.

In addition, the Catholic schools' emphasis on AB as opposed to ABC model had its own influence on what the teachers brought to class. According to the model, A stood for abstinence, B for being faithful and C for correct and consistent condom use. In the selective teaching of HIV education using the ABC MoE approved models, teachers were emphasising abstinence at the expense of being faithful and correct and consistent condom use, which to some extent was deprivation of correct information which learners needed much.

Teachers were of the opinion that discussing condom use was tantamount to encouraging learners to have sex. In addition, there was contention on the ABC model that the MoE wanted teachers to use in class. Some teachers argued that the Catholic Church's position on Abstinence was justified because of the conflict in messages that ensue from preaching about Being faithful to one partner and Correct and consistent use of the Condom along side Abstinence. Teachers' predicament in HIV education as illustrated earlier was consistent with the findings reported by Rasing (2003), that some teachers thought that children were not to be taught about condoms, because they were too young to have sex. In addition, Rasing observed that *although HIV and AIDS education at school has largely contributed to the knowledge about HIV and AIDS, there are still certain aspects that remain doubtful for some learners,* (2003, p. 12). Such doubts can only be attributed to the selective teaching and inadequacies associated with HIV and AIDS education taking place in our schools.

In this approach, teachers resorted to specialised teaching of HIV and AIDS related topics. They either taught, linking HIV and AIDS to certain components of the topics in an already existing curriculum or simply restrict it to basic components (biomedical facts). Selective teaching fragmented HIV and AIDS into a number of distinct subjects. Some of the subjects that had the topic of HIV, AIDS and related issues incorporated into their curriculum included, Biology (science), English (literature) and Religious Education.

In the case of the former, HIV and AIDS is placed within a biomedical framework as it relates to the human body. The topic is referred to as an example of the pathogenic diseases and its discussion focuses on *causative agents, signs and symptoms, methods of transmission and control* (MoE, 2002: 25), this manner of teaching adopted the medical or scientific discourse of HIV and AIDS.

In the English course for high school, HIV and AIDS is covered under unit three of English Comprehension. Using a passage on *healthy living*: Pupils read about different diseases including HIV and AIDS. Teachers facilitate learning through discussions to ascertain pupils' understanding of healthy living. Equally, the teacher can resort to teaching pronunciations using the same passage through pair work and plenary discussion, or the teacher can use the section to teach spellings by dictating words for pupils to spell (write). The teacher can also opt to use the same passage to teach summary and suggested methods are group work followed by class discussion. This can be grasped from the experience as explained by one of the male class teacher: *I normally talk about it [...] when I am teaching comprehension in English using a passage on HIV/AIDS, then I would go into details* (I_9, School G). The above circumstance will cover HIV and AIDS as it relates to healthy living, thus HIV and AIDS discussions and explanations will focus on nutrition for healthy living.

In Literature, pupils read about HIV and AIDS from a book on poems: *Echoes of Despair,* which contains various poems with HIV and AIDS information. For instance, *The Land Mine*; *The Commentator*; *HIV/AIDS Vs Humanity*; *Listen My Child*; and *who Will Burry us - the Young, the Old.* Teachers use different methods to relay the HIV and AIDS messages in the poems to pupils. This is done through plenary sessions, classroom presentations, and group discussions. However, the weakness with the Literature in English syllabus is the rotation of literature textbooks used. The book (*Echoes of Despair)* is the only one which has HIV and AIDS content and if the teacher chooses not to use it, then there is no guarantee that pupils will learn something related to HIV and AIDS during their course of study. The situation worsens when the rotation of books to be covered for a particular examination year takes place, implying that the next time the book will be used in the syllabus will be after three years.

The other subject that may cover HIV and AIDS is Religious Education (RE), which has two syllabi at high school level. These syllabi are RE 2046 and RE 2044 (MoE, 1984). The component on HIV and AIDS in the former (RE 2046) comes under Unit 7 and the theme of the unit is: *Jesus' power over diseases and nature.* RE 2044, which is commonly taught in all Catholic schools, HIV and AIDS as a topic is incorporated into the pupils' books but not included into the teachers' handbooks. As such, those teaching RE 2044 are not guided on how to integrate HIV/AIDS and related topics in their lessons. HIV and AIDS information is reflected as follows; Pupils should be able to: Understand the causes and effects of HIV/AIDS; understand the ways through which HIV can be contracted; and how to prevent themselves from infection. The RE 2044 syllabus content restricts HIV education to basic knowledge on the topic. Such objectives, which focus on pupil's understanding need to go beyond understanding to change in behaviour and ways of life among youths.

Any teacher may decide to leave out HIV and AIDS components taking for granted that other subject areas will look at them, especially in the sciences. If such occurs, selective teaching will go on unchallenged since the decisions of what to teach rest with the teacher, as a curriculum implementer at the classroom level. The preceding observation can be deduced from the reflections quoted from two (male) teachers, one from the girls' school and the other from the boys'. Both teachers are club patrons, the former coordinates debate club and the latter sports activities. One of them commented that, *people have talked too much about HIV and AIDS, hence people have the information* (I_2, School G). Such a concern may relate to information fatigue that results from uncoordinated approach to HIV education.

Teachers lack the knowledge of what colleagues cover in other subject areas and this results in ignorance of what pupils may already know about the topic from other study areas. Another example of selective teaching at the boys' school was cited when a male teacher explained how he taught the topic in his subject. An Industrial Arts teacher had the following to say;

In my subject, Technical Drawing, HIV and AIDS is infused into the topic on personal safety rules taught when handling sharp tools in the (Woodwork) workshop. Therefore, prevention information as it relates to injuries in the workshop avails the opportunity to talk about the risks involved in using sharp tools. We tell pupils that it is not only through sex that people contract HIV, but also through accidents that may occur when using sharp objects that have become contaminated with infected blood (I_{12}, School B).

The example given by the Arts teacher shows how teachers may relate their topics to HIV and AIDS. HIV and AIDS as was taught by this teacher was restricted to preventive information (ways of contracting HIV) with regards personal safety rules when handling sharp instruments that may be infected, not just in the workshop but in other places of work too. HIV education when taught selectively may lack the due visibility and is prone to disappear within the topics of host subject areas.

A review of some school textbooks showed that the theme is restricted to one or two units only. These units or topics are covered once in a school term. If the teacher in a specific subject area does not prioritise HIV and AIDS related topics, then pupils will have not learnt anything about it in that particular subject. Textbooks that touch on HIV and AIDS limit it to an example, which teachers can either regard or disregard. In class, teachers retain the autonomy of what to teach and what not to teach, especially if they are not guided in their teaching materials. They may decide not to integrate HIV education and pupils will be disadvantaged. Above all, selective teaching restricts HIV education.

Another way of relating to selective teaching of HIV education in the schools include use of slogan or catchy adages, recitation of poems, role - playing, use of posters (distributed by NGOs) and short briefings at the start of a lesson or during school assembly. Some of the factors that have been attributed to this approach of *selective teaching* of HIV and AIDS education include, cultural taboos that discourage elders from conversing about sexuality to youths, parental reluctance to entrust their children to others on matters that border on sexuality, teacher's positionalities – some teachers could be experiencing HIV and AIDS in their lives thus express discomfort, teacher unpreparedness in integrating the content in their subject area, and lack of teaching materials. Added to the list, is the school proprietors' position on HIV education that should be taught to learners. The catholic schools have been associated with Abstinence only approach. This strategy differs from the ABC model proposed by the Ministry of Education.

Learners' Right to Access HIV Education as a Social Justice

Presented with the challenge of HIV and AIDS, the government through the Ministry of Education, the Catholic schools and other stakeholders agreed on integrating HIV and AIDS education (Sex education, comprehensive sex education) in the school curriculum. The learner was the end user of the integrated content, and the justification for this target group was based on research findings that indicated the low HIV prevalence rates among the youths, also low knowledge levels of HIV and AIDS prevention knowledge.

Using the school as a social vaccine, the Ministry of Education prescribed age appropriate, subject specific content to be embedded in the school curriculum. An example of the official discourse on HIV and AIDS prevention that schools had to teach was the ABC model. Schools through its teachers and administrators had to relate to ABC messages in the school curriculum and co-curriculum activities. According to the model A stood for abstinence, B for being faithful and C for correct and consistent condom use. This anthem was to be blended with knowledge or information on HIV and AIDS (facts about HIV and AIDS), exposure to life skills and attitudes appropriate for behavioural change in the face of HIV and AIDS.

Like any other school, the Catholic schools were to be guided by the Ministry of Education position on HIV education. But, the school experience of HIV education in the Catholic schools revealed limitation in the implementation of HIV education. The content of HIV and AIDS education remained basic – knowledge about HIV and AIDS, modes of transmission and prevention (with emphasis on A - abstinence). The scenario depicted *selective teaching* depending on circumstances at play.

The Catholic schools are careful about the content that accompany HIV and AIDS education, thus the insistence on A as opposed to including B and C for learners at secondary school level. With that situation in place, learners are deprived of certain information which some of their colleagues are likely to receive in other learning space. Because of the different factors that lead to selective teaching in Catholic schools, learners' right to access HIV information is infringed upon. As expected, the Catholic schools are supposed to educate learners in a fair and just manner that prepare the latter to be change agents in society, but in the advent of HIV and AIDS, this role is overshadowed with selective teaching. Learners leave the schools inept in negotiating their way into the world of HIV and AIDS. Selective teaching of HIV and AIDS education leaves room for doubt on the type of learners that such schools would have prepared. It is assumed that with HIV education integrated in the school curriculum, learners would have acquired increased information, knowledge, and awareness on HIV and AIDS, that such learners' behaviour will change faster in terms of delaying their sexual debut and that they would take action that may lessen the risk of infection.

SOLUTIONS AND RECOMMENDATIONS

The major issue, which this chapter grappled with was the selective teaching of HIV and AIDS education in Catholic schools, to learners who had the right to access HIV and AIDS education from the school context. Given that teachers accounted for the major factor in the selective teaching of HIV and AIDS education, there is need for continued capacity building among teachers in pedagogical approaches that would help them integrate emerging issues of the curriculum. This should go hand in hand with appropriate curriculum reviews and integration of cross cutting issues in the twenty first century.

Ultimately, selective teaching of HIV and AIDS education in this chapter mirrored the inadequacies at different levels of education system (Ministry of Education, Catholic School Administration, Teachers in Catholic Schools and Community). Therefore, interventions should start with the reorientation of different stakeholders on HIV and AIDS education in the schools in relation to the guiding policies from the Ministry of Education.

CONCLUSION

The chapter reflected on learners' right to access HIV and AIDS education in the Catholics schools from a social justice perspective. It was established that HIV and AIDS education in the Catholic schools sampled was inadequate and failing learners in acquiring the necessary knowledge, skill and attitudes that would foster behavioural change in the face of HIV and AIDS. The schools as a social vaccine failed to play its role in preparing learners for social transformation.

REFERENCES

Breidlid, A., Cheyeka, A. M., & Farag, A. I. (Eds.). (2015). *Perspectives on youth, HIV/AIDS and indigenous knowledges in Africa*. Boston: Sense Publishers. doi:10.1007/978-94-6300-196-0

Carmody, B. (2004). *The evolution of education in Zambia*. Lusaka: Bookworld.

Central Statistical Office (CSO), Ministry of Health (MOH), and ICF International. (2014). *Zambia Demographic and Health Survey 2013-14*. Rockville, MD: Central Statistical Office, Ministry of Health, and ICF International.

Central Statistics Office. (2016). *Projected mid year population & projected eligible voter population*. Lusaka: CSO.

Chikwanda, T. (2015). HIV and AIDS and teacher education in Zambia. In A. Breidlid, A. M. Cheyeka, & A. I. Farag (Eds.), *Perspectives on youth, HIV/AIDS and indigenous knowledges in Africa* (pp. 61–76). Boston: Sense Publishers. doi:10.1007/978-94-6300-196-0_5

Kelly, M. J. (2000). *What HIV/AIDS can do to education and what education can do to HIV/AIDS*. Lusaka: UNZA.

Kelly, M. J. (2010). *HIV/AIDS: A social Justice Perspective*. Nairobi: Paulines Publications.

Kelly, M. J., & Bain, B. (2005). *Education and HIV/AIDS in the Caribbean*. Paris: IAN Randle Publishers.

Ministry of Education. (1996). *Educating our future*. Lusaka: Ministry of Education.

Ministry of Education. (2003). *HIV/AIDS guideline for educators*. Lusaka: Ministry of Education.

Ministry of Education. (2008). *Teaching in the window of hope: HIV/AIDS education for Zambian teachers*. Lusaka: Ministry of Education.

Munachonga, H. (2015). School and home sexuality discourse in selected girls' secondary schools in Lusaka. In A. Breidlid, A. M. Cheyeka, & A. I. Farag (Eds.), *Perspectives on youth, HIV/AIDS and indigenous knowledges in Africa* (pp. 77–96). Boston: Sense Publishers. doi:10.1007/978-94-6300-196-0_6

Mwanakatwe, J. M. (1968). *The Growth of education in Zambia since independence*. Lusaka: Oxford University Press.

National AIDS Council & Ministry of Health. (2015). *Global AIDS response progress reporting - Zambia country report: Monitoring the declaration of commitment on HIV and AIDS and the universal access*. UNGASS.

Rasing, T. (2003). *Love check: A game for children to prevent HIV/AIDS: Report of the game love check in Zambia*. WEB Foundation, Unpublished Report.

Snelson, P. (1974). *Educational development in northern Rhodesia 1883 – 1945*. Lusaka: Kenneth Kaunda Foundation.

UNESCO. (2007). *UNESCO's strategy for responding to HIV and AIDS*. Paris: IIEP.

World Bank. (2002). *Education and HIV/AIDS: A window of hope*. Washington, DC: World Bank.

ZEC. (2004). *A pastoral letter from the catholic bishops of Zambia on education: Empowerment through education*. Mission Press.

KEY TERMS AND DEFINITIONS

Catholic Education: Education provided by the Catholic Church in grant-aided schools with a catholic ethos in post-colonial Zambia.

Children: These are pupils in the age bracket 7-18 years in primary and secondary schools.

Curriculum: Sum total of learners' experiences in and outside the class as a subject package.

Fragmented: In relation to information, that which is delivered in piece meals.

HIV Education: Education about HIV and AIDS meant for the schools.

HIV/AIDS: A condition with multiple diseases that result in chronicle illness.

MoE: Ministry of Education – Zambia.

Teaching: The process in which pupils and teachers interact to bring about learning.

ZEC: Zambia Episcopal Conference – Mother body of the Catholic Church in Zambia, consisting of Catholic Bishops overseeing dioceses.

Chapter 9
Interagency Collaboration to Improve School Outcomes for Students With Mental Health Challenges

Kristina Bixler
Indiana University, USA

Jeffrey Alvin Anderson
Indiana University, USA

ABSTRACT

Students with significant emotional-behavioral concerns and mental illness tend to experience poor educational and social outcomes. This chapter describes some of the challenges facing schools that are responsible for educating students with and at-risk for mental health challenges. Although some students encounter numerous risks, thereby increasing the chances of developing mental illness and failing school, there are also protective factors that can be identified and harnessed to counterbalance such risks and promote higher levels of resilience. By examining relationships among factors such as poverty, mental well-being, family engagement, resiliency, and school performance, a school-focused, community-based framework is suggested for responding to and overcoming these challenges. This chapter provides practical guidelines for schools, community agencies, and families to work together to support and engage young people who are at-risk for school failure due to emotional-behavioral concerns and mental health challenges.

INTRODUCTION

Partnerships among families, schools, and communities can be created and harnessed to support academic achievement for students with mental health needs (e.g. Adelman, & Taylor, 2006a; Adelman & Taylor, 2006b; Anderson, 2002; Conwill, 2003). Practitioners and researchers alike are now calling for a broader focus on collaborative efforts in schools and children's social services that include

DOI: 10.4018/978-1-5225-2578-3.ch009

prevention, in addition to targeted early and intense interventions, across child-serving systems (e.g., education, health, child welfare, etc.) (Anderson & Cornell, 2015). The significance of this chapter is that it provides a practical orientation for schools and community agencies to work together, along with families, to successfully engage students, particularly young people who are at-risk for school failure due to emotional-behavioral concerns and mental health challenges. First, the chapter describes some of the challenges facing primary and secondary schools that are responsible for educating students with mental health challenges by examining the interconnected relationships among poverty, mental health, and school performance. The authors then argue that in this field, much of the research base examining academic failure has been limited by focusing on risk factors, often to the exclusion of critically important individual variation within subgroups of children with and at-risk for mental health challenges. While such research has uncovered important risks that correlate with school failure, our narrow attention on risks has reduced our ability to understand how resiliency influences academic and social development.

Once a better understanding of risk and resiliency has been established, the second goal of this chapter is to provide a practical guide for developing interagency prevention and intervention approaches, designed to bring together the entire community resource pool to reduce the number of students who fail in school due to unmet mental health needs. Interagency collaboration has been defined as "the process of agencies joining together for the purpose of interdependent problem-solving which focuses on improving services to children and families…" (Hodges, Hernandez, & Nesman, 2003, p. 292). Current policy implications supporting school-based interagency collaboration also are presented. It is further argued that by using resiliency within a collaborative model consisting of individual, family, community, and school assets, effective pedagogical and social approaches can be applied that allow young people with and at-risk for mental illness to succeed in and out of school. A number of well-known preventative and early intervention models are described. Finally, some specific steps for creating models of interagency collaboration are discussed.

BACKGROUND

Although the relationships between school functioning and mental health challenges are not fully understood (Epstein, Nelson, Trout, & Mooney, 2005), scholars have suggested wide-ranging interactions among school and non-school factors may be at fault, which can include clinical, familial, and environmental variables (Anderson, 2011). Explanations for the poor academic achievement for students with emotional challenges have included (1) poor grades leading to aggression; (2) aggression leading to poor grades; (3) a reciprocal relationship between poor grades and emotional challenges; and (4) other underlying factors that cause both poor grades and emotional challenges (Epstein et al., 2005; Barriga, Dorans, Newell, Morrison, Barbetti, & Robbins, 2002). Adelman and Taylor (2006a; b) described a continuum with causes from environmental factors, causes coming from within the person, and a transactional view caused by an interaction between the environment and the individual.

STUDENTS WITH MENTAL HEALTH RISKS

In the United States (U.S.), students with mental illness often have been labelled by the mental health community as having *serious emotional disturbances* and/or by schools as having *emotional disabilities*[1] (e.g., Anderson & Mohr, 2003). These terms can encompass numerous other labels and diagnoses such as conduct disorders and emotional-behavioral disabilities. Furthermore, this chapter expands the focus beyond young people with the most significant mental health challenges to also include students who may not be formally labelled but nonetheless are at great risk for school failure due to mental health challenges. While the percentage of young people identified as having significant mental health challenges has been estimated in the 3-6% range, when students who are at-risk are included, this figure increases significantly (e.g., Anderson, 2016). The purpose of taking the more expansive position of including youth who are at-risk is to promote capacity building for models in schools and communities for earlier intervention and prevention of mental illness (Anderson & Cornell & Cornell, 2015).

Overall, the population of students who have or are at-risk for mental health challenges has been documented as failing or risking failure across a wide range of domains, including home, school, and community (see e.g., Bradley, Henderson, & Monfore, 2004). Although researchers have indicated that as much as one-fifth of children in the United States has been diagnosed with a mental health disorder, only a small percentage of them will receive treatment (Rones & Hoagwood, 2000). It is estimated further that more than 40% of the young people experiencing these kinds of challenges will exhibit externalising behaviours aggressive enough to result in school suspensions. It is doubtful that students with serious behavioural challenges are effectively serviced by their schools (e.g., Walker, Ramsey, & Gresham, 2004); thus, the authors argue, schools need additional supports to assist this population of students in succeeding in school.

In fact, poor progress and outcomes for this population of young people has been documented in every school domain, including attendance, achievement, school behavior, social skills such as friendships with peers or relationships with teachers, involvement in extra-curricular activities, secondary graduation, and successful progression to post-high school work or training (Bub, McCartney, & Willet, 2007; Lopes, 2007; Reinke, Herman, Petras, & Ialongo, 2008; U.S. Department of Education, 1998; 2001; Vitaro, Brendgen, Larose, & Trembaly, 2005). Although researchers who study risks and resiliency for youth with mental health challenges advocate for increased focus on modifying negative trends (Edgeland, Carlson, & Stroufe, 1993; Wong, & Donahue, 2002), the continued reliance on using methods that emphasize risks to the exclusion of identifying protective factors may be limiting the growth and development of the field (Anderson, Howland, & McCoach, 2015).

Risk and Resiliency

Risk factors for mental illness can include internal influences, such as biological and psychological risks, as well as external influences like family and community risks (Trussell, 2008). Biological risks include those that can impact the central nervous system and development of the child and can increase the potential that students will have difficult dispositions and poor social and problem-solving skills (Garmezy, 1993; Trussell, 2008). Such difficulties can stem from prenatal damage such as exposure to alcohol, drugs, and/or malnutrition during pregnancy (Trussell, 2008). Psychological factors are described as "individual personality characteristics that are associated with poor future outcomes" (Trussell, 2008, p. 150). Depression, substance abuse, other mental health issues, and ineffective parental role models are some examples of psychological risk factors (Reid & Eddy, 1997). These kinds of psychological concerns also appear to be more prevalent in people who experience socioeconomic disadvantages and the consequential environmental stresses (Webster-Stratton, 1990; Webster-Stratton & Hammond, 1998).

The relationships children form with their families and the people around them help develop their personalities and their ability to connect with others (e.g., Anderson & Mohr, 2003). Children who grow up in abusive or neglectful homes may have difficulty forming healthy, loving relationships with others and struggle to regulate their own emotions (Toth & Cicchetti, 2004; Trussell, 2008; Barnett, 1997). Research has shown that those who have difficulty developing healthy relationships are at greater risk for depression and substance abuse (Toth & Cicchetti, 2004). Children who have grown up in abusive environments also may avoid intimacy or displaying emotions and may have higher rates of aggressive behaviour or harming others (Trussell, 2008). Children with these risk factors are almost twice as likely to be arrested during adolescence (Toth & Cicchetti, 2004).

Family difficulties, stressful life events, and community risks such as crime and high levels of poverty, are examples of external influences that can negatively impact students with mental health challenges. Family risks are considered to include those characteristics of a family that can be detrimental to a child's development such as "severe parental conflict, overcrowding within the home, and a parental history of criminal behaviour or psychopathology" (Trussell, 2008, p. 150; Toth & Cicchetti, 2004). Families experiencing significant poverty or economic difficulties may experience higher levels of stress, increasing risks for abuse or neglect due to lack of parental engagement (Baydar, Reid, & Webster-Stratton, 2003). Stressful life events, which cause undue hardship on a family, such as the death of a parent, parental divorce, and surviving a life-threatening experience (Trussell, 2008), can also increase the risks for school challenges. Living in situations of significant poverty can increase exposure to parental stress during infancy. This can lead to emotional dysregulation, which in turn increases children's risks for developing more negative symptoms in elementary school (Essex, Kraemer, Armstrong, Boyce, Goldsmith, Klein, Woodward, & Kuper, 2006).

Risk factors, experienced in isolation or cumulatively, can increase the likelihood of negative or undesirable outcomes in school and other life domains. However, the presence of risk alone does not lead to poor outcomes for all children (Oldfield, Hebron, & Humphrey, 2016). Although greater risk is associated with the likelihood of experiencing negative outcomes, such as school failure (Garmezy & Marsten, 1986; Rutter, 1985; Werner & Smith, 2001), not everyone in a given risk group will fail; nor will all of the members of a specific group experience similar levels of risk. Indeed, when data are aggregated, risk status is not equal for all students with mental health challenges (Anderson, Howland, & McCoach, 2014). Students who are resilient to various risks tend to possess protective factors. For example, Werner and Smith (1992), described five factors or attributes that may reduce the negative influences of risks: 1) having an even temperament; 2) having a positive and meaningful relationship with an adult; 3) having an outside support system to help develop self-confidence; 4) having an interest in one's own future by setting goals and making decisions; and 5) being of average intelligence. Researchers have noted that students who are more resilient may possess certain protective skills, know their self-worth, and/or have had effective parenting (Masten, 2006).

Resiliency also appears better developed when students have parents who are caring, nurturing, and communicate openly with their children (Trussell, 2008). Likewise, scholars have pointed out that schools need to be considered among the most potentially powerful protective factors. Through instructional practices, curriculum, teacher perceptions, social support, and community building, schools can encourage and support resiliency in children (Masten, 2006; Trussell, 2008). Young people come to school with a variety of academic, behavioural, and social strengths and needs. In spite of the levels of individual need, attending an effective school correlates with how successful a student will be in school (Masten, 2006). On the other hand, attending under-resourced or ineffective schools can present another set of risks to students' learning and social development (e.g., Chen, Anderson, & Watkins, 2016). The literature examining what it means to be an ineffective school has identified common themes, including a) lack of materials and supplies, b) overcrowded classrooms, c) teachers who are inadequately trained, d) staff turnover, e) high absence rates by students and staff, and f) a highly mobile student population (Trussell, 2008). Therefore, researchers have demonstrated that learning best occurs when healthy, reciprocal relationships exist among families, schools, and communities (Kim, Sheridan, Kwon, & Koziol, 2013).

Legal Support for School-Based Interagency Collaboration

Unfortunately, under-resourced schools tend to have a harder time building and sustaining resiliency in their students (Chen et al., 2016). In the U.S., during the years following the passage of the Federal No Child Left Behind (NCLB) legislation in 2001, it became increasingly clear that the patterns of poor academic outcomes observed in many under-resourced schools were going to be difficult to reverse (Blank, Melville, & Shah, 2003; Dryfoos, 2005; Tagle, 2005). During this time period, advocates called for more and better involvement of families in schools and more support from community social service agencies, especially in schools serving poor and disadvantaged neighbourhoods and populations (Dryfoos, 2000; Harris & Wilkes, 2013). With the U.S.'s recent passage of Every Student Succeeds Act (ESSA), which replaced NCLB in late 2015, some of those same advocates are expressing hope because the new law emphasises authentic family engagement in schools, as well substantive community involvement. According to the National Center for Mental Health in Schools (NCMHS, 2016), ESSA is intended to "(1) significantly improve the academic and developmental outcomes of children living in the most distressed communities of the United States, including ensuring school readiness, high school graduation, and access to a community-based continuum of high-quality services; and (2) provide support for the planning, implementation, and operation of full-service community schools that improve the coordination and integration, accessibility, and effectiveness of services for children and families, particularly for children attending high-poverty schools, including high-poverty rural schools." Moreover, the authors stated that ESSA clearly acknowledges that the coordination and integration of community support services in schools is necessary for overcoming barriers to learning and teaching (NCMHS, 2016). This follows efforts by the U.S. Department of Education (2000) to set expectations for schools to deliver practices that foster mental health well-being. Schools are the ideal environment for students to learn the academic, behaviour, and social skills necessary for developing into healthy young adults (e.g., Anderson, 2016; Anderson, 2016; Powers, 2002).

Supporting Under-Resourced Schools

Scholars have argued that service coordination and integration can help under-resourced schools increase their effectiveness (Anderson & Cornell, 2015; Dryfoos, 1994; 2005). By strengthening family social support networks, interagency collaboration can help to expand opportunities for parents, schools, and agencies to work together. Interagency collaboration also can help increase the interconnectedness of schools and their neighbourhoods (e.g., Coleman, 1988). For example, support for finding stable housing and employment counselling can be offered to parents and caregivers within their children's schools by community agencies (Anderson, 2000). Mental health screenings can be provided in schools by clinicians from nearby community mental health centres. Moreover, by providing the organizational framework for schools, communities, and families to work together in creating multi-tiered systems of supports, school-based approaches can provide the kinds of supports necessary to help children and youth with or at-risk for emotional-behavioral challenges succeed in school, while simultaneously supporting youths' families and teachers (Anderson & Cornell, 2015).

Drawing from *community schools* approaches (Dryfoos, 2005) in education and systems of care initiatives in the children's mental health field (Stroul & Friedman, 1986; Stroul & Blau, 2010), contemporary interagency frameworks in schools provide children and their families, as well as teachers and administrators, access to a variety of community supports (e.g., caregiver support groups, behavioral training for adults who work with students) and services (e.g., family case management, therapeutic services, residential treatment facilities) to address the wide range of possible physical, emotional, academic, and social needs students may be experiencing that can interfere with learning (Rones & Hoagwood, 2000). In such a framework, each system, agency, and school commit to operating under a community-wide tiered network or system of support. Partners, including families, collaborate with the goal of supporting individuals, schools, and families, to improve the overall functioning of students with and at-risk for mental health challenges and school failure (e.g., Chen et al., 2016).

As the focus of these collaborative efforts has shifted from children with mental illness and their families to the entire population of young people within a community, broader, more comprehensive approaches to interagency collaboration that include prevention are being created (Anderson, 2016). Services and supports are not only being offered in schools, but agencies and schools are starting to collaborate in new and innovative ways (Anderson & Cornell, 2015). For example, in one interagency model called the Full Purpose Partnership (FPP), located in Indianapolis, Indiana, *care coordinators* who act as case managers for the school and community are housed within participating schools (Anderson et al., 2010). These care coordinators are responsible for implementing four components core to the FPP model: (a) effective curricula and instruction; (b) inquiry driven, data-based decision-making; (c) systems of care and wraparound principles (including authentic family involvement; strengths-based practice; cultural competence; and interagency collaboration); and (d) school-wide positive behavior supports. Each of these components is conceptualised through a three-tiered system of school-wide supports (Sugai & Horner, 22002), focusing on prevention, early intervention, and comprehensive intervention. Borrowing heavily from positive behavior interventions and supports, which in turn was adopted from the field of public health (Walker, Ramsey, & Gresham, 2004), the multi-tiered system simultaneously coordinates prevention (what schools do to ensure that all students are successful); early intervention (what schools do to intervene quickly and effectively when students experience challenges); and comprehensive intervention (what happens when students are experiencing chronic levels of school challenges).

Community-school collaborations like the FPP make it easier to identify gaps in community service networks, thus allowing for the creation of new services and supports to fill those gaps. The ultimate goal is that each child serving system or agency, including schools, will collaborate to offer prevention efforts at the base level and more intensive targeted services to smaller numbers of individuals as needed (Anderson et al., 2010). Another goal is to move away from children's social services systems that historically were expert-driven, overly restrictive, fragmented and uncoordinated, costly, absent, or separated from the natural settings where children's challenges occur (Johnson, Zorn, Yung Tam, Lamontagne, & Johnson, 2003; Stroul & Blau, 2010). By offering services and supports that are family-driven, youth-guided, and grounded in strengths orientations, caregivers are empowered to become decision-making partners in the planning of such services (e.g., Anderson, Wright, Smith, & Kooreman, 2007; Atkins, Hoagwood, Kutash, & Seidman, 2010).

Educating Students At-Risk for School Failure

With the passage of ESSA in the U.S., schools now have a clear legislative mandate to connect school and community supports through collaborations among educators, families, and communities. A beginning framework for the systematic integration will require schools and their communities to "(1) coalesce existing student and learning supports into a cohesive component and (2) over a period of several years, develop the component into a comprehensive intervention system that is fully interwoven into instructional efforts. Such a component is key to enabling all students to have an equal opportunity to learn at school and all teachers to teach effectively. This type of systematic approach is especially important where large numbers of students are not succeeding" (NCMHS, 2016; p. 15). It is clear that students need to experience success to increase their resiliency and that schools are ideal places for success to occur (e.g., Keogh, 2000). Thus, a critical area of importance for schools is the use of effective classroom methods (Wang, Haertel, & Walberg, 1998). For example, teachers can use evidenced-based practices for instruction to improve opportunities for students to succeed. This is particularly important for students who are at-risk for various types of school failure. Researchers have shown that teachers improve learning by creating safe and caring environments where students feel comfortable taking risks and by using positive behavioural techniques such as verbal praise and positive reinforcement to enhance student learning and classroom management (e.g., Jones & Jones, 2015). Most teachers understand that their own teaching styles can create increased risks for students (Trussell, 2008). It is well understood that teachers should avoid yelling or using negative verbal remarks, which may potentially cause students to be disruptive or disengaged (e.g., Anderson & Mohr 2003). Educators should also realise that some students have deficits in prerequisite skills that may interfere with their ability to meet the grade level requirements. Likewise, curricular content should be interesting and flexible enough to address the individual strengths and needs of students (e.g., Adelman, & Taylor, 2006a; b). When developing school curriculum, educators should not only incorporate student interests into the curriculum, they should plan for the necessary attention and instructional remediation, to ensure that their students who are at-risk for failure have necessary opportunities to succeed (Trussell, 2008; Brooks, 2006).

Teacher perceptions and expectations of their students also influence how successful students are in school (Anderson, Howland, & McCoach, 2014). Both teachers and students view antisocial peers in negative ways (Walker et al., 2004); therefore, teachers need to be trained in classroom management skills such as posting rules and consequences, setting behavior goals for classrooms and individuals, and following through with the management plan for the class (Jones & Jones, 2013). Educators who spend time with and learn to understand both the challenges and strengths of their students who are at higher risk for school failure can serve as an important protective factor for this population of students (Brooks, 2006; Trussell, 2008). At-risk students who have a positive relationship with an adult tend to be more successful in dealing with challenging situations and are more likely to succeed (Werner & Smith, 1992; Trussell, 2008). Another protective factor for students at-risk is social support. Friendships with peers and adults provide an important source of social support, which can act as a buffer for students who have experienced a stressful life event (Werner & Smith, 1992; Brooks, 2006; Trussell, 2008). Resilient students are more likely to turn to their friends during times of crises (Werner, 1989). Thus, schools should provide opportunities for students who are at risk for failure to develop relationships with peers and adults. In fact, an important goal of schools should be to help students develop social competence (Consortium on the School-Based Promotion of Social Competence [CRPSC], 1994). Social competence involves students working on their citizenship skills, which include: problem-solving, assertive decision-making, communicating clearly, regulating emotions, managing and resolving conflict, resisting pressure from peers, and developing positive personal relationships (CRPSC, 1994; Farrell, Meyer, & White, 2001; Griffin, Botvin, Nichols, & Doyle, 2003).

Schools can work to improve and ensure positive outcomes for all students, including students at higher risks for failure, and promote resiliency by building a strong sense of community both in classrooms and throughout the entire school (Battistich, Schaps, Watson, & Solomon, 1996). By creating warm and caring environments where students feel safe and valued and by teachers providing effective instruction, educators are helping students succeed (Battistich et al., 1996). At the school level, a governance body is established, directly involving parents and caregivers as decision-making partners, designed to eliminate territorial issues among partnering community agencies. Support for teachers to use the best, evidenced-based instructional and classroom management practices is provided, as is assistance for teachers to connect and stay connected with the families of their students. Incentives, benchmarks and expectations for interagency collaboration are developed, implemented, and monitored. The governance group systematically builds linkages among schools, families, systems, and agencies to support broader goals of community wellness and improved overall functioning for students, their families, as well as teachers and administrators (see, e.g., Anderson & Cornell, 2015).

Examples of School-Based Approaches

School-based interagency programs should incorporate universal preventative interventions that focus on students' social and problem-solving skills (Anderson et al., 2010). Preventative interventions need to target all students, with a specific focus on young people who are at a higher risk for developing emotional-behavioral difficulties. This is especially important for youth who may "fall through the cracks"; which is when students exhibit symptoms and signs but do not qualify for services (Chen et al., 2016). Many different preventative programs have been developed for schools. Such approaches can vary but they typically assist students in developing and using appropriate social and emotional skills. For example, Promoting Alternative Thinking Strategies (PATHS) is a school-based prevention program that "aims to increase children's ability to discuss and understand emotions, facilitate the development of self-control, promote a positive peer climate, and enhance interpersonal problem-solving skills" (Rones & Hoagwood, 2000, p. 229). Another prevention program, Linking the Interests of Families and Teachers (LIFT), is designed to prevent or reduce aggressive and antisocial behaviour for elementary students who live in neighbourhoods with high crime rates (Rones & Hoagwood, 2000). The Family and Schools Together (FAST) Track program targets kindergarten students who are oppositional and aggressive. Researchers have noted that students who completed FAST were less likely to be referred to special education and exhibited less aggressive and oppositional behaviour than those who did not receive these services (Rones & Hoagwood, 2000). The Life Skills Training (LST) Program is a skills-based substance abuse program, which teaches students skills on how to manage anxiety, build self-esteem and relationships, communicate effectively, be assertive, and resist peer pressure (Rones & Hoagwood, 2000).

In addition, the Kaleidoscope program is a rapid response program designed by the Indianapolis Public School system in Indiana to provide supports for students who are experiencing difficulties with their behaviour in the school setting, as well as for their teachers and families (Wang, Cornell, & Anderson, 2016). In brief, the program theory is that students who start exhibiting behaviour problems in school can be assisted through intensive, comprehensive interventions before challenges escalate. While the purpose is to intervene early to prevent the need for more intensive interventions and placements, when necessary, the program also guides the process for students who require more intensive support (e.g., special education services). Kaleidoscope uses a team-based approach, pairing a behaviour specialist and social worker who provide coordinated services and supports across home, school, and community. An example of team efforts can include: 1) designing intervention plans, which include interventions at home and school; 2) relationship building among caregivers and school personnel; 3) educating parents about how to communicate with professionals in their community; 4) educating teachers and other school professionals about classroom management; 5) educating families, teachers, and other school professionals about how mental health related issues can affect learning; 6) conducting environmental assessment and modifications to increase opportunities for learning; and 7) easing frustrations among the adults living and working with youth experiencing mental health challenges. Kaleidoscope staff members are also trained to navigate the organisational culture already in place in the schools in which they work and then assist educators in building healthy engagement with the parents of students in those schools.

School-based interagency programs tend to have similar components, such as flexibility and individualization (e.g., Chen et al., 2016). Programs often include opportunities for teaching parents and teachers to use effective behaviour management skills. These preventative programs can be integrated into the general education curriculum and, of course, need to be developmentally appropriate for the students (Rones & Hoagwood, 2000). To be successful, Rones and Hoagwood (2009) stated that clear, specific guidelines are needed clarifying how the program should be implemented. Teachers, caregivers, and others actually implementing the program should receive feedback about their efforts and school leaders need to support teachers by funding both the training and maintenance sessions as well as monitor program fidelity (e.g., Anderson et al., 2010).

Guidance for Developing Interagency Frameworks

Interagency collaboration can reduce fragmentation and redundancy and allow service gaps to be identified and filled. However, to have effective interagency collaboration, schools and community agencies must have dedicated staff, be willing to understand and respond to philosophical differences, and have appropriate funding and time for such engagement (Anderson-Butcher & Ashton, 2004; Gonsoulin & Read, 2011). While most child-serving agencies have their own funding and management systems, these functions may conflict with the ability of the agencies to work together (Anderson, 2000; Anderson, 2000; Tapper, Kleinman, & Nakashian, 1997; Johnson et al., 2003). Thus, systems, schools, and agencies have to be willing to share relevant information to coordinate the most effective configurations of services and supports for each participating child and her or his family (Johnson et al., 2003; Gonsoulin & Read, 2011).

Arguably the key component of effective interagency collaboration is sustaining clear and open communication and cooperation with the other agencies (e.g., Chen et al., 2016). When students are involved with two or more agencies, someone will need to coordinate meetings and facilitate shared decision-making. Scheduling these meetings is not easy and takes time and resources (Tapper et al., 1997; Gonsoulin & Read, 2011). One straightforward task to develop frameworks and infrastructure for interagency collaboration is the creation of memoranda of understanding (MOU). The MOU can serve many purposes but at a minimum, it can clearly outline how participating agencies and schools will share information regarding the needs of specific students, such as demographic information, information about strengths and challenges and data related from student records (Gonsoulin & Read, 2011). For example, if a goal is improved school attendance, information about current and future performance will be needed. Developing MOUs allows all partners to delineate both how and what information will be shared, which can include medical records, information about the family, and educational records (Gonsoulin & Read, 2011). MOUs should also clearly address confidentiality and specific procedures in terms of what information can be shared, how it can be shared, with whom the information can be shared, and who from each agency will grant permission for the sharing of information (Tapper et al., 1997; Gonsoulin & Read, 2011). By outlining the information and goals shared, this establishes trust among the partners. Leaders from all partnering agencies and schools, along with legal staff, can help navigate the MOU, ensuring compliance with national, state, and local laws (Gonsoulin & Read, 2011). Further, by sharing fiscal responsibility and staff, the interagency team can benefit from the expertise of multiple disciplines (e.g., health, education, social work), while working to eliminate duplication of services and fill in service gaps (Tapper et al., 1997; Gonsoulin & Read, 2011). However, the sharing of funds can be a complicated process, which often requires changes in existing policy and law. Many public and private agencies have to provide evidence regarding their collaboration efforts in order to receive funding (Gonsoulin & Read, 2011).

These partnerships continue to benefit all stakeholders in the community (Anderson-Butcher, 2004). The benefits include teachers, families, and counsellors understanding the many issues students may be facing; increased support among school professionals and the families; and more effective psycho-educational programs for youth with mental challenges (Tourse & Sulick, 1999). Research has shown that students have increased academic achievement and reduced behaviour issues due to interagency collaboration (Smith, Armijo, & Stowitschek, 1997). Collaboration among agencies has helped improve school attendance for students in addition to the quality of the students' learning experiences (Hatch, 1998). Anderson (2011) found that school functioning significantly improved between the time students enrolled in a local community-based interagency system of care and up to 36 months, post-enrollment. Moreover, these longitudinal improvements also were found to be significantly associated with improved clinical functioning over time. In an earlier study, Manteuffel, Stephens, and Santiago (2002) also reported that school performance and attendance improved from enrollment in a system of care to two years post enrollment for a national sample of young people served by interagency systems of care.

CONCLUSION

Emphasising a strengths orientation to service provision and authentically partnering with families have dramatically changed how society works with young people with mental illness, and their families (Anderson, 2011). Indeed, best practices now require that children's mental health and social services be *family-driven* and *youth-guided* (Stroul & Blau, 2010). Perhaps the most challenging aspect of such interagency initiatives is building and then sustaining trusting relationships not only among service providers but with the child and family. Personnel from schools and child-serving agencies must first acknowledge that children and their families are experts about their own circumstances. Thus, students and families will be considered as full partners in all teaming, treatment, and decision-making processes. Gonsoulin and Read (2011) provided a number of practical suggestions for working with families: 1) schedule meetings when it is convenient for the family; 2) ask the family to define their basic interests and needs; 3) define roles of family and participating professionals; 4) find local support groups for the family; 5) provide child care for the family to facilitate meeting attendance; 6) arrange for transportation for families to attend the meetings; 7) provide food, snacks, and beverages when meetings occur during mealtimes; 8) use technology (email, phone conferences, and web conferences) to eliminate unnecessary face-to-face meetings; 9) ensure that children and family are empowered not only to share their own stories but to take leadership roles in these processes; and 10) eliminate the use of professional jargon. The authors recommend that professionals start by adopting and adhering to these simple suggestions.

Viewed as a way to overcome intractable patterns of educational failure occurring in many seriously under-resourced communities, interagency collaborative initiatives are emerging in schools and children's social services across the U.S and elsewhere. Combined with other recent innovations such as multi-tiered student supports (MTSS), Response-to-Intervention (RtI), and trauma-informed service provision, these kinds of partnerships offer multiple pathways for schools to better achieve their primary goal of academic growth for all students, including young people at higher risks of school failure. Moreover, the recent ESSA legislation in the U.S. highlights the importance of supporting learning through organised networking and collaboration among educators, families, and community social services agencies. However, it is critical that school-community partnerships and authentic family involvement in schools do not become just another educational "fad" that comes along, consumes a lot of time and resources, and then fades away. With appropriate development and support for communication, coordination and wide-ranging community backing, schools and community agencies can begin to think and act in new ways.

REFERENCES

Adelman, H. S., & Taylor, L. (2006a). *The school leader's guide to student learning supports New directions for addressing barriers to learning*. Thousand Oaks, CA: Corwin Press.

Adelman, H. S., & Taylor, L. (2006b). *The implementation guide to student learning supports in the classroom and schoolwide: New directions for addressing barriers to learning*. Thousand Oaks, CA: Corwin Press.

Anderson, J. A. (2000). The need for interagency collaboration for children with emotional and behavior disabilities and their families. *Families in Society*, *81*(5), 484–493. doi:10.1606/1044-3894.1050

Anderson, J. A. (2011). Patterns of school functioning over time among students served in a system of care. *Remedial and Special Education*, *32*(6), 482–495. doi:10.1177/0741932510364545

Anderson, J. A. (2016). Is an ounce of prevention still worth a pound of cure? Community-based interagency collaboration to enhance student and family wellbeing (guest editorial). *School Community Journal*, *26*(1), 9–29.

Anderson, J. A., & Cornell, H. (2015). *Full Service Community Schools: A comprehensive education model for providing comprehensive supports for students and their families.* In 8th Annual International Conference on Education, Research and Innovation, ICERI2015. Retrieved from http://library.iated.org/view/ANDERSON2015FUL

Anderson, J. A., Houser, J. H., & Howland, A. A. (2010). The Full Purpose Partnership model for promoting academic and socio-emotional success in schools. *School Community Journal*, *20*(1), 31–54.

Anderson, J. A., Howland, A. A., & McCoach, B. (2015). Modeling resiliency in the prevention of special education identification. *Preventing School Failure*, *59*(2), 63–72. doi:10.1080/1045988X.2013.837811

Anderson, J. A., & Mohr, W. K. (2003). A developmental ecological perspective in systems of care for children with serious emotional disturbances and their families. *Education & Treatment of Children*, *26*(1), 52–74.

Anderson, J. A., Wright, E. R., Smith, J. S., & Kooreman, H. E. (2007). Educational profiles of students at enrollment in a system of care. *Remedial and Special Education*, *28*(1), 9–20. doi:10.1177/0741932 5070280010201

Anderson-Butcher, D., & Ashton, D. (2004). Innovative Models of Collaboration to Serve Children, Youths, Families, and Communities. *Children & Schools*, *26*(1), 39–53. doi:10.1093/cs/26.1.39

Atkins, M. S., Hoagwood, K. E., Kutash, K., & Seidman, E. (2010). Toward the integration of education and mental health in schools. *Administration and Policy in Mental Health and Mental Health Services Research*, *37*(1-2), 40–47. doi:10.1007/s10488-010-0299-7 PMID:20309623

Barnett, D. (1997). The effects of early intervention on maltreating parents and their children. In M. J. Guralnick (Ed.), *The effectiveness of early intervention* (pp. 147–170). Baltimore, MD: Brookes.

Barriga, A. Q., Dorans, J. W., Newell, S. B., Morrison, E. M., Barbetti, V., & Robbins, B. D. (2002). Relationships between problem behaviors and academic achievement in adolescents: The unique role of attention problems. *Journal of Emotional and Behavioral Disorders*, *10*(4), 233–240. doi:10.1177/1 06342660201000405O1

Battistich, V., Schaps, E., Watson, M., & Solomon, D. (1996). Prevention effects of the Child Development Project: Early findings from an ongoing multisite demonstration trial. *Journal of Adolescent Research*, *11*(1), 12–35. doi:10.1177/0743554896111003

Baydar, N., Reid, M. J., & Webster-Stratton, C. (2003, September). The role of mental health factors and program engagement in the effectiveness of a preventive parenting program for head start mothers. *Child Development*, *74*(5), 1433–1453. doi:10.1111/1467-8624.00616 PMID:14552407

Blank, M. J., Melville, A., & Shah, B. P. (2003). *Making the difference: Research and practice in community schools.* Retrieved from ERIC database. (ED499103)

Bradley, R., Henderson, K., & Monfore, D. A. (2004). A national perspective on children with emotional disorders. *Behavioral Disorders*, *29*, 211–223.

Brooks, J. E. (2006). Strengthening resilience in children and youths: Maximizing Opportunities through Schools. *Children & Schools*, *28*(2), 69–76. doi:10.1093/cs/28.2.69

Bub, K. L., McCartney, K., & Willett, J. B. (2007). Behavior problem trajectories and first-grade cognitive ability and achievement skills: A latent growth curve analysis. *Journal of Educational Psychology*, *99*(3), 653–670. doi:10.1037/0022-0663.99.3.653

Chen, M. E., Anderson, J. A., & Watkins, L. (2016). Parent perceptions of connectedness in a full service community school project. *Journal of Child and Family Studies*, (25): 7, 2268–2278. doi:10.1007/ s10826-016-0398-5

Consortium on the School-Based Promotion of Social Competence. (1994). The school-based promotion of social competence: Theory, research, practice, and policy. In R. J. Haggerty, L. R. Sherrod, N. Gramezy, & M. Rutter (Eds.), *Stress, risk, and resilience in children and adolescents: Processes, mechanisms, and interventions* (pp. 268–316). Cambridge, UK: Cambridge University Press.

Conwill, W. L. (2003). Consultation and collaboration: An action research model for the full-service school. *Consulting Psychology Journal: Practice and Research, 55*(4), 239–248. doi:10.1037/1061-4087.55.4.239

Dryfoos, J. (2000). *Evaluation of community schools: Findings to date.* Retrieved from ERIC database. (ED450204)

Dryfoos, J. (2005). *Community schools in action: Lessons from a decade of practice.* Oxford University Press.

Dryfoos, J. G. (1994). *Full-Service Schools.* San Francisco: Jossey-Bass.

Egeland, B., Carlson, E., & Stroufe, L. (1993). Developmental Psychopathology: Vol. 5. *Resilience as a process.* Cambridge University Press.

Elder, G. H. Jr. (1998). The life course as developmental theory. *Child Development, 69*(1), 1–12. doi:10.1111/j.1467-8624.1998.tb06128.x PMID:9499552

Epstein, M. H., Nelson, J. R., Trout, A. L., & Mooney, P. (2005). Achievement and emotional disturbance. In M. H. Epstein, K. Kutash, & A. J. Duchnowski (Eds.), *Outcomes for children and youth with emotional and behavioral disorders and their families: Programs and evaluation best practice* (2nd ed.; pp. 451–477). Austin, TX: Pro-ed.

Essex, M. J., Kraemer, H. C., Armstrong, J. M., Boyce, W. T., Goldsmith, H. H., Klein, M. H., & Kupfer, D. J. et al. (2006, November 1). Exploring Risk Factors for the Emergence of Children's Mental Health Problems. *JAMA Psychiatry, 63*(11), 1246–1256. doi:10.1001/archpsyc.63.11.1246 PMID:17088505

Farrell, A. D., Meyer, A. L., & White, K. S. (2001). Evaluation of Responding in Peaceful and Positive Ways (RIPP); a school-based prevention program for reducing violence among urban adolescents. *Journal of Clinical Child Psychology, 3*(4), 451–463. doi:10.1207/S15374424JCCP3004_02 PMID:11708233

Garmezy, N. (2015, January). Children in poverty: Resilience despite risk. *Psychiatry, 56*(1), 127–136. doi:10.1080/00332747.1993.11024627 PMID:8488208

Garmezy, N., & Masten, A. S. (1986). Stress, competence, and resilience: Common frontiers for therapist and psychopathologist. *Behavior Therapy, 17*(5), 500–521. doi:10.1016/S0005-7894(86)80091-0

Gonsoulin, S., & Read, N. W. (2011). Improving Educational Outcomes for Youth in the Juvenile Justice and Child Welfare Systems through Interagency Communication and Collaboration. Washington, DC: National Evaluation and Technical Assistance Center for Children and Youth Who are Neglected, Delinquent, or At-Risk (NDTAC).

Griffin, K. W., Botvin, G. J., Nicholas, T. R., & Doyle, M. M. (2003). Effectiveness of a universal drug abuse prevention approach for youth at high risk for substance use initiation. *Preventive Medicine, 36*(1), 1–7. doi:10.1006/pmed.2002.1133 PMID:12473419

Harris, E., & Wilkes, S. (2013). Partnerships for learning: Community support for youth success. Cambridge, MA: Harvard Family Research Project. Retrieved from www. hfrp. org

Hatch, T. (1998). How community action contributes to achievement. *Educational Leadership, 55*(8), 16–19.

Hodges, S., Hernandez, M., & Nesman, T. (2003). A developmental framework for collaboration in child-serving agencies. *Journal of Child and Family Studies, 12*(3), 291–305. doi:10.1023/A:1023987710611

Johnson, L. J., Zorn, D., Yung Tam, B. K., Lamontagne, M., & Johnson, S. (2003). Stakeholders views of factors that impact successful interagency collaboration. *Council for Exceptional Children, 69*(2), 195–209. doi:10.1177/001440290306900205

Jones, V. F., & Jones, L. S. (2015). *Comprehensive classroom management: Creating communities of support and solving problems* (11th ed.). New York: Pearson.

Kim, E. M., Sheridan, S. M., Kwon, K., & Koziol, N. (2013). Parent beliefs and childrens social-behavioral functioning: The mediating role of parent-teacher relationships. *Journal of School Psychology, 51*(2), 175–185. doi:10.1016/j.jsp.2013.01.003 PMID:23481083

Lopes, J. A. (2007). Prevalence and comorbidity of emotional, behavioral, and learning problems: A study of 7th-grade students. *Education & Treatment of Children, 30*(4), 165–181. doi:10.1353/etc.2007.0027

Manteuffel, B., Stephens, R. L., & Santiago, R. (2002). Overview of the national evaluation of the Comprehensive Community Mental Health Services for Children and Their Families Program and summary of current findings. *Childrens Services (Mahwah, N.J.), 5*(1), 3–20. doi:10.1207/S15326918CS0501_2

Masten, A. S. (2006). Promoting resilience in development: A general framework for systems of care. In R. J. Flynn, P. M. Dudding, & J. G. Barber (Eds.), *Promoting resilience in child welfare* (pp. 3–17). Ottawa: University of Ottawa Press.

National Center for Mental Health in Schools (NCMHS) in the Department of Psychology at UCLA. (2016). *ESSA, equity of opportunity, and addressing barriers to learning.* Retrieved from ERIC database. (ED565303).

Oldfield, J., Hebron, J., & Humphrey, N. (2016). The role of school level protective factors in overcoming cumulative risk for behavior difficulties in children with special education needs and disabilities. *Psychology in the Schools*, 1–17. doi:10.1002/pits.21950

Reid, J. B., & Eddy, J. M. (1997). The prevention of antisocial behavior: Some considerations in the search for effective interventions. In D. M. Stoff, J. Breiling, & J. D. Maser (Eds.), *The Handbook of Antisocial Behavior* (pp. 343–356). New York: Wiley.

Reinke, W. M., Herman, K. C., Petras, H., & Ialongo, N. S. (2008). Empirically derived subtypes of child academic and behavior problems: Co-occurrence and distal outcomes. *Journal of Abnormal Child Psychology, 36*(5), 759–770. doi:10.1007/s10802-007-9208-2 PMID:18205038

Rones, M., & Hoagwood, K. (2000). School-based mental health services: A research review. *Clinical Child and Family Psychology Review, 3*(4), 223–241. doi:10.1023/A:1026425104386 PMID:11225738

Rutter, M. (1985). Resilience in the face of adversity: Protective factors and resistance to psychiatric disorders. *The British Journal of Psychiatry, 147*(6), 598–611. doi:10.1192/bjp.147.6.598 PMID:3830321

Stroul, B., & Friedman, R. M. (1986). *A system of care for children and youth with severe emotional disturbances* (Rev. ed.). Washington, DC: Georgetown University Child Development Center, CASSP Technical Assistance Center.

Stroul, B. A., & Blau, G. M. (2010). Defining the system of care concept and philosophy: To update or not to update? *Evaluation and Program Planning, 33*(1), 59–62. doi:10.1016/j.evalprogplan.2009.06.003 PMID:19836078

Sugai, G., & Horner, R. H. (2002). Introduction to a special series on positive behavior support in schools. *Journal of Emotional and Behavioral Disorders, 10*(3), 130–136. doi:10.1177/10634266020100030101

Tagle, R. (2005). Full service community schools: Cause and outcome of public engagement. *New Directions for Youth Development, 2005*(107), 45–54. doi:10.1002/yd.128 PMID:16315516

Tapper, D., & Kleinman, P., & Nakashian. (1997, July). An Interagency Collaboration Strategy for Linking Schools with Social and Criminal Justice Services. *Social Work in Education, 19*(3), 176–188.

Toth, S. L. & Cicchetti, D. (2004, December). Child maltreatment and its impact on psychosocial child development. In *Encyclopedia on Early Childhood Development.* Mt. Hope Family Center & University of Rochester.

Tourse, R. W. C., & Sulick, J. (1999). The collaborative alliance: Supporting vulnerable children in school. In R. Tourse & J. F. Mooney (Eds.), *Collaborative practice: School and human service partnerships* (pp. 59–78). Westport, CT: Praeger.

Trussell, R. P. (2008). Promoting school-wide mental health. *International Journal of Special Education, 23*(3), 149–155.

U. S. Department of Education. (1998). *Twentieth annual report to congress on the implementation of the Individuals with Disabilities Education Act.* Washington, DC: Author.

U. S. Department of Education. (2001). *Twenty-third annual report to Congress on the Implementation of the Individuals with Disabilities Education Act.* Washington, DC: Author.

Vitaro, F., Brendgen, M., Larose, S., & Trembaly, R. E. (2005). Kindergarten Disruptive Behaviors, Protective Factors, and Educational Achievement by Early Adulthood. *Journal of Educational Psychology, 97*(4), 617–629. doi:10.1037/0022-0663.97.4.617

Walker, H. M., Ramsey, E., & Gresham, F. M. (2004). *Antisocial behavior in schools: Evidence-based practices* (2nd ed.). Belmont, CA: Wadsworth.

Wang, M. C., Haertel, G. D., & Walberg, H. J. (1998). *Educational resilience (Publication Series No. 11).* Philadelphia: National Research Center on Education in the Inner Cities.

Wang, T. Q., Cornell, H., & Anderson, J. A. (2016). *IPS Kaleidoscope Program Evaluation Report: 2007- 2015.* Indianapolis Public Schools. Bloomington, IN: Families, Communities, and Schools.

Webster-Stratton, C. (1990). Stress: A potential disruptor of parent perceptions and family interactions. *Journal of Clinical Child Psychology*, *19*(4), 302–312. doi:10.1207/s15374424jccp1904_2

Webster-Stratton, C., & Hammond, M. (1998). Conduct problems and level of social competence in Head Start children: Prevalence, pervasiveness, and associated risk factors. *Clinical Child Psychology and Family Psychology Review*, *1*(2), 101–124. doi:10.1023/A:1021835728803 PMID:11324301

Werner, E. (1989). High-risk children in young adulthood: A longitudinal study from birth to 32 years. *The American Journal of Orthopsychiatry*, *59*(1), 72–81. doi:10.1111/j.1939-0025.1989.tb01636.x PMID:2467566

Werner, E. E., & Smith, R. S. (2001). *Journey from childhood to midlife: Risk, resilience, and recovery*. New York: Cornell University Press.

Wong, B., & Donohue, M. (2002). *The social dimensions of learning disabilities*. Lawrence Erlbaum.

KEY TERMS AND DEFINITIONS

Family-Driven: Families are the primary decision-makers in the care of their own children and authentically contribute to all policymaking and procedures governing care for all children in their community.

Interagency Collaboration: Systematic communication and cooperation among child-serving agencies (school systems, mental health services, welfare services).

Mental Health: The field of study and practice that focuses on the psychological and emotional well-being of an individual.

Prevention: Stopping something before it happens.

Protective Factors: Qualities that people possess or interactions with others that predict better outcomes for people who face adversity.

Resiliency: The ability to recover from risks or difficult life experiences.

Risk Factors: External and internal influences that can lead to poor outcomes for people.

School-based Interventions: Strategies or techniques used by the school to help students improve their academics, behavior, and/or social skills.

Systems of Care: Clusters of organizational strategies that are focused on improving outcomes and grounded in a set of principles, including cultural competence, strengths-focused, family-centered, and least restrictive/community-based.

Youth-Guided: Young people are fully involved in all decision-making role related to their own lives and authentically contribute to all policymaking and procedures governing care for all children in their community.

ENDNOTE

1 In 1997, the Individuals with Disabilities Education Act was reauthorized and the term SED was shortened from 'Serious Emotional Disturbance' to 'Emotional Disturbance' (ED) (Anderson and Mohr (2003) and Anderson (2000) discuss labels and diagnoses in education and mental health).

Chapter 10
Maasai Girls' Subjectivities and the Nexus of Gender Justice and Education Rights Discourse

Serena Koissaba
University of Illinois at Urbana-Champaign, USA

ABSTRACT

Global development discourse around the interplay between social justice and childhood issues are complicated when interpreting these ideas contextually through translocational gender and cultural lenses. This chapter attempted to address some of the following questions: How do international gender and education interventions problematize the transition for Maasai girls as they transition from childhood to adulthood? Can Amartya Sen's 'capability framework, work effectively for African children in Kenya who by their cultural norms become adults before the age of 18? In what ways are the social justice schemes producing disaggregated cultural structures for Maasai Girls? This chapter, therefore examined how Maasai girls' subjectivities are affected by gender and education rights mediation through Amartya Sen's 'capabilities approach' and a human rights framework. The experiences and perspectives of female subjects have seemingly been distorted within feminist and geopolitical rhetoric. Transnational feminism in this work is positioned as a postcolonial project that employs theories of human rights, capabilities, and multiculturalism as lenses in which to interrogate practices of erasures of voice and representation of active participants within the movement, but reconsider what feminist theory can do to move the conversation away from male-centric ideologies.

INTRODUCTION

Current analyses of the condition of African girls are in direct contestation to their cultural norms. The "intervention factor" (Nsamenang, 2013) by international actors with the goal of defining and promoting Western sensibilities in non-Western contexts are at work to restructure the lives of girls living outside of those spaces by using social justice and emancipatory-based instruments to position non-western girls to contribute to the global economy. Funding sources for these initiatives are based almost entirely on

DOI: 10.4018/978-1-5225-2578-3.ch010

foreign aid (Nsamenang, 2013) with development ideologies regarding 'children' and their wellbeing, which in some ways reflects a poor attitude towards African social systems. The critique of these African social systems are framed around human rights and multiculturalism binaries that do not consider global hegemonic forces and these forces tend to produce structural inequalities that disrupt the lives of the people they claim to desire to help (Tamale, 2013) There is a movement of neoliberal "market-oriented politics" (Kjørholt, 2013), connected to gender and education rights discourses that shape how African girlhood is imagined. Education is seen globally as the mechanism for economic growth worldwide. Youth from aboriginal settings are situated between concepts of human-child rights and human capital strategies. Maasai females live in a communitarian social ontology which means that members of the community participate as a political collective to design their shared knowledge of social goods and standards (Kang, 2008). There are disadvantages to the distribution of power both in and outside of the political community for women and girls.

This interpretation of Maasai girls' rights to gender justice and education is framed using a 'capabilities approach' and a sociological analysis to conceptualise their childhood. Traditionally, Maasai girls transition into adulthood at puberty. This is problematic due to theoretical and practical implications regarding children's rights and considerations of the complexities of the sociological norms in which they live. Standards for the transition to adulthood should be reconsidered in light of international human rights and children's rights precepts as enshrined in the UN Convention on the Rights of the Child, and congruent to various processes and definitions of childhoods globally. Sen's (1999)'s capability approach does not limit what 'freedom' means in terms of a child's development, access to jurisprudence, or enacting their own agency when desired (Peleg, 2013). Global development discourse around the interplay between social justice and childhood issues are complicated when interpreting these ideas contextually through global and local gender and cultural lenses. For example, how do international gender and education interventions problematize the transition for Maasai girls as they transition from childhood to adulthood? Can the Sen's capability approach be effective for African females who by their cultural norms become adults before the age of 18? In what ways are social justice schemes producing disaggregated cultural structures for Maasai Girls? This chapter sought to establish an understanding of how the Maasai girls' subjectivities are constructed by gender and education rights mediation by looking at childhood through Sen's capabilities approach, multiculturalism, and the human rights framework.

BACKGROUND

Fieldwork

My fieldwork with Maasai schoolgirls began in the Maasai Mara Game Reserve in Kenya. The field site for my initial research took place in Narok County from 2000-2006 with follow-up interviews from 2007 to the present. I conducted interviews with both women and men on their views concerning female circumcision as well as laws passed by the Kenyan government to restrict customary rituals. My primary research site was the Maasai Mara Game Reserve. The Maasai Mara is a challenging site to conduct research regarding FGM because of the amount of tourism and external influences from outsiders. I attended numerous circumcision ceremonies for both boys and girls while having the opportunity to talk to them and the community about the meanings of this ritual before and after the event. During the first six years of my fieldwork, I was further involved in establishing two primary schools that are located in the villages on the outskirts of the Game Reserve. My interest in providing educational opportunities to the children in the area was my primary goal. The 'body' politics of Maasai girls, as well as girls from other tribes in Kenya, became a hot topic in global development conversations. I began to notice in my own work the role that sexuality played in the lives of the girls in the villages where I lived. Since the year 2000, I have continued conducting ethnographic research in the Maasai communities primarily in Kenya, but also in Tanzania as well. Over the course of my fieldwork, I have witnessed and participated in socio-political advocacy activities within these communities. I conducted focus groups with local women and girls and also attended community meetings led primarily by males and interviews with political officials. This longitudinal ethnographic study is important to the chapter because it provides a narrative about how Maasai girls have adapted to social changes brought about through global interventions aimed at recruiting them into the marketplace by reconfiguring their identities and cultural norms.

Multicultural Worldview

The lives of African indigenous women and girls are shaped by cultural norms that conflict with political dynamics globally which work to restructure the way they live (Maiga, 2014; Sylvain, 2010). There is no monolithic mould for indigenous gender analysis yet there is a need to interrogate the motives and underpinning of Western neoliberal schemes as it pertains to gender politics in Africa. It is, therefore, important to discuss the role of multicultural debates in shaping global ideologies about human rights, and capabilities that frame cultural imperialism on minority groups. At its core multiculturalism as a theoretical plan is to alter the historical exclusions of marginalised groups (Kymlicka, 1995, p. 18). These groups are often excluded because of their difference from the norms of the dominant group. This is what makes multiculturalism problematic for people who are not members of the dominant group because the ideologies of the dominant are imposed upon the subaltern in the name of interventions that seeks to integrate them into the mainstream pluralist culture of the dominant group.

Feminist Worldview and Girlhood Rights

Feminism is as Adrienne Rich (2007) noted, the history of women's movements globally which deals with the universality of embedded patriarchy in discourses and frameworks concerning how women and girls can connect and create a space where domination over them by men is abolished. This notion is problematic because it makes body politics, that is, male/female binaries central in conceptualising feminists and as to what interventions should be. Tamale (2013) commented on the complexities and the necessity for exploring methodologies and epistemological tools to think about the construction of knowledge outside of the colonial project. Tamale (2013) further challenges us to review the interlocking mechanisms concerning African sexualities. It is important to note that there is no 'feminism' that is all inclusive and representational of all of the issues females face globally. Patrizia Violi drawing on work by Teresa de Lauretis links the development of subjectivity to the "relation of narrative, meaning and desire whereby the narrative engages the subject with positions of meaning," (Violi, 1992, p. 169). Embedded in female subjectivity are alliances to one's self and experiences. These social forms of self-representation are not individualistic or absent of influence by a patriarchal culture. This chapter seeks to interrogate ideas about African childhood sexualities that looks at the agency and choice of these young people to participate in sexual relations that disrupt Western neoliberal sensibilities.

Drawing on empirical work in Sub-Saharan Africa with indigenous children on sexuality issues, I began to observe their lives in conjunction with international neoliberal development agendas that target girls for participants in capitalist societies through interpretive transnational feminism. Maasai schoolgirl's sexualization in this chapter is used as an archetype to critically examine how global political power structures are connected to "the making of persons" (Stoler, 2006, p. 25) where girls' bodies are considered "Flesh and Bone of empire." (Ballantyne and Burton, 2009, p. 4) This notion of reorienting the intimate extends into the social order of people's private lives and decisions and interventions become global (Runyan & Marchand, 2011). A global political push for universalism with some forms of feminist theories may be the source for gender myth-making within socio-political contexts that show essentialized images of girlhood, especially in indigenous settings (Cornwall et al., 2007). The result of these gender myths and the direct outcomes from legal feminist policies reveal a gap in the agenda anticipated and the realities on the ground. International education schemes are essential in controlling the production and reproduction capabilities of girls in the Global South by isolating them in school settings where they are trained in Western ideologies about human rights and feminist tenets that are antithetical to the customs of their culture (Decker, 2015). The education and childhood sexualities nexus is problematic in international development discourses due to a moral panic around the issue of childhood sexualities (Blaise, 2010). Forms of power and agency for Maasai schoolgirls are encapsulated by gender-identity norms.

SEN'S CAPABILITIES APPROACH AND AFRICAN GIRLHOOD

The Capabilities Approach

The interconnection between Sen's capability approach (1999), human capital theory, and African childhood studies is the notion of freedom and how those freedoms are accessed and controlled. The capability approach as a framework is useful in understanding the implications for how education is situated in and through the education system. (Gale & Molla, 2015) The term justice denotes a mechanism that is used to bring conflict resolutions that help individuals who want to advance (Gale & Molla, 2015; Harvey, 2009). Ball (1998) believes international education policies are the result of colonisation whose premise is based on a human capital approach which positions education systems in terms of economics. The objective of neoliberal movements is to increase children's access to education are based on an economic rationale and not one of social justice. The recent attraction around global girl education schemes draws upon intersectionality of gender and education rights to create public discourse around these girls abandoning their traditional social norms and entering formal education in preparation for positions in the marketplace. The interworking of the human capital approach to gender and education is political and does not take into consideration the freedom and well-being of human beings. The politics of education creates inequalities and disaggregates social systems that are in direct contradiction to human rights frames. Sen (2005) believes that capabilities and human rights can complement each other as concepts except when assessing the attainment of freedoms.

The Counter-Narrative

Nussbaum (2003) counters Sen's argument regarding the position of freedoms in discourses around the capability approach and human rights. She argues that Sen's notion of freedom is too ambiguous. She continues to state that concepts of social justice have the potential to offer something to issues of gender. Nussbaum's definition of gender is limited to male and female relations which exclude other forms of gender. The role of human agency in human development is defined as a focus on civil and political freedoms (Fukuda-Parr, 2003; Birdsall, 2014). There is a dichotomy presented politically when evaluating human capabilities through the lens of human rights. The capability approach in the context of this chapter is intertwined with human rights and critical democratic theories. There have been numerous international human rights and development agendas with ambitious aims to make development a right for all. These efforts have become ensnared with North-South politics (Birdsall, 2014; Ibhawoh, 2011). Politics of social justice work to unravel social norms of aboriginal societies based on interpretations of social justice and feminism based on Western sensibilities (Keddie, 2014). The Universal Declaration of Human Rights (UDHR) article 1 states that "all human beings are born free and equal in dignity and rights," (UDHR, 1948). Where do we place the agency in feminist scholarship where females under the age of 18 years of age are faced with the decision of whether they want to adhere to the social norms of their societies or explore what neoliberal feminism and global capitalism have to offer them?

Walkerdine (2009, p11) asserts that "an adolescent cannot exist as a person or become a subject in his or her own right" unless they are capable of putting themselves in conflict with other generations. If this view is taken by the global community to situate children as it relates to their sexuality and position of being, then these would not qualify under the Articles 6 and 15 of the Universal Declaration of Human Rights to be recognized as a person under the law and the right to nationality as outlined under the tenets of their tribe for nationhood. (UNDHR, 1948) The social representation of Maasai girls is constructed through a lens of victimisation that does not reflect the fact that they are a human being with rights and capabilities that exhibited in their daily lives. Paradigms of childhood sociology are rethinking what childhood should be at a global level. These paradigms must move away from Western conceptualizations (Prout & James, 1990) and global child rights apparatus that alienate positive and constructive aspects of African childhoods and should further abandon notions that stigmatise the conceptions of an African childhood. (Nsamenang, 2013) Conditioning the girl child for a life in the economic market will ultimately afford her the opportunity to have some financial freedom and an escape from her household responsibilities. (Abosede, 2014) These so call freedoms are subjective because although a female may work outside of the home, their income and activities are often controlled by her husband. Women who live in polygynous marriages are more likely to work outside of the home or be self-employed. Variables such as age and education gap are lower than amongst these women than their spouses. (De Giusti & Kambhampati, 2015, p. 88) Sen (1990) argues that women devalue themselves and their contribution to their households. Their comparative assessment to the work of market and non-market labour is problematic leaving many females to put their families' well-being above their own.

This chapter contributes to the literature on social justice education and labour force participation of girls living in the global South while framing the argument through an agency-based approach. Children are groomed from birth to adulthood for an independent life. Girls and boys are circumcised at puberty as part of their rite of passage into adulthood. The purpose of childhood is contextually a stage for socialising young people for family, economic and community leadership responsibilities (Okwany et al., 2011, p.93). Due to aspects of colonialism and globalisation, this social system has come under attack by those who want to alter it to conform to a more Western universal view. Where do indigenous girlhood sensibilities fit in transnational feminism discourses? Opportunity structures are hidden within discourses around multiculturalism and racial and ethnic differentiation. Ideas and possibilities for new forms of citizenship are obscured by over emphasising ways in which the transnational body is different.

CONTEXTUALISING MAASAI GIRLHOOD IN LIGHT OF TRANSNATIONAL FEMINISM

Sexuality is defined as "a means of organisation of generations and of marking age-related positions," (Voléry, 2016; Diasio & Vinel, 2010). The symbolism in which sexuality as a function is modelled in Maasai girlhood and later in their transitional position to adulthood has created a moral panic within international feminist rights movements. There is a need to contextualise social and political analyses of this occurrence in order to understand the hypersexualizing of Maasai girls. The hypersexualizing of Maasai girls shifts political attitudes regarding the marginalised children who need to be saved from harmful cultural practices, such as female circumcision or female genital mutilation (FGM) and early marriage. Although it may seem from a Western vantage point that these practices should be abolished, such movements tend to prolong the Maasai girls in the category of a child, which eliminates levels of agency and social protection they may need within their community to survive. Female circumcision is the rite of passage into womanhood for Maasai girls in which they are expected to marry and have children soon after this period. The economies of identity for Maasai girls are tied to (FGM) because the practice is their rite of passage into womanhood. After circumcision, Maasai girls are now considered women who are ready to be married and have a home and children. If females do not become wives and mothers their value diminishes to practically nothing. Their ability to survive and be accepted amongst their people becomes lost. The older women in the community are the gatekeepers of the tradition. (Coyne & Coyne, 2014) Once girls participate in (FGM) they become the new gatekeepers of the practice for future generations. They retain the benefits that their foremothers experienced. Girls who consciously refuse to participate in (FGM) often experience feelings of guilt that they have abandoned their families and community members (Kradin, 2012). Oftentimes, girls who have been allowed to attend school are most likely to refuse or object to the FGM practice. The most invasive threat to uprooting this cultural system for traditional Maasai girls are the new imaginations of Maasai females who are experiencing life outside of the local setting who are challenging changes and customary laws within the nation. This form of body politics restructures the dichotomy between interpretations concerning practices related to the body and for this chapter the female indigenous body (Ballantyne, 2015) and how these meanings translate into market-based regulations for labour purposes. There is a need to draw attention to agency and sexualities within childhood studies that go beyond viewing it as dangerous. (Bhana, 2016) The regulation of female sexualities and surveillance in the global South is problematic. Maasai girls are sexual agents who use their sexualities within relations of power and pleasure. Sexuality is a social function where male and females are positioned in a power hierarchy. (Bhana, 2016; Allen, 2005) Conceptions of African childhoods that depict girls as innocent victims exploited by patriarchal structures cannot provide an adequate analysis of indigenous African girlhood.

THE NEXUS OF GENDER JUSTICE AND EDUCATION RIGHTS DISCOURSE

Educating girls has long been a centrepiece in human rights discourse since the Beijing Platform for Action in 1995 (Purewal, 2015). Such frameworks ushered in an era for the universalization of education in which girls began to be prominent symbols of the movement. The synthesis of targeting the girl-child in international education policy rights discourse positioned them mythically as victim/heroine (Cornwall et al, 2007) while using the human rights scheme as the basis for equality and peace rhetoric. (Purewal, 2015) According to Francis Fukuyama (1992), development policies were constructed around concepts of rights, global citizenship, and markets rather than capitalism and communism. "Children's rights agenda is the way that Western fantasies of childhood dependence and innocence have come to assume universal status," (Manzo, 2008; Manzo, 2005; Moore, 2000). Access to educational institutions has played a key role in aiding colonial and neocolonial ideologies to combat and influence female circumcision. "Human rights are grounded in the experiential realm of power politics at the local level…human rights are practice seeking a theory," (Birdsall, 2014, p.14) The 1920s saw an increase in British colonial influence in Kenya especially through Christian missionaries and colonial government agencies. By 1925, the missionaries continually denied girls from enrolling in their schools if they did not denounce (FGM) practices. (Boulanger, 2008, p.66) Maasai girls who want to continue to practice female circumcision as a rite of passage into womanhood found themselves having to fight against the state as well as global actors in the name of development who wanted to exploit the issue for gain. NGO feminism has a "power-knowledge nexus" (Gore, 1993) that contribute to oppression. Switzer (2010) discusses how the subjectivity of Maasai school girls reassures them of their position as children and not women yet; they lose their agency when they are relegated to the girl-child category The same loss of agency is present for girls who may or may not be in school but do not undergo circumcision. The ritual is the threshold when girls transition to womanhood whether they become married or remain in school. The families of these girls are also able to place her with a husband if she becomes pregnant out of wedlock and without the ability to provide for herself and her child. This idea may not seem like a positive intervention, but it assures that the girl and her baby will not be left without social and economic provisions. As noted by gender and women's studies scholar Switzer (2013 p. 347), global representational regimes like The Girl Effect are paradigms of hegemonic discourse that propagates a form of girl power that is only obtained through formal education. Formal education becomes a mechanism in which to control the adolescent females' productive and reproductive capabilities through the guise of global poverty remedies. Maasai feminists who are against FGM seem to use their agency to align themselves with the state and global development actors who fund their agenda. Fabienne Peter (2003) drawing on Sen's commentary regarding social choice theory posits that agency evaluation requires noticing explicit motivations and constraints in which people behave. She goes on to state that the tasks in which a person is able to accomplish successfully within their social structure are their level of capabilities. Globalisation accelerates the integration of global economies into one with political and cultural corollaries embedded within its process. (Kang, 2008; Jagger 2001). Schools are social systems that hold the possibilities of mediating tensions between multiculturalism, group rights, and feminisms. (Keddie, 2014) They also contribute to social fractures and segregation by supporting Western liberalist ideals that problematize patriarchal cultures without context and empirical evidence. Dilemmas of multiculturalism and feminism debates are about more than gender relations. Social justice is contextual. These dialogical politics should re-conceptualize what gender equality is within these social systems. (Anthias, 2002) Can choice exist in a capitalist society? Multiculturalism and feminism "are not just an issue of patriarchy or an issue of ethnic culture. Women exploit other women as in the experience of domestic maids," (Anthias, 2008, p. 276) The increase of women entering the workplace produce new forms of marginalisation and oppression. Systems of care are gendered relations seen as non-commodities. (Fraser, 2013; Anthias, 2008) Polarity is established between the modern and the traditional girl in the global South. Global campaigns that target educating girls in the global South use a human rights approach that is connected to an international economic agenda. (Keddie 2014; Davies 2000, p. 66) The identity politics and economies of Maasai girlhood are vastly different from those of girls in the North.

Interventions

The interventions imposed contextually on Maasai girls use education and human rights arguments to displace these girls from their traditional social norms and places them in educational spaces where they can learn the tenets of 'Smart Economics.' "Gender Equality as Smart Economics" (Calkin, 2015), has underpinned much of the mediation for girls' empowerment movements. This form of advocacy is a source for contestation in indigenous communities because they endeavour to eradicate cultural norms that position women and girls in domestic roles, in order to encourage their participation in the marketplace. Girls living in the Global South have become mythical symbols of the ultimate cure for global poverty through campaigns such as Nike Foundation's Girl Effect and the UN's Girls' Education initiative (UNGEI). The girl effect campaigns have created slogans that promote girls as ideal stewards of financial resources. (Skalli, 2015) These campaigns quote unfounded data which says to educate a girl can raise the national economy in her country. As noted by Nancy Fraser (2013), gender rights and social justice discourses are framed by flexible capitalism which seeks to make two-earner households a modern norm in the global South. It encourages girls from poor working class families to pursue formal education in order to create a cohort of middle-class females whose lives reflect the standards of Western feminist ideologies. Flexible capitalism is defined by Fraser (2013) as a feminist critique of family wage to justify exploitation while promoting an idea that women's emancipation is synonymous with capital accumulation. The African female body and its social organisation and cosmological significance use sexuality to explicate the politics of intimacy at the margins. (Ballantyne, 2015; Foucault, 1979) What is protected is neoliberal bonds that are perpetuated on other groups through a globalised marketization of feminism.

Conflicting Dialogues

The conflicts presented in multiculturalism are often a problem in gender justice dialogues. Susan Okin's (1999) seminal work entitled "Is Multiculturalism Bad for Women?" has been greatly contested by feminist scholars regarding her views on minority cultures and whether or not their group rights and privileges should be protected. Okin's view of cultures, in general, were that they are patriarchal, thus place women in a subservient position to men. However, the debate around this issue goes beyond Western liberalism versus patriarchal culture debates. It prohibits the creation of gender frames that privileges marginalised voices and build spaces of possibilities that are significant to minority groups. (Keddie, 2014; Anthias, 2002; Davies, 2000) Another interesting question is how multiculturalism is situated within international education rights conversation? Sutton (2005 p. 98) noted there are two binaries involving multicultural education as a global phenomenon: 1) educational access as equality for all and 2) institutional and historical recognition of inequalities for those who have been denied access to educational opportunities. She continues to note that the term illustrates how students are taught about their social identity and the identity of others. The quest to give girls in the global South more equal educational opportunities is a modern project (Sutton, 2005) with aims to recruit more females to the marketplace. Multiculturalism in this context is different from the views outlined by Okin. The global capitalist agendas have replaced the position of patriarchal systemic determinants for women and girls worldwide. Feminism needs to go beyond a conversation about female experiences and their relationships to and with men. Feminist ideas about what freedoms they should have are based on patriarchal parameters in public and private spaces. Self-governance and the redefining of the feminine self and body subjectivities are necessary to reject traditional and universal notions of our bodies. How do feminists construct subjectivity? The body becomes a triptych of material, symbolic, and social categories.

GLOBAL SOCIAL JUSTICE INTERVENTIONS AND DISAGGREGATED SOCIAL STRUCTURES

Educational campaigns for girls make Maasai communities antagonistic because of the impact it has on shaping girls' thinking concerning local norms (Cloward, 2015). International social justice movement disaggregates the social order from within the space they live. Cultural relativism is defined by Anthias (2002) as the notion that there are established universal principles of justice that apply to everyone and reflecting positivist epistemologies. Many Maasai girls who are afforded the opportunity to attend school become pregnant and married at a young age. Education systems are not equipped to override a lifetime of cultural indoctrination of self and identity or the expectations the girls have for how they want to live their lives. Gendered politics must rethink its relationship on how they would like the state to mediate on their behalf without causing "the destruction of social institutions" (Calkin, 2015) that are valued by the other when crafting policies that limit certain females from benefiting within their social spheres. For example, abortion-related deaths are the leading cause of mortality for Kenyan girls (Oduor-Ombaka, 2010; Kenya Ministry of Health, 2007) yet NGO feminists are not working hard to end abortion but FGM practices because abortion is more in line with acceptable 'rights' rhetoric from Western feminism. The legal framework around FGM does not offer protection for females over the age of 18. Globalisation offers a political paradox where it can create opportunities for aboriginals on the one hand and neocolonial injustice on the other. (O'Sullivan, 2012) These new international incentives require that locals renegotiate their 'nationalism,' social norms, and ethnic identities in their struggle to maintain control over their land while mobilising resources to support the nation. (Lynch, 2011) Global causal support of gender policies enables girls to control and restrict their reproductive health and probability for early marriage. Contextually, early marriage is used in Maasai communities as an alternative to shame and alienation within the community when girls become pregnant out of wedlock. Early marriage is seen as a measure to provide girls and their children with social and financial support. FGM as a ritual is the process in which girls' transition into women are eligible to marry and have children. I posit that the crises that these imperialist projects give global feminists an opportunity to turn away from discourses around resistance/vulnerability binaries in order to assess international apparatus such as the UN Human Rights approach that works to stratify and control means of transnational female subjects' abilities of production and reproduction in the name of liberation. The challenge to move beyond esoteric divisions of subjectivities in modern transnational feminism practices is the question of choice and agency within capitalist and neoliberal structures. Can female subjects see themselves as autonomous within the public sphere? Women and girls' empowerment interventions want to populate the public sphere with females while theoretically there is a void as to how their empowerment affects her private life. Active public participation by females in capitalism reconfigures their private life in ways that can be destructive to those who intimately occupy her private spaces. Traditional/modernity binaries continue to display the roles of the female subject and define how she is to function in public and private roles.

THE MAKING OF MODERN INDIGENOUS GIRLHOODS: CONCLUDING THOUGHTS FOR TRANSNATIONAL FEMINISM

The findings in this chapter raise three key questions for how we might continue this discourse within international education development and transnational feminism circles:

1. How do we deal with the polarity and inequalities within systems of care and labour created by flexible capitalism for girls who are not educated?
2. The economy of many indigenous girls is steeped in their ability to function as wives and mothers. How can the issues related to home economics and marketplace participation converge in an agency-oriented manner to serve the females who choose to participate in it?
3. How can global education initiative be used to expose and counter destructive iconographic representations of who the indigenous girl is based upon empirical evidence that does not seek to polarise the conversation about the desires and struggles of these females in order to advance neoliberal market-based agendas?

Wall (2008) states that children's rights will "transform societies" when human rights frames are conceptualised in light of childhood. In essence, concepts of human rights are not limited to age or responsibilities but are centred on being human. Indigenous girls like many other girls around the world are targets for neoliberal campaigns that seek to influence how these females use their lives to invest in the global economy. International discourses around issues of gender and education as related to girls in the global South uses policies and ideologies to marginalise them in the name of empowerment and social justice. Discourses that attempt to use universal methodologies based on Western economic agendas place non-Western women and girls at risk for rationalising freedom through Western economic standards. Contestations over traditional versus modern practices can put non-Western females in a position to destroy traditional customs (where they have agency and resources) to advocate for a romanticised notion freedom from a global system that cannot guarantee anything to them.

ACKNOWLEDGMENT

I would like to thank Pradeep Dhillon at the University of Illinois for her helpful comments on earlier versions of this chapter.

REFERENCES

Abosede, A. (2014). *Making modern girls: A history of girlhood, labour, and social development in colonial Lagos*. Ohio University Press.

Allen, L. (2005). *Sexual Subjects: Young People, Sexuality and Education*. Basingstoke, UK: Palgrave Macmillan. doi:10.1057/9780230500983

Anthias, F. (2002). Beyond Feminism and Multiculturalism: Locating Difference and the Politics of Location. *Womens Studies International Forum*, *25*(3), 275–286. doi:10.1016/S0277-5395(02)00259-5

Ballantyne, T. (2015). *Entanglements of Empire: Missionaries, Maori, and the Question of the Body*. Durham, NC: Duke University Press.

Ballantyne, T., & Burton, A. (2009). *Moving subjects: gender, mobility, and intimacy in an age of global empire*. Chicago, IL: University of Illinois Press.

Bhana, D. (2016). Sex isnt better than love: Exploring South African Indian teenage male and female desires beyond danger. *Childhood*, *23*(3), 362–377. doi:10.1177/0907568216642828

Birdsall, W. F. (2014). Development, Human Rights, and Human Capabilities: The Political Divide. *Journal of Human Rights*, *13*(1), 1–21. doi:10.1080/14754835.2013.824268

Blaise, M. (2010). Kiss and tell: Gendered narrative and childhood sexuality. *Australian Journal of Early Childhood*, *35*(1), 1–9.

Boulanger, S. (2008). A puppet on a string: The manipulation and nationalisation of the female body in the "female circumcision crisis" of colonial Kenya. *Wagadu*, *6*, 61–74.

Calkin, S. (2015). Feminism, interrupted? Gender and development in the era of Smart Economics.. *Progress in Development Studies*, *15*(4), 295–307. doi:10.1177/1464993415592737

Cloward, K. (2015). Elites, Exit Options, and Social Barriers to Norm Change: The Complex Case of Female Genital Mutilation. *Studies in Comparative International Development*, *50*, 378–407. doi:10.1007/s12116-015-9175-5

Cornwall, A., Harrison, E., & Whitehead, A. (2007). Gender myths and feminist fables: The struggle for interpretive power in gender and development. *Development and Change*, *38*(1), 1–20. doi:10.1111/j.1467-7660.2007.00400.x

Coyne, C. J., & Coyne, R. L. (2014). The identity economics of female genital mutilation. *Journal of Developing Areas*, *48*(2), 137–152. doi:10.1353/jda.2014.0036

Davies, B. (2000). *A Body of Writing 1990-1999*. New York: Alta Mira Press.

De Giusti, G., & Kambhampati, U. S. (2015). Women's Work in Kenya: The Role of Social Institutions and Household Gender Attitudes. *Feminist Economics*, *22*(2), 87–113. doi:10.1080/13545701.2015.1115531

Decker, C. (2015). The elusive power of colonial prey: Sexualizing the schoolgirl in the Zanzibar Protectorate. *Africa Today*, *61*(4), 43–60. doi:10.2979/africatoday.61.4.43

Declaration of the Rights of the Child G.A. (1959). res. 1386 (XIV), 14 U.N. GAOR Supp. (No.16) at 19, U.N. Doc. A/4354.

Diasio, N., & Vinel, V. (2010). Objets de soin, objets á soi. La fabrication d'un corps intime chez les enfants de 9 á 13 ans. In 9 émes journées de sociologie de l'enfance, Paris, France.

Fraser, N. (2013). How Feminism became Capitalism's Handmaiden and How to Reclaim It. *The Guardian*. Retrieved from www.theguardian.com/commentisfree/2013/oct/14/feminism-capitalist-handmaiden-neoliberal

Fukuda-Parr, S. (2003). The Human Development Paradigm: Operationalizing Sens Ideas on Capabilities. *Feminist Economics*, *9*(2-3), 301–317. doi:10.1080/1354570022000077980

Fukuyama, F. (1992). *The end of history and the last man*. New York, NY: Penguin.

Gale, T., & Molla, T. (2015). Social justice intents in policy: An analysis of capability for and through education. *Journal of Education Policy*, *30*(6), 810–830. doi:10.1080/02680939.2014.987828

Goldberg, D. T. (1993). *Racist culture*. Cambridge, UK: Blackwell.

Gore, J. (1993). *The Struggle for Pedagogies: Critical and Feminist Discourses as Regimes of Truth*. New York: Routledge.

Harvey, D. (2009). *Social Justice and the City* (Revised ed.). Athens, GA: The University of Georgia Press.

Ibhawoh, B. (2011). The Right to Development: The Politics and Polemics of Power and Resistance. *Human Rights Quarterly*, *33*(1), 76–104. doi:10.1353/hrq.2011.0001

Jaggar, A. (2001). Is Globalization Good for Women? *Comparative Literature*, *53*(4), 298–300. doi:10.1215/-53-4-298

Kang, H-R. (2008). Transnational Women's Collectivities and Global Justice. *Journal of Social Philosophy*, *39*(3), 359-377.

Keddie, A. (2014). Identity Politics, Justice and the Schooling of Muslim Girls: Navigating the Tensions between Multiculturalism, Group Rights, and Feminism. *British Journal of Sociology of Education*, *35*(3), 353–370. doi:10.1080/01425692.2013.776930

Kjørholt, A. T. (2013). Childhood as social investment, rights and the valuing of education. *Children & Society*, *27*(4), 245–257. doi:10.1111/chso.12037

Kradin, R. L. (2012). When ancestral heritage is a source of discomfort: Culture, pre-object relatedness and self-alienation. *The Journal of Analytical Psychology*, *57*(2), 207–222. doi:10.1111/j.1468-5922.2011.01962.x PMID:22444356

Kymlicka, W. (1995). *Multicultural Citizenship: A Liberal Theory of Minority Rights*. Oxford, UK: Clarendon Press.

Lynch, G. (2011). Kenyas new indigenes: Negotiating local identities in a global context. *Nations and Nationalism*, *17*(1), 148–167. doi:10.1111/j.1469-8129.2010.00465.x

Maiga, S. (2014). Gender and Indigenous Peoples' Rights. In Indigenous People in Africa: Contestations, Empowerment and Group Rights. African Institute of South Africa.

Manzo, K. (2005). Exploiting West Africas Children: Trafficking, Slavery, and Uneven Development. *Area*, *37*(4), 393–401. doi:10.1111/j.1475-4762.2005.00644.x

Manzo, K. (2008). Imaging Humanitarianism: NGO Identity and the Iconography of Childhood. *Antipode*, *40*(4), 632–657. doi:10.1111/j.1467-8330.2008.00627.x

Ministry of Health (Republic of Kenya). (2007). *National Reproductive Health Policy: Enhancing Reproductive Health Status for All Kenyans*. Nairobi: Government of Kenya.

Moore, K. (2000). Supporting Children in their Working Lives: Obstacles and Opportunities within the International Policy Context. *Journal of International Development*, *12*(4), 531–548. doi:10.1002/1099-1328(200005)12:4<531::AID-JID689>3.0.CO;2-J

Nsamenang, A. B. (2013). Dilemmas of rights-based approaches to child well-being in an African cultural context. In D. J. Johnson,... (Eds.), Vulnerable children: Global challenges in education, health, well-being, and child rights (pp. 13–25). New York: Springer. doi:10.1007/978-1-4614-6780-9_2

Nussbaum, M. C. (2003). Capabilities as Fundamental Entitlements: Sen and Social Justice. *Feminist Economics*, *9*(2-3), 33–59. doi:10.1080/1354570022000077926

Oduor-Ombaka, C. (2010). Girls in Transition: Negotiating, constructing and re-constructing girlhood after the Fall in rural Kenya. *Girlhood Studies*, *3*(2), 109–128. doi:10.3167/ghs.2010.030207

Okin, S. M. (1999). Is Multiculturalism Bad for Women? In S. M. Okin (Ed.), *Is Multiculturalism Bad for Women*. Princeton, NJ: Princeton University Press.

Okwany, A., Muhangi, A., & Mulongo, E. M. N. (2011). *The role of local knowledge and culture in child care in Africa: A sociological study of several ethnic groups in Kenya and Uganda*. Lewiston, NY: Edwin Mellen Press.

OSullivan, D. (2012). Globalisation and the Politics of Indigeneity. *Globalizations*, *9*(5), 637–650. doi:10.1080/14747731.2012.732424

Peleg, N. (2013). Reconceptualising the childs right to development: Children and the capability approach. *International Journal of Childrens Rights*, *21*(3), 523–542. doi:10.1163/15718182-02103003

Peter, F. (2003). Gender and the Foundations of Social Choice: The Role of Situated Agency. *Feminist Economics*, *9*(2-3), 13–32. doi:10.1080/1354570022000078006

Prout, A., & James, A. (1990). A new paradigm for the sociology of childhood? Provenance, promise and problem. In A. James & A. Prout (Eds.), *Constructing and reconstructing childhood: Contemporary issues in the sociological study of childhood* (pp. 7–34). London: The Falmer Press.

Purewal, N. (2015). Interrogating the rights discourse on girls education: Neocolonialism, neoliberalism, and the Post-Beijing platform for action. *IDS Bulletin*, *46*(4), 47–53. doi:10.1111/1759-5436.12156

Rich, A. (2007). Notes towards a Politics of Location. In S. B. Freedman (Ed.), *The Essential Feminist Reader*. Modern Library.

Runyan, A. S., & Marchand, M. H. (2011). *Gender and Global Restructuring: Sightings, Sites, and Resistances*. Routledge.

Sen, A. (1990). Gender and Cooperative Conflict. In I. Tinker (Ed.), Persistent Inequalities, (pp. 123-49). New York: Clarendon Press.

Sen, A. (1999). *Development as Freedom*. New York: Knopf.

Sen, A. (2005). Human Rights and Capabilities. *Journal of Human Development*, *6*(2), 151–166. doi:10.1080/14649880500120491

Skalli, L. H. (2015). The Girl Factor and the (In)security of coloniality: A view from the The Middle East. Alternatives: *Global, Local. Political*, *40*(2), 174–187.

Stoler, A. L. (2006). Tense and tender ties: the politics of comparison in North American history and (post)colonial studies. In A. L. Stoler (Ed.), *Haunted by empire: Geographies of Intimacy in North American history*. London: Duke University Press. doi:10.1215/9780822387992-002

Sutton, M. (2005). The Globalization of Multicultural Education. *Indiana Journal of Global Legal Studies*, *12*(1), 97–108. doi:10.2979/GLS.2005.12.1.97

Switzer, H. (2010). Disruptive Discourses: Kenyan Maasai Schoolgirls make themselves. *Girlhood Studies*, *3*(1), 137–155. doi:10.3167/ghs.2010.030109

Switzer, H. (2013). (Post)Feminist development fables: The Girl Effect and the production of sexual subjects. *Feminist Theory*, *14*(3), 345–360. doi:10.1177/1464700113499855

Sylvain, R. (2010). At the intersections: San women and the rights of indigenous people in Africa. *International Journal of Human Rights*, *15*(1), 90.

The United Nations and Human Rights. (1995). *1945-1995, Department of Public Information*. New York: United Nations.

Violi, P. (1992). Gender, subjectivity and language. In G. Bock & S. James (Eds.), *Beyond Equality and Difference: Citizenship, Feminist Politics and Female Subjectivity*. Routledge.

Voléry, I. (2016). Sexualization and the transition from childhood to adulthood in France: From age-related child development control to the construction of civilizational divides. *Childhood*, *23*(1), 140–153. doi:10.1177/0907568215576525

Wall, J. (2008). Human rights in light of childhood. *International Journal of Childrens Rights*, *16*(4), 523–543. doi:10.1163/157181808X312122

KEY TERMS AND DEFINITIONS

Capability: The opportunity of what a person is able to do or be.

Flexible Capitalism: A feminist critique of family wage to justify exploitation of women for the purpose of capital accumulation.

Polygyny: The practice of a man marrying more than one wife.

Sexualities: Norms that are described as immoral, defiling and even unnatural.

Subjectivities: Refers to how one's judgment is shaped by personal opinions and feelings instead of outside influences.

Chapter 11
Social Justice and Inclusion of Children With Diverse Needs in Mainstream Schools

Velisiwe Gasa
University of South Africa, South Africa

ABSTRACT

This chapter opens with a broad statement that coins the social justice and inclusion as prominent concepts. The foundation is laid by giving a clear background using a South African context where there is a gap between the policy and implementation of social justice and inclusion of children in mainstream schools. This explanation goes further when the social justice, inclusion, and related concepts are conceptualised and the relationship brought forth. The main issues that temper social justice and inclusion in the mainstream schools are debated. Furthermore, there is an engagement regarding practices that hamper social justice and inclusivity of children with diverse needs. Finally, the solutions and recommendations that can be considered in dealing with the issues, controversies, or problems presented in this chapter are highlighted.

INTRODUCTION

Social justice is a requirement for a democratic society, and so is inclusive schooling. It is a cornerstone of inclusive education because a socially just system of education embraces inclusive schooling. This is highlighted by Nieuwenhuis (2010: 280-283) and Pendlebury and Enslin (2004: 40) when providing the indicators of a socially just system of education. These indicators are also prevalent in inclusive education and points to the interconnectedness between these concepts. These indicators demonstrate that a socially just system of education:

- Excludes no children from access to education. In a social justice context, it respects the equal right to education for all, whereas in the inclusive education context it calls for the increase of access and participation of all the learners in schools that are inclusive.

DOI: 10.4018/978-1-5225-2578-3.ch011

- Excludes no children from access to learning within schools. In a social justice context, it guards against internal exclusion, whereas in the inclusive education context it propels change in discriminatory attitudes and calls for the creation of welcoming communities and the development of an inclusive society.
- Provides opportunities and support for all children to exercise the range of functions necessary for developing their mature adult capabilities;
- Reduces or, better, abolishes structural forms of oppression that restrict peoples' access to resources and opportunities for developing and exercising their capacities or capabilities for living a decent human life. Without social justice and educational inclusion, groups and individuals are deprived of opportunities for developing those capabilities essential to living a fully human life.
- Takes human agency seriously and enables the self-development and self-determination of all citizens. In social justice as well as in inclusive education, self-development and self-determination are exactly what is required for disadvantaged and marginalised people – such as those living with a disability, those differed in class, ethnicity, gender, sexuality, religion and language as well as those from a poverty stricken homes or homeless. These will help them to break out of the cycle of exclusion.

This chapter makes a case for a conception of social justice, inclusion and inclusive education in order to highlight the diverse needs of disadvantaged and marginalised children.

BACKGROUND

School inclusion has been a tool of South African government over the last decade to try to address some of the social injustices that happened particularly during apartheid era and which disadvantaged a large number of learners. The lack of school inclusion has been labelled as affecting both the quality of life of individuals and the equity and cohesion of society as a whole. The indicators for this exclusion are the lack, or denial of resources, rights, goods, and services. It also involves the inability of the individuals or designated groups to participate in the normal activities available to the majority of the people in a society. This is a concern for social justice as it propagates that people should have sufficient financial and other resources to participate in economic, social, cultural and political life (National Pro Bono Resource Centre, 2011).

Moreover, social justice advocates the creation of fair institutions and institutional frameworks that provide schools that are socially inclusive in such a way that they justly cater, accommodate and support learners with diverse needs. It is about making the systems and structure of society more just, rather than seeking justice in individual cases. This is the main principle of inclusive education which states that it is incorrect to assume that barriers to learning reside primarily within the learner. Therefore, it calls for the shift in focus from individual learner to the entire learning system. It can be said that both social justice and inclusive education advocate the positive intervention of government to tackle structural inequalities or barriers (Department of Education, 2001; The International Forum for Social Development, 2006).

In the general inclusion discourses or school inclusion, in particular, a nexus is shown between inclusive education, human rights, democracy and social justice (National Pro Bono Resource Centre, 2011). The interesting readings on the above concepts propel that the idea of inclusive education provides a useful focus for an account of social justice. This link is also put forth when defining inclusive education as it means overcoming the barriers to the participation of all in education, so as to extend to all learners the human right to education and the right to participation in an inclusive polity (Pendlebury & Enslin, 2004).

CONCEPTUALIZING SOCIAL JUSTICE

Social justice is a very broad concept and it is fluid in nature. It involves how fairly people handle the poor, the needy, and the successful. It is concerned with the opportunities of all children. It typically means distributive justice. It is both a process and a goal. Its goal is to ensure that full and equal participation of all groups in a society is realised and their needs are met. Its vision ensures that the distribution of resources is equitable and all members are physically and psychologically safe and secure. It calls for a society in which individuals are both self-determining (able to develop their full capacities) and interdependent (capable of interacting democratically with others). It points to a need to acknowledge the injustices of the past in order to understand and remedy the situation of marginalised groups. This can be done only if environments were adjusted and barriers removed through redistributive measures in order to accommodate the marginalised groups (Oppenheimer, 2002; Riddell, 2009).

Social justice tackles oppression, privilege, social advantage, exclusion, and isms. It focusses on how people, policies, practices, curricula, and institutions are used to liberate rather than oppress the marginalised groups. It enables individuals to see and act, giving them the courage to resist unfairness and inequity while enhancing freedom and possibility for all. It also guides the individuals about the matrix of unequal relationships and its implications, analysis of the mechanisms of oppression, and the ability to challenge these hierarchies (Sensoy & DiAngelo, 2009; Ayers, 2010).

CONCEPTUALIZING INCLUSION, INCLUSIVE EDUCATION AND INCLUSIVE SCHOOLING

In a South African context, inclusive education has been recognised as an embracing term that includes a philosophy of acceptance, catering and accommodating learners with diverse needs in an unclassified school. Learners with diverse needs include those who were previously disadvantaged due to disability, class, ethnicity, gender, sexuality, religion, language, poverty; and those who are homeless or working, as well as those from remote or nomadic populations, from cultural minorities, etc. (Department of Education, 2001; Ainscow, Booth & Dyson, 2006; Ruairc, Ottesen & Prece, 2013).

Learners with 'diverse needs' or 'barriers to learning' are the most preferred terms used in South Africa rather than learners with special needs. The latter term is less preferred because it has been sometimes used to focus on learners with physical disabilities, thereby ignoring or having less focus on learners with other needs. As a way of becoming more embracing to inclusive schooling, South Africa has recognised physical disabilities as well as other socio-economical barriers as having a detrimental effect (if not properly addressed) on the academic achievement of these learners.

Consequently, to the above indicators, the South African government acknowledge that many learners experience learning difficulties and thus have barriers to learning at some time during their schooling. Schools have to find ways of successfully educating all learners, including those who have serious disadvantages and disabilities. The consensus has been reached that learners with diverse needs should be included in the educational arrangements made for the majority of learners. This has led to the concept of the inclusive schooling which encompasses all those learners whose diverse needs arise from disabilities, socio-economic factors or those who are disadvantaged by circumstances beyond their measure. In a nutshell, inclusion has been variously conceptualised as a process of decreasing exclusion from mainstream settings and communities. This has been done in order to increase access and participation of all the learners in schools that are inclusive (Culham & Nind, 2003).

Coined to the above concepts are respect, equality, collective belonging and positive responses to diversity. Furthermore, Florian (1998: 16) confirms that these concepts tend to ''transcend the concept of normalisation by using language that emphasises participation over normalcy''. He further clarifies that they transcend traditional boundaries between those with and without a disability. This is done by focussing on the actions and responsibilities of everyone and not just on those disadvantaged, with a disability or previously marginalised. In this way all learners are respected as individuals, their strengths, abilities and diverse learning needs are recognised as their foundation for learning and their learning challenges are identified, understood and accommodated. This has paved the way whereby the common learning environment, including curriculum and instruction, is structured and adapted such that all learners learn to their best potential. Furthermore, the government through policies has put in place systematic measures aimed at prevention, and early identification, timely assessment of need and evidence-based intervention (Culham & Nind, 2003).

Worldwide, these concepts were embraced when the right of every child to an education was proclaimed in the Universal Declaration of Human Rights and was forcefully reaffirmed by the World Declaration on Education for All. The World Declaration on Education for All which was adopted in Jomtien, Thailand 1990 did set out an overall vision. Inclusive education was taken as the key strategy to achieve Education for All. It became a process of strengthening the capacity of the education system to reach out to all learners (Haddad, Colletta, Fisher, Lakin & Rinaldi, 1990). UNESCO (2008, 2009) defines inclusive education as a process that looks at giving quality education to all learners, acknowledges the diversity of learners, their needs and aims at eliminating any form of discrimination. This process includes the transformation of school and centres of learning in terms of structure and curricula change to provide learning opportunities to all. Inclusive education is central to achieving high-quality education for all learners, identification of the barriers that many encounters when accessing education and how to overcome them. It is also essential to achieve social equity and is an important element of lifelong learning.

The broad aims of inclusive education are to accommodate all learners, regardless of their differences which may be physical, intellectual, social and emotional or other conditions. This includes learners with a disability, gifted, street or working, disadvantaged or marginalised. It also aims at eliminating exclusion that is a consequence of negative attitudes and a lack of response to diversity. If one considers inclusion it should not be taken only as a process that changes the existing structures to make them accessible, but it should be taken as a process that brings change to societies and schools by making them sensitive to diversity through appropriate curricula, organizational arrangements, teaching strategies, resource use, and partnership with their communities (European Agency for Development in Special Needs Education, 2010).

Furthermore, the Education White Paper 6 (Department of Education, 2001:16) emphasises that inclusive education is about:

- Acknowledging that all children can learn and need support.
- Accepting and respecting the fact that all learners are different in some ways and have different learning needs which are valued.

- Enabling education structures, systems and learning methodologies to meet the needs of all learners.
- Acknowledging and respecting differences in learners, whether due to age, gender, ethnicity, language, class, and disability or HIV status.
- Acknowledging that learning is broader than formal schooling and it can also occur in the home and community.
- Changing attitude, behaviour, teaching methods, curricula, and the environment to meet the needs of all learners.
- Maximising the participation of all learners in the culture and curricula of educational institutions and uncovering and minimising barriers to learning.
- Empowering learners by developing their individual strengths and enabling them to participate critically in the process of learning.

The whole concept of inclusion comes with a number of benefits. According to Westwood (2013:4), the inclusion of learners with diverse needs may enhance appreciation and acceptance of individual differences. It may encourage recognition, understanding, respect, and acceptance of diversity. Increased opportunity for social interaction and the forming of friendships as well as greater development of communication skills can be achieved. Learners with diverse needs may have access to the same mainstream curriculum, exposure to higher standards of academic achievement and increased independence in all areas of functioning. They can meet peers in a mainstream school who provide good role models of appropriate behaviour and social skills. This may yield higher expectations for behaviour and schoolwork and better preparation for adult life in an inclusive society.

Furthermore, Westwood (2013:4) states that inclusion may also benefit the schools through greater school collaboration and teamwork. Increased parent communication and participation can be witnessed. The special education staff can have an opportunity to work more closely with classroom teachers. This may improve methods of teaching, ensure more effective use of material and human resources as well as greater access to outside services. With all these benefits in place, the needs of all learners may be met successfully.

To sum it up inclusion, inclusive education and inclusive schooling should be understood as an effort to make sure that diverse learners with diverse needs such as those with disabilities, different languages and cultures, different homes and family backgrounds, different interests and ways of learning are taken care of and their needs are met in a non-discriminatory institution.

RELATIONSHIP BETWEEN INCLUSION, INCLUSIVE EDUCATION AND SOCIAL JUSTICE

Social justice and inclusivity are interlinked concepts. Where there is social justice, there should be inclusivity, and where there is no social justice there is probably no inclusivity. This inter-linkage is best uttered by Schraad –Tischler (2011: 11) when saying: 'social justice depends less on compensating for exclusion than it does on investing in inclusion'. The broader concept of inclusion should be understood as embracing recognition, redistribution, empowerment and justice. Ideally, inclusion is used as a means to promote justice (Ngwenya, 2014). Alongside inclusion is inclusive education which evolves from human rights and social justice (Tirussew, 2005; Asrat, 2013). Inclusive education originates from the idea of a "just and fair society" in opposition to the discriminatory educational systems (Armstrong, Armstrong & Spandagou, 2010). That is why it enjoys the support of international human rights declarations such as the United Nations Convention on the Rights of the Child (1989), the Universal Declaration of Human Rights (1948) and the Convention on the Rights of Persons with Disabilities (2006).

Pendlebury and Enslin (2004:40) indicate that a combination of these concepts may bring a socially just system of education that:

- Takes human agency seriously and enables the self-development and self-determination of all citizens;
- Provides opportunities and support for all children to exercise the range of functions necessary for developing their mature adult capabilities (and so meets a crucial set of intrinsic needs);
- Reduces or, better, abolishes structural forms of oppression that restrict peoples' access to resources and opportunities for developing and exercising their capacities or capabilities for living a decent human life;
- Excludes no children from access to schooling (that is, respects the equal right to education for all);
- Excludes no children from access to learning within schools (thus guarding against internal exclusion).

Social justice has created a vital necessity to the field of education. It has brought a debate regarding the inequality that disadvantaged learners are exposed to and the importance of education to minimise marginalisation. It gives useful strategies on how to alleviate inequalities. It is then possible to say that learners with diverse backgrounds can benefit from their educational provisions when the learning environment is set in a way that diverse learner groups could get a 'just' education (Provenzo & Renaud, 2009).

According to European Agency for development in Special Needs education (2010:11) inclusive education is concerned with issues of social justice, which means teachers must know how to create a classroom where issues of respect, fairness, and equity are addressed. This is because the traces of injustices such as isolation and rejection of learners with disabilities as well as discrimination by gender, poverty and racism, are still witnessed in the mainstream schools. According to UNESCO (2009:9) working towards inclusion has three justifications:

1. Educational justification: the requirement for inclusive schools to educate all children together means they have to develop ways of teaching that respond to individual differences and that therefore benefit all children.
2. Social justification: inclusive schools are able to change attitudes toward diversity by educating all children together, and form the basis for a just and non-discriminatory society.
3. Economic justification: it is less costly to establish and maintain schools that educate all children together than to set up a complex system of different types of schools specialising in different groups of children.

In furthering the links between these concepts, Humpage and Fleras (2001) together with Hay and Beyers (2011) table three models of social justice. The first one is the distributive model whereby the resources (scarce) are distributed equally to individuals. The second one is the retributive model, also known as "market-individualism", which is about punishing or rewarding based on the performance.

This type of model also reimburses individuals who were unfairly treated in the past. The last one is the re-cognitive model which is about appreciating the diversity that corresponds with inclusion. This model "take differences seriously, recognition of the collective rights of groups, support for indigenous models of self-determination, and commitment to inclusiveness through meaningful involvement in decision-making processes" (Gale, 2000: 259).

The Theory of Justice comes to mind when one thinks how these concepts advocate for the recognition, redistribution, empowerment and justice for those who are less fortunate. John Rawls is one of the theorists who developed the Theory of Justice in 1971. John Rawls' aim was to create the Theory of Justice that is better than utilitarianism. Furthermore, he developed it in order to criticise the utilitarianism for its misrepresentation of different people with different backgrounds and for not considering the differences which are found between/among people (Arneson, 2008). In addition, utilitarianism was further criticised for promoting unequal distribution of resources among societies. It also disregarded the rights of the disadvantaged people. It gave more right to upper-class people at the cost of the lower class society (National Pro Bono Resource Centre, 2011).

Rawls Theory of Justice entails two principles known as liberty (freedom) and social equality. While the first principle emphasises the right to freedom that every citizen or individual should have, the second principle advocates that the social and economic discrepancies should be avoided in order to include the disadvantaged or marginalised people and that the resources should be shared equally. This theory advocates that all people regardless of their disabilities or adversities should enjoy their freedom and benefit from social and economic aspects. In other words, this theory is the foundation for the pursuit of social justice by which the disadvantaged people can benefit from social services such as education. It is also viewed as open to extending into further developments such as the inequality in education (Arneson, 2008; Terzi, 2010; National Pro Bono Resource Centre, 2011; Hay & Beyers, 2011).

INCLUSIVE EDUCATION AND SOCIAL JUSTICE ISSUES IN THE MAINSTREAM SCHOOLS

Effective inclusive practice is subject to a number of constraints and challenges that tempers more on social justice issues. The challenge confronting the inclusive schools is that of developing a child-centred pedagogy capable of successfully educating learners with diverse needs in one school setting. This challenge borders on the willingness of the personnel to change discriminatory attitudes and into creating the welcoming communities who geared towards the development of an inclusive society (UNESCO, 1994). For social justice to take its course in inclusive education, a change in social perspective is imperative. It can be acknowledged that most of the people in South Africa support the notion of inclusion and understand that it is a journey or process of continual societal adjustment. But their actions towards realising it has been minimally achieved. For example, the challenges of people with disabilities have been compounded by a disabling society that has focused upon their impairments rather than their potential.

Another challenge that impacts on inclusive education and social justice is the school culture. The culture of a school affects the manner in which schools operate and the way in which the problem of translating inclusive policy into inclusive practice is solved. It is believed that the culture of a school should reflect collective understandings among members that envisaged inclusive education. This is a wish that has taken too long to be fully realised. But on a more understanding mode, people have to realise that inclusion is an unending term, so it will take a lot of planning, action, provision and implementation to have something called an inclusive school. One has to bear in mind the poor status of South Africa. Nieuwenhuis (2010) argues that the challenge of poor or developing countries is that they may not have the economic resources or political will to provide the type of quality education for all in an inclusive setting. But even if they have the resources and political will, cultural beliefs and practices may work against these ideals. It is, therefore imperative to look at the social realities of the situation in order to achieve social justice that may pave the way to inclusive schooling.

One may say that whilst individuals verse in inclusion rhetoric they are also constructing many other barriers that stall its realisation. The promotion of inclusive education does not enmesh with the provision of resources. Whilst committed to inclusion the implementers are not adequately trained. In some instances, inclusion has succumbed to mere integration or placement without adequate provision. The policy is silence on whether the inclusion of learners with physical disabilities to the mainstream schools is by choice or compulsory. This has led to a misunderstanding of which some parents who cannot afford certain schools pushing their children to mainstream schools with no adequate support. This situation is leaving no doubt that inclusion has led to a tension in how it is defined and operationalised not only by parents but also by government and educational practitioners. It is these tensions within parents, government and teachers' definitions and operation of inclusion in schools that needs to be looked through the lens of social justice (Hodkinson & Devarakonda, 2011).

Barriers on Social Justice and Inclusion for Children With Diverse Needs

Social justice and inclusion of children with diverse needs are often hampered by external and internal exclusion. Externally excluded groups are those who are kept out of both the distributive domains for public resources and the platforms of public deliberation. Internally excluded groups are those who are brought into a public deliberative domain but remain on the margins of deliberation. The latter is more destructive and harmful because it is done under the pretence of inclusion. For example, learners with special needs may be brought into the mainstream schools under the pretence of inclusion, but their needs, aspirations, and participation remain on the perimeter. This means social justice is far from being achieved regarding educational access, participation, and outcomes, especially for learners with special needs and those who are poor, illiterate or semi-literate as well as those residing in far-flung rural or remote areas (Ngwenya, 2014).

In South Africa, many layers of exclusions were fostered through imbalances and injustices of the past, apartheid practices, and local tradition. Most of the learners with special needs were cast at the bottom of the heap. Education White Paper 6, which requires ordinary schools to accommodate learners with disabilities and other barriers to learning, came as a rescue (Department of Education, 2001). Although it was widely adopted but the implementation of its principles is at a snail pace and sometimes haphazardly or unsystematically implemented. There is still a long way to go in order to fully attend to the patterns of educational exclusion arising from poverty, disease, conflict and other societal marginalisations. The continual exclusion of learners with special needs from social goods associated with education reflect the persistence of social injustice despite an impressive suite of policies (Pendlebury & Enslin, 2004).

Furthermore, research suggests a continuing scepticism and lack of confidence amongst teachers in mainstream schools to effectively teach learners with special educational needs (Pather, 2011). Inclusion often requires a shift in people's attitudes and values. The effect of transforming structures and societies is not possible without a radical shift from one set of assumptions, beliefs, values, mutual acceptance, respect, diversity and social justice (UNESCO, 2009; European Agency for Development in Special Needs Education, 2010). In developing countries, there are a large proportion of children who are still out of schools. Those who get enrolled are unable to complete a minimum prescribed number of school years due to institutional barriers. The nature of such barriers involves the physical location of schools as some schools are located in areas that are not easily accessed, non-availability of schools, social stigmatisation and economic conditions of children (Jha, Online: n.d.).

Teaching for Inclusion and Social Justice

It is important to note that thinking has moved beyond the narrow idea of inclusion as a means of understanding and overcoming a deficit and it is now widely accepted that it concerns issues such as social conditions, health and human rights, gender, ethnicity, class, access, participation and achievement (Ouane, 2008). Inclusion should be a guiding principle for educational policies and programmes so that education can cater for the diverse needs of all learners. It should respond to various needs of learners by increasing participation in education while preventing segregation and alienation in schools and in the larger society. There should be a genuine advancement of the Education for All (EFA) agenda and an in-depth transformation of the education systems. The values, ethos, and culture of an education system committed to excellence by promoting education opportunities for all learners should be emphasised (UNESCO, 2008).

There should be an understanding that inclusive education is about building a more just society and therefore it should ensure that the right to education for all learners regardless of their individual characteristics or difficulties is upheld. Quality education for all and the development of schools which receive learners from different socio-cultural contexts and with different capacities are powerful tools to contribute to social cohesion. The legal frameworks which should establish the rights and responsibilities, as well as the provision of the necessary resources in order to strengthen the existing systems for guaranteeing the right to education, are required. It has to be theoretically and practically shown that people with disabilities, those belonging to an ethnic or linguistic minority, those from isolated or poor areas, children from migrant families, those affected by HIV/AIDS, as well as those victimised by armed conflict or violence have a right to a high quality education (Daniels & Garner, 1999; UNESCO, 2008).

Dyson (2001) states that inclusion requires major changes and not just a tinkering of the education system. He sets out the broad principles of inclusion as social justice, educational equity and school responsiveness to learner diversity. He suggests that these principles should be interpreted and applied by policy makers and practitioners according to the specific context, culture, and circumstances of a particular country.

SOLUTIONS AND RECOMMENDATIONS

The scenario depicted in this chapter shows that strategies are required to ensure substantive inclusion and the elimination of marginalisation and oppression of children with diverse needs. These strategies are discussed below:

Children's Participation

There is a strong believe that children should be involved in decision-making because they belong at the centre of efforts to build inclusive schools – not just as beneficiaries, but as agents of change (UNICEF, 2013). Save the Children (2002) suggests two ways in which children can participate in the creation of inclusive learning environments. The first strategy is called child-to-child methodology. This strategy shows that children are a valuable and often under-used resource in education. Children can be actively involved in challenging negative attitude in their communities towards disability and in identifying children who are excluded from school. They are among the people who are carrying or pushing to school children with disabilities in wheelchairs; writing notes for children with visual impairments in class, and tutoring children with disabilities in their homes. If these efforts of children are coordinated, encouraged and rewarded, many children will enjoy learning in inclusive classes. Children's involvement is also evident in child-centred pedagogy where teachers can use teaching methods such as peer tutoring, small group instruction, project work, among others to allow children to help one another.

The second strategy is the creation of groups for children with different needs. Such groups could be encouraged to meet regularly. The benefits of such groups are that children will develop a positive self-identity; they will be exposed to different role models, and such groups may provide these children with opportunities to share experiences about the particular difficulties they may be facing. Adults and organisations can be very helpful in supporting the development of such groups. When children learn to participate, have the ability to play, learn and develop along with their peers, they often benefit something. The outcome and the results are positive for all involved – the child, his/her family, and the adults who provide programmes and services (Synodi, 2010).

Community Participation

It is important to note that educational institutions should not see themselves as the only experts on education. There are many community members who can contribute to the development of inclusive education: community-based rehabilitation (CBR) workers; community elders; religious leaders; parents; adults and children themselves. Making use of locally available human and material resources helps to develop links between schools, families, and communities, as well as promoting community ownership of inclusive education programmes. Community participation results in support and collaboration (Save the Children, 2002; Swart & Pettipher, 2013).

With the realisation that factors impacting the creation of inclusive learning environments operate at the macro, meso and micro levels of educational systems, active involvement of all stakeholders and positive interaction between multiple systems should be pursued for the successful implementation of inclusive education (Stofile, 2008). There is a need to facilitate local synergies between stakeholders in the education system, including the employment sector, the welfare sector, and the health sector in order to strengthen inter-institutional complementarities. This may ensure that inclusive societies are promoted (Ebersold, Schmitt, & Priestley, 2011).

Ensuring Access and Policy Development

Education exclusion should be addressed in such a way that all learners from marginalised backgrounds are genuinely included in education programmes. According to Sayed, Subrahmanian, Soudien and

Carrim (2007: xi), this could be achieved by an inclusive system that secures funding, resourcing, and mechanisms of distribution that ensures the provision of compulsory education to all learners. Economic access through strategies which reduce the cost of education such as scholarship, conditional and unconditional cash grants need to be addressed. They, further, suggest that schools situated in wealthy areas that are largely inaccessible to learners from poorer areas should address the politics and culture of difference through the curriculum, to help ensure that they do not remain islands of exclusion. It may also be helpful to consider twinning programmes which are structured to ensure that these schools interface with and prepare their learners for the real world in ways that celebrate rather than tolerate differences.

Furthermore, Sayed, et al. (2007) reiterates that policies that emphasise inclusion of those 'previously excluded' learners should be developed. These policies need to address the human resource development of all staff, especially teaching staff. There should be awareness of the particular forms of differentiation associated with caste and race that give rise to discrimination against marginalised groups. An engagement in inclusive discourses at all levels of the school environment including governance as well as teaching and learning should be encouraged. They emphasise that inclusive governance structures and processes should be created. These school governing structures that facilitate inclusion should include stakeholders and the school management team.

Provision of Adequate Teaching and Learning Resources

The success of inclusion that culminates social justice rests on how existing resources are used in new ways and how additional resources are acquired (Swart & Pettipher, 2013). The provision of adequate resources, equipment and teaching material suitable for learners with diverse needs is recommended. These include provision for training and courses for teachers and other professionals, development and dissemination of materials and methods, support for mainstream schools and parents, short-time or part-time help for individual learners and support in entering the labour market (Meijer, 2010).

Ensuring Acceptance

Inclusion that embraces social justice can only be successful if teachers elicit an attitude of acceptance towards all learners. Teachers should take responsibility for all learners in the classroom and demonstrate their commitment to a culture of inclusivity. The proclamation that every child has a right to education should be upheld. Schools should ensure that all learners are accommodated in the education system regardless of their intellectual, physical and any other conditions. Teachers should ensure that all children feel included in the classroom and that the opportunity to achieve and maintain the level of learning is given (Sayed, et al., 2007).

Role players in inclusive education should move away from pedagogy informed by traditional perspectives towards approaches that hinge on the 'No Child Left Behind Philosophy'. This paradigm shift, also known as an 'organisational paradigm' of inclusive education requires an analysis and action on the barriers to participation and learning (Ainscow, et al., 2014).

Whole School Intervention

If inclusion is to be successful, the whole school community should play a part. Westwood (2013:5) suggests that a genuine commitment and leadership by school heads and senior staff should be upheld.

There should be a 'whole school approach' to creating and maintaining an inclusive culture, with a positive attitude and willingness among teachers. Supportive school team, which clearly understands its roles and responsibilities is needed. Teachers should be able to collaborate as members of a team, and able to work cooperatively with support personnel. Coordinated on-going communication between special education teachers, mainstream teachers, and teaching assistants should become a practice.

Westwood (2013) further suggests that teachers should be given adequate time to meet, plan and evaluate. Teachers with appropriate skills should develop strategies for adapting the curriculum and teaching methods when necessary. Appropriate use of cooperative learning and peer tutoring methods alongside effective research-based instruction need to be prioritised. There should be adequate provision of support personnel (special education teachers, teaching assistants, volunteer helpers) as well as access to any necessary outside services. Parental involvement and support should take precedence in the whole planning and collaboration.

CONCLUSION

This chapter has demonstrated that there is a problem regarding the viability of social justice and the inclusion of learners with diverse needs. It has shown the wide gap that exists between the policy and implementation of social justice and inclusion of children in mainstream schools. It has debated that no matter how South Africa has tried to embrace social justice and the inclusion of all learners in the mainstream schools, the process has proved to be impossible. The feasibility of a smooth transition into inclusive schooling has proved to be impossible because of the embedded nature of the imbalances and injustices of the past. For these reasons, this chapter calls for everyone to genuinely address injustices such as race and class distinction which produce unequal effects. But it has been acknowledged that beyond race and class there are other socio-economic factors that crop in. For example, poverty and unemployment, violence and child abuse, child neglect and oppression, and many others always work against achieving the type of social justice that everybody envisaged. The enormous gap in the distribution of wealth, income and public benefits is growing wider and wider, leaving those who are disadvantaged helpless. This reflects a trend that is morally unfair, politically unwise and economically unsound. That is why this chapter is outlining solutions and recommendations. These solutions and recommendations call for South Africa to go back to the basics or drawing board, to re-orient, to engage in soul searching, to change the way of doing things, to make an effort where effort is required, to embrace inclusion and portray social justice in its true sense.

REFERENCES

Ainscow, M., Booth, T., & Dyson, A. (2006). *Improving Schools, Developing Inclusion*. London: Routledge.

Armstrong, A., Armstrong, D., & Spandagou, L. (2010). *Inclusive Education: International Policy and Practice*. London: SAGE Pub Ltd.

Arneson, D. (2008). *John Rawls's Theory of Social Justice: Notes for Theories of Justice*. Retrieved July 15, 2016, from http://philosophyfaculty.ucsd.edu/faculty/rarneson/

Asrat, D. (2013). Factors Affecting the Implementation of Inclusive Education in Primary Schools of Bahir Dar Town Administration. *Education Research Journal*, *3*(3), 59–67.

Ayers, W. C. (2010). Social Justice. In C. Kridel (Ed.), *Encyclopedia of Curriculum Studies*. Thousand Oaks, CA: SAGE Pub, Inc. doi:10.4135/9781412958806.n418

Culham, A., & Nind, M. (2003). Deconstructing normalisation: Clearing the way for inclusion. *Journal of Intellectual & Developmental Disability*, *28*(1), 65–78. doi:10.1080/1366825031000086902

Daniels, H., & Garner, P. (Eds.). (1999). *Inclusive education: supporting inclusion in education systems*. London: Kogan Page.

Department of Education. (2001). *Education White Paper 6: Special needs education: Building and inclusive education and training system*. Pretoria: Government Printer.

Dyson, A. (2001, March). *Varieties of Inclusion*. Paper presented at the conference VI Jornadas Cientificas de Investigacion sobre Personas con Discapacidad, Salamanca, Spain.

Ebersold, S., Schmitt, J. M., & Priestley, M. (2011). Inclusive Education For Young Disabled People in Europe: Trends, Issues, and Challenges. A synthesis of evidence from ANED country reports and additional sources. Academic Network of European Disability experts (ANED) – VT/2007/005. Human European Consultancy, University of Leeds.

European Agency for Development in Special Needs Education. (2010). *Teacher Education for Inclusion: International Literature Review*. Odense, Denmark: European Agency for Development in Special Needs Education.

Florian, L. (1998). Inclusive practice: what, why and how? In C. Tilstone, L. Florian, & R. Rose (Eds.), *Promoting inclusive practice*. London: Routledge.

Gale, T. (2000). Rethinking social justice in schools: How will we recognise it when we see it? *International Journal of Inclusive Education*, *4*(3), 253–269. doi:10.1080/13603110050059178

Haddad, W., Colletta, N., Fisher, N., Lakin, M., & Rinaldi, R. (1990). *Final Report: World Conference on Education for All: Meeting Basic Learning Needs*. New York: The Inter-Agency Commission.

Hay, J., & Beyers, C. (2011). An Analysis of the South African Model of Inclusive Education with regard to Social Justice. *Africa Education Review*, *8*(2), 234–246. doi:10.1080/18146627.2011.603226

Hodkinson, A. & Devarakonda, C. (2011). Conceptions of Inclusion and Inclusive Education: A Critical Examination of the Perspectives and Practices of Teachers in England. *Educational Futures, 3*(1), 52-65.

Humpage, L., & Fleras, A. (2001). Intersecting Discourses: Closing the Gaps, Social Justice and the Treaty of Waitangi. *Social Policy Journal of New Zealand*, *16*, 37–54.

Jha, M. M. (n.d.). *Barriers to Access and Success: Is Inclusive Education an Answer?* Retrieved August 10, 2016, from http://citeseerx.ist.psu.edu/viewdoc/download?doi=10.1.1.431.6785&rep=rep1&type=pdf

Meijer, J. W. (2010). *Special Needs Education in Europe: Inclusive Policies and Practices*. Retrieved August 10, 2016, from http://www.inklusion-online.net/index.php/inklusion-online/article/view/136/136

National Pro Bono Resource Centre. (2011). *What is social justice?* Retrieved July 15, 2016, from http://probonocentre.org.au/wp-content/uploads/2015/09/Occ_1_What-is-Social-Justice_FINAL.pdf

Ngwenya, M. C. (2014). *External and internal exclusion of black undergraduate students from impoverished township schools in historically advantaged universities in the Western Cape* (Unpublished Masters thesis). Stellenbosch University, Stellenbosch, South Africa.

Nieuwenhuis, J. (2010). Social justice in education revisited. *Education Inquiry, 1*(4), 269–287. doi:10.3402/edui.v1i4.21946

Oppenheimer, J. (2002). Considering Social Justice: A Review of David Millers Principles of Social Justice. *Social Justice Research, 15*(3), 295–311. doi:10.1023/A:1021066630225

Ouane, A. (2008, November). *Creating education systems which offer opportunities lifelong learning.* Paper presented at UNESCO International Conference on Inclusive Education: The way of the future 48th session, Geneva, Switzerland.

Pendlebury, S., & Enslin, P. (2004). Social justice and inclusion in education and politics: The South African case. *Journal of Education, 34*, 31–50.

Provenzo, E. F., & Renaud, J. P. (Eds.). (2009). *Encyclopaedia of the Social and Cultural Foundations of Education*. SAGE Pub, Inc.

Riddell, S. (2009). Social justice, equality and inclusion in Scottish education. *Discourse (Berkeley, Calif.), 30*(3), 283–297.

Ruairc, G. M., Ottesen, E., & Prece, R. (2013). *Leadership for Inclusive Education Values, Vision, and Voices*. Rotterdam: Sense Publishers. doi:10.1007/978-94-6209-134-4

Save the Children. (2002). *Schools for All: Including disabled children in education.* Retrieved June 30, 2016, from www.savethechildren.org.uk/development

Sayed, Y., Subrahmanian, R., Soudien, C., & Carrim, N. (2007). *Education Exclusion and Inclusion: Policy and Implementation in South Africa and India*. London: DFID Publications.

Schraad-Tischler, D. (2011). Social Justice in the OECD – How Do the Member States Compare? Gütersloh, Germany: Bertelsmann Stiftung.

Sensoy, O., & DiAngelo, R. (2009). Developing social justice literacy: An open letter to our faculty colleagues. *Phi Delta Kappan, 90*(5), 350. doi:10.1177/003172170909000508

Stofile, S. Y. (2008). *Factors affecting the implementation of inclusive education policy: A case study in one province in South Africa* (Unpublished doctoral dissertation). University of the Western Cape, Cape Town, South Africa.

Swart, E., & Pettipher, R. (2005). A framework for understanding inclusion. In E. Landsberg, D. Kruger, & N. Nel (Eds.), Addressing barriers to learning (pp. 3-23). Pretoria: Van Schaik.

Synodi, M. (2010). *Early Childhood Special Education Update*. Retrieved July 30, 2016, from http://www.sde.ct.gov/sde/lib/sde/PDF/DEPS/Early/preschoolSE/B5Spring10.pdf

Terzi, T. (2010). *Justice and Equality in Education: A Capability Perspective on Disability and Special Educational Needs*. New York: Continuum International Publishing Group.

The International Forum for Social Development. (2006). *Social Justice in an Open World: The Role of the United Nations.* New York: United Nations Publication.

Tirussew, T. (2005). *Disability in Ethiopia: Issues, Insights, and Implications.* Addis Ababa: Addis Ababa University Printing Press.

UNESCO. (1994). *The Salamanca Statement and Framework for action on Special Needs Education.* Paris: UNESCO.

UNESCO. (2008). Inclusive Education: The Way of the Future. *International Conference on Education: 48th Session in Geneva*. Paris: UNESCO.

UNESCO. (2009). *Policy Guidelines on Inclusion in Education*. Paris: UNESCO.

Westwood, P. (2013). *Inclusive and Adaptive Teaching: Meeting the Challenge of Diversity in the Classroom*. Oxon, UK: Rutledge.

KEY TERMS AND DEFINITIONS

Children With Diverse Needs: It means children with different needs such as disabilities, developmental delays, healthcare needs, barriers to learning, challenging behaviours, disadvantaged backgrounds and marginalised.

Diversity: Recognising individual differences and uniqueness.

Educational Equity: It means fairness whereby personal or social circumstances are not obstacles to achieving educational potential.

Inclusion: Is a process to reconstruct and reform to increase participation and decrease exclusion of marginalised groups from mainstream settings.

Inclusive Education: It is a process where all learners participate and learn together in one class and school regardless of disability, class, ethnicity, gender, sexuality, religion, language and home background. It addresses and responds to the learners' diverse needs by increasing participation and reducing exclusion within and from education.

Mainstream School: It is a school that includes all learners regardless of special educational needs. Regular education classes are combined with special education classes.

Social Justice: Is a process of promoting tolerance, freedom, and equality for all people, support for their human rights, a right to equitable treatment, and a fair allocation of community resources.

Chapter 12
The Socioeconomic Status Label Associated With Mathematics

Nosisi Nellie Feza
University of South Africa, South Africa

ABSTRACT

The socioeconomic status of learners has implications for research and the provision of mathematics education. Literature has shown that learners from a disadvantaged socioeconomic background begin their education with a gap. Hence, a lot of research advocates for quality early childhood stimulation, aiming to close such gaps. The South African government-commissioned reviews which discovered that the challenges faced by ECD provision are inequities and poor quality education in some schools. Furthermore, mathematics assessment studies' results point to poor foundational knowledge of learners, especially those from low socioeconomic backgrounds. However, little is known about the level of numeracy knowledge possessed by these learners before they enter the reception class. Interviews with 26 reception class learners conducted at the beginning of the year revealed that they demonstrate numeracy knowledge and skills that are above the curriculum expectations which shows a challenge to the kind of educator these learners are exposed to as they do not have formal teacher training.

INTRODUCTION

Young children are learners. They learn in different situations about different things. They learn from parents and from other children. They learn by interacting with things. They learn by helping others (Fuson et al, 2015:63).

Fuson et al (2015) highlight the important components in education: the learner, the abilities and the elasticity that only belong to young learners when it comes to learning. Hence, discussions that label learners without empirical evidence might mislead practice. This quote, therefore, questions practice and research on what happens to these learners when they enter school. What happens to the learners who cannot solve problems efficiently in higher grades, such as the findings of the Southern and Eastern African Consortium for Monitoring Educational Quality (SACMEQ) that indicate that Grade 6 learners

DOI: 10.4018/978-1-5225-2578-3.ch012

of South Africa use strokes (ones) when solving problems (Venkat & Spaull, 2015). Jung et al (2007, 50) confirm that "mathematics is a science of patterns and relationships and young children have far more ability to see those patterns than we may think." All these researchers ignore what socioeconomic variable researchers discovered: that preschool learner and those learners entering school for the first time demonstrate sound reasoning abilities on quantitative concepts (Nunes et al, 2015, Schalk et al., 2016). With such evidence of young learners' abilities before entering school, is it their low socioeconomic status that prevents extension of their prior learning and knowledge? Is their background an excuse for poor provision?

The socioeconomic status variable in learning has become a labelling obstacle in allowing and acknowledging young children's ability to learn and do mathematics. Inequities experienced globally have influenced investigations focusing on this variable. Van der Berg (2008) and Spaull and Kotze (2015) suggest that the socioeconomic status of a home and a school has a significant influence on performance. Spaull (2011) also highlights the gap caused by coming from a poor home, schooling in a poor school using the SACMEQ results to support this argument. However, South African national certificate results have indicated continuously the ability shown by children from poor homes attending poorly resourced schools. Several studies have also revealed innate abilities as universal (Duncan et al, 2007, Clements & Sarama, 2009, Lee & Ginsburg, 2010; Feza, 2012). Furthermore, Borman and Overman (2004) argue for schools that promote resiliency among learners from deprived socioeconomic backgrounds. In their paper, they revealed that resilient learners are those who are actively engaged in their academic activities, enjoy school, have a positive self-concept, and show mathematics efficacy. Reflecting on Borman and Overman's list of characteristics, it can be deduced that school plays a significant role in either developing or suppressing learners. The literature on early years of learning shows that young learners learn effectively through play, learner-directed activities, using their senses, the extension of learner curiosity and intuitive ideas. These aspects link very well with the characteristics of resilient learners mentioned by Borman and Overman (2004). It challenges schooling, as Sarama and Clements (2015) indicate that young children's transition to school has an impact on their success. This claim points to the school's capabilities in developing the child, extending what the child brings with to school. Visser et al (2015) add to this literature by indicating that the resiliency of learners defeats the low socioeconomic variable.

In support of this argument, there is an abundance of literature that has proved the positive influence that quality early learning experiences have on school and career success. Starkey et al (2007) have shown how both literacy and mathematics stimulation in early years eliminated grant-seekers, school dropouts and decreased numbers of offenders. In layman terms, this literature argues that one's background does not determine one's future. Hence, this chapter, therefore, aims to critically scrutinise the socioeconomic variable by investigating mathematical abilities showed by young children before formal schooling and aligning these abilities with curriculum expectations. The main questions this chapter responds to are: (1) Do learners from socioeconomically deprived homes lag the curriculum expectations in mathematics when they enter formal school? (2) How do these young children perceive themselves socioeconomically?

BACKGROUND

All schools participating in this study are no-fee schools or quintile 1 schools. In the South African context, this means that these schools service only learners from poor homes and those with parents who cannot afford to pay for school fees. The schools also offer food to the learners. In terms of resources, educators who teach these learners do not have professional qualifications. Out of the six schools, only one school has resources for motor development, relevant learner furniture and a playground for these learners. All other schools accommodate these learners as if they were older learners, including classrooms containing furniture that is not custom-made for five-year-old children. The schools' heads of department (HODs) who supervise the educators of these learners also lack understanding of how these learners learn. Furthermore, the school environments these learners are exposed to are not conducive to their holistic development. In one school learners are in a second-floor classroom that has a broken balcony that could lead to an accident. In the same school, another classroom is in a shack near the school gate. In two other schools, Grade R classrooms are situated near dysfunctional bathrooms with a lot of leaking. This is where these learners play during playtime and it is a health hazard. If the bathrooms are not leaking, they are in a terrible smelly condition and right next to the Grade R classrooms.

Socioeconomic Status of the Home

Semi-Rural

The town in which these schools are situated is a semi-rural town. By semi-rural is meant that this town does not have enough opportunities to provide job opportunities for its residents. Before 1994 the residents of this town were too dependent for the sustainability of the cash flow of their small businesses on the trains that were passing by the town. The railway company at the time offered a significant number of jobs to the residents. As soon as some rail lines were closed, a number of jobs were lost and not much was done to replace this source of income. In addition, it is surrounded by villages and farms that also contribute to the economy of the town. Most learners from these schools have moved from farms and villages to stay in the township for better opportunities, however limited. Most homes depend on children's grant money from the Department of Social Development.

Housing

Most of the learners in this study live in informal settlements with no proper sanitary and water provision. This condition is made worse by the number of family members in each shack as most of these learners come from extended families. Those who have elders will have an opportunity to be part of their old-age grant. However, those with grandparents that are still younger are at the mercy of the child grant of R320.00 that is equivalent to $20.

Parent Structure

Ten out of the 26 learners come from single-mother extended families. Seven learners have both parents within extended families. Only one learner comes from a single-father home, four learners come from a single-mother home only and the last four come from a nuclear home with both parents. The extended family structure dominates this group of learners followed by single parenting, especially single mothers. Most of their mothers are quite young, younger than 23 years.

LITERATURE REVIEW

Influence on Education by Socioeconomic Status

Global literature indicates the negative influence and impact of socioeconomic status in education (Borman and Overman, 2004, Van der Berg, 2008, Spaull, 2011). A lack of resources for learning and teaching has been highlighted as an influential factor towards the successful learning of mathematics (Enu et al., 2015; Visser et al., 2015; Bayat et al., 2014). Wang et al (2014) also support these studies by indicating that in China: learners from low socio-economic status backgrounds perform poorly in mathematics. This study suggests that the education of parents also has a significant role to play in learners' mathematics performance. The latter variable is also common to South African learners as indicated by Visser et al (2015). This debate has been raging for more than a decade as Bowman et al (2001), and Denton and West (2002) showed that children from low socioeconomic backgrounds performed very poorly in mathematics compared to their peers. This poor performance has been claimed to increase with time (Denton & West, 2002; Wright, Martland & Stafford, 2000).

Schmidt et al (2010) bring different findings compared to other researchers on the inequalities in mathematics learning. In their findings, they reveal that regardless of socioeconomic status there is no level playground for mathematics learning in the schooling system. Although their study is based in the United States their findings speak to the global community. When it comes to mathematics learning the major challenge is school provision and curriculum provision. Some schools offer multiple opportunities for learning mathematics while others do not. Some curriculums in other countries offer more than others, whether more in terms of quality or quantity. Providing all learners with quality early mathematics can level the ground, as Smidt et al (2010) argue. Quality early stimulation has yielded positive results as Hutchinson and Pournara (2011) discovered that learners, regardless of their socioeconomic status after having received quality stimulation, were able to copy extended patterns. Hoppenbrouwer (2011) shares the same findings for South African learners who were exposed to quality mathematics stimulation that yielded to developed numeracy skills. Fuson et al (2015) argue for the levelling of the ground for mathematics learning in preschool and during reception class by providing quality mathematics learning that is structured.

This chapter adds to this argument by focusing on recognising learners' actual levels of thinking and mathematical activity versus their background. Literature falls short in highlighting the thinking levels of learners from a poor socioeconomic background today. It falls short in investigating how prior experiences impact a learner's performance before a school starts developing mathematical ideas of young learners. It falls short on looking at how a young learner develops cognitively in this context. Feza (2013) adds to this debate by highlighting the exclusion of young learners from quality early-stimulation as quality provision can only be accessed by means of money. This emerging literature argues that learners from low socio-economic backgrounds can perform well in their mathematics education if relevant opportunities for learning are provided.

Successful Opportunities for Mathematics Learning

Wang et al (2013) suggest that more opportunities to learn mathematics at home and at preschool play a significant role in nurturing low-income learners' mathematics performance. Wilson et al (2009) explored the influence of a number race game in nurturing the number sense of socioeconomically deprived learners. Their findings revealed that since the number of access to these learners was improved learners could make links with symbolic and non-symbolic representations of number. Atweh et al (2014) highlight quality educators as significant in nurturing mathematics learning of learners from deprived socioeconomic backgrounds. According to these authors, the characteristics of the quality educators are a high morale, content knowledge of mathematics, and understanding mathematics progression. Cross et al (2009) and Fuson et al (2015) highlight the importance of supporting learners to be self-directed and self-initiating so that all learners can experience success in learning mathematics.

Importance of Early Mathematics Stimulation

Earlier research has suggested that early mathematics stimulation in schooling has been successful. Ginsburg (2010) and Duncan et al (2007) proved that mathematics skills attained in early years influence successful academic experiences in schooling and tertiary education. Barnett (2008) highlighted that quality preschool education leads to school success, improves performance, eliminates repetition of grades, and reduces crime and misbehaviour. Inequities globally cause provision of poor quality preschool and work against levelling the ground for all children. This literature shows that the schooling system and government ignore the most important challenge, which is levelling the ground by providing equal opportunities for all learners. This does not suggest the downsizing of quality but setting high expectations and providing high-quality provision for all.

Reception Class (5 to 6-Year-Old Learners) Number Development Alignment

This chapter is influenced by the learning trajectories in making sense of learners' levels of numeracy. Table 1 below presents the alignment followed by global curriculum expectations.

Learning Trajectories Expectations on Counting From Ages 0 to 5

The multiple concepts towards becoming a meaningful counter cannot be ignored; also the natural abilities young learners possess play a significant role (Feza, 2015). Clements and Sarama, (2009, 2014) state that the developmental progressions that a learner experience assist the learners to become meaningful counters. By the time the learner is five years old, the learner should be able to demonstrate mastery of the following:

Oral Counting

Counting begins before a child can even speak. However, when the child starts uttering words, a need for the correct words becomes important for his/her development. 'Many' becomes an important concept to young children as they begin to develop a sense of ownership and competitiveness such as "I have many toys, many sisters, and much food". This is the time to quantify 'many' through verbal descriptions and number names become handy. Two important concepts become crucial in developing this verbal counting: number names and sequence. Oral counting begins as number names. Sometimes young children do not even separate them as a number name but use them as one name such as "one two three". Baroody and Wilkins (1989) describe this stage as just a memorization of chucks with no meaning. This skill has been proved to develop too early in life (Sadler, 2009, Feza, 2016).

Table 1. Aligning the CAPS Mathematics Curriculum for Grade R/5 to 6 Years With Learning Trajectories

CAPS Expectations for Grade R	Learning Trajectories
Count objects **Count concrete objects.** Estimate and count to at least 10 everyday objects reliably.	**One-to-one correspondence**
Count forwards and backwards in ones from 1 to 10; use number rhymes and song.	**Counting backwards**
Recognise, identify and read numbers • Recognise, identify and read number symbols 1 to 10. • Write number names 1 to 10.	**Number recognition**
Describe, compare and order collections of objects up to 10. • Describe whole numbers up to 10. • Compare which of two given collections of objects is big, small, smaller than, greater than, more than, less than, equal to, most, least, fewer up to10. • Order more than two given collections of objects from smallest to greatest up to 10.	**Comparison and ordinality**
Use ordinal numbers to show order, place or position Develop an awareness of ordinal numbers, for example first, second, third up to sixth and last.	**Ordinality**

Rote Sequential Counting

Number names can be memorised easily but the order becomes an important skill for matching the name with quantity. For example, one of the young boys was playing in a preschool in the US started counting cars. In his counting touching each car as he touches, he continued "one, four, five, two," and the teacher asked him "How many cars are there, Naithling?" (pseudonym). He responded "one, five, seven, three" touching each car again. This indicates that Naithling knows number names and knows that when counting objects, you need to match a number with an object. However, the sequence of numbers makes it impossible for him to count the objects accurately. Thus, verbal counting is not enough without the correct sequence. It is important to mediate these number words individually. For example, when feeding a child, the mother needs to count each spoon at least to three repeatedly so that the child can memorise the number words. The child will be able to say such numbers separately as their speech begins to open up.

Object Counting/One-To-One Correspondence

Naithling's example reveals the importance of mastering sequential verbal counting before object counting, to match number and object accurately. One-to-one correspondence is an important concept of counting that a learner demonstrates when he or she can count each object, matching it with a correct number name. Some learners are challenged by this concept; therefore, keeping track of the objects counted becomes an important component of object counting. In the picture below Grade R, learners arrange the counting objects strategically to make their counting accurate.

Figure 1 shows that the learner has a structure for object counting of arranging objects in a row. This structure will make object counting easy and accurate. However, in the picture below many possibilities could occur:

Figure 2 shows that the learner grouped objects together with no structure. In this case, the learner stands a chance of either counting one object twice or skipping some objects. This indicates that for a learner to be a one-to-one correspondence counter or object counter, he or she has to have a structure

Figure 1. Learner structured manipulatives

Figure 2. Learner unstructured manipulatives

first: whether it is taking away the object as it is counted, but a structure that avoids inaccuracy. Some learners are so advanced that they use their eyes instead of their fingers in object counting. This means their structure cannot be observable but it is there. It is important to note this possibility in object counting. Fuson (1988) supports the development of structure in counting as an important skill of accurate object counting.

Cardinality/ How Many?

This concept is an inclusive concept where a learner understands that the last object counted is inclusive of those counted before it. This concept is not easily developed as is shown in Naithling's example. Cardinality means the learners' understanding that the last number in counting includes all numbers counted before, the whole group (Lee and Md-Yunus, 2016).). For example, Lindiwe counted six oranges and her friend asked her: "How many oranges are there?" Lindiwe responded "6". Lindiwe's response shows that she understands that 6 includes 5, 4, 3, 2 and 1. This concept is developed through repetition as literature has shown that young learners love repetition and it influences their development (Fuson et al, 2015). This is where the subitising skill becomes handy for learners and is an important skill for number sense development. Subitizing is discussed later in this chapter.

Counting On

Counting on is described as simple adding. Clements and Sarama (2009) describe it in a short form as 6+. For example, Lindiwe received five marbles from her friend to play with and the friend asked her to count them. Lindiwe counted the marbles, touching each as she is counting until 5. When she reached 5, Sally, her friend, asked her how many marbles she had. She responded, "5" then Sally gave her three more and asked her how many she had in total. Lindiwe counted, "6, 7, 8," and said, "8". Then Sally asked her how she knew without having counted them again. Lindiwe replied: "Remember, I had five marbles already, then the next one was six, then seven, then eight. There are eight marbles." Lindiwe's scenario shows in detail the meaning of counting on. Sarama and Clements (2008) extend this discussion as they reflect that children use counting on as both a taking-away strategy and an adding-on strategy. They share an example of a learner who was solving a problem of eight apples, of which five were given to her friends. They show that this learner used his fingers to solve this problem. He started by showing up fingers counting on from 5 and said: "6, 7, 8" showing a finger per count and then counted those three fingers as the remaining three apples. In Vygotsky's theory of social constructivism, this process is unpacked as a process of formation of mental structures as learners use their fingers to symbolise the apples. It is important to note that counting on can develop efficiency in counting if learners have attained cardinality and the subitising skill.

Subitising

Subitizing is described as the simultaneous acknowledgement of numbers in a collection. Clements (1999: 400) describes subitising as "instantly seeing how many". In this paper, Clements introduced two types of subitising: Perceptual subitising that demands no mathematical abilities, and conceptual subitising that demands the use of patterns (Clements, 1999). Subitising is being able to see a group of objects within a second and being able to give their number immediately (Feza, 2015). It is important to note that natural subitising cannot happen beyond four; however, conceptual subitising can be mediated by the teachers for bigger numbers. Hence, patterning becomes essential in the learning of number for young learners. The subitising skill links with multiple-number concepts, for example, if learners' subitising skills are developed, these learners find it easy to understand cardinality as it refers to the group of objects you see (Clements, 1999).

Composing and Decomposing of Number

Young children learn by composing and decomposing. For example, when they get toys they dismantle them with the hope of seeing how they were made in the first place. These concepts connect well with them. It is important to play games where learners can see different compositions of numbers, for example, the number 9 is composed of 9 and 0, 8 and 1, 7 and 2, 6 and 3, 5 and 4. The literature describes these concepts as number bonds that need to be developed at early ages (Venkat & Spaull, 2015). There are many games that can be used to develop the number bond knowledge of learners, for example, a circle game. Learners can play in pairs taking turns. They draw a circle on the floor or use a string to form a circle. They choose the number they want to decompose and collect the counters representing the number, for example, they choose 9. The first player will stand 0.5 metres away from the circumference of the circle and throw all the counters into the circle. Then he/she counts the counters that fell inside the circle and then count those outside the circle recording each number, for example, 6 and 3, 4 and 5, 3 and 6, 8 and 1. The composition of numbers develops young learners' number sense. At this stage, they begin to see the number as a unit that has units in it. They begin to acknowledge diverse ways of composing numbers versus one way. This becomes an efficient problem-solving skill needed in the schooling years, as they proceed with their arithmetic development. It also develops independence and curiosity of exploring more numbers.

METHODOLOGY

Qualitative inquiry is used to get insight into learners' backgrounds, and levels of numeracy prior to formal schooling. This method is employed for its strength in allowing individual learners display their numeracy knowledge through gestures, play, and learner language. Qualitative inquiry allows for multiple techniques of data collection, such as capturing of gestures, learner-directed play and formal activity directed by a skilled adult. It unravels reasons behind certain actions. In this chapter, the aim is to unravel and tease out the socioeconomic status of these learners and the influence their experiences has on developing their numeracy knowledge. Denzin & Lincoln (2000) describes qualitative inquiry as an inquiry that allows for careful disentangling of the multifaceted situated situation with the aim to gain insight into buried motives of experienced actions through attention and time given to the particularly studied behaviour. In their argument, Denzin and Lincon also highlight that this inquiry advises and assists in problem-solving.

Research Design

A case study of 32 learners from six primary schools in the Eastern Cape was conducted with the aim of highlighting the learners' levels of numeracy during their first week of entering formal school. The levels of numeracy are integrated with learning trajectories and aligned with curriculum expectations. Only 26 learners participated in this study due to the fact that one school with three classes could not participate because of a school outing. The data was collected at the beginning of the year before serious instruction begins. The aim for doing this was to get the data before Grade R stimulation happens. In addition, learners' interviews also had questions that were aimed at unravelling learners' perceptions of their homes.

Participants

Five-to-six-year-old children who had just entered primary school in the Lukhanji district of the Eastern Cape of South Africa were selected randomly from all Grade R offering schools. There are six schools offering Grade R with 16 Grade R classes in the selected community; in each class, two learners were selected randomly (apart from the fact that it had to be one girl and one boy) by using ballot papers. One school with three classrooms could not participate due to a school outing. Two learners were selected randomly from each of the 13 classrooms using a ballot paper system that allowed the boys' names to be in the separate hat while the girls' names were also grouped separately for selection. This allowed for an equal number of 13 girls and 13 boys being selected. The data reported is for these 26 learners.

Instruments

Structured clinical interviews were adapted from a previous project were designed for eliciting the numeracy levels of learners guided by the learning trajectory theory of Clements and Sarama (2009). The interviews were informally piloted to young children of 5 to 6-year-old gathered at church with parental consent. This pilot leads to minor changes in language and materials used to collect data. The bottle tops that were used as counters had to have brighter colours and had to come from the same brand of bottles as the difference leads to disruption. Children were more attracted into sorting similar bottle tops taking too much of their given play time during interviews. Unstructured interviews were also developed mostly to familiarise learners with the manipulatives and to observe their initiated play when they received the manipulatives. Some questions were used to explore learners' perceptions about their homes. In total, these interviews lasted 20 minutes each inclusively.

Data Collection

A cohort of six researchers worked together in two groups, composed of three members each. Prior to data collection, a one-day field work training was conducted on how to conduct the interviews with a high focus on time spent on unstructured interviews, following of questions on the script as they are and providing relevant materials per question before asking the learner. The fieldworkers then practised on one another repeatedly until they were able to focus on the questions and provision of material timeously. They visited schools in these separate groups to conduct learner individual interviews that lasted about 20 minutes each. The three researchers had different roles; one was videotaping all the interviews, the other wrote down field notes of the interviews and the third member ensured that learners had all the manipulatives needed. The data collection took two full days. Interviews highlighting the five-year-old children's mathematical abilities, accompanied by unstructured interviews focusing on how these young children perceived their status, were conducted. This data was kept separately preparing for the analysis, that is the field notes were separate from the videotaped data. This chapter is part of an ongoing project that has attended to all ethical processes with the Department of Education requirements of South Africa, and the University of South Africa's ethical board and received ethical clearance certificate. Therefore, parental consent and learner consent were obtained with learners allowed to provide only information they are happy to share.

Data Analysis

All clinical interviews were transcribed and typed for analysis in a separate Word document. The responses were grouped according to the questions asked to all learners in each document. The researchers' field notes were also typed in a separate document and grouped according to the interview questions. The unstructured interviews were also transcribed into a separate Word document. A thematic analysis was conducted by analysing the structured interviews. The data was triangulated with learning trajectories by Clements and Sarama (2009, 2014). This analysis was then aligned with the Grade R mathematics curriculum (CAPS, 2011). Learners' unstructured interviews and their biographical information from field notes were coded separately from those transcribed from the videotapes that were also coded. The two different codes were then triangulated revisiting empirical data for trustworthiness. Analytical memos were written by two researchers interpreting the emerging themes. Both researchers presented their themes with empirical evidence and these themes were then triangulated producing the themes presented in this chapter.

FINDINGS

The thematic report presented here has three main themes with sub-themes: The three main themes are learners' background, socio-economic status of the home and learners' numeracy levels aligned with the CAPS and learning trajectories.

Learners Numeracy Levels Aligned With CAPS and Learning Trajectories

Verbal Counting/Rote

All 26 learners in the study were able to count sequentially verbally to 100. An outcome that is not included their CAPS curriculum. They recited the numbers together with the letters of the alphabet.

Count Concrete Objects/One-To-One Correspondence and Cardinality

The concept of object counting is numerically demonstrated by 12 learners at different levels.

- One learner counted all 55 objects accurately moving each object after a count. This learner went further into responding to the "how many?" question, and her response was "55" without hesitation. It was clear that if the counters were more than 55 this learner would have continued to count beyond 55 objects.
- Eight of these learners counted objects accurately with a minimum of counting to 29 and a maximum of 49. All eight learners were able to respond accurately and promptly to the "how many" question.
- The last three learners of the 12 were able to count from one to 23, with one learner ending at 20-object counting. Again these learners responded to the cardinality question promptly and accurately.

The following learners' concept of object counting was below the quantity of 15. For example:

- All eight learners were able to count objects from one to 10, with a maximum of 13 for two of them followed by a prompt accurate response to the "how many" question.

The last group of six learners showed that their counting was still developing:

- Five learners could not count objects beyond six and also could not respond to the "how many" question at all.
- One of the six learners refused to count as he responded by saying "andikwazi kubala", meaning "I cannot count".
- Recognise, Identify and Read Numbers

The same student who counted correctly to 55 also wrote numerals to 20 as shown in Figure 3. It is not clear if the learner could proceed to more numerals because she asked for a break and did not come back.

Only two students of the eight who counted meaningfully to 29 minimum could write numerals as shown in Figure 4.

One of the three students who counted to 23 could write numbers from one to 10 and the other two were not able to write numbers. Figure 5 is evidence of the writing of one of the students.

Only two of the eight learners who counted to maximum 13 could write numbers. Others wrote letters, some zigzags, and some only three numbers (see Figure 6).

DISCUSSION

The key findings of this chapter indicate four main things: complex learners' backgrounds, learners from poor homes disputing their home status as the predictor of their abilities, the CAPS curriculum imposing lower expectations, and curriculum gaps on developing counting. These findings demand more research on exploring the advantages of extended families that have been revealed to be a beneficiary in families

Figure 3. Learner writing 1 to 20

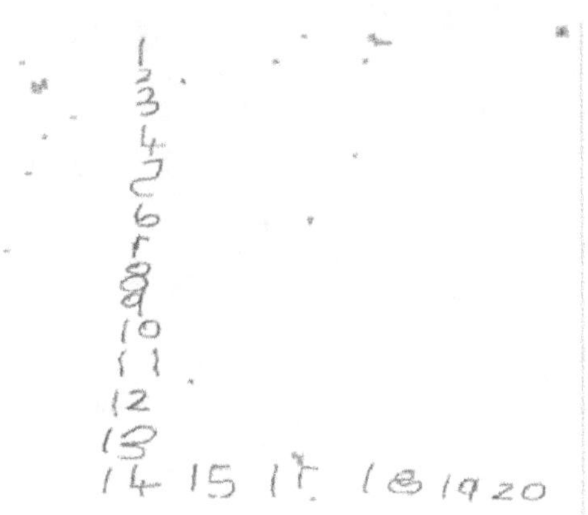

Figure 4. Two learner numerals

a.

b.

Figure 5. One student numerals

Figure 6. Two learner numerals

a.

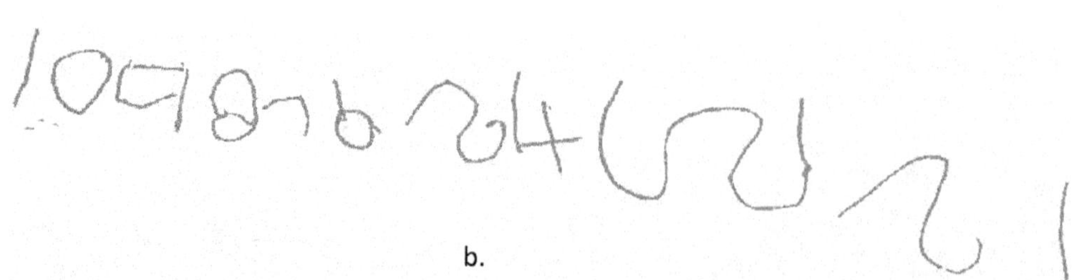

b.

affected by HIV in South Africa, where the name "orphan" has no existence. In this case, this variable needs to be studied looking at its benefit for schooling and the challenges it carries. Mafumbate (2013) revealed the influence of extended families in easing the burden of orphans caused by HIV/AIDS. Mathambo and Gibbs (2009) argue for the resilience of South African extended families, highlighting the role of grandparents in taking care of their grandchildren. As I have indicated, the extended family's influence on education needs to be studied so as to inform schooling and education policies, as it continues to dominate the family structure of low socioeconomic households in South Africa.

Complex Learners' Backgrounds

The findings indicate clearly that the learners studied in this chapter live below poverty levels at home with complex families. The family structures these learners come from are diverse, dominated by extended single-parenting skewed towards mothers. The sources of income of parents in these homes are not stable and too small.

Learners Dispute Low Socioeconomic Variable

The literature on low socioeconomic learners has argued convincingly about the relationship between the variable and learner knowledge that is disadvantaged. However, their numeracy levels give a different view on the kind of experiences they receive before entering formal schooling. Out of 26 learners, only six could not count to objects beyond 10, which is the minimum CAPS requirement. The learners studied also demonstrate abilities beyond Grade R CAPS expectations, such as number recognition to number writing. These findings question the role played by the school in the development of learners that result in them performing poorly in ANA assessments, TIMSS numeracy assessment, and SACMEQ assessments. If these learners enter school with high levels of numeracy, what happens to them that result in them using strokes (counting in ones) in Grade 6 (Venkat & Spaull, 2015). Another possibility might be Clements and Sarama's (2008) argument that learners from preschools are challenged by the transition they go through from preschool to formal school. This demands more attention in research to see how Grade R itself extends their knowledge, and if so, what are the practices that seem not to extend what learners already know.

CAPS Curriculum with Lower Expectations

The alignment of the CAPS Grade R Curriculum with the studied learners' numeracy levels reveals that the curriculum expectations are low compared to the learner in the classroom. The CAPS curriculum requires a minimum of 10-object counting while the learners demonstrated minimum is 29 for object counting. The learners' numeracy skills go beyond the CAPS expectations of cardinality and the writing of numerals beyond recognition and reading, which is a CAPS requirement. South Africa needs to improve the curriculum expectations for Grade R rigorously. Also, it is important for levelling the ground for all learners in the country. Professional teacher training for Grade R educators cannot be left for too long anymore. The South African curriculum in higher grades has improved, however, the inclusion of Grade R in the curriculum is based mainly on the holistic development of these learners. The mathematics stimulation curriculum indicates huge gaps that will have a negative impact on how these learners develop. Grade R CAPS need revision so as to build the desired foundation for these learners.

Curriculum Gaps

The CAPS curriculum is too limited regarding developing counting concepts and might impede meaningful learning opportunities as most of the Grade R practitioners follow the curriculum under the guidance of their supervisors. The Grade R CAPS curriculum needs rigorous revision if, as literature states, this level of stimulation is vital for successful schooling and career paths. The gaps in the curriculum neither assist educators nor align with advanced learners' abilities. Smidt et al (2010), Pournara (2011), Hoppenbrouwer (2011) and Fuson et al (2015) revealed that the curriculum and mathematics provision received by learners globally is unbalanced. Some receive rigorous varied mathematics opportunities, while some receive very little mathematical stimulation. In this chapter, the school and CAPS curriculum fall short in educating the learner the society presents. The school needs to train head of departments and educators that understand this learner and the CAPS curriculum requires revision that sets high expectations that will nurture the development of meaningful numeracy for learners and extended their prior experiences.

IMPLICATIONS

Learners have outstanding abilities even if they come from poor homes. The socioeconomic variable research debates need to use empirical evidence on learners' abilities for it to influence practice. The responsibility for poor performance does not lie with learners but with provision received or provided by the education system. The international assessment studies' findings speak to more of the education system than to the learner. All the assessments are pointing to the education system that is unable to service its learners rather than learner inabilities. The learners studied here indicate that as they enter school, their numeracy levels are high and misaligned to the curriculum. This chapter's findings suggest that enrichment of the CAPS curriculum for Grade R needs to be done.

In levelling the playground for learning, this chapter recommends provision of professional training to Grade R educators. The status of Grade R teachers is an embarrassment to the country as these learners are in their prime time for learning. More research is also needed to assist understanding the role of the extended family structure in a child's development. There seems to be limited research on the impact of extended family to learning and human development.

Lastly, White Paper 1 of Education promises to provide quality education to all learners. However, this promise seems not to be understood by the education system. Smidt et al (2010) describe it better when they assert that it implies the levelling of the education ground. The diverse education quality the South African system provides should not be embraced as it is the cause for inequity and continues to celebrate inequalities. This chapter challenges policies as they seem to fail to deliver the main right for all children. Quality education for all is a right, not a necessity. The universality of Grade R has been achieved well in South Africa, however, the urgency of quality cannot be exaggerated.

REFERENCES

Atweh, B., Bose, A., Graven, M., Subramanian, J., & Venkat, H. (2014). *Teaching numeracy in preschool and early grades in low-income countries. Deutsche Gesellschaft für Internationale Zusammenarbeit (GIZ).*

Bayat, A., Louw, W., & Rena, R. (2014). The impact of socioeconomic factors on the performance of selected high school learners in the Western Cape Province, South Africa. *Journal of Human Ecology (Delhi, India)*, *45*(3), 183–196.

Baroody, A. J., & Gatzke, M. R. (1991). The estimation of set size by potentially gifted kindergarten-age children. *Journal for Research in Mathematics Education*, *22*(1), 59–68. doi:10.2307/749554

Barnett, W. S. (2008). *Preschool education and its lasting effects: Research and policy implications.* Boulder, CO: Education and the Public Interest Center & Education Policy Research Unit. Retrieved 14 July 2016 from http://epicpolicy.org/publication/preschooleducation

Borman, G. D., & Overman, L. T. (2004). Academic resilience in mathematics among poor and minority students. *The Elementary School Journal*, *104*(3), 177–195. doi:10.1086/499748

Bowman, B. T., Donovan, M. S., & Burns, M. S. (Eds.). (2001). *Eager to learn: Educating our pre-schoolers*. Washington, DC: National Academy Press.

Clements, D. H., & Sarama, J. (2009). *Learning and teaching early math: The learning trajectories approach*. New York: Routledge.

Clements, D. H., & Sarama, J. (2014). *Learning and teaching early math: The learning trajectories approach* (2nd ed.). New York: Routledge.

Cross, C., Woods, T. A., & Schweingruber, H. (2009). *Mathematics learning in early childhood: Paths toward excellence and equity*. Washington, DC: National Research.

Denton, K., & West, J. (2002). *Children's reading and mathematics achievement in kindergarten and first grade*. Retrieved by 29 June 2011 from http://nces.ed.gov/pubsearch/pubsinfo.asp?pubid=2002125

Denzin, N. K., & Lincoln, Y. S. (2000). *Handbook of Qualitative Research*. London: Sage Publications.

Duncan, G. J., Claessens, A., Huston, A. C., Pagani, L. S., Engel, M., Sexton, H., & Duckworth, K. et al. (2007). School Readiness and Later Achievement. *Developmental Psychology*, *43*(6), 1428–1446. doi:10.1037/0012-1649.43.6.1428 PMID:18020822

Enu, J., Agyman, O. K., & Nkum, D. (2015). Factors Influencing Students' Mathematics Performance in Some Selected Colleges of Education in Ghana. *International Journal of Education Learning and Development*, *3*(3), 68–74.

Feza, N. (2012). Can we afford to wait any longer? Young children in pre-school are ready to learn mathematics. *South African Journal of Childhood Education*, *2*(2), 58–63. doi:10.4102/sajce.v2i2.12

Feza, N. N. (2013). Inequities and lack of professionalisation of early childhood development practice hinder opportunities for mathematics stimulation and realisation of South African policy on quality education for all. *International Journal of Inclusive Education*. doi:10.1080/13603116.2013.855266

Feza, N. N. (2015). Teaching 5- and 6-Year-Olds to Count: Knowledge of South African Educators. *Early Childhood Education Journal*, *43*(5), 483–489. doi:10.1007/s10643-015-0736-z

Fuson, K. C., Clements, D. H., & Sarama, J. (2015). Making early math education work for all children. *Kappan*, *97*(3), 63–68.

Feza, N. N. (2016). Basic numeracy abilities of Xhosa Reception year students in South Africa: Language policy issues. *Issues in Educational Research, 26*(4), 576–591.

Hoppenbrouwer, E. M. (2011). *Introducing a child-centered numeracy play-center intervention in three rural preschools in Dennilton, South Africa* (Master's Thesis). University Utrecht.

Hutchinson, E., & Pournara, G. (2011). Preschool childrens mathematical understanding. *South African Journal of Childhood Education, 1*(2), 92–111. doi:10.4102/sajce.v1i2.87

Jung, M., Kloosterman, P., & Macmullen, M. B. (2007). Young Children's Intuitions for Solving Problems in Mathematics, *Young children. NAEYC, 2*(3), 50–57.

Lee, J., & Ginsburg, H. P. (2009). Early childhood teachers' misconceptions about mathematics education for young children in the United States. *Australian Journal of Early Childhood, 34*(4), 37–45.

Lee, J., & Md-Yunus, S. (2016). Investigating Childrens Abilities to Count and Make Quantitative Comparisons. *Early Childhood Education Journal, 44*(3), 255–262. doi:10.1007/s10643-015-0707-4

Mafumbathe, R. (2013). Sustainability of the role of extended families on orphan care in the era of HIV and AIDS in the Zimbabwean society. *Journal of Emerging Trends in Educational Research and Policy Studies, 5*(1), 91–99.

Mathambo, V., & Gibbs, A. (2009). Extended family childcare arrangements in a context of AIDS: Collapse or adaptation? *AIDS Care, 21*(1), 22–27. doi:10.1080/09540120902942949 PMID:22380975

Nunes, T., Bryant, P., Evans, D., & Barros, R. (2015). Assessing quantitative reasoning in young children. *Mathematical Thinking and Learning, 17*(2-3), 2–3, 178–196. doi:10.1080/10986065.2015.1016815

Sadler, F. H. (2009). Help! They Still Don't Understand Counting A Feature Article. *Teaching Exceptional Children Plus, 6*(1), 1-12. Retrieved 14 November 2016 from http://www.files.eric.ed.gov/fulltext/EJ875422.pdf

Sarama, J., & Clements, D. H. (2008). Mathematics in early childhood. In Contemporary perspectives in mathematics in early childhood education (pp. 67-94). Information Age Publishing.

Sarama, J., & Clements, D. H. (2015). Scaling up early mathematics interventions: transitioning with trajectories and technologies. In Mathematics and Transition School, Early Mathematics Learning and Development (pp. 153-169). doi:10.1007/978-981-287-215-9_10

Schalk, L., Saalbachb, H., Grabnerc, R. H., & Stern, E. (2016). Relational Quantitative Reasoning in Kindergarten Predicts Mathematical Achievement in Third Grade. *Journal of Numerical Cognition, 2*(2), 77–90. doi:10.5964/jnc.v2i2.29

Spaull, N. (2011). *Primary school performance in Botswana, Mozambique, Namibia and South Africa.* Paris: Southern and Eastern African Consortium for Monitoring Educational Quality (SACMEQ) Working Paper no.8.

Spaull, N., & Kotze, J. (2015). Starting behind and staying behind in South Africa: The case of insurmountable learning deficits in mathematics. *International Journal of Educational Development, 41*, 12–24. doi:10.1016/j.ijedudev.2015.01.002

Van der Berg, S. (2008). How effective are poor schools? Poverty and educational outcomes in South Africa. *Studies in Educational Evaluation*, *34*(3), 145–154. doi:10.1016/j.stueduc.2008.07.005

Venkat, H., & Spaull, N. (2015). What do we know about primary teachers mathematical content knowledge in South Africa? An analysis of SACMEQ, 2007. *International Journal of Educational Development*, *41*, 121–130. doi:10.1016/j.ijedudev.2015.02.002

Visser, M., Juan, A., & Feza, N. N. (2015). Home and school resources as predictors of mathematics performance in South Africa. *South African Journal of Education*, *35*(1), 1–10. doi:10.15700/201503062354

Wagner, S., & Walters, J. (1982). A Longitudinal Analysis of Early Number Concepts: From Numbers and Numbers. In Action and Thought, (pp. 137-161). New York: Academic Press.

Wang, L., Lee, X., & Li, N. (2014). Socio-economic status and mathematics achievement in China: A review. *ZDM Mathematics Education*, *46*(7), 1051–1060. doi:10.1007/s11858-014-0617-8

Wang, A. H., Shen, F., & Byrnes, J. P. (2013). Does the opportunity–propensity framework predict the early mathematics skills of low-income pre-kindergarten children? *Contemporary Educational Psychology*, *38*(3), 259–270. doi:10.1016/j.cedpsych.2013.04.004

Wright, R. J., Martland, J., & Stafford, A. K. (2000). *Early numeracy: Assessment for teaching and intervention*. London: Chapman.

KEY TERMS AND DEFINITIONS

Innate Abilities: Innate abilities are natural capabilities shown by human being in early years of life without any training.

Labelling: Labelling means giving a category to a thing. In this case it means categorizing learners using a certain characteristic and this label influences perceptions and can create stereo typical myths.

Learning Trajectories: Learning trajectories refer to learning progressions or advances experiences through a learning process as a path to attain full understanding of an idea or concept.

Leveling the Ground: Leveling the ground is stolen from builders when they prepare to build a structure, which means providing equal opportunities for human development.

Resiliency: Resilience is a trait shown by human beings who succeed under unfavorable conditions.

Stimulation: Stimulation means arousing interest and extends it through activities and experiences.

Unravelling: Dismantling or entangling of a phenomenon to make sense of it.

Section 5

Understanding and Confronting Social Injustice in Childhood

Chapter 13
Words Were All We Had:
Confronting Social Injustices Facing Hispanic Students in American Schools

Elizabeth Goulette
Georgia State University, USA

ABSTRACT

Language and identity are inextricably intertwined. Over the years, countless Hispanic students have been categorized dichotomously in schools in ways that marginalize their language practices and restrict their evolving identities. American public schools often unjustly force Hispanic students to deny who they are, stripping them of the ability to retain their self-claimed identity and linguistic freedom. This common practice in American schools is nothing short of social injustice. Therefore, the overall purpose of this study was to illuminate and more deeply understand Hispanic youth's experiences in schools and to examine closely through analysis of classroom discourse and interaction the identities and ideologies that come into play in FLL-HLL mixed classrooms. The analysis presented in this chapter reveals critical information about how these diverse students see themselves, information that might otherwise be constrained by schooling practices (i.e. labeling and categorization), which marginalize rather than empower diverse students.

INTRODUCTION

Throughout my schooling, I refused to allow myself to be categorized as either 'a Spanish speaker' or 'an English speaker.' I spoke both; I was bilingual. I remained obstinate about retaining all of what I was and possessed. In spite of my insistence on linguistic freedom and success in achieving this for myself, English hegemony was the rule in schools and in the communities around me. That's how it was then and, sadly, how it is now (Halcón, 2011, p. 94).

As Halcón (2011) so poignantly proclaimed, his perceived obstinacy at school was simply rooted in an intense desire to retain, as he wrote, "all of what I was and possessed" as a bilingual in a world of English hegemony (p. 94). What distinguishes Halcón's tale from a U.S./Mexico border town in the 1950s

DOI: 10.4018/978-1-5225-2578-3.ch013

to that of the scores of bilingual youth today is a sense of agency that Halcón held firmly on to amidst a restrictive environment that confronted him daily. While there are, of course, some ethnolinguistic crusaders like Halcón in American schools now, the voices of the vast majority are silenced by English-only policy and practices and powerful monolingual ideologies.

Over the years, countless Hispanic students have been categorized dichotomously in schools in ways that marginalize their language practices and restrict their evolving identities. Halcón (2011) desired a basic human right, afforded by his U.S. citizenship but which was not enacted accordingly in schools: to be exactly who he already was and to retain what he already possessed (culturally, linguistically, etc.) in spite of the outside world he encountered which attempted to strip him of that inalienable right. González (2011) underscored this point by coining the catchy phrase "words were all we had" to illuminate the notion that by forcibly eliminating the usage of Spanish from Hispanic students in impoverished communities, schools were in effect taking away the very last thing these people felt that had. He wrote of this very situation "nearly everyone in our border town was poor. Perhaps we imagined that words were all we had, and we were not about to give any of them up" (González, 2011, p. 27). With only a sliver of empathy, any human being would see the grave consequences of such a dire situation for Hispanic students, like González and Halcón (2011), who truly believed that schools forced them to give up the very last thing they had, the very essence of who they were and wanted to be. There is only one way to interpret a scenario whereby powerful institutions, here American public schools, unjustly force Hispanic students to deny who they are, stripping them of the ability to retain their self-claimed identity and linguistic freedom. This all-too-common practice in American schools is nothing short of social injustice.

Therefore, the overall purpose of this case-study of an American Spanish/English bilingual middle school (typically ages 11-13) was to illuminate and more deeply understand emergent bilingual youth's experiences and to examine closely through analysis of classroom discourse and interaction the identities and ideologies that come into play in FLL-HLL mixed classrooms. The following research questions were developed with this goal in mind. The overarching question is: In a heterogeneous Spanish class of so-called heritage language learners (HLLs) and foreign language learners (FLLs), what does the classroom discourse reveal about students' experiences as language learners and users? 1.) What positions, if any, do HLLs assume and in what ways are they positioned by other classroom participants? 2.) What positions, if any, do FLLs assume and in what ways are they positioned by other classroom participants? 3.) What do these positions suggest about the students' local identity negotiation processes and ideologies they may subscribe to? As is customary in case study research, generalizations to other classroom contexts are not intended. However, there is much to be learned about what transpired in this culturally and linguistically diverse classroom that could benefit other 'super-diverse' schools around the globe, namely an acknowledgement of a disconnect between the dichotomous school classification system and students' own self-claimed identities. Byrd-Clark (2010) also noted this disconnect in her study of Canadian youth of Italian origin who were studying French as a Foreign Language,

...many individuals find themselves in a perpetual tension between self-chosen, invested identities and the attempts of others to position them differently. This tension between a dominant ideology of national homogeneity and actual heterogeneity has important implications in liberal states for multilingual identities and social justice (p. 385).

BACKGROUND

Super-Diversity in Schools Worldwide

The world today has shrunk from the vastness that previous generations experienced. Since the advent of the internet, information from across the globe can be accessed in mere seconds. Similarly, the convenience of travel has created a reality in which many people are able to move freely across borders, and even continents, in little time. Globalization has led to the so –called 'super-diversity' of many first world regions, namely the United States, Canada, and the United Kingdom. This increased mobility worldwide "generates cultural and linguistic diversity within schools" (Moskal, 2016). For example, in the case of Scotland, migrant children and youth from Poland currently constitute the most rapidly growing portion of the school-age population, yet their cultural capital is disvalued in schools where mainstream education which excludes the home language is the norm (Moskal, 2016). According to the 2011 National Household Survey of Canadians, 20.6% of the respondents were immigrants, with the majority being of South Asian and Chinese descent (Census Program, 2017) In the 2011 Canadian census, over 200 languages were reported as home languages or mother tongue. However, in Canada, no one specific minority ethnic group dominates quite the same way the Hispanic population does in the United States.

Current demographics of the United States provide staggering numbers with respect to the exploding Spanish-speaking population. The most recent census estimates the number of U.S. Hispanics at 52 million, which is about 16.7% of the total population. In fact, Hispanics are widely acknowledged to be the current largest ethnic minority in the U.S. Consequently, a wide variety of schools all across the United States are enrolling Hispanic students. This trend will only continue as predictions are for the Hispanic population to more than double from 52 million in 2012 to an estimated 128.8 million in 2060 (www.census.gov). These projections are based partially upon a 43% increase in the Hispanic population between the 2000 and 2010 census recordings.

While the ethnolinguistic profiles of Canada, the United Kingdom, and the United States are quite distinct, they share the complex issue of educating a significant number of students for whom the official or de facto language is not their home language. Research from all three regions reports unequivocally that these migrant or linguistically diverse pupils are disadvantaged in schools. Moskal (2016) identified school practices in Scotland which created barriers to inclusion for migrant students. For example, she noted that there is a high correlation between academic achievement and language proficiency when it comes to standardized tests, with migrant students attaining much lower scores than their native-born peers (Moskal, 2016). In their study of a super-diverse area called Flanders, which is located in Dutch-speaking Flemish Region of Belgium, Clycq et al. (2014) found that "pupils with a different socio-ethnic background than the dominant majority and middle class seem to be confronted with a lot of difficulties in this school system" (p. 796). They discovered that variables such as educational background and socio-economic status were directly linked to educational track and grade retention in their large-scale survey of students, parents, teachers, and principals in Flanders (Clycq et al., 2014). Despite the fact that each distinct area has the autonomy to deal with the 'super-diversity' of their schools, research indicates that marginalization of minority students persists.

Bilingual Classrooms: Sites of Social Injustice

Fuller's (2013) notion of language ideologies strengthened the view of heterogeneous bilingual classrooms as potential sites for producing and reproducing social injustice, privileging certain types of students while marginalizing others. Language ideologies as defined by Fuller (2013) are "ideas about language structure and use relative to social contexts" (p. 4). Language ideologies and hegemony are intricately intertwined. They are particularly detrimental because of the fact they often persist unchallenged, particularly in schools: "the state of hegemony means that one entity (usually one social group) is dominant over another and this dominance is thought of as 'just the way it is'" (Fuller, 2013, p. 4). However, power inequalities that are displayed and reinforced by language ideologies cannot be ignored.

This issue is particularly acute in schools where language ideologies serve to both produce and reproduce social injustice (Fuller, 2013). As Fuller (2013) explained, one common ideology regarding bilingualism in schools is that bilingual schools are full of students who are all immigrants and for that very reason, so-called immigrant bilingualism is linked to the working class and therein not prestigious (Fuller, 2013). So, while bilingualism for monolingual English speakers has by and large been perceived as a resource for social mobility, it has the very opposite meaning for Spanish speakers for whom bilingualism is connected unfairly to immigration and a lack of prestige. Therefore, a monoglossic language ideology has flourished in schools where languages are seen as "distinct, pure entities; if they are mixed, they lose value and are not taken seriously" (Fuller, 2013, p. 12). While schools have long been promoting a normative monolingual discourse, this has been to the detriment of heteroglossia or the notion that "all ways of speaking include multiple voices" (Fuller, 2013, p. 12). These prevalent language ideologies provide affordances for certain students (monolingual English speakers learning a second language) while constraining opportunities for others (Spanish-speakers are expected to forego their first language in pursuit of the normative monolingual English ideal).

Even within a given classroom, some groups of students are viewed as powerful and thereby influence the class' prevalent ideologies. In language classrooms, where individual and collective identity is enveloped in language and culture, it is of the utmost importance to consider the implications of intergroup positioning on the social justice of the classroom. Intergroup positioning is defined by Harré and Van Langenhove (1999) as "the process by which individual persons or groups of persons position themselves and other individuals on the basis of group membership and the process whereby persons or groups position their own or other groups" (p. 183). Since classrooms necessarily involve multiple participants, intergroup positioning, and its effects are crucial points of consideration in any analysis of classroom discourse.

In an explanation of his struggles in school, Halcón (2011) recalled having to fight for his "linguistic freedom and success," going against the grain in school at the expense of being labeled obstinate for his desire to maintain his sense of self (p. 94). Not every student back in the 1950s or even now is so lucky - able to actively resist English hegemony in schools. Therefore, educators should carefully consider both Halcón and González's (2011) accounts of what was (and what remains) regarding the state of education in the United States from a multilingual and multicultural perspective. It is paramount to consider all of the effects (both positive and negative) of the decisions made about how to run schools, as well as the enacted curriculum on diverse student populations. Not much has changed regarding the education of Hispanic bilingual students in the sixty years that have elapsed between Halcón and González's (2011) experiences in schools and the students you will meet in this chapter.

SOCIALLY UNJUST LABELING PRACTICES IN SCHOOLS

Various labels in use in educational institutions and practice have been contested as artificial and exclusionary, but they are nonetheless an ever-present part of mainstream U.S. society. Educational institutions have adopted terminology to represent diverse people for as long as they have existed. Labels were (and will likely continue to be) necessary to categorize a diverse population into manageable groups for logistical purposes. However, care and consideration must be taken with both the choice of labels as well as their use in schools (García & Sylvan, 2011; Holland & Lave, 2009; Hopewell & Escamilla, 2013; Reyes; 2006). This is because naming practices are not merely referential. The labels we give carve up the world in particular ways, and in that respect, they do not just name what is, they create and sometimes constrain what can be. Ngo reiterated this important point, writing "expectations from others of *who we are or should be* may collide and conflict with *how we want to identify ourselves*" (2010, p. 65).

Top-down decisions about labels and their corresponding definitions reflect the power imbalance that has long existed in schools between the administration and the students. When educational stakeholders label students they have underlying intentions, the least concerning of which is logistical. Schools implement categorization systems as a means to place students in like groups and so-called educationally appropriate courses. While the grouping and placing are definitely necessary when there are hundreds or thousands of students in one given school, particular attention should be given to the labels that schools adopt to categorize their diverse student bodies and to the criteria used in assigning labels. For example, a study of a fifth-grade bilingual classroom conducted by García (2009) illustrated how homogeneous grouping of students does not accurately reflect the nuances of students' ethnolinguistic backgrounds. While the teacher in the study offered two labels to the class (Latino or Anglo), the dichotomized structure had clear implications for students. As García (2009) explained, "the individual experiences of the children were far more complex than simply those of two ethnic or linguistic groups. Among the so-called 'Latinos,' there were monolingual Spanish speakers, monolingual English speakers, and bilingual and trilingual speakers." (p. 390). Reducing students' vibrant ethnolinguistic backgrounds to one school-issued label simply does not do them justice.

Problematizing Restrictive Institutional Categories

This case-study of a Spanish/English bilingual middle school in the United States begins to illuminate the clash between school-issued categories and students' own self-claimed identities. Since the school-issued categories were so limiting, offering only two options to an extremely diverse study body, students' self-claimed identities, helped to reveal their personal perspectives which complexified the dichotomous institutional categories ascribed to them. In this bilingual school, students were initially assessed using a state battery test to ascertain their linguistics skills, in order to place them in language classes. Then, the school categorized each student based on the test results using the dichotomous labels "Spanish-dominant" or "English-dominant." While the school used a two label system for student categorization, the researcher discerned at least three salient categories of students in her classroom observations, which are presented in this chapter. As the student profiles presented below illustrate, even within these three categories, great diversity existed. The school's restrictive classification system is called into question as it appeared to efface the subtleties of students' evolving identities in this heterogeneous Spanish class in a bilingual school.

Participants

All thirteen students completed a short survey in class which asked about their language experiences at home and in school. The story of the nine HLLs in this class problematizes the commonly held notion that HLLs are a monolithic group. Instead, the demographic survey reveals the nuances in their experiences as diverse HLLs in a bilingual school and heteroglossic community. Please refer to Figure 1 below for demographic details about the students.

Data Collection and Analysis

Ethnographic data collected originate from six months of classroom visits. Acting as a participant observer, the researcher became an active part of the classroom community. Over the course of the study, the students became comfortable with the researcher and offered important insight into their experiences and perspectives. Data analyzed for evidence of positioning and evolving identities include audio recordings, observation field notes, samples of student work, and informal chats between classroom participants and the researcher. Student work was particularly informative for answering research questions about classroom positioning.

Data analysis was an ongoing, recursive process. It began with observational field notes of the classroom interactions. Then, analytic memos were used to assist with reflection and analysis of the observations. Audio recordings of informal chats with the researcher were transcribed verbatim to provide an accurate portrayal of students' perspectives. In combination with transcripts of the informal chats, open-ended class assignments afforded an opportunity to ascertain students' self-claimed identities without the restrictions inherent in the school-issued dichotomous categorization system.

Figure 1. Student Profiles

Name	HLL or FLL	Dominant Language	Ethnicity (Self-Reported)	Spanish Literacy Level (by Ms. F.)	Gender
Antonio	HLL	English	Puerto Rican	intermediate	M
Araceli	HLL	Spanish	Puerto Rican	advanced	F
Cristina	HLL	Spanish	Puerto Rican	advanced	F
David	HLL	English	American – ties to Spain	beginner	M
Destiny	FLL	English	African American	beginner	F
Dylan	FLL	English	African American	beginner	M
Hernando	HLL	English	Puerto Rican American	beginner	M
Ignacio	HLL	Spanish	Puerto Rican	advanced	M
Jamarion	HLL	English	African American/ Puerto Rican	beginner	M
Jessie	FLL	English	American	beginner	F
Jimena	HLL	Spanish	Dominican	advanced	F
Liliana	HLL	Spanish	Puerto Rican American	intermediate	F
Logan	HLL	English	Puerto Rican American	beginner	M
Madison	FLL	English	American	beginner	F

Students' Self-Claimed Identities V. School's Classification System

"Spanish-Dominant" HLLs

Jimena, age 13, came to the United States via the Dominican Republic where she was born. Jimena self-identified as "Dominicana." Jimena's family moved to the northeastern United States when she was nine years old. She had been learning English for nine years and for this reason, she was most confident using English despite the fact that she identified her first language as Spanish.

In one particularly informative conversation with the researcher, Jimena noted that she was "tired of learning Spanish" which she felt she had already mastered. In the home and community, Jimena explained that she spoke only Spanish. Jimena articulated a desire to learn French because she was "bored with Spanish and English." Her boredom was likely a consequence of not being sufficiently challenged in school because Jimena underscored her affinity for learning languages and the desire to add more to her repertoire. Jimena said during class time, "I cannot wait to be multilingual. It's my goal. I know I can get a good job being bilingual but it would be even better for me to speak French, too." Jimena's comment alluded to the possibility of studying French next year in high school, an opportunity which was not available to her at school, which only offered Spanish and English classes. Clearly, Jimena valued language learning for career opportunities, expressing a desire to set herself apart from her future job competition. She also repeatedly demonstrated a love for her Dominican heritage and was quite proficient in all areas of Spanish.

In Spanish class, Cristina was always very quiet and reserved. This fact initially shrouded her in mystery. However, over the course of the school year, Cristina opened up little-by-little, enough that toward the end of the study, it became well-understood how she felt about learning both Spanish and English. Unlike some of her HLL peers, Cristina was reticent to comment on her ethnicity or language background. It seemed that she was proud of her Puerto Rican heritage but in a much different way than her vocal friend, Jimena, who chattered on excitedly about her Dominican background. Cristina's upbringing was similar to Jimena's in that she also was born in a predominantly Spanish-speaking country (in this case, Puerto Rico). Cristina's family immigrated to the northeastern United States much like her HLL peers' families, to improve their quality of life. Cristina explained that she spoke only Spanish at home with her parents and siblings but that she began learning English early on at her Puerto Rican preschool. Cristina enrolled at this school in third grade and attributed her strong English proficiency solely to school instruction, explaining that in the home and community, Spanish predominated. Quiet Cristina self-identified as a Spanish speaker but much like her HLL peers vocalized a preference for using English. "I feel most confident when I can use English to explain how I am feeling or what I am thinking," she said in an informal group conversation.

Bright-eyed, curious Ignacio was a talented young eighth-grade boy from Puerto Rico. Ignacio self-identified as "puertoriqqueño" (Puerto Rican) and often enjoyed talking about his heritage with the other classroom participants. Ignacio was highly proficient in both Spanish (his first language) and English (his second language), repeatedly demonstrating his strong receptive abilities. Ignacio was very proud of his dual language skills and Puerto Rican heritage, coming alive during a country project where he was able to showcase pieces of his Puerto Rican culture (like Puerto Rican customs, dance, music, clothing, food, etc.) with his classmates. Ignacio sought out opportunities to chat with the researcher about his home life on a farm in Puerto Rico after learning of the researcher's recent trip there. Ignacio's upbringing had been tough; consequently, he explained that he had moved ten times in his young life. However, instead of seeing his nomadic lifestyle as a disadvantage, Ignacio expressed an appreciation for having lived in different settings that was beyond his thirteen years of life.

Unlike some of her classmates also of Puerto Rican descent, Liliana was born in the northeastern United States and lived with her grandparents. Still, she was referred to by the teacher and likewise self-identified as "Spanish-dominant." Liliana typifies the variability of heritage learners because she self-identified as Puerto Rican despite being born in the United States. In the home, Liliana spoke only Spanish as her grandparents had limited English proficiency. In interactions with other Spanish-speakers in her community, Liliana indicated that she was able to successfully communicate with them. However, in school Liliana demonstrated a relatively low Spanish proficiency for her confidence level, often using English first on speaking and writing tasks and then attempting to translate the content into Spanish.

Araceli and Liliana had one important attribute in common: they were both born in the United States to Spanish-speaking families who had emigrated from Puerto Rico. Araceli self-identified as Puerto Rican and an HLL, preferring to use Spanish over English in classroom conversations. Other than that the girls were polar opposites. Araceli was a feisty, strong-willed, sassy young lady who often found herself in trouble in school (she was suspended a few times during the study). She ended up embroiled in verbal disputes with classmates when conversations over trivial topics like music, sports, and pop culture escalated.

Araceli likewise had issues with authority figures and over the course of the study, clashed often with her teacher and other school personnel. One important clue to her behavior could lie in her high Spanish proficiency level as Araceli frequently expressed her boredom in Spanish class. Engaging in loud verbal disputes with Ms. Flores who attempted to redirect her disruptive behavior, Araceli shouted: "I already know this stuff [Spanish content]. I'm sick of this class! I know how to do this so I don't see why I'm even here – it's a waste of my time!" Ms. Flores time and again urged Araceli to be a Spanish helper for her "English-dominant" peers in obvious attempts to curb her distracting behavior but Araceli never appeared to rise to the challenge. Even if she was asked to read a passage aloud to the class, Araceli would simply rush through and resume off-task chatter. Perhaps, she resented her school-ascribed position as a "Spanish-dominant" student.

"English-Dominant" HLLs

One student who often collided with Araceli and other peers was Hernando, a very tall and intimidating young man. Hernando was an HLL, born in the local community to Puerto Rican parents. However, Hernando's family made a decision not to speak Spanish in the home in service of their larger goal of helping Hernando assimilate and acculturate to the United States. Since Hernando surrounded himself with Spanish-speaking friends and frequented Spanish places in the community, he was sometimes able to understand Spanish conversations. However, other than slang terms and vulgar language, Hernando was neither fluent nor literate in Spanish.

A son of Puerto Rican immigrants to the United States, Antonio was born in the Bronx but moved to the local community at age seven. He was an intelligent, studious young man who articulated a desire to learn and be successful in school. In Antonio's home, English predominated despite the fact that his parents came from Puerto Rico and were Spanish speakers. Antonio explained that his parents and grandparents spoke to him mostly in English. What Antonio lacked in Spanish literacy, he made up for with knowledge of Puerto Rican culture, which he often shared during classroom discussions.

At the beginning of the study, when the teacher provided the researcher some background on her students, Jamarion was labeled "English-dominant" without a heritage connection to Spanish. In fact, Jamarion self-identified as African American in class. Fascinatingly, months into the study, one side conversation between two young boys, problematized his case. The school labeled Jamarion based on the information that had been made available at the time: namely, that Jamarion hardly spoke Spanish, was "English-dominant," lived with paternal grandparents in an English-speaking home, and self-identified as African American. However, one day in class, Jamarion revealed that he was actually half African American and half Puerto Rican. Jamarion's primary familial contacts were his paternal African American grandparents who spoke only English. He also had occasional visits with his father, an African American monolingual English speaker. The side that was unknown to school personnel was that Jamarion's mother was reportedly Puerto Rican American, a fact that he proudly announced to his peers during class time. Due to very limited contact with his mother, Jamarion did not have frequent access to her spoken Spanish; therefore, his English-speaking side predominated.

Much like the case with Jamarion, Logan's heritage connection to Spanish did not appear on the radar until about half-way through the study. Logan was always very enthusiastic about learning and speaking Spanish in class, volunteering to read aloud and always participating in class. It was clear that he had a real interest in learning Spanish despite the fact that he was "English-dominant." Logan lived in the local community with an American family of English speakers (mother, stepfather, and siblings). It became evident one day during a discussion with Jamarion that Logan also considered himself to be a heritage learner of Spanish. Logan explained that his biological father, with whom he had infrequent contact, was Puerto Rican. Logan's preference for English was due to being brought up in an English-speaking home environment yet he expressed a genuine desire to learn Spanish.

It was not revealed until halfway through the study that David had a slight heritage connection to Spanish. During the country project, David brought his cultural knowledge about Spain into the classroom discussion. He appeared to know a great deal about many cultural elements of Spain (music, food, dance, etc.) despite almost no ability to understand or speak the language. David's demographic survey and writing piece shed some light on his feelings about his Spanish background. David reported feeling closer to the cultural elements of his Spanish background than the linguistic ones, classifying his relationship with the Spanish language as "distant." He explained that he was more interested in pursuing his cultural ties to Spain via dance, art, and music than through learning the language of his ancestors.

"English-Dominant" FLLs

This Spanish classroom also had students who were "English-dominant" FLLs with no heritage connection to the language. One such example was a kind and smart young African American boy named Dylan. Dylan was a great friend to his peers in the Spanish classroom; he could always be seen helping his various partners with classroom tasks. Dylan had a natural aptitude for learning languages. He seemed to pick up the Spanish content relatively easily. In fact, at times, Dylan was better able to explain grammatical answers to his peers than the teacher. Somehow, Dylan had an ability to teach others about the language that he himself was busy learning.

Another monolingual English speaker in the class was Destiny, an extremely shy, sweet young African American girl. For the first entire semester of Spanish, Destiny was painfully shy in Spanish class, only answering questions in the softest whisper when called upon by Ms Flores. Destiny did not speak much in class nor did she take an active role in group work, instead opting to be the reserved, quiet one.

Jessie was a very quiet, shy young lady who appeared disinterested in engaging with the Spanish language during observations. She rarely participated in classroom tasks even when called upon by Ms Flores. In dyadic interactions, she generally was the quiet one – letting her HLL peer do the majority of the task individually. Her general demeanor during class was one of disinterest and apathy. She appeared to do the bare minimum of what was expected of her during class. However, she did not present any behavior problem to the environment but rather generally quietly abstained from classroom discussions and activities.

STUDENT SELF-POSITIONING IN SCHOOLS

While the previous section detailed a disconnect between the dichotomous school classification system and students' self-claimed identities, the present section moves the discussion toward a deeper exploration of the ways students both self-positioned and articulated their identities in a classroom activity. When given an open-ended activity where they had the freedom to explore all aspects of their classroom identities, the students' own responses revealed that the restrictive school categorization system did not adequately account for the nuances of their evolving identities as language learners and users in a heterogeneous Spanish class. Therefore, teachers of emergent bilinguals should offer more opportunities for students to position themselves in school through open-ended tasks which allow them to work through the development of their dynamic socially situated identities.

Foreign-Born HLLs

Despite the fact that they were all labeled "advanced" by their teacher, each of these students had diverse language skills, preferences, and priorities. Two of the five "advanced" HLLs were born and educated for some time outside of the continental United States. Jimena was born in the Dominican Republic and in the survey self-identified as "Dominican." She reported going to school in the Dominican Republic for about five years and entering U.S. public school at the age of nine when she moved to her current community. Jimena reported learning to read as a young child in Spanish. Ignacio was the other foreign-born HLL of the group, born in Puerto Rico. In the survey, he self-identified as Puerto Rican. He lived and was educated in Puerto Rico until the age of nine when he moved to the United States with his mother. Ignacio reported that he began learning to read first in Spanish in Puerto Rico.

Both Jimena and Ignacio wrote that their family wanted them to continue learning Spanish. However, Jimena reported using Spanish more often than Ignacio. While Ignacio explained that he used English most of the time, Jimena said she used both equally. Both students used mostly Spanish at home but Jimena reported speaking with friends in both English and Spanish whereas Ignacio recounted his language experiences with friends as occurring mostly in English. Similarly, when asked in general which language they preferred to speak, Ignacio selected English while Jimena listed both English and Spanish as her preferences. Through these two examples of foreign-born "advanced Spanish-dominant" students, different language use and preferences reveal some nuances of their HLL experiences.

Despite living in Spanish speaking homes in the very same community, Ignacio and Jimena had distinct attitudes towards learning and using Spanish. Jimena demonstrated a preference for using both languages in multiple settings. Ignacio definitely spoke Spanish at home but tended to prefer using English as well as sought out friendships with English speakers rather than Spanish speakers like Jimena.

Interestingly, both "advanced" HLLs clearly valued the ability to speak multiple languages. Recall that Jimena exhibited an intense desire to be multilingual - expressing to the researcher the advantages it would afford her in life, in particular, for her career. Ignacio was less outspoken about the importance of being multilingual but in his survey and some informal chats with the researcher, he detailed a desire to learn Chinese and live in China one day.

In addition to the language background survey, students completed a task in which they were asked by the teacher in an activity during class time, to create a visual depicting their relationship to the Spanish language. Then, they were asked to provide a short written explanation of the visual. On this activity, Ignacio drew both countries where he had lived. His drawing incorporated a sketch of the island of Puerto Rico with his home city, Ponce, included. The text below the drawing read "I was born here." Then, Ignacio sketched the United States and wrote beneath "Move here when I was nine." In his own words, an explanation of the drawing is as follows: "I was born in Puerto Rico, learn Spanish and English until [*sic*] I was nine. My mom wanted to move to the US for I can have a better life than in Puerto Rico. I would like to live in China and learn Chineis [*sic*]." Ignacio decided to share not only the basis for his family's move but also provided the rationale his mother had given him for moving, one very common for immigrants to the United States.

Jimena's visual was quite different than Ignacio's. Jimena drew herself helping her Spanish-speaking friend understand the English sign on a nearby building. In Spanish, Jimena's friend is saying "Que dice eso. No hablo ingles." [sic] [What does that say? I don't speak English.] Jimena is answering, "película en la esquina" [movie on the corner]. Clearly, Jimena viewed her bilingualism primarily as an avenue to assist others. In her own description of the drawing, Jimena explained, "I could help people translate. I love speaking Spanish but when I get older I'll know more than just two languages like French and Chinese." Jimena was consistent as she repeatedly mentioned her goal for multilingualism. At times, she indicated an expectation that her multilingualism would open up career opportunities. In this writing selection, Jimena informed the researcher of her desire to use Spanish and other languages she wanted to learn in the future, to help others by translating for them. Jimena's given classroom role and responsibility very much mirrored this statement, as she was constantly referred to as a "teacher" for her "English-dominant" classmates.

The United States Born HLLs

Of the five "advanced Spanish-dominant" HLLs, three were born in the United States. In this class, all three U.S. born "advanced" HLLs had Puerto Rican heritage. All three of these students self-identified as Puerto Rican American in their surveys whereas the two foreign-born HLLs mentioned above self-identified with their home country and not the United States.

There were some very interesting similarities in this small group of students. For example, all three of them described learning to read first in English as a young child. Their answers contrasted with the foreign-born group (Jimena and Ignacio) who started reading first in Spanish. When asked which language they spoke more often, all three students listed English. Interestingly, all three reported speaking both English and Spanish at home. While Antonio described speaking both English and Spanish with friends, the two girls (Liliana and Araceli) explained that they usually spoke with friends in English.

In the picture section of the language-identity activity, both girls depicted the importance of friends in their lives as bilinguals. Both Araceli and Liliana drew pictures of their school and labeled their classmates as their friends with whom they spoke Spanish. Their drawings are not included in this paper because they did not use pseudonyms for the school nor their friends' names. Both girls considered themselves friends as they included one another in their pictures, along with two other classmates, Madison and Dylan (FLLs). Araceli also wrote about speaking Spanish at school with friends in Spanish class. She wrote:

I only speak Spanish in school with my friends because I feel more comfortable speaking Spanish with them because they won't judge me speaking Spanish. By them laughing at me and saying I can't speak Spanish because I can't speak that much Spanish.

Araceli referred to her Spanish as "ghetto Spanish" informally in class during the observations. Since she was quite fluent in Spanish but not literate, it seems that Araceli was devaluing her dialect more than indicating that she truly did not speak Spanish. She appeared to be conveying a comfort of speaking her Spanish variety with other Spanish learners and users in Spanish class. To Araceli, the classroom environment provided a safe place where she could use the Spanish variety she learned at home, what she called "ghetto Spanish," meanwhile learning the standard Spanish variety along with her peers.

Another U.S. born HLL, Liliana, wrote about self-identified gaps in her knowledge as a Spanish-speaking HLL in an English-dominant world. In Liliana's writing piece, she devoted considerable time and attention to her home connections to Spanish. In her case, both her home and the school were Spanish learning environments where she could obtain significant Spanish input and expand her horizons as a Spanish language learner and user. She wrote:

I speak Spanish in school and at home. My mother and father both are Puerto Rican and both like to speak Spanish. There are some words I don't know in Spanish but sooner or later I will learn them. My grandma and grandpa speak Spanish so I must know how to speak it because they only know Spanish they don't really understand English.

For Liliana, using Spanish was the norm in life. She reported speaking Spanish at home with various family members. It is important to note that Liliana's family structure is typical of many Latinos in that her grandparents lived in her home. So, she had frequent daily contact outside of school with four adult Spanish speakers (her mother, father, grandfather, and grandmother). Liliana perceived that as a reason to continue learning and using Spanish as an emergent bilingual. She definitely desired to achieve successful communication ability with her grandparents in Spanish out of necessity because they were unable to communicate in English. The family connection appeared to provide Liliana incentive to continue expanding her linguistic repertoire inside and outside of school.

Three other heritage language students in this class were also born in the United States but in contrast to Antonio, Araceli, and Liliana they were labeled as "English-dominant." Certainly, their family exposure to Spanish was more limited than the "Spanish-dominant" group who lived in exclusively Spanish-speaking homes. However, they were still considered HLLs by the broad definition, which includes a Spanish heritage connection as well as some Spanish content knowledge.

Interestingly, all three of these "English-dominant" HLLs self-identified as "mixed" on the survey. David self-identified as "mixed" but listed white, black, Spanish from Spain, Italian, and Native American on his paper. He took the opportunity to include all of the facets of his heritage on the survey and detailed where his Spanish side came from Spain. Despite the eclectic nature of his heritage, David drew and wrote specifically about his relationship to the Spanish language and culture, noting that he was distant from it. In David's drawing, he incorporated many aspects of Spanish culture to a center box entitled "me." Branching off from the word "me" David included cultural items like "art," "music," "clothes," "dance," "entertainment," and "food." He then added two linguistic elements to the drawing "Italian language" and "English" that he explained directly connected to him. In contrast, David drew a line off of the "food" section, which included the phrase "Spanish language." In his own words, David provided his rationale for the placement:

I am very distant from the Spanish language. We eat Spanish food, listen to music, and dance. However, the language I am distant from. For me, Spanish branches off of food and music witch [sic] is what I like. Also now I'm attempting to learn the language for me and my family when I really want to learn Italian.

Clearly, David felt much more connected to the cultural aspects of his Spanish heritage. He explained that he was "distant" from the Spanish language but contrasted it with his closeness to Spanish cultural aspects like "food, music, and dance."

Jamarion was another young man who was labeled by the school as an "English-dominant HLL" and self-identified as "mixed." Under the word "mixed" Jamarion included the following additional features of his heritage: "Puerto Rican American, African American, and Native American." On the drawing activity, Jamarion's visual depicted both sides of his family as he drew a stick figure labeled "Mom" with the words "Puerto Rican" beneath her. On the other side of the page, Jamarion included another stick figure labeled "Dad" and the words "African American" below the drawing. To explain further, Jamarion completed the writing exercise with the following excerpt:

Mom speaks Spanish. My mom's family is from Puerto Rico. My Dad speaks English. I would want to speak Spanish. My Grandma and Grandpa speaks [sic] English and Spanish. My entire side of my Mom's family speak [sic] both.

Jamarion expressed a desire to speak Spanish in his writing "I would want to speak Spanish" yet during the observations he did not appear to take Spanish class very seriously as a means to that end. Perhaps, though, the apparent disconnect between Jamarion's classroom behavior and his statement about wanting to speak Spanish was a consequence of the fact that his Spanish class did not really provide him an opportunity to learn Spanish seriously. A possible reason for Jamarion to learn to speak Spanish was the family connection; he explained that his mother's entire side of the family spoke Spanish. Spanish could have been seen as an avenue for him to reconnect with his mother's side, particularly since he lived with his father.

Logan was also an "English-dominant" HLL in Ms. Flores' class with a mixed heritage. On the demographic survey, Logan responded to the self-identification question with both the terms "Puerto Rican-American" and "American." His choice to include both terms is noteworthy and corresponds to his actions in class regarding his family background. Even though the term "Puerto Rican-American" includes the word American and therein the American heritage, Logan added "American" to the category "Puerto Rican American." This choice might reflect a more fractured identity representative of Logan's feelings about his heritage expressed in class during the observations.

Due to a geographic separation from his Puerto Rican side (Dad's side) Logan repeatedly spoke of a desire to re-connect with his father via the Spanish language. In his drawing, Logan included two stick figures, one was his father and the other was Logan himself. In order to contact his father's side of the family, Logan had to call on the telephone so his picture included a phone up to the ear of the stick figure. To explain his drawing, Logan wrote: "My father is Puerto Rican and Hungarian. He usually talks in Spanish to his friends and to me and whenever my grandma calls I ask him to help me understand what she says and helps me tell her things in Spanish." Logan's father was an intermediary between Logan and his grandmother who could not easily communicate with two different dominant languages. Logan's father's bilingualism was a resource that facilitated communication between two generations of the family who had different language abilities. Also, like many other heritage learners, Logan's family connection to Spanish propelled him in his motivation to be bilingual.

The United States Born FLLs

In this class, there were three FLLs enrolled: Destiny, Jessie, and Madison. All were English monolinguals beginning to learn Spanish in this bilingual school. However, they each had a very different relationship with Spanish.

Jessie self-identified as "American" in the survey and listed only English under the question about languages were spoken. She clearly did not perceive herself as a "Spanish speaker" at the time of the survey which took place during the second semester. This perspective was evident in her classroom demeanor. She was very quiet in Spanish class and did not appear to be learning much Spanish in class over the course of the study. Since she was so quiet in class, a fascinating revelation about her family was revealed in the survey when she reported that her family did not want her to learn Spanish. This perspective is interesting particularly since they had deliberately enrolled her in the school which was marketed as a Spanish/English bilingual school.

Likewise, her general disinterest evident in classroom interactions was surprising considering what she drew and wrote about her relationship to Spanish. Regarding the picture she drew of herself and her pet cat, Jessie reported: "I don't speak Spanish. I want to learn in high school. I have a cat named Kevin. I am going to take Spanish classes in high school. I want to learn Spanish for fun." Jessie's perspective clearly was that she did not speak Spanish. She likely equated speaking Spanish with having Spanish heritage like many of her HLL classmates.

Destiny shared many of Jessie's sentiments regarding learning the Spanish language. Destiny self-identified as "African American" on her survey. Destiny also reported only speaking English under the section about language is spoken on the survey. Destiny wrote about her rationale for studying Spanish: "I want to learn Español in high school because it's fun, and I can use it to travel around the world. Teach other people Spanish who doesn't [*sic*] know Spanish like English speakers." Destiny clearly desired to continue learning Spanish during high school which was not too surprising because she had both made significant progress in Spanish and seemed to enjoy it during the observations. Like her monolingual classmate, Jessie, she appeared to subscribe to the ideology that for her, a monolingual English speaker, learning Spanish was "fun" but not at all constitutive of her identity. Instead, Destiny's writing revealed a goal of helping non-Spanish speakers (for example, the English speakers she wrote about) learn Spanish. Destiny clearly subscribed to the ideology that English speakers "do not know Spanish." This ideology likely had implications for how she viewed herself as a Spanish language learner and might explain why she did not consider herself a Spanish speaker despite being a successful language learner in Spanish class.

The third FLL in Ms. Flores' class also indicated that she did not speak Spanish on the survey. Madison self-identified as American and reported a preference for speaking English. Her classroom behavior supported this position as she was typically reluctant to speak Spanish in class. Madison's writing affords an opportunity to better understand her experience as an FLL in this heterogeneous Spanish class. Madison wrote the following:

I only speak Spanish in school with my friends or I wouldn't be speaking Spanish. When Im [sic] at my friends [sic] house her family speaks Spanish I hear them and I understand them and I respond back in English. The only reason why im [sic] learning Spanish is because I have to at school.

Here, Madison explored her feelings about learning Spanish in school. It appears that Madison viewed Spanish learning as compulsory at the bilingual school she attended. However, she did not seem to find much value in doing so. Possibly, she was required by her parents to attend the bilingual school since she reported in the survey that her family did, in fact, want her to learn Spanish. Madison's behavior during class corroborated this writing sample's perspective as she did not usually put much effort into learning or speaking Spanish in class.

For Madison, speaking Spanish was more about a general school obligation than a personal area of interest. However, she clearly valued the friendships she garnered while being enrolled at the bilingual school. Interestingly, Madison's closest school friends were fairly diverse; the two girls were "English-dominant" HLLs (Araceli and Liliana) and one boy was an "English-dominant" FLL (Dylan). In the writing piece, Madison recalled times when she encountered Spanish at her friend's home. Interestingly, Madison created a firm boundary for her Spanish at Liliana's home. Despite reporting to speak Spanish at school amongst friends, Madison explained that she only spoke English at her friend's house. Madison recounted solid receptive ability with Liliana's family of native speakers (whom she reported being able to understand in Spanish) yet elected to respond to them in English. In a separate conversation with Madison, she explained that Liliana would translate her responses in English to Spanish so that Liliana's family could understand. The personal choice not to speak Spanish to Liliana's family resonated with Madison's general disinterest in learning and speaking Spanish. It appeared that her friendship with HLLs provided minimal motivation for speaking Spanish at school and did not prompt her Spanish language use to transcend the physical boundary of the school.

SOLUTIONS AND RECOMMENDATIONS

"Emergent Bilingual": An Attractive Alternative

These findings detailed identity tensions between the school's classification of students and the students' own self-claimed positions. The school's attempts to categorize their diverse student body using the labels "Spanish-dominant" and "English-dominant" created a rigid hierarchical structure that students were largely unable to traverse. These dichotomous labels engendered serious identity tensions in the classroom as students either succumbed to or negotiated the social identities ascribed to them by the school and classroom participants who took up the school's labels. Official school discourse and practices constrained identity options available to students and had a significant impact on the ways that the teacher and students assumed classroom positions. However, as the researcher grew well acquainted with the school and classroom participants, the complexity of the classroom positionings became salient.

In order to resolve identity tensions like the ones presented above, the researcher set out to find a more inclusive term for these dynamic students and others like them in American schools. García (2009) has argued that the term "emergent bilingual" be used because it not only emphasizes the positive characteristics of emergent bilinguals by putting bilingualism at the center but also because it is perceived to be much more inclusive. For example, including the word "emergent" highlights the learner's potential in developing their bilingualism rather than focusing on the end-product of achieving bilingualism (García, 2009, p. 322). As a result, García (2009) believed the term "emergent bilingual" inherently recognized bilingualism as a cognitive and social resource for these students, "emergent bilinguals are seen as having an advantage over those who speak English only and for whom becoming bilingual will be more difficult" (p. 322). The term "emergent bilingual" has the potential to reflect the extreme diversity of these students' linguistic repertoires, "emphasizing the students' emergent bilingualism places students on a bilingual continuum of more or less accessibility to languaging bilingually" (García, 2009, p. 323).

A fundamental change in perspective comes with the new label "emergent bilingual." Now, a positive spin has been given to students who have previously been viewed as having a deficit to overcome in schools. Furthermore, emergent bilinguals' potential for language and literacy development is expanded rather than constrained as it so often has been in the past. Reyes (2006) explained this new label's ("emergent bilingualism") impact on early learners:

for emergent bilingual children, their zones of proximal development are expanded because they have the opportunity to transact with two overlapping and interacting literate worlds and to enhance their learning by thinking and exploring their social worlds with others in two languages (p. 286).

This shift from an orientation of deficit to a language as a resource perspective allows educators to conceive of all students in their classes as capable of achieving success in schools (Fuller, 2013). As Hornberger and Link detailed, teachers can and should create "a learning environment that recognizes and builds on the language and literacy repertoires students bring to school" (2012, p. 243). Instead of tearing our diverse learners' down, we need to build them up to appreciate their dynamic identities.

FUTURE RESEARCH DIRECTIONS

It is concerning that so few studies have been published thus far which investigate classroom talk for evidence of HLL and FLL students' experiences in a heterogeneous class. The field of heritage language education has only very recently begun to receive researchers' attention. So far, there is only one specific heritage language conference in the U.S. One relatively new educational research journal, called the *Heritage Language Journal* (*HLJ*), makes it a priority to report research studies dealing with heritage language education. However, the need is great for future research in the previously unchartered territory of heritage language education, particularly classroom-based studies like the one presented in this chapter.

In large part, the scant existing heritage language research is dominated by studies of either affective aspects of being an HLL or specific linguistic skills and funds of knowledge (Moll, 1992) that HLLs bring to the classroom. Even at these heritage language conferences, pure, theoretical linguistic studies clearly dominate. The *HLJ* is heavily biased towards theoretical linguistics rather than applied linguistics research like the study present here. On the other hand, educational research is critical because HLLs are already in a great deal of American public classrooms today. Teachers are largely unaware of *how* to effectively teach HLLs and as an extension, *how* to approach the heterogeneous classes that are quickly becoming commonplace in our nation's schools. Therefore, urgent attention must be given to applications of heritage language education. More studies such as the one presented here are desperately needed to provide language instructors with more information about how to better meets the needs of the diverse students that end up in classrooms today.

CONCLUSION

Using data gleaned from twenty-six ethnographic observations of Ms Flores' class, this chapter presented identity tensions that arose in classroom interaction. In order to handle their diverse student population, school-issued labels not only dichotomously categorized students with very complex linguistic and cultural backgrounds, but resistance to this rigid classification system spilled over into the classroom in the form of serious identity tensions. One particularly enlightening, open-ended assignment allowed students' to explore their connections to the Spanish language through image and writing. With the freedom to explore any and all aspects of their relationship to Spanish, the students' images and writing complexified the dichotomous labels handed down to them by the school. Without this sort of open-ended assignment, we might not have understood the students' true feelings about learning and using Spanish in this heterogeneous class and the surrounding community. The takeaway point is that without the freedom to express themselves, students either tended to adopt school-wide labels that constrained them by failing to capture their linguistic and cultural complexity or behaved in ways that appeared to resist this rigid classification system. In both situations, the school is doing these students an injustice.

The concept of language dominance and its incorporation in labeling practices at this school reveal an underlying conceptualization of bilingualism as dichotomous. That is to say, bilingualism was viewed as two separate language systems existing within one person. The transitional bilingual school model adopted by the bilingual school focused on the acquisition of English as the primary goal for their diverse student body, which often appeared to come at the expense of Spanish. García and Sylvan (2011) provided an example of this outmoded view, "there is a conception of two autonomous languages - an L1 and an L2 - and of bilinguals as two monolinguals within one individual" (p. 387). However, diverse students' varied linguistic and cultural background in multiple languages is in reality much more complex than this simple conceptualization. In fact, scholars have recently urged a view of bilingualism as a continuum that includes all of the speakers' linguistic resources or essentially in terms of linguistic repertoire, which refers to the totality of languages and communicative resources available to speakers (García, 2009; Hornberger & Link, 2011).

As an alternative perspective to the linear models, dynamic bilingualism "suggests that the language practices of all bilinguals are complex and interrelated; they do not emerge in a linear way" (García & Sylvan, 2011, p. 388). To underscore this point, this study shows what happens when bilingual students are characterized by language dominance. It was discovered that language dominance becomes the most salient feature and the bilingualism component fades away. Students are labeled as and assume their subscribed identities as either "Spanish-dominant" or "English-dominant" since no labels existed to capture the realities of their individual and collective linguistic heterogeneity.

There was no label available to students in Ms. Flores' class which emphasized their emergent bilingualism. Every student regardless of language proficiency and heritage status must fit into the rigid dichotomous duo of labels available to them: "Spanish-dominant" or "English dominant." Holley et al. (2009) explored the problem caused by schools which often force linguistically diverse students into pre-established categories and explained, "it is within the school context that youths often first encounter pressures to select a racial category…many children of color are forced to figure out their places within pre-established racial and ethnic groups" (p. 15). The notion of language dominance excludes that possibility that any given student could utilize a single linguistic repertoire potentially including multiple languages for communicative purposes.

In actuality, be(com)ing bilingual is a process but in this school, it clearly was conceptualized as product or end-goal, something that is fixed and static instead of fluid, dynamic, nuanced, and situational. The notion of bilingualism as a process is complicated and messy; students who are in the process of be(com)ing bilingual do not fit nicely into dichotomous boxes for the purpose of categorization. He (2010) spoke to this very dangerous issue: "HL learning provides fertile ground for us to reconsider dichotomous concepts such as native language versus target language, native speech community versus target speech community, instrumental versus integrative motivations…" (p. 78). Schools like the one examined here force an extremely nuanced process into a limited binary: conceptualizing bilingualism as a product which results in the dominance of one language at the expense of another.

Though the labels currently utilized by the school are convenient for the grouping of students, they clearly limit possibilities available to students, making the process of bilingualism a black or white one (Abdi, 2011; García and Sylvan, 2011; Reyes, 2006). A fundamental change in perspective by the administration regarding labeling practices would widen the scope of bilingualism as a continuum and influence the enacted curriculum. Instead of viewing these language learners as two monolinguals in the same skin, an emergent bilingual view would definitely allow the students an opportunity to embrace the exciting process of be(com)ing bilingual.

Language and identity are inextricably intertwined. The language(s) people speak impacts how they define themselves and how they are defined by others. Therefore, it is important to (re)conceptualize emergent bilinguals as both language learners and users because neglecting either aspect would fail to capture the emergent nature of their bilingualism. All emergent bilinguals are to varying degrees both learners and users of two languages. Emergent bilinguals are not only learning and using multiple languages but they are also involved in identity negotiation inherent in the language learning process. The analysis of classroom discourse presented in this chapter, reveals critical information about how emergent bilinguals see themselves, information that might otherwise be constrained by schooling practices which marginalize rather than empower diverse students.

REFERENCES

Abdi, K. (2011). She really only speaks English: Positioning, language ideology, and heritage language learners. *Canadian Modern Language Review*, *67*(2), 161–189. doi:10.3138/cmlr.67.2.161

Byrd-Clark, J. (2010). Making "wiggle room" in French as a second language/Français langue seconde: Reconfiguring identity, language, and policy. *Canadian Journal of Education*, *33*(2), 379–406.

Census Program. (2017, January 27). Retrieved from http://www12.statcan.gc.ca/census-recensement/index-eng.cfm

Clycq, N., Ward Nouwen, M. A., & Vandenbroucke, A. (2014). Meritocracy, deficit thinking, and the invisibility of the system: Discourses on educational success and failure. *British Educational Research Journal*, *40*(5), 796–819. doi:10.1002/berj.3109

Fuller, J. M. (2013). *Spanish speakers in the USA*. Tonawanda, NY: Multilingual Matters.

García, O. (2009). Emergent bilinguals and TESOL: Whats in a name? *TESOL Quarterly*, *43*(2), 322–326. doi:10.1002/j.1545-7249.2009.tb00172.x

García, O., & Sylvan, C. E. (2011). Pedagogies and practices in multilingual classrooms: Singularities in pluralities. *Modern Language Journal*, *95*(3), 385–400. doi:10.1111/j.1540-4781.2011.01208.x

González, J. M. (2011). Words were all we had: Reflections on becoming biliterate. In M. Reyes (Ed.), *Words were all we had: Becoming biliterate against the odds* (pp. 26–35). New York, NY: Teachers College Press.

Halcón, J. J. (2011). Obstinate Child. In M. Reyes (Ed.), *Words were all we had: Becoming biliterate against the odds* (pp. 85–95). New York, NY: Teachers College Press.

Harré, R., & Van Langenhove, L. (Eds.). (1999). *Positioning theory: Moral contexts of international action*. Malden, MA: Blackwell Publishers Ltd.

Holland, D., & Lave, J. (2009). Social practice theory and the historical production of persons. *Actio: An International Journal of Human Activity Theory*, *2*, 1–15.

Hopewell, S., & Escamilla, K. (2013). Struggling reader or emerging, biliterate student? Reevaluating the criteria for labeling emergent bilingual students as low achieving. *Journal of Literacy Research*, *46*(1), 68–89. doi:10.1177/1086296X13504869

Hornberger, N. H., & Link, H. (2012). Translanguaging in todays classrooms: A biliteracy lens. *Theory into Practice*, *51*(4), 239–247. doi:10.1080/00405841.2012.726051

Moskal, M. (2016). Language and cultural capital in school experience of Polish children in Scotland. *Race, Ethnicity and Education*, *19*(1), 141–160. doi:10.1080/13613324.2014.911167

Ngo, B. (2010). *Unresolved identities: Discourse, ambivalence, and urban immigrant students*. Albany, NY: State University of New York Press.

Reyes, I. (2006). Exploring connections between emergent biliteracy and bilingualism. *Journal of Early Childhood Literacy*, *6*(3), 267–292. doi:10.1177/1468798406069801

Chapter 14
The 'New Paradigm' of the Sociology of Childhood:
Reflections on Social Justice Through the Italian Alternative Pedagogies

Stefano Ba'
Leeds Trinity University, UK

ABSTRACT

This chapter aims at developing a critique of the so-called "New Paradigm" of the sociology of childhood, which was developed in British sociological schools between the 1960s and 1980s. The New Paradigm represented a substantial challenge to mainstream sociology of childhood and from this basis, Childhood Studies were capable of producing influential thinking about childhood and practices involving childhood. The main idea of this chapter is that the New Paradigm cannot constitute an adequate theoretical basis for ensuring the fulfilment of children's lives in terms of freedom and social justice. Its central point, that childhood is socially constructed, is not articulated coherently and is internally inconsistent. Italian alternative pedagogical practices are used to provide a concrete backdrop for the theoretical objections raised against the New Paradigm. These alternative critical practices commonly assert that theory cannot be separated from practice and that ideals of social justice for children are based on the struggles of marginalised communities.

INTRODUCTION

This chapter aims at assessing some of the principal tenets of the 'New Paradigm' of sociology of childhood (James and Prout 1990) in the light of current development of critical pedagogies, as elaborated in the alternative realities of Italy (e.g. *Gruppo Pedagogia Libertaria* of Reggio Emilia, the Parents' Pedagogy Group [e.g. Fraire and Colapinto 2012], the 'slow school' movement [Zavalloni 2008] and the critical testimonies collected in Marielisa Muzi [2009]). This New Paradigm in the sociology of childhood finds its theoretical expression especially in Jenks (1996 [1982]), James and Prout (1990), James Jenks and Prout (1998) and Wyness (2012) more recently (for a brief history of the 'New Paradigm'

DOI: 10.4018/978-1-5225-2578-3.ch014

see also: Woodhead 2009). The New Paradigm has been very successful in transforming the discipline of Childhood Studies, advancing a new agenda that highlights children's agency, but also undermining conceptually important social factors that sustain children and families' livelihood, as we will see later.

The new sociology of childhood, which was mainly developed in British sociological schools and hereafter will be referred to as 'New Paradigm', cannot constitute an adequate theoretical basis for ensuring the fulfilment of children's lives, less so for their liberation. A more precise articulation of critique of social factors around childhood can be found in the alternative Italian critical pedagogy (e.g. *Pedagogia dei Genitori* [Parents' Pedagogy Group] and *Rete per l'Educazione Libertarian* [Libertarian Education Network]), which will be used as a theoretical and practical base to move a critique to the sociology of childhood.

The notion that 'childhood is socially constructed' has become a mantra for the New Paradigm, but the point raised in this chapter is that this social construction is simply postulated and not actually articulated. We will show that the sociology of childhood misses what exactly is 'socially constructed' and forgets to ask who the subject of the construction is. Despite the explicit reference to child's agency, this agency is conceptualised in an abstract manner, which has unhelpful consequences for policies around childhood and children's rights. Here the example of child soldiers can be the most befitting one: are they victims of war (structural constraints) or moral agents (agency) that should be held responsible for their bellicose actions? In this chapter we will try to show that the New Paradigm facilitates this type of questions, which are so abstract that cannot have a practical answer: using alternative Italian Pedagogies will link theoretical matters, like 'agency' and 'structure', with the practical orientation of pedagogies, that is: how in this modern world our values may have a practical foundation and what do these values say about the nature of childhood, subjectivity and modernity.

CHILDHOOD, SUBJECTIVITY, AND MODERNITY

In this chapter, we will use general concepts such as 'subjectivity' and 'modernity', in order to advance the critique of the New Paradigm into the practical terrain. The question of subjectivity (and agency) is central. Subjectivity is considered against the forms of modernity as elaborated both in Critical Theory (Bonefeld 2014) and in the practice of alternative Italian critical pedagogy (see the previous section). The question is: how the agency may or may not emerge in the social context of modernity? The stress has to be in the dialectical relationship between the social context and the subject that is in process of formation. There is a particularity of childhood, as there is a particularity of family life that needs to be taken into account, and child's agency needs to be seen through and against the integration of childhood into social life. More importantly: theoretical matters (and the issues of 'values') must converge with considerations around practice, as we maintain that the field of ideas and values cannot be severed by social practice (Bonefeld 2014, but see also Zavalloni 2012).

Modernity is here understood as capitalist modernity and the analysis of the sociology of childhood will be compared and contrasted with that of Critical Theory. We will see in the section 'Socialisation and childhood' how there is a need to understand the way children are integrated into their society because this integration is rather a complex concept which includes resistance to mainstream values and norms and creativity from the part of children and families. The context for integration is capitalist modernity and the need to reproduce human types, rather than human beings (Holloway 2010). This view is explored further in the next section.

Capitalist Modernity and Childhood

According to Adorno (1976), late capitalism has halted its production of differentiation thus directing its mechanism of homogenisation at every individual human being, including children, absorbing differences and producing uniformity (Holloway 2010; Tischler 2006). The free market economy of the 1970s and 1980s simply accentuated this tendency: the need for profit often means acceleration and intensification of labour time, which has effects on families and children in particular. Globalisation, as we understand it to be the most recent phase of capitalism, has had and is having a major social impact in the world in term of exploitation of labour, which often includes child labour, especially in the 'Global South'. However, in the 'Global North', even if the problem of child labour is less marked, families struggle through the intensification of work (Cooper 2014) and children are increasingly under the pressure to perform in education systems that treat them as material for completing tests and as competent actors who need to choose a path for their careers at an early age (Rikowski 2002). In other words, children in the Global South are often treated as economic capital and children in the Global North as human capital, that is, capital that can find employability later on.

A critical sociology cannot oversee the equation of human capital and labour force, and more in particular how labour force is treated as a commodity. Since the sociology of childhood is centred around debates on 'social construction' and agency, it tends to naturalise the so-called economic forces into a social structure which is largely exterior to the agency of children and their families. It tends to reproduce the dualism of systemic reality on the one side and subjective actions on the other. Whereas Italian critical pedagogy maintains there is only one social reality, not two (*Gruppo Pedagogia Libertaria,* 2015), the neo-liberal emphasis on self-worth on the part of children and the optimistic view on the transformation of their natural talents into human capital has become a 'discourse' that sits easily with the supposedly critical views of the New Paradigm. Critical Theory and the alternative pedagogies groups whose practice is based on the critique of economic logic, spell out clearly the equation of human capital and labour force and the consequence of this assimilation, which is the 'commodification' of labour, and therefore the 'commodification' of people that need to perform labour within capitalism (Holloway 2010; Rikowski 2002; Bernardi 2009). The form of labour as a commodity is the form through which childhood appears in capitalist modernity. Thus, we need to link capitalist modernity and childhood to make clear the dangers of economic exploitation of children in the 'Global South' and the transformation of childhood into a path to wage-based employment for children in the 'Global North'.

The Sociology of Childhood

The approach of the sociology of childhood to its subject matter is an idealist at best, if not complicit with the logic of the market that 'perverts' forms of life. From the use of a 'structuralism without structures' to the subjectivism of social interaction theory, the New Paradigm is undecided about the direction to give to its theoretical foundation and opt for the easiest option: abstract relativism on one hand and empty subjectivism on the other. There is an insistence on the fact that childhood is socially constructed, but this is only vaguely explained in general terms. The New paradigm simply comments on historical cases and ethnographic material and does not critically reflect on the terms of the construction of childhood in a way that may have validity for the socio-economic circumstances that families and children are actually experiencing. In other words, it does not fully consider social relations around childhood and children's rights. This is especially the case for the form 'human capital' and how children in the Global

North must be trained as the future knowledgeable labour force, while child labour remains an issue for children in the Global South. These forms are often accepted because of this theoretical foundation that emanates from the 'New Paradigm' which simply describes the forces that produce childhood, and in so doing postulate that nothing else is possible in its stead.

The main difficulty of the sociology of childhood is the construction of its own object of study: what is childhood? In trying to sever the link between the 'physical and abstract features of children' (Wyness 2012: 10) there is already the defining contradiction of the discipline, it cannot reduce childhood to nature but equally, cannot articulate the assertion that 'childhood is culturally constructed'. They refer to childhood as a 'bundle of ideas and sentiments that characterise the socially constructed nature of childhood' (Wyness 2012: 10), which is indicative of an approach that considers social dynamics as abstract and separated by the 'sentiments' of children. This peculiar mix of relativism and positivism is particularly evident in the main equations that e.g. Wyness (2012) posits at the beginning of his analysis of the contemporary culture of childhood. He observes that, in the developed economies, the cultural definition of contemporary childhood is about linking childhood with 'play' and adulthood with 'work'. Our contention here is that what should follow from this observation, would be the critical analysis of the forms that associate adulthood with a particular version of work (that is: wage labour) and how childhood is constructed in opposition to, but also in function of the general form of work as a commodity. As Adorno (1995) observed in the 1950s, sociology cannot afford to be a dilettante about 'economics' and the general forms that impose on society. In this case (Wyness 2012), it is clear that the category of 'work' is to be considered largely neutral and of course 'normal' category for the adults. There, the focus is about the effect of this category on children, that is: children do not have any abstract choice in that regard, other than taking up the role of playful human beings. In this case, the socio-economic background is somehow naturalised in order to focus on the abstract formation of childhood. 'Play' is considered a social construction at the expense of work, which is now a normal condition for the adults. The point is that it is actually not (Infoaut-Gruppo di discussione 2016). Below we consider a different approach.

An Alternative Qualitative Approach

Let's see the contrasting views of the collective work and practice of *Gruppo Pedagogia Libertaria* [Libertarian Pegagogy Group] (2015), the *Rete per l'Educazione Libertaria* [Libertarian Education Network] (Bernardi 2009) and *Pedagogia dei Genitori* [Parents' Pedagogy] (Atgabbes 2015; Fraire and Colapinto 2012), as well as the above-mentioned work of pedagogists such as Trasatti (2004), Zavalloni (2008) and others collected in Muzi (2009). Assessing these contributions is crucial here, because of the Italian critical pedagogy and pedagogical practice articulates the concrete aspects of childhood in the backdrop of the analysis of socio-economic changes. This is where issues affecting children and adults are not merely abstract issues that can be either evaluated as cultural phenomena or 'normalised' as economic phenomena. In these contributions, the analysis of work is done bearing in mind capitalist modernity and the conditions of wage labour (Bernardi 2009) as well as considering play in terms of its concrete potentials for liberation not only for children but also for adults (Atgabbes 2015; Fraire and Colapinto 2012). In the above case, work and play are not simply abstract variables, but these are considered elements inscribed in a critical practice that needs to take into consideration the adult world, as well as the world of children.

Through these approaches, culture (e.g. the way play and childhood are represented) is not a process 'unfolding itself on the back of the subjects', but something humans do in an active way, which contains elements of resistance to the most repressive and exploitative aspects of work (Bianchi 2012). History and culture are not seen as a system reproducing itself and it is not possible to exclude something qualitatively different from the outset (Adorno 1995: 66).

THE THEORY BEHIND THE 'NEW PARADIGM'

The New Paradigm has the aim to build an understanding of childhood in opposition to the scientism of most psychological research and the functionalism of sociological approaches, which tend to naturalise the child (Prout and James 2015). The explicit reference is to phenomenology and social interactionism, but there are also many references to Foucault and post-structuralism as the main theoretical frame for developing concepts (James, Jenks and Prout 1998; Jenks 2009). Historical and anthropological data is usually mobilised to show the relative status of childhood's concepts (the obvious example here is the study of Aries [1962]). The methodology used by these sociologists to elaborate their theory of childhood and society is usually the phenomenological 'bracketing': this means in order to create their theory and their most important concepts, they select a specific aspect of childhood (let's say play), they isolate it (they put it in brackets) and they can then elaborate this specific aspect of childhood reality. However, the implication of their analysis is that they have to, first of all, accept current meanings of childhood, which then can be elaborated and 'deconstructed', but the fact is that –at this precise point– the New Paradigm has to accept concepts and categories as given by selected reality. In other words: the analysis needs to take 'things' (childhood) as they are, and so accept them as they are.

This theoretical foundation has important implications: the critical approach to social reality is weakened because, as we said, sociologists need first of all to accept aspects of childhood (like play) as given, beyond the possibility of critique (so, in principle the value of play cannot be considered within the New Paradigm's approach, as play needs to be taken as fact). Another important implication is that the phenomenological 'bracketing', that is the selective use of social phenomena, takes them to an abstract point of view, which necessarily disregards values in operation within the aspect of the social reality of childhood. To keep with the same example, play may be considered as an aspect of childhood that has social reasons to happen, but the values that play refer to are considered as separate from the actual practice of children playing together (or with adults). Thus, in the parents' pedagogic practices (*Pedagogia dei Genitori* 2016) the considerations around play are embedded in their community's issues and children's rights, and so the value of play is not separated from the actual phenomenon, but values and aspects of social reality are considered part of their social reality that needs to be reflected and discussed, and ultimately affirmed (Fraire and Colapinto 2012; Borghi 2000).

Therefore, the difference between the New Paradigm and the Italian alternative pedagogical practices is the difference between a theoretical approach that necessarily abstract *from* social reality and a theoretical-practical approach that constructs its concepts *through* engagement with social reality (see Muzi [2009] on the unity of theory and practice).

Children's Rights and the Contradictions of the New Paradigm

The New Paradigm's contradiction lies in simultaneously requiring, on one hand, strong subjectivities from the part of children, to counter functionalist explanations, and on the other hand, the formation of social structures to explain the lack of freedom which has to be postulated for childhood's situation.

Thus, we have supposedly spontaneous acting subjects (children) which are an active part of the social construction of reality, but who are also constituted by discourses that make them 'real' subjects. In other words, the New Paradigm has to postulate freedom and lack of freedom at the same time: children have an agency, they are considered capable of constructing their own social worlds, but at the same time their social world is formed by others (the educations system, the parents etc.) in a way that they have little choices about their time and their favourite course of actions. This contradiction (which some of the authors seems to be partially aware of - Prout and James 2015: 22) follows the abstract formation of concepts and the lack of explanation for social structures mentioned above.

This contradiction can be analysed further. Sociology of childhood needs to relate the 'agency side' of its argument with the social and structural side. For its particular analyses e.g. childhood and the education system, the New Paradigm needs to find social structures (of oppression) that constrain or even determine the social reality of the child, whilst still asserting the agency of the child, the freedom of children in elaborating their social reality (Wyness 2012). This type of approach is unhelpful to understand neither sides: on one hand, we have social structures that are seemingly unchangeable or changeable on an arbitrary way. For instance: the education system can be seen as an oppressive structure that reproduces itself according to its function in society. On the other hand, the child has an agency that makes her or him a free subject, although this agency is simply postulated, it is an abstract subject that is represented by the New Paradigm. We have then social structures that are beyond rational comprehension as to their dynamics, and we have abstract ideas around the subjects of childhood (Bonefeld 2014; Dinerstein 2014).

Necessarily this inconsistency prevents any analysis aiming at really demonstrating that 'childhood is socially constructed', rather, the re-construction of their concepts simply forces the analysis at presenting their issue (around childhood) in a historically relative manner. Within this approach, at every possible historical period, we may have a corresponding radically different historical child, these differences being arbitrary and completely contingent. Hence we have the tension in most of these studies between coherent historical and cultural relativism and the need for accounting for children's freedom, 'truth' and 'authenticity'. Then, for the New Paradigm, the problem of understanding childhood is identified in the reflexivity (James, Jenks and Prout 1998) of the researcher. Only through this reflexivity, the values of truth, authenticity, freedom and justice may be introduced into the considerations of research, but crucially they ought to be introduced from an external point of view.

It is clearly a position whereby values do not find a place in the construction of the 'object' of their discipline (childhood), but it needs to be taken into the argument through a voluntarist act. This, of course, happens in the best output of sociology of childhood, because in some of its production, the discussion usually finds its closure in social policy recommendations. However, is it possible to reconstruct this 'object' (childhood) taking into account freedom and social justice as intrinsic and internal to its reconstruction? Is it possible to see childhood as subject, in the sense that adults and children alike are involved in a project of social change? These questions are further explored in the next section.

What is Critical About the New Paradigm?

The previous section sought to demonstrate that the very theoretical foundation of the sociology of childhood leads to a dualism, where the agency of children is found in the reality of everyday life, despite the claim that childhood is actually supposed to be socially constructed. But it is precisely the way childhood is formed socially that is not spelt out theoretically and it actually cannot be precisely specified. The New Paradigm seems to fall into the same pitfall as other sub-disciplines in sociological studies. It identifies the forms through which childhood appears (e.g. the playful child, the obedient child, the educated child, child as human capital) but does not explain how we arrive at that 'form'. The only explanations are contingent: these are relative to a specific moment in time and to a specific culture. However, 'the critique of reification is not about reified things as such' (Bonefeld 2014: 69).

What do we mean with the above? We have seen above that through its theoretical approach, the New Paradigm needs to accept certain social facts as they are, because these provide the foundation of its categories. In this case, accepting social facts as they are, means closing the analytical eyes on the processes that produce these facts. For example, on the family and childhood: the New Paradigm claims that the family is a social structure existing independently from children, and consequently elaborates its explanation of childhood on the basis of a social fact that require further attention. Italian critical pedagogy importantly has a different approach that is based on the unity of theory and practice, thus, in this case, the explanation would include how childhood is intimately involved in family life. The critique of the family as a site of oppression is part of the parents' practice of overcoming this oppression within and through the formation of childhood (Codello 2005). Thus the family may be a 'reified' form, but the aim of critique is not about the reified form of childhood (and family life), but the process of reification, that is: the process that (in this example) distorts the life of parents as well as that of the children (Bernardi 2009).

This is what happens necessarily to the New Paradigm: it calls into question the determined form of childhood (or using critical theory terminology, its reified form) and then it stops there. Through the phenomenological bracketing, and through the historical and anthropological data, every form of childhood that is possible to be identified (e.g. innocent child, the evil child, the playful child etc.) is abstractly considered in its lack of freedom. Social phenomena are taken as such and then relativised to a particular place and time – these are then proclaimed to be culturally constructed. However, what is really constitutive of social reality, and what represents the 'sheer unrest of human life' (Dinerstein 2014), that is, conflict, as well as mutual aid? These do not enter into the analysis of the New Paradigm.

Conflict, social antagonism as well as social cooperation are of paramount importance not only to the understanding of the position of children in modern societies but also their place in often exploitative capitalist modernity. In the sociology of childhood, the social construction of childhood always happens in a relativistic vacuum: there are abstractly indeterminate varieties of forms in which childhood may manifest itself. Considerations around the constitutions of forms of social life around childhood, family, education, work are not connected to social processes that include conflicts and mutual aid. As we said above, Italian critical pedagogies and pedagogical practices are based on the unity of theory and practice: struggles are seen as shaping reality and struggles are part of practices that are informed by a theoretical understanding of the social environment. For example, parents of children with autism (Atgabbes 2015) constitute a community in which pedagogical practices are formative of social realities for parents and children, where these social realities are grounded in the struggle against discrimination and in the struggle for dignity. It is not simply a humanistic idea: these values are inscribed in the understanding of their social world (Zavalloni 2008).

The theoretical weakness of the New Paradigm is matched by the positivist solution to it: the social reality ends up as accepted as 'real', without the possibility of figuring out one better. On the contrary, Critical Theory, and the type of pedagogical practice that is associated with it construct a theory of social (and human) relations, as long as this relation can be unmasked as inhuman (Adorno 1995). Atgabbes (2015) unmasks social relations for children with autism as yet inhuman. From this position, we also have, for instance, the struggles for better education and for better early years conditions as promoted by the practices of parents, children and practitioners in working class areas of Italy (Moletto and Zucchi 2011; Infoaut-Gruppo di discussione 2016).

Socialisation and Childhood

Socialisation is called into question by the New Paradigm: such a concept is considered untenable because the theory that underpins it implies that children are simply passive receptors of social norms and values. The objection that is raised here is that children do not naturally internalise roles and normative ideas about social roles. However, the New Paradigm stops there. It does not ask where socialisation (which in a sense can be understood as the social process which implies the reification of personhood) may come from and through what kind of struggles may be imposed or resisted. Critical Theory and pedagogical practices of liberation take the 'socialisation' concept as complex determination showing what kind of social form people have to constitute for themselves (as a class) and how they may struggle against the limits imposed by social class. As we said at the beginning, socialisation is integration into capitalist modernity, that is 'social destruction' (Holloway 2010). However, childhood is better understood as tension between the particularity of an event in human life, which is not reducible to a concept and drives towards social integration. It is this resistance in reducing human life to socialisation (and to culture) that natural tendencies are called into question: not as a biological foundation of human behaviour, but as a negation of societal norms as positive and universal (Fraire and Colapinto 2012; Zavalloni 2008).

Similarly, for childhood, socialisation then comes to represent processes of reification – that is, children are formed into a certain type of human beings so that fundamental values of capitalist modernity are internalised and reproduced. Obviously, being formed of a 'type' of human being goes against the principles of many alternative pedagogical practices (e.g. parent's pedagogy, see Trasatti 2004). One of the critical points of the Italian critical pedagogy (Muzi 2009, but also see: Rikowski 2002) is that childhood and socialisation are linked to the dominant social form (capitalism) which is reproduced through the daily activities of parents and children in order to form them as human capital. Socialisation as reification can be then read in terms of actual social relations that are extended to childhood as such, however, these social relations are contradictory and they imply the capricious struggle of children to resist and negate their transformation into human types (Bernardi 2009; Codello 2005). Criticising the reified form of childhood does not help to get rid of reification processes since the sociology of childhood shows its lack of focused critique and, like its deconstructionist counterparts, 'calls everything into question and criticises nothing' (Adorno 1995: 37).

The New Paradigm and Psychoanalysis

Along with the abstract critique of social relations surrounding childhood and the misplacement of reification with reified things, another important instance must be flagged up in this chapter, which is rather telling of the New Paradigm's ideas around the child as a subject. In this section, we discuss New Paradigm's critique of the psychoanalytical theory and of what it has been called the 'unconscious child'. According to this view, Freud's theory would dispossess childhood of 'intentionality and agency', as his emphasis goes on 'drives and instincts', especially the sexuality drives of the child (James, Jenks and Prout 1998: 19-21). But it is exactly the analysis of an inextricable mix of culture and nature, individual and species in the determination of individual agency that makes Freud's contribution still important (Fraire and Colapinto 2012), and it is exactly the 'reification' of individual agency here that is problematic, both in terms of its formation (assumed spontaneous) and in its positive existence in society. The New Paradigm's critique of the 'unconscious child' is telling exactly because it has to assume a solid, transparent subject who is conscious of her / his own desires and possibly 'rational' about her / his own actions. Drives and instincts are inseparable from the formation of personality and its social repression (Adorno 1976). Not seeing a conflict in these areas is not only sign of conceptual superficiality, but it is tantamount to endorse the conception of a transparent and rational subject which has purchasing powers in the free market thinking of society (Trasatti 2004).

NEW PARADIGM AND VALUES

So, why Critical Theory and pedagogies of liberation try to establish a link between capitalist modernity and childhood? It is vital from this point of view to understand how childhood is socially formed, that is: what kind of *social relations* are in place not only around childhood but also around parenting, education and the world of work (as no phenomenon can be analysed in isolation). In this way, Italian critical pedagogies places issues around childhood within the frame of capitalist modernity, because only through this frame (characterised, as we have seen, by the understanding of labour force as commodity), the features of childhood (in a spectrum that goes from play to human capital), becomes clear in their social relevance (Codello 2005; Trasatti 2004; Zavalloni 2008). Constructing an understanding of theory in this way, it avoids the separation of issues from values, like freedom and social justice. It is the unity of theory and practice which we have discussed above.

Whereas the New Paradigm has to introduce values from outside (Prout and James 2015: 25), Italian critical pedagogies understand childhood within social relations that need social justice and freedom to become intelligible. However, social justice and freedom are not there yet. Indeed, social relations are trapped in quantities (mainly paid work hours) that need to be exchanged according to the unequal mechanism of the market. In modern capitalism then childhood acquires an immediate sense in terms of social reproduction, the formation of human capital and social integration to the social order (*Infoaut-Gruppo di discussione* 2016). However, this social order can only be understood in relation to values around freedom and social justice (e.g. Atgabbes 2015; *Gruppo pedagogia libertaria* 2015). Values such as freedom and social justice are intrinsic to the conceptualisation of childhood in its negation of an existing unequal social order (*Infoaut-Gruppo di discussione* 2016; Trasatti 2004).

The New Paradigm has to move from a relativistic position as for freedom and social justice: these are necessarily socially constructed concepts, however, this social construction happens in the vacuum. As we have seen, the New Paradigm has to invoke reflexivity from the part of researchers in order to introduce values that may be of benefit to children. We claim that once the separation of values and issues is postulated, then it is only possible to introduce values from the outside of the field of study, in a way that has to rely on voluntarism.

Our critique to the New Paradigm is mainly about the way it conceptualises childhood, which happens through abstraction, a type of abstraction which is not useful for advancing determinate, concrete critique. As Adorno (1995: 44) would remind us, this type of indeterminate abstraction is all about superficial aspects of the issue under examination. 'The insight into a basic matter of ideology evaporates into mere finesse', which aims at no specific target, surely not at the commodity form that social relations are taking, including the one involving children and their transformation into human capital. Indeed, from the part of the New Paradigm there always has been hastiness about the 'new': claiming a new area to colonise for their academic purposes, rather than because of any internal necessity of the issue to be investigated. 'All previous thought on childhood is to be sent to the dustbin' (James, Jenks and Prout 1998: 23): it seems clear that the New Paradigm of sociology of childhood 'dreams of new academic fields to conquer' - as Adorno accused sociology of knowledge of doing, more than fifty years ago (Adorno 1995: 48). Although in the end, the way they dream of doing it boils down to little more than simply adding a new variable along gender, race and sexuality to the analysis (Prout and James 2015: 20).

Childhood as 'Human Capital'

The 'social construction' of childhood is then central, but we need to understand what it really means. The critique of the sociology of childhood showed that their social categories are empty, abstracted from determined social relations. The social construction of childhood becomes then a kind of meaningless formula which can be renewed with any content. A concrete critique of forms of 'social construction' (e.g. socialisation) is needed instead of an abstract critique of the forms of social relations around childhood. How do the Italian critical pedagogical practices achieve this concrete critique? For reasons of space, we will discuss the general lines of this critical enterprise, showing their links to Critical Theory more in general.

Childhood is not simply socially constructed, as the orthodoxy in sociological thinking would maintain, rather: it is subject to social integration, which is part of the wider, essential phenomenon of capitalist integration of society as such (Adorno 1976), or as John Holloway (2010) calls it: the social synthesis. Following Adorno (1990), we consider exchange value as one of the principal features of capitalism and we then conceptualise individual beings as subjects that are entrapped within a quantity measuring mechanism (Bonefeld 2014; Holloway 2010; Tischler 2008). Within this frame, Critical Theory and Italian critical pedagogical practices highlight conflicts and struggles in operation in society. Thus childhood, as an object to be reconstructed in theoretical terms, is to be re-interpreted as an area of tensions: namely between the formation of human capital and the liberation of children as creative beings – 'childhood as subject' (Codello 2005).

Italian critical pedagogical practices place a special emphasis on the way children, as well as parents, are active agents of their own lives through their own activities – or their 'doing' ('*l'operare*' proposed by the *Gruppo Pedagogia Libertaria* [2015] and Trasatti [2004]). However, these activities always take place in a social context characterised by exchange value and the capitalist need to transform human labour into a commodity. Ultimately, it is this commodity form of human activities that transforms relations between people into relations between things (Holloway 2010). Thus, this general form of social relations, the commodity form, 'perverts' the activity (*operare*) of the families and of children into something that may have an exchange value, either directly or in the long term. Hence we can see why families would 'invest' (as this term is currently used) in their children's activity in order to form a set of capabilities that may have some use in life: in other words, it is through these mechanisms and rationales that we have the formation of *human capital*. The outcome of this investment often signifies the disruption of routines and family rituals, transforming them in distorted routines (Ba' 2016; Bianchi 2012).

Alternative Pedagogical Practices and Resistance

Sociology of childhood can criticise the ideology that assigns to children the role of learners when these are deemed to be immature beings, human beings simply in the process of forming their own individual personality (Wyness 2012). However, criticising the ideology and its alleged final product does not say anything about the process transforming children into 'individuals', that is: how the commodity form od social relations actually shapes our individual selves. It is for this reason that critical pedagogies are turning into alternative pedagogies (Allman 2001; McLaren 2000; Rikowski 2002) and that in Italy (as in other countries) networks of alternative and antagonistic realities around parenting and education are emerging (e.g. *Gruppo Pedagogia Libertaria*, *Pedagogia dei genitori*, Infoaut-Gruppo di discussione). Negating the absolute validity of free market thinking is part of the *critique of political economy*, which aims to unmask social relations and identities as lacking freedom and social justice.

There is a number of ways whereby this commodity form articulates itself in the social relations constituting childhood. Education and training are the formalised moments through which capitalist modernity includes childhood in the mechanism of social reproduction: in capitalism, the social production of labour-power takes the specific social form of human capital (Rikowski 2002). The way in which labour force is connected to the commodity form, the way exchange value enters into the social relations of people, leave its mark not only in the human activities (*operare*) but also in those who do the activities (*operai*, that is: *workers* in the general sense of the word) (Fraire and Colapinto 2012). Once we understand this frame, it becomes easy to see how children become potential labour force and that education and training as provided by the institutions have now the function of making children useful human capital for the good of 'the economy' (Infoaut-Gruppo di discussione 2016).

Thus, the issue for Italian critical and practical pedagogies is around the resistance to processes of dehumanisation generated by the social production of labour power. The main point is then the resistance to becoming human capital. Capitalism requires the recasting of human as human capital, which deforms (and reforms!) education as an element of this process, with the added pitfall of linking this recasting to freedom of choice (Infoaut-Gruppo di discussione 2016; Trasatti 2004, Zavalloni 2008; Rikowski 2002: 204). One of the answers that are possible to gather from these critical pedagogies and current practices is linked to the autonomy of educational networks and to the claim of the radical particularity of children in their interaction with adults. We can see that in the next section.

The Role of Autonomy and Narration

It is exactly because the way parenting and education are entangled in the production of human capital that many groups place a decisive emphasis on autonomy and self-managed forms of education. Freedom and social justice are not simply contextualised in a particular time and place: in most of the cases, these values are directly linked to existing struggles of particular communities (Atgabbes 2015). However, it needs to be clear that autonomy is never a fully achieved autonomy, but a struggle that is experienced by that particular community, be it a community of parents of disabled children (Atgabbes 2015), a dispossessed working class community (*Infoaut – Gruppo di discussione*) or an anarchist community (*Rete per l'Educazione Libertaria*). Coherent with the suggestion of Paulo Freire, education (but also parenting – see Bianchi [2012]) links narration of knowledge with experience, and the narration is always situated through specific struggles, against the backdrop of social and political awareness of social relations. The actors of these narrations (parents, educators, and children alike) are always implicated in struggles, and the narration of struggles are about substantiating autonomy as reality and autonomy as aspiration (Moletto and Zucchi 2011). We do not have here the space to go into the details of the experiences of autonomy in alternative realities in some of the Italian-speaking areas, but it is important here to point at the way that (e.g.) the *Gruppo Pedagogia Libertaria* (Bernardi, 2009; Borgi 2000) overcomes a distorted concept of childhood through the mechanisms of self-managed assemblies that see the convergence of parents, educators, and children (Gruppo Pedagogia Libertaria 2015). Concepts such as multiplicity and freedom of choice, dear to neo-liberal ideology, find their realisation in the particular needs of narratives around struggles. We need to add here that, where the term 'struggle' suggests (especially in English) chaos and clashes, in Italian and in particular in the terminology of the alternative practices, the term struggle (*lotta*) is associated with an aim, a wilful spirit of going in the direction of a socially shared (and treasured) aim.

Their starting point is 'why are we struggling': their narration always springs from a situation which describes exclusion instead of inclusion (Bianchi 2012), inequality instead of social justice (Bianchi 2012). Just as an example is worth citing the way math as a subject is elaborated in the *Pedagogia dei Genitori*: math 'is learned' through the number of attacks and bullying occurrences children with a disability suffer during the course of their early life (Moletto and Zucchi 2011). This raises the issue of 'particularity' around childhood and its social interaction, a particularity that shows the universal social construction of identities as 'rule and repression' (Ba' 2016; Tischler 2009: 109). However, it is not only the antagonistic subjectivity that is privileged here: daily interaction is not devalued, exactly because the daily interaction with children, adults, and educator is the source of social activities (*operare*) constituting social reality. This is also potentially the place of childhood as 'subject', rather than 'object' of study (Bernardi, 2009; Codello 2005; Zavalloni 2008).

CONCLUSION

The aim of this chapter has been to critique the 'New Paradigm' of the sociology of childhood and to explore the relevance of this critique in relation to values such as social justice and freedom. The frame of reference for this critique is represented by Critical Theory and by the pedagogical practice in place in antagonistic and alternative realities in Italy. We argued that the New Paradigm calls everything into question and criticises nothing.

We have tried to show that despite the mantra that 'childhood is socially constructed', the New Paradigm does not articulate how childhood is implied in social relations and how these social relations shape children and adults alike. The emphasis on children as active subjects is equally misplaced in the sociology of childhood, as the concept of personality in use is reified and ultimately borrowed from neo-liberal ideologies. We argued also that critiquing socialisation does not get rid of socialised (or reified) forms of identity, but leave mechanisms of segregation untouched. The New Paradigm does not deal with processes that may turn human action into something distorted: we have seen the crucial example of work, as a concept that, according to Wyness (2012) separate adults from children in the 'Global North'. This concept is to an extent naturalised by the proponents of the New Paradigm, in order to possibly show the concept of play as a segregating factor for children. Conversely, in the Italian alternative pedagogical practices, play and narrations around play are considered a constitutive of social reality: there, the unity of theory and practice makes necessary the thinking of the value of play as something intertwined with the way we practice parenting and education.

We have further argued that we need to contextualise childhood in capitalist modernity, which features labour power as a commodity. It is important to critically reflect on that because the commodity form that life takes under capitalism shapes adult in their interaction with children. The commodity form turns children into bearers of economic and human capital (as it may happen respectively in the Global South and Global North).

Finally, we considered antagonistic practices around education and childhood: we highlighted how the unity of theory and practice follows the conception of childhood as something linked to the narration of struggles, both personal and social. We considered 'autonomy' and 'particularity' as approaches that are formed through a concrete critique of the transformation of childhood as human capital and in particular how these approaches aim at subverting the neo-liberal appropriation of education.

Freedom and social justice for childhood are then here linked to everyday struggles of children, parents, educators and committed scholars, rather than a set of political or legislative principles. It is substantiated by the creative imagination of these actors that run against the freedom as constructed through the commodity form of capitalist modernity.

REFERENCES

Adorno, T. W. (1976). *Scritti Sociologici*. Torino Einaudi Editore.

Adorno, T. W. (1990). *Negative Dialectics*. London: Routledge.

Adorno, T. W. (1995). *Prisms*. Cambridge, MA: MIT Press.

Allman, P. (2001). *Critical education against global capital: Karl Marx and revolutionary critical education*. Westport, CT: Bergin and Garvey.

Ariès, P. (1962). *Centuries of Childhood: A Social History of Family Life*. New York: Vintage.

Atgabbes. (2015). *La Pedagogia dei Genitori*. Lugano: Dossier Rivista dell'associazione Atgabbes.

Ba', S. (2016). Teoria Critica e Nesso Lavoro-Famiglia. *Quaderni di Teoria Sociale*, *16*(2), 11–38.

Bernardi, M. (2009). *Educazione e libertà*. Milano: Rizzoli.

Bianchi, A. M. (2012). Alla scoperta di ali e radici. Narrazioni di cittadinanza attiva. Metodologia Pedagogia dei Genitori. *Handicap & Scuola*, *27*(162), 3–14.

Bonefeld, W. (2014). *Critical Theory and the Critique of political Economy*. London: Bloomsbury.

Borghi, L. (2000). *La città e la scuola*. Milano: Elèuthera.

Codello, F. (2005). *Vaso, creta o fiore? Né riempire, né plasmare ma educare*. Lugano: La Baronata.

Cooper, M. (2014). *Cut Adrift: Families in Insecure Times*. University of California press.

Dinerstein, A. (2014). Too bad for the facts: Confronting value with hope. *The South Atlantic Quarterly*, *113*(2), 367–378. doi:10.1215/00382876-2643675

Fraire, W. & Colapinto, L. (2012). *Genitori e figli... cercatori d'oro. La metodologia 'Pedagogia dei Genitori'*. Saluzzo: Fusta editore.

Gruppo Pedagogia Libertaria. (2015). *Dalla parte dei bambini: Costruire una società diversa partendo dalla scuola*. Reggio Emilia: Pedagogia Libertaria ltd.

Holloway, J. (2010). *Crack Capitalism*. New York: Pluto Press.

Infoaut – Gruppo di discussion. (2016). *Per la ripresa di un movimento antagonista nelle scuole e nelle università*. Retrieved 1 October 2016, from: http://www.infoaut.org/index.php/blog/segnalazioni/item/16802-appunti-per-una-riflessione-collettiva-su-apparati-educativi-e-sistema-scolastico

James, A. (2007). Giving voice to childrens voices: Practices and problems, pitfalls and potentials. *American Anthropologist*, *109*(2), 261–272. doi:10.1525/aa.2007.109.2.261

James, A. (2009). Agency. In J. Qvortrup, W. Corsaro, & M. S. Honig (Eds.), *Palgrave Handbook of Childhood Studies* (pp. 34–45). London: Palgrave MacMillan.

James, A., Jenks, C., & Prout, A. (1998). *Theorising childhood*. Cambridge, UK: Polity.

James, A., & Prout, A. (Eds.). (2015). *Constructing and reconstructing childhood*. Abingdon, UK: Routledge.

Jenks, C. (1996). *Childhood*. Abingdon, UK: Routledge.

Jenks, C. (2009). Constructing childhood sociologically. In M. J. Kehily (Ed.), *An introduction to Childhood Studies*. Maidenhead, UK: Open University Press.

McLaren, P. (2000). *Che Guevara, Paulo Freire and the pedagogy of Revolution*. Lanham, MD: Rowman and Littlefield.

Moletto, A., & Zucchi, R. (2011). Famiglia e cittadinanza attiva. *Handicap & Scuola*, *26*(158), 11–43.

Muzi, M. (Ed.). (2009). *Pedagogia critica in Italia*. Bari: Carocci.

Pedagogia dei Genitori. (2016). Retrieved 5 October 2016, from: http://www.pedagogiadeigenitori.com/

Prout, A. (2011). Taking a step away from modernity: Reconsidering the new sociology of childhood. *Global Studies of Childhood*, *1*(1), 4–14. doi:10.2304/gsch.2011.1.1.4

Prout, A., & James, A. (2015). A new paradigm for the sociology of childhood? provenance, promise, and problems. In A. James & A. Prout (Eds.), *Constructing and reconstructing childhood*. Abingdon, UK: Routledge.

Rete per l'Educazione Libertaria. (2016). Retrieved 2 October 2016, from: http://www.educazionelibertaria.org/

Rikowski, G. (2002). Fuel for the living fire: labour-power! In A. Dinerstein & M. Neary (Eds.), *The labour debate*. Aldershot, UK: Ashgate Publishing Company.

Tischler, S. (2008). *Tiempo y Emancipación – M. Bajtín y W. Benjamin en la Selva Lacandona*. Guatemala: F&G Editores.

Trasatti, F. (2004). *Lessico minimo di pedagogia libertaria*. Milano: Elèuthera.

Woodhead, M. (2009). Childhood studies: past, present and future. In M. J. Kehily (Ed.), *An introduction to Childhood Studies*. Maidenhead, UK: Open University Press.

Wyness, M. (2012). *Childhood and society* (2nd ed.). London: Palgrave MacMillan. doi:10.1007/978-0-230-35725-9

Zavalloni, G. (2008). *La pedagogia della lumaca*. Bologna: EMI.

Chapter 15
Child Resilience, Survival, and Development:
Voices of Orphans in Zimbabwe

Racheal Mafumbate
University of South Africa, South Africa

ABSTRACT

This chapter draws on a study which was conducted over a period of one and half years on orphans in Zimbabwe. While this chapter discusses extensive issues around resilience, survival and development of children, the highlights on their wellness are critically engaged with as well. The aim is to provide empirical insights to current and emerging debates on experiences of orphans especially from a developing country's perspective and Zimbabwe in particular. Drawing on the Ubuntu theory and the Wellness theory, the chapter consists of two sections. In section one; the chapter shall conceptualise the notions of Child Resilience, Survival and Development and further explore Ubuntu and Wellness through a theoretical lens. In section two there will be an in-depth discussion on issues around resilience, survival and development of orphans and how these are impacting their wellness.

INTRODUCTION

Historically, it is argued that in African Traditional Communities, there were "no orphans" since every child belonged to the whole community. The whole community ensured that each orphan got proper support and care, thereby confirming Mbiti's (1969) proverbial saying; "I am because we are". People cherished living in large numbers sharing whatever they had as well as observing the expected norms and values and imparting them to their children. The African community used to be one but extended large family and all African languages generally still have words for uncles, aunts' cousin and niece who comprise the entire family (Kanu, 2010). Marriage was taken as a good and serious commitment in the sense that it is a covenant between two (extended) families, kindred and villages. "Living together" and the sense of "community of brothers and sisters" are the basis of, and the expression of, the extended family system in Africa. This arrangement guaranteed social security for the poor, old, widowed, and

DOI: 10.4018/978-1-5225-2578-3.ch015

orphaned children which is one of the most admired values in the traditional African socio-economic arrangement. This communitarian culture does not exist in the Western perspective which is characterised by individualism and the nuclear family structure. In the African community, a man had the obligation to cater for the widow and orphans of his deceased relative. Failure to do so earned him strong public rebuke and as a result, it was difficult to find someone in the community without help (Kanu, 2010). In essence, the extended family was a veritable instrument in the family cohesion and community continuity and stability. However, it is noted that with the advent of urbanisation and westernisation, most of the families are now a nuclear family in nature and as consequence weakened the social security structures.

BACKGROUND

The Traditional Family

In the African traditional family, the community was the custodian of the individual; hence the individual was to go where the community goes. In light of the above statement, a popular African proverb to express the African sense of community says "Go the way that many people go; if you go alone, you will have reason to lament" (Thumi & Horsfield, 2004). This implies that the African idea of security and its value depended on personal identification with and within the community. In the Traditional family, harmony was rated as the most important value for all family members (Shizha & Charema, 2008). In light of the above view, Foster, Makufa, Drew and Kralovec (1997) maintain that traditional life was characterised by brotherhood, a sense of belonging to a large family and by groups rather than individuals. Children in general and orphans, in particular, were expected to grow up accustomed to expectations of the community just like any other children who had parents. Therefore, the whole community had an obligation to see to it that, orphans were engaged in community activities all the time.

A sense of hospitality used to be inherently indispensable in the survival of African values. There used to be a spontaneous welcome and accommodation to strangers and visitor (Ekeke & Ekeopora, 2010). Africans would easily incorporate strangers and give them land to settle hoping that they would one day leave and the land would revert to the owner (Kanu, 2010). It was, thus, the willingness to give, to help, to assist, to love and to carry one another's burden without profit or reward as the driving force. Unlike in the Western culture, no appointment and special invitation were needed for one to visit a distant relation or neighbour. On arrival when there is food, the visitor is invited to eat. The visitor would be treated kindly, just as one would wish to be treated when visiting another home.

The extended family heads would be seen inculcating this value of among orphans. This value, particularly in the Zimbabwean Shona philosophy, is based on the proverb which says *Mweni haapedzi dura* literary translated means "a visitor does not finish the contents of the granary". Another aspect of hospitality which was highly cherished among African cultures was sharing with the needy neighbours who came for assistance (Kanu, 2010). In this circumstance, anybody who did not assist was regarded as a bad community member (Soro, 2007). The extended family heads welcomed and co-opted orphans into their families. This action was meant to reinforce the African idea that orphans were not strangers in a community hence the African community emphasised on the value of giving and sharing with other community members (Nyaumwe, & Mkabela, 2007). This value is based on the Zimbabwean Shona philosophy which says *Chaibva chaora* literary translated in the Shona language means "food which has been cooked cannot be kept for a longer time for future use, it is already spoilt." Extended family heads had a duty to empower orphans with skills and techniques in order to be able to live in the community in peace as well as solving problems amicably whenever faced with difficult situations.

The family setup plays a paramount role in the development of a child as children do not develop into competent adults, simply through the unfolding of their genetic endowment (Kanu, 2010). Instead, they require direction and delimitation of their vast potential to develop into integrated individuals capable of living amicably in their society together with their fellows. Thus the family is of unique importance to a child in that it provides a buffer and mediates between the child and the world (Wiredu, 1990). The family unit also ensures the promotion of emotional, cognitive and other higher order needs amongst children to enable them development to optimal potential (Seedat, Duncan & Lazarus, 2001). Tartar and Myers (2010) maintain that cultural background is also an important consideration for the well-being of children.

Challenges on Traditional Family Culture

The extended family system has come under immense pressure as a result of the death of many bread-winners being either ill or death from the HIV and AIDS pandemic. Also as a result of the economic meltdown in most African countries, few relatives can afford to support extra children (Bhargawa & Bigombe, 2003). Those who take in orphans face increasing challenges leading to worsening poverty and failure to meet basic needs (UNICEF, 2003). The above situation has been exacerbated by population movement due to economic or political instability. Thus, Foster (2000:202) argues that "the once seemingly limitless network of extended family, which expanded through geographic areas and generations, is depleting because of migration, westernisation, demographic changes and AIDS." Many households who are likely to take care of orphans are headed by grandparents, siblings, or other relatives (UNICEF, 2005). In some cases, grandmothers are caring for multiple orphans.

Most theories on child development, social interaction and communication are developed based on the "normal" family and a "normal" society, this means that most children grow up with at least one parent and are able to interact and communicate with people in the community. African societies have always been a communitarian society (Shizha & Charema, 2008). Westerners have on many occasions been surprised at the Africans' capacity for talking to each other, not for the sake of arriving at a particular conclusion but merely to enjoy the communication for its own sake. Conversations used to be only amongst groups and these were determined by age and division of labour (Biko, 2006). All commonly shared their secrets, joys and woes. As a result, no one felt an intruder into another person's life. The attitude to see people as not themselves but as agents for some particular function either to one's disadvantage or advantage was foreign to traditional Africans society (Biko, 2006). Africans, regarded their living together not as an unfortunate mishap warranting endless competition among them, but as a deliberate act of God to make them a community of brothers and sisters jointly involved in the quest for a composite answer to the varied problem of life (Biko, 2006:46). Traditionally, African culture was designed to make slower progress in an effort to make sure that there was agreement among all community members through extensive consultation. To instil a sense of discipline and to discourage dissent in society, folk laws and myths were used. In this way, the community was viewed as central, the custodian of the individual, and each member one to observe the norms and values of the community.

In an endeavor to get a deeper understanding on issues surrounding child resilience, survival and development particularly in developing countries, an interpretive qualitative paradigm which involves studying things in their natural settings, attempting to make sense of, or to interpret, phenomena in terms of the meanings people bring to them" (Denzin and Lincoln, 2000:3), was employed. A significant amount of time was spent in the field observing the lives of the orphans and extended family from within their naturalistic setting (Creswell, Ebersohn, Ivankova, Jansen, Nieuwenhuis, Clark & van der Westhuizen, 2011). The chapter is underpinned by integrative lenses of *Ubuntu* theory and Wellness theory which intersect in their emphasis on a holistic and interrelated approach to the achievement of wellness. Various sources of literature relating to this area were reviewed. Some interviews to explore and get a deeper understanding of activities being pursued as survival strategies to promote the wellness of orphaned learners were conducted. In this way, I was in a position to make sense of the inherent meanings of gestures, displays, symbols, activities, songs, sayings and everything else that has some implicit or tacit meaning in their culture which is in consistency with Creswell et al. (2011). Ethnographic research methods are very crucial in research studies in that they can give shape to new constructs or paradigms, and new variables, for further empirical testing in the field or through traditional, quantitative social science methods (Thomas, Nelson & Silverman, 2009).

CONCEPTUALIZING CHILD RESILIENCE, SURVIVAL AND DEVELOPMENT

Child Resilience

The notion of child resilience is broadly perceived. Resilience is defined as an individual's ability to successfully adapt to life tasks in the face of social disadvantage or highly adverse conditions (Newman, 2002). Mastein (2014) maintains that resilience is important because it is the human capacity to face, overcome and be strengthened by or even transformed by the adversities of life. There are three kinds of resilience (Jameel, Shah & Gainaie, 2015). The first type is represented by children who do not succumb to adversities, in spite of their high-risk status, for example, low birth weight babies. The second type concerns children who develop coping strategies in situations of chronic stress, such as children of drug using or alcoholic parents. Thirdly, children who have suffered extreme trauma, for example through disasters, sudden loss of a close relative or abuse, and who have recovered and prospered may be described as resilient (Gibson 1998). It is important to stress at the outset that no child is, or can be rendered, invulnerable to emotional or physiological stress. Where adversities are continuous and extreme, and not moderated by factors external to the child, resilience will be very rare (Cichetti and Rogosch 1997). In this chapter, child resilience will be referring to the third type of resilience which involves children who have suffered extreme trauma but managed to prosper through survival strategies to manage their lives.

Child Survival

The United Nations Declaration of the Rights of the Child states that all children are "entitled to grow and develop in health; to this end, special care and protection shall be provided with both to him/her (UNICEF, 2005). The international community has responded to the crisis in child health with increased efforts to alleviate the suffering of the world's poor. In the year 2000, leaders from 189 nations of the world developed eight Millennium Development Goals (MDGs) to reduce poverty around the world by the year 2015. The fourth goal aims to reduce the rate of child mortality in every country around the world by two-thirds. The child shall have the right to adequate nutrition, housing, recreation, and medical service. Most developing countries fail to meet the millennium development goal and also to meet the needs of the world's poorest developing countries due to limited resources. Consequently, they fail to meet their obligations to provide appropriate environments for child survival. It is in light of this background that the chapter will provide an empirical insight into how children in difficult circumstances are surviving. This survival enhances child development.

Child Development

Child development refers to the biological, psychological and emotional changes that occur in human beings between birth and the end of adolescence, as the individual progresses from dependency to increasing autonomy (Parham & Fazio, 2008). In this chapter, from a wellness perspective, child development will be referring to how a child develops physically, emotionally, spiritually, socially, intellectually and also entrepreneurship. Families and communities have a great influence on a child's ability to be resilient. Children who demonstrate resilience come from families and communities that provide caring and support, hold high expectations and encourage children's participation (Bernard 1991). When adults provide responsive care to infants, toddlers, and preschoolers, children learn to trust others. When children are held to high expectations by their parents or other caregivers, children begin to believe in themselves and realise that they are capable (Barros, Silver, & Stein, 2009). Therefore, adults should encourage children to participate in the family or classroom by giving to them responsibilities and offering them choices about their environment. In this way, young children feel a sense of belonging, get directions and develop competencies.

Physical Wellness

Cultural background is an important consideration for the physical well-being of children (Cluver & Gardner, 2007). Differences regarding the well-being of adolescents from various countries have stressed the importance and relevance of understanding the impact of culture in shaping children's world (Tatar & Myers, 2010). Likewise, the different families' way of life; have a great impact on children's physical well-being. The physical wellness incorporates the Exercise, for example, I am physically active most of the time, and on Nutrition, for example, I eat a healthy diet (Tatar & Meyers, 2010). Children need high-quality care, opportunities for developing and maintaining relationships, adequate nutrition, and support from families, educators, and communities. When these and other protective factors are in place, children experience positive development in all domains and have the internal adaptive resources to cope with trauma and stress they encounter. These aspects promote the physical wellness of an individual. Regrettably, in most cases, a balanced nutritional diet is rarely found among orphans in developing countries, hence negatively affecting their physical growth. However, the area of physical wellness, children in most African context are often engaged in household chores which include; gardening activities, such as watering vegetable beds in the garden, digging, making vegetable beds, as well as pulling out weeds. In this way, their physical wellness is being promoted through their involvement in these traditional activities.

METHODOLOGY

In an endeavour to get a deeper understanding on issues surrounding child resilience, survival and development particularly in a developing country, an interpretive qualitative paradigm was used. This approach involved studying phenomena in their natural settings and attempting to make sense of, or to interpret, phenomena in terms of the meanings people bring to them" (Denzin and Lincoln, 2000:3), was employed. A significant amount of time was spent in the field observing the lives of the orphans and extended family members from within their naturalistic setting (Creswell, Ebersohn, Ivankova, Jansen, Nieuwenhuis, Clark & van der Westhuizen, 2011). This chapter is underpinned by integrative lenses of *Ubuntu* and Wellness theories which intersect in their emphasis on a holistic and interrelated approach to the achievement of wellness. Various sources of literature relating to this area were reviewed to establish a deeper understanding of meanings. Some interviews were conducted to explore the activities being pursued as survival strategies to promote the wellness of orphaned learners were conducted. In this way, a position was reached to make sense of the inherent meanings of gestures, displays, symbols, activities, songs, sayings and everything else that had some implicit or tacit meanings in orphaned children's culture which consistent with Creswell et al. (2011). Ethnographic research methods are very crucial in research studies in that they can give shape to new constructs or paradigms, and new variables, for further empirical testing in the field or through traditional, quantitative social science methods (Thomas, Nelson & Silverman, 2009).

DISCUSSION OF FINDINGS

Findings on the involvement of extended families on the wellness of orphans revealed that children in general and orphans in particular need motivation, stimulation combined with nutrition and health programmes to enable them to grow well from childhood to adulthood. When one of the participants was asked if they are getting adequate support for enhancement of their physical development, the following emotional response was given;

Playing with our friends at home is history to us. We do not get time for that. Even time to do homework at home, we do not have. That is why I do my homework while I am still here at school. In most cases, our caregivers only afford one meal per day but we are very grateful because they love us. We thank God because the Action Faim has given us gardens and drilled boreholes inside. We, therefore, grow nutritional vegetables inclusive beans which have the highest protein content. We are always boasting to our friends at school by telling them that we always eat meat with no bones and they think we are referring to mincemeat while we will be referring to beans. However, we do not want them to know that we hardly eat meat because they will laugh at us. We hardly get luxury things including time to play while at home.

The above response is indicative of the orphans' need for stimulation and help from the community, caregivers and other stakeholders for them to live a healthy life. These children also need to be accorded time to play and socialise with their peers as this promote their physical, social and emotional wellness. In most circumstances, these basic requirements are rarely prevalent due to commitments given to orphans by caregivers.

As children enter school age, parents and other primary caregivers should continue to be important providers of physical and emotional security. When adolescents feel teachers care about them, they are more likely to do well academically and less likely to get involved in a number of risky behaviors, including substance use, early sexual activity, and suicide attempts (Murphey, Statford, Gooze, Bringewatt, Cooper, Carney & Rojas 2014), in this way, growth is enhanced.

Emotional Wellness

Emotional wellness is conceptualised as awareness and control of feelings, as well as a realistic, positive, and developmental view of the self, conflict, and life circumstances, coping with stress, and the maintenance of fulfilling relationships with others (Rossouw, 2003. Van Den Berg (2006) defined emotional wellness as related to one's level of depression, anxiety, well-being, self-control, and optimism. On the other hand, he views emotional wellness as a situation whereby an individual experiences satisfaction, curiosity, and enjoyment in life, as well as having a positive anticipation of the future, or optimistic outlook.

The above definitions imply that an individual should have the capacity to feel positive and enthusiastic about oneself and about life. When an individual is well equipped in this dimension, the individual will have the ability to motivate oneself and persist in the face of frustrations and to delay gratification and suppress impulsiveness (Zhao et al, 2007). Although most of the orphans are cared for by extended family members, these orphans are more likely to live in households with less favorable dependency ratios and greater experiences of financial hardship (Monasch & Boerma, 2004; Nyambedha, Wandibba, & Aagaard-Hansen, 2006; Oleke, Blystand, & Rekdal, 2005; Safman, 2004). Thus as evidenced by the above scholars, one can safely conclude that orphans experience increased internalised problems and anxieties. The school system has a curriculum which promotes emotional wellness through physical education but the system may not cater for all children as some may not afford to be in school. However, caregivers are enhancing emotional wellness by encouraging traditional games where children are to observe certain games rules. For example, respect, tolerance, control of emotions and being accommodative are some of the aspects instilled by these games.

Social Wellness

Social/Environmental wellness focuses on the aspect of the need for personal identity and a feeling of belonging (Jager, Bensley & Jager, 2003). It may also include the extent to which a person works toward supporting the community and environment in everyday actions, such as volunteer work (Richter, Manegold & Pather, 2004). Included in the definition of social wellness is getting along with others and being comfortable and willing to express one's feelings, needs, and opinions; supportive, fulfilling relationships (including sexual relations), and intimacy; and interaction with the social environment and contribution to one's community (Ohnishi, Nakamura, Kizuki, Seino, Inose & Takano, 2008). In the promotion of social wellness, an individual has to establish meaningful relationships as well as demonstrate an on-going commitment to the common good of the community and the environment. Identity, uniqueness as a person and a sense of personal continuity give a child a sense of the future and direction in life if a child fails to achieve all these, he/she may therefore experience a sense of alienation and become apathetic with a low self-esteem and lack of direction (Loening, Voysey & Wilson, 2001). Unlike children in developed countries who are over-protected resulting in them failing to cope with stressors and obstacles, children in developing countries are exposed to challenging situations, resultantly they develop resilience and coping mechanisms. The challenging situations sometimes deprive them their right to enjoy playing and socialising with their peers. On the other hand, this scenario exposes them to the acquisition of entrepreneurship skills. For example, one of the respondents echoed the following concerns;

The selling of sweets, vegetables, popcorn and fruits is depriving me the opportunity of playing with other siblings. Just imagine seating on that stool for more than 4 hours almost every day (pointing at an empty 5-litre container). I cannot socialise with my friends because the time does not warrant that. I am expected to sell every day since that is where we get the money for rent and food comes from.

However, they are more likely to suffer damage to their cognitive and emotional development and to be subjected to the worst forms of child labour. To minimise excessive child labour, mitigation measures need to be put in place. Such measures may include; education of the caregivers on observing and promotion of the right of the child, enforcement of child protection laws by state agents and partners interested in child protection. Also necessary would be the provision of assistance by stakeholders to orphans and children in need. Various researchers established that nurturing relationships by caregivers and other stakeholders are essential for enhancement and maintenance of physical, social, intellectual, career and emotional wellness of children (Cluver & Gardner, 2007; Murphey, Statford, Gooze, Bringewatt, Cooper, Carney & Rojas, 2014). The supportive relationships can also provide a buffer or a protective shield. Review of related literature from various African countries suggests that although the extended family heads might alleviate orphans' plight, it is unrealistic to assume that children can escape from poverty without massive support from external sources (Bhargava & Bigombe, 2003).

Intellectual Wellness

Intellectual development is all about language and cognitive development. It is about how individuals organise their minds, ideas and thoughts to make sense of the world they live in. The two important tools of intellectual development are language and communication skills. In order to enhance intellectual wellness, there is a need for one to be exposed in creative and stimulating activities, as well as the use of resources to expand knowledge and focus on the acquisition, development, application, and articulation of critical thinking. The perception of intellectually stimulating activity that involves critical reasoning, as well as development of a sense of humour, is also important in enhancing intellectual wellness (Sirin, 2005).

An orphan's lack of enrolment in school causes psychological distress as children often associate school with the possibility of being able to care for themselves and their siblings as they enter adulthood (Cluver & Gardner, 2007). Even when orphaned children are enrolled in school, they are not necessarily able to take advantage of their enrolment. Bereaved African children are less likely to do their homework, study, or read, because of chores at home, engaging in economic activities before and after school, as a way of impressing those who take care of them. Paxan and Abledinger's (2004) study on the impact of orphanhood on children's school enrolment in sub-Saharan countries established that besides poverty, lack of care and love from caregivers contributed to orphans' absenteeism from school. Consequently, orphans in this situation may be forced into child labour for them to survive.

Nevertheless, orphans who are forced into child labour situation would eventually develop resilience and also enhance their intellectual wellness through other facets. The other facets which promote intellectual wellness are embedded in some of the wellness dimensions, for example, in physical wellness, where learners are exposed to games involving calculation of distance, time and speed. Other than intellectual wellness being enhanced in school, caregivers engage children in activities such as selling; and that involves calculations of quantities of goods, prices, profits, losses and changes during selling commodities to enhance their intellectual wellness.

Career, Entrepreneurship, and Wellness

Career development can be defined as the "services and activities intended to assist individuals of any age and at any point throughout their lives, to make educational, training and occupational choices and to manage their careers" (OECD & EC, 2004). Career readiness includes career and research, job seeking skills, network systems, career soft skills and also personal finance skills. Career readiness/maturity is thought to be the interaction between an individual's resources (what he brings to his encounter with reality) and reality demands (Horn, 2006). Career/ *Entrepreneurship* is a programme of activities put in place for learners to acquire specific information on career options; to identify interests, values, and aptitudes; to use this information in career planning and course selection and to change plans when pertinent information is presented. The above situations apply under normal circumstances which may not be the case for orphans and disadvantaged children. Orphans are aware of their predicament hence accepting their situation and devising survival strategies as is being highlighted below by one of the orphans in Masvingo;

We are living in a very challenging environment. However, we have decided to turn those challenges as stepping stones to opportunities. Life is not all that easy but we have just devised survival strategies. As soon as we get home, we will be busy selling at the market. If we do not do that, then at the end of the month water and electricity will be disconnected by the municipality if we fail to pay for it, so, we just have to work very hard. However, we have learned to set realistic goals and expectations. Through the support we get from our grandmothers, we have developed abilities to solve problems and make decisions and more likely to view mistakes, hardships and obstacles as challenges to confront rather than as stressors to avoid.

Amongst ourselves, we are aware of our weaknesses and vulnerabilities but we also recognize our strong points and talents. Consequently, we have developed effective interpersonal skills with peers and adults and are able to seek out assistance and nurturance in appropriate ways. We try by all means to focus on the aspects of our lives over which we have control rather than those over which we have little or no influence.

The above statement clearly shows that children in this study are overwhelmed with work (child labour) at the expense of other activities which promote their physical, emotional, social, intellectual and career wellness. However, they are showing resilience through involvement into various activities to earn a living. Their interpersonal skills are also being developed as they sell commodities by the roads sides.

Ubuntu and Wellness as Theoretical Lenses

The *UBUNTU* principle's moral philosophy is premised on the reciprocal belief that an individual's humanity is expressed through personal relationships with others in a community and in turn other people in that community recognise the individual's humanity (Nyaumwe & Mkabela 2007).The maxim *munhu munhu navanhu (*Shona), *Umuntu ngumuntu ngabantu* (Ndebele) or a person's success is through other persons (Mkabela & Lithuli, 1997), implying that, a person's wellbeing and achievement is through the support he/she gets from others. Hence the above maxims emphasise the importance of *ubuntu* to people within a given community, through the spirit of mutual support and the principle of caring for each other.

In Zimbabwe the extended family has been the principal orphan-care unit as the practice of inheriting a widow and her children was extensively practised (Nyamukapa & Gregson, 2005). However, the advent of HIV and AIDS pandemic has rendered this practice extremely risk hence it is tended to be discouraged. The system of westernisation and migration leading to social profound changes had already weakened the traditional 'system' of absorbing orphans (Nyamukapa & Gregson, 2005; Richter & Manegold, 2004). As a result, the deep-rooted kinship care system became extremely stretched as many people lacked the capacity to take care of additional children.

The traditional African *Ubuntu* system instilled a lot of values and expected norms to the children at an early age (Mafumbate & Magano, 2016). Thus, the community was viewed as the custodian of the individual, and one had to observe the norms and values of the community. Hence, Thumi and Horsefield (2004) maintain that, in the African mentality, the community as an entity remains, while individuals, as persons, come and go. Therefore, the Africans emphasised community life and communalism as a living principle of which the basic ideology was community-identity. Therefore, this chapter attempts to discuss issues around resilience, survival and development of orphans in developing countries, with special attention to Hettler's (1980) five of the six dimensions which are intellectual, social, physical, career, and emotional wellness.

The notion of Wellness has grown from conceptualizations with the attempt to capture a positive perspective of health which although no longer defined simply as freedom from illness, still connotes a reactive or more negative-reducing notion of enhancing human functioning (Hettie, Myers & Sweeney, 2011). Wellness is a dynamic state of being in which a person's awareness, understanding and active decision-making capacity are aligned to some extent with their values and aspirations for a more satisfying life (Botha & Brand, 2009). Orphans assisted to live a wellness lifestyle will aim to enhance their alignment to reach their highest potential (Diener, 2002; Hawks, 2004). The outcome of a wellness lifestyle is a capacity to contribute in a positive and meaningful ways to one's community, society and the welfare of the earth. A wellness enabling environment produces orphans who manage to live a wellness lifestyle which will help them to adapt and balance the multiple dimensions of their health and wellbeing in concert with others and their environment.

FUTURE RESEARCH

In African traditional Community, a child belonged to the whole community. With the adverse of urbanisation and westernisation, families have turned from being extended families into nuclear ones. Seemingly, this has contributed to a number of challenges to orphaned children who find it very difficult to live a meaningful life. Basing on the emergency challenges encountered by orphaned children as evidenced in this chapter, the researcher recommends a future research within the domain of child resilience in other developing countries to determine the level of challenges being experienced by this target population/ group in order to find out strategies which could being employed by stakeholders in various developing countries as they will be trying to promoting wellness of the orphaned child. A future research study would also be necessary to ascertain the suitability and sustainability of the strategies employed by children for survival and development as well as for the promotion of various wellness dimensions.

CONCLUSION

It is evident from the findings of this study that there are certainly more issues emanating from orphans as they travel the road of life. The study also revealed that extended family heads who are trying to support these children are even suffering more due to the scarce or limited resources. The study revealed that orphans in developing countries, particularly in Zimbabwe, are experiencing a lot of challenges which amongst other causes, have been caused by the economic meltdown in the country. However, the children under study have used the encountered challenges as stepping stones towards devising survival strategies. Some children sell various commodities to earn money while others are being involved in gardening activities. These activities in one way or another have enabled them to develop effective interpersonal skills. One would safely conclude that the ones discussed in this chapter, are just but tips of an iceberg as has been brought forth in this chapter. Nevertheless, as much as orphans are encountering challenges here and there, it is inspiring that they are using these challenges as stepping stones to achieve desired outcomes. The extended family ties have been affected by demographic changes (population movement, effects of HIV/AIDS) and economic instability. Also, cultural changes as a result of westernisation which emphasises on the nuclear family, have adversely affected the traditional *Ubuntu* way of life, hence orphans' quest for the revival of African traditional values. Integration of health, nutrition, education, social and economic development and collaboration between government agencies and civil society is also important in addressing issues of orphans' wellness. The community plays a key role in supporting the disadvantaged learners in developing countries. Through the use of Ubuntu principle, extended family members as partners with teachers or caregivers are encouraged to continuously support children's development and wellness through providing those opportunities which initiate and instigate their own learning and exploration of their surroundings with age-appropriate activities.

REFERENCES

Anspaugh, D., Hamrick, M., & Rosato, F. (2004). *Wellness: Concepts and Applications* (6th ed.). Boston: McGrawHill.

Atwine, B., Cantor-Graae, E., & Bajunirwe, F. (2005). Psychological Distress among AIDS Orphans in Rural Uganda. *Social Science & Medicine*, *61*(3), 555–564. doi:10.1016/j.socscimed.2004.12.018 PMID:15899315

Barros, R. M., Silver, E. J., & Stein, R. E. K. (2009). School recess and group classroom behaviour. *The Journal of Psychology*, (7): 431–436.

Biko, S. (2006). *I write what I like: A selection of his writing*. Johannesburg: Picador.

Botha, P.A & Brand, H. (2009). Development of a holistic wellness model for management in tertiary institutions. *S. A. Journal of Human Resources Management, 7*(1), 166-175.

Bhargava, A., & Bigombe, B. (2003). Public policies and the orphans of AIDS in Africa. *British Medical Journal, 326*(740), 1387–1389. doi:10.1136/bmj.326.7403.1387 PMID:12816831

Cicchetti, E., & Rogosch, F. (1997). *Predictors of Resilience in Maltreated and None maltreated Latino Children*. Academic Press.

Cluver, L., & Gardner, F. (2007). The psychological well-being of children orphaned by Aids in Cape Town. *South Africa Journal, 7*(19), 5–8.

Creswell, J. W., Ebersohn, L., Ivankova, E. R. F., Jansen, J. D., Nieuwenhuis, J. P., Clark, V. L. P., & van der Westhuizen, C. (2011). *First Step in Research*. Pretoria: Van Schawk Publishers.

Diener, E. (2002). Subjective Well-Being: The Science of Happiness and Proposal for a National Index. *The American Psychologist, 55*(1), 34–43. doi:10.1037/0003-066X.55.1.34 PMID:11392863

Ekeke, C. E., & Ekeopara, C. A. (2010). God's divinities in African traditional religious ontology: A Conceptual and Philosophical Analysis. *American Journal of Social and Management Sciences., 1*(2), 209–218.

Engle, L.P., Castle, S., & Menon, P. (n.d.). Child development: Vulnerability and resilience. *Journal of Education, 4*(1), 621-635.

Foster, G., Makufa, C., Drew, R., & Kralovec, E. (1997). Factors leading to the establishment of child-headed households: The case of Zimbabwe. *Health Transition Review, 2*(7), 155–168.

Hawk, S. (2004). Spiritual Wellness, Holistic Health, and the Practice of Health Education. *American Journal of Health., 35*(1), 11–16. doi:10.1080/19325037.2004.10603599

Hettler, B. (1980). Wellness promotion on university campus. *Family & Community Health, 3*(1), 77–95. doi:10.1097/00003727-198005000-00008 PMID:10246133

Jameel, S. N., Shah, S. A., & Gainaie, S. A. (2015). Perceived Social Support and Resilience among Orphans: A Systematic Review. *The International Journal of Indian Psychology., 3*(1), 1–6.

Jarger, A.G., Bensley, J. R., & Jarger. M. (2003). *Wellness from the Western and African Perspective: The Merging Point*. Academic Press.

Kanu, G. A. (2010). The Indispensability of the Basic Social Values in African Tradition: A philosophical appraisal. *African Health Sciences Journal, 7*(5), 125–138.

Loening-Voyse, H., & Wilson, M. (2001). *Approaches to caring for orphaned and vulnerable children: Essential elements for a quality service*. Institute for Urban Primary Health Care.

Mafumbate, R. (2011). *Academic performance of Child-Headed and Parent Headed Children: A Comparative Study, Masvingo Urban, Zimbabwe*. Leipzig: Lombard Academic Publishing.

Mafumbate, R., & Magano, D. M. (2016). The Ubuntu Principle amongst the Shona Speaking People in Promoting the Wellness of HIV and AIDS Orphaned Learners in Zimbabwe. *African Journal of Indigenous Knowledge Systems, 15*(1), 28–45.

Mastein, A. S. (2014). *Ordinary magic: Resilience in development*. New York: Guilford Press.

Monash, R., & Boerma, J. T. (2004). Orphan -hood and Childcare patterns in sub-Saharan Africa: An analysis of national surveys from 40 countries. *AIDS Care, 18*(2), 55–65. doi:10.1097/00002030-200406002-00007

Mkabela, N. Q., & Lithuli, P. C. (1997). *Towards an African Philosophy of Education*. Durban: Kagiso Publishers.

Mbiti, J. S. (1969). *African Religions & Philosophy*. Durban: Heinemann Educational Books.

Mwoma, T., & Pillay, J. (2016). Educational support for orphans and vulnerable children in public primary school: Challenges and interventions. *Issues in Educational Research, 26*(1), 82–97.

Mwoma, T, & Pillay, J. (2015). Psychosocial support for orphans and vulnerable children in public primary schools in Soweto South Africa. *South Africa Journal of Education*.

Nakamura, A. R., & Takano, T. (2008). Healthy lifestyle behaviour risks of being bullied, violence and injury. *Open Access Journal., 3*(2), 10–25.

Newman, T. (2002). Promoting Resilience: A Review of effective Strategies for child Care Services. Prepared for Centre for Evidence-Based Social Services, University of Exeter.

Nyamukapa, C. A., & Gregson, S. (2005). Extended family and womens roles in safeguarding orphans education in AIDS-afflicted rural Zimbabwe. *Social Science & Medicine, 60*(1), 2155–2167. doi:10.1016/j.socscimed.2004.10.005 PMID:15748665

Nyaumwe, L. J., & Mkabela, Q. (2007). Revisiting the Traditional Cultural Framework of Ubuntuism: A Theoretical Perspective. *African Journal of Indigenous Knowledge, 6*(2), 152–163.

Nyambedha, E., Wandibba, S., & Aagaard-Hansen, J. (2006). Changing Patterns of Orphan Care Due to the HIV Epidemic in Western Kenya. *Social Science & Medicine, 5*(1), 301–311. PMID:12765710

Ohnishi, M., Nakamura, K., Kizuki, M., Seino, K., Inose, T & Takano, T. (2008). *Caregivers' and non-caregivers' knowledge regarding HIV/AIDS and attitude towards HIV/AIDS and orphans in Nigeria*. Academic Press.

Oleke, C., Blystad, A., & Rekdal, O. (2007). Experiences of orphan care in Amach, Uganda: Assessing policy implications. *Journal of Social Aspects of HIV/AIDS, 4*(1), 1-12.

Parham, L. D., & Fazio, L. (2008). *Play in occupational therapy for children* (2nd ed.). St. Louis, MO: Elsevier.

Richter, L., Manegold, J., & Pather, R. (2004). *Family and Community Interventions for Children Affected by AIDS*. Cape Town: HSRC Publishers.

Rossouw, D. (2003). *Intellectual tools skills for the learners*. Pretoria: Van Schaik.

Safman, R. M. (2004). Assessing the impact of orphanhood on Thai children affected by AIDS and their caregivers. *AIDS Care*, *16*(1), 11–19. doi:10.1080/09540120310001633930 PMID:14660140

Seedet, M., Duncan, N., & Lazarus, S. (2001). *Community Psychology Theory, Method and Practice*. London: Unisa Press.

Sirin, S. R. (2005). Socioeconomic status and academic achievement: A meta-analytic review of the research. *Educational Research Journal*, *75*(3), 417–453.

Soro, A. (2007). Living Together: African Community-Based Values in Toni Morrison's Song of Solomon. *Nouvelle Serie*, *9*(2), 1–10.

Shizha, E., & Charema, J. (2008). *Counseling Indigenous Shona People in Zimbabwe: Traditional Practices* versus Western Eurocentric Perspectives. *Journal of Psychology and Counseling*, *4*(5), 59–67.

Tatar, M., & Myers, J. E. (2010). Wellness of children in Israel and the United States: A preliminary examination of culture and well-being. *Journal of Psychological Being.*, *23*(1), 17–33.

Thumi, K. C., & Horsefield, G. E. (2004). *Traditional African values, guide to effective community-based health care*. Presented at the International Conf. AIDS.

UNICEF. (2005). *Africa's orphaned generations*. New York: UNICEF.

Van Den Berg, E. (2006). *Factors influencing the capacity of Extended Families to provide psychological support to AIDS orphans*. Academic Press.

Wiredu, K. (1990). Are there cultural universals? Quest: An African International. *The Journal of Philosophy*, *4*(2), 5–19.

Zhao, L., Fang, X., Zhao, J., Yang, H., & Bonita, S. (2007). Care arrangement, grief, and psychological problems among children orphaned by AIDS in China. *AIDS Care*, *19*(9), 1075–1082. doi:10.1080/09540120701335220 PMID:18058390

KEY TERMS AND DEFINITIONS

Child: Any minor/teenager under the age of 18 which is considered as age of maturity in Zimbabwe.

Development: It is a process of growing within an individual whereby one is maturing from one stage to the other. The growth encompasses the physical growth and the cognitive growth.

Orphans: A child who has lost one or both biological parents.

Resilience: A state of being able to withstand challenges as one survives.

Survival Strategies: These are ways being employed by an individual to earn a living in difficulty circumstances.

Traditional Community: This refers to the old generations and how they lived together, caring for one another within their geographical area.

Wellness: Is a continuous state of being in a stable being with the self, the mind, the environment and others.

Compilation of References

Abbie. A., Olson, A. A., & van Brederode, T. M. (2001, April). *The effects of violent video game habits on adolescent aggressive attitudes and behaviours*. Academic Press.

Abdi, K. (2011). She really only speaks English: Positioning, language ideology, and heritage language learners. *Canadian Modern Language Review*, *67*(2), 161–189. doi:10.3138/cmlr.67.2.161

Abosede, A. (2014). *Making modern girls: A history of girlhood, labour, and social development in colonial Lagos*. Ohio University Press.

ActionAid. (2005). *A Study on the Impact of —Operation Murambatsvina/Restore Order in 26 Wards of Harare High-Density Housing Areas. ActionAid International in Collaboration with Combined Harare Residents Association*. CHRA.

Adelman, H. S., & Taylor, L. (2006a). *The school leader's guide to student learning supports New directions for addressing barriers to learning*. Thousand Oaks, CA: Corwin Press.

Adelman, H. S., & Taylor, L. (2006b). *The implementation guide to student learning supports in the classroom and schoolwide: New directions for addressing barriers to learning*. Thousand Oaks, CA: Corwin Press.

Adorno, T. W. (1976). *Scritti Sociologici*. Torino Einaudi Editore.

Adorno, T. W. (1990). *Negative Dialectics*. London: Routledge.

Adorno, T. W. (1995). *Prisms*. Cambridge, MA: MIT Press.

Africa, O. (2016). *State of children*. Retrieved October 13, 2016, from: http://www.our-africa.org/state-of-children

Ahmed, J. U. (2010, Spring). Documentary research method: New dimensions. *Indus Journal of Management & Social Sciences, 4*(1), 1-14. Retrieved from https://www.academia.edu/4900830/Documentary_Research_Method_New_Dimensions

Ainscow, M., Booth, T., & Dyson, A. (2006). *Improving Schools, Developing Inclusion*. London: Routledge.

Ake, C. (1996). *Democracy and development in Africa*. Washington, DC: Brookings Institution.

Akwara, P., Noubary, B., Lim Ah Ken, P., Johnson, K., Yates, R., Winfrey, W., & Luo, C. et al. (2010). Who is the Vulnerable Child? Using Survey Data to Identify Children at Risk in the Era of HIV and AIDS. *AIDS Care*, *22*(9), 1066–1085. doi:10.1080/09540121.2010.498878 PMID:20824560

Allen, L. (2005). *Sexual Subjects: Young People, Sexuality and Education*. Basingstoke, UK: Palgrave Macmillan. doi:10.1057/9780230500983

Allman, P. (2001). *Critical education against global capital: Karl Marx and revolutionary critical education*. Westport, CT: Bergin and Garvey.

Alvy, K. (1975). Preventing child abuse. *The American Psychologist*, *30*(9), 921–927. doi:10.1037/0003-066X.30.9.921 PMID:1180422

Anderson, J. A., & Cornell, H. (2015). *Full Service Community Schools: A comprehensive education model for providing comprehensive supports for students and their families.* In 8th Annual International Conference on Education, Research and Innovation, ICERI2015. Retrieved from http://library.iated.org/view/ANDERSON2015FUL

Anderson-Butcher, D., & Ashton, D. (2004). Innovative Models of Collaboration to Serve Children, Youths, Families, and Communities. *Children & Schools*, *26*(1), 39–53. doi:10.1093/cs/26.1.39

Anderson, J. A. (2000). The need for interagency collaboration for children with emotional and behavior disabilities and their families. *Families in Society*, *81*(5), 484–493. doi:10.1606/1044-3894.1050

Anderson, J. A. (2011). Patterns of school functioning over time among students served in a system of care. *Remedial and Special Education*, *32*(6), 482–495. doi:10.1177/0741932510364545

Anderson, J. A. (2016). Is an ounce of prevention still worth a pound of cure? Community-based interagency collaboration to enhance student and family wellbeing (guest editorial). *School Community Journal*, *26*(1), 9–29.

Anderson, J. A., Houser, J. H., & Howland, A. A. (2010). The Full Purpose Partnership model for promoting academic and socio-emotional success in schools. *School Community Journal*, *20*(1), 31–54.

Anderson, J. A., Howland, A. A., & McCoach, B. (2015). Modeling resiliency in the prevention of special education identification. *Preventing School Failure*, *59*(2), 63–72. doi:10.1080/1045988X.2013.837811

Anderson, J. A., & Mohr, W. K. (2003). A developmental ecological perspective in systems of care for children with serious emotional disturbances and their families. *Education & Treatment of Children*, *26*(1), 52–74.

Anderson, J. A., Wright, E. R., Smith, J. S., & Kooreman, H. E. (2007). Educational profiles of students at enrollment in a system of care. *Remedial and Special Education*, *28*(1), 9–20. doi:10.1177/07419325070280010201

Anspaugh, D., Hamrick, M., & Rosato, F. (2004). *Wellness: Concepts and Applications* (6th ed.). Boston: McGrawHill.

Anthias, F. (2002). Beyond Feminism and Multiculturalism: Locating Difference and the Politics of Location. *Womens Studies International Forum*, *25*(3), 275–286. doi:10.1016/S0277-5395(02)00259-5

Ariès, P. (1962). *Centuries of Childhood: A Social History of Family Life.* New York: Vintage.

Armstrong, A., Armstrong, D., & Spandagou, L. (2010). *Inclusive Education: International Policy and Practice*. London: SAGE Pub Ltd.

Arneson, D. (2008). *John Rawls's Theory of Social Justice: Notes for Theories of Justice.* Retrieved July 15, 2016, from http://philosophyfaculty.ucsd.edu/faculty/rarneson/

ASH. (2016). *Key Dates in the History of Anti-Tobacco Campaigning.* Available at: http://www.ash.org.uk/files/documents/ASH_741.pdf

Asrat, D. (2013). Factors Affecting the Implementation of Inclusive Education in Primary Schools of Bahir Dar Town Administration. *Education Research Journal*, *3*(3), 59–67.

Atgabbes. (2015). *La Pedagogia dei Genitori*. Lugano: Dossier Rivista dell'associazione Atgabbes.

Atkins, M. S., Hoagwood, K. E., Kutash, K., & Seidman, E. (2010). Toward the integration of education and mental health in schools. *Administration and Policy in Mental Health and Mental Health Services Research*, *37*(1-2), 40–47. doi:10.1007/s10488-010-0299-7 PMID:20309623

Atweh, B., Bose, A., Graven, M., Subramanian, J., & Venkat, H. (2014). *Teaching numeracy in preschool and early grades in low-income countries. Deutsche Gesellschaft für Internationale Zusammenarbeit (GIZ).*

Atwine, B., Cantor-Graae, E., & Bajunirwe, F. (2005). Psychological Distress among AIDS Orphans in Rural Uganda. *Social Science & Medicine*, *61*(3), 555–564. doi:10.1016/j.socscimed.2004.12.018 PMID:15899315

Ayers, W. C. (2010). Social Justice. In C. Kridel (Ed.), *Encyclopedia of Curriculum Studies*. Thousand Oaks, CA: SAGE Pub, Inc. doi:10.4135/9781412958806.n418

Azar, S. T. (1991). Models of Child Abuse A Metatheoretical Analysis. *Criminal Justice and Behavior*, *18*(1), 30–46. doi:10.1177/0093854891018001004

Azorín, J. M., & Cameron, R. (2010). The application of mixed methods in organisational research: A literature review. *Electronic Journal of Business Research Methods*, *8*(2), 95–105.

Ba', S. (2016). Teoria Critica e Nesso Lavoro-Famiglia. *Quaderni di Teoria Sociale*, *16*(2), 11–38.

Babu, A. M. (1981). *African socialism or socialist Africa?* Harare: Zimbabwe Publishing House.

Ballantyne, T. (2015). *Entanglements of Empire: Missionaries, Maori, and the Question of the Body*. Durham, NC: Duke University Press.

Ballantyne, T., & Burton, A. (2009). *Moving subjects: gender, mobility, and intimacy in an age of global empire*. Chicago, IL: University of Illinois Press.

Bangladesh Bureau of Statistics (BBS). (2006). *Report on national child labour survey 2002-2003*. Dhaka: BBS.

Bardi, M., & Borgognini-Tarli, S. (2001). A survey on parent-child conflict resolution: Intrafamily violence in Italy. *Child Abuse & Neglect*, *25*(6), 839–853. doi:10.1016/S0145-2134(01)00242-3 PMID:11525528

Barnett, W. S. (2008). *Preschool education and its lasting effects: Research and policy implications.* Boulder, CO: Education and the Public Interest Center & Education Policy Research Unit. Retrieved 14 July 2016 from http://epicpolicy.org/publication/preschooleducation

Barnett, D. (1997). The effects of early intervention on maltreating parents and their children. In M. J. Guralnick (Ed.), *The effectiveness of early intervention* (pp. 147–170). Baltimore, MD: Brookes.

Baroody, A. J., & Gatzke, M. R. (1991). The estimation of set size by potentially gifted kindergarten-age children. *Journal for Research in Mathematics Education*, *22*(1), 59–68. doi:10.2307/749554

Barriga, A. Q., Dorans, J. W., Newell, S. B., Morrison, E. M., Barbetti, V., & Robbins, B. D. (2002). Relationships between problem behaviors and academic achievement in adolescents: The unique role of attention problems. *Journal of Emotional and Behavioral Disorders*, *10*(4), 233–240. doi:10.1177/10634266020100040501

Barros, R. M., Silver, E. J., & Stein, R. E. K. (2009). School recess and group classroom behaviour. *The Journal of Psychology*, (7): 431–436.

Basu, M. (2012). *The invisible world of domestic work: Report documents abuses*. Retrieved from http://inamerica.blogs.cnn.com/2012/11/27/the-invisible-world-of-domestic-work-report-documents-abuses/comment-page-2/

Battistich, V., Schaps, E., Watson, M., & Solomon, D. (1996). Prevention effects of the Child Development Project: Early findings from an ongoing multisite demonstration trial. *Journal of Adolescent Research*, *11*(1), 12–35. doi:10.1177/0743554896111003

Bayat, A., Louw, W., & Rena, R. (2014). The impact of socioeconomic factors on the performance of selected high school learners in the Western Cape Province, South Africa. *Journal of Human Ecology (Delhi, India)*, *45*(3), 183–196.

Baydar, N., Reid, M. J., & Webster-Stratton, C. (2003, September). The role of mental health factors and program engagement in the effectiveness of a preventive parenting program for head start mothers. *Child Development*, *74*(5), 1433–1453. doi:10.1111/1467-8624.00616 PMID:14552407

BBC. (2015). *Breck Bednar murder: How Lewis Daynes manipulated his victim.* Available at: http://www.bbc.co.uk/news/uk-england-essex-30730807

Beeld, A. R. (2011). Corporal punishment still in schools. *News 24 Archives*. Retrieved 13 November 2016, from http://www.news24.com

Belsky, J. (1980). Child maltreatment: An ecological integration. *The American Psychologist*, *35*(4), 320–335. doi:10.1037/0003-066X.35.4.320 PMID:7386966

Benvengnú, L. A., Gastal Fassa, A., Augusto Faccini, L., Wegman, D. H., & DallAgnol, M. M. (2005). Work and behavioral problems in children and adolescents. *International Journal of Epidemiology*, *34*(6), 1417–1424. doi:10.1093/ije/dyi187 PMID:16144859

Berger, S., & Thornycroft, P. (2008). *Zimbabwe's Cholera Victims Ten Times More Likely To Die.* London: Telegraph (UK). Retrieved December 8, 2008, from, http://www.telegraph.co.uk/news/worldnews/africaandindianocean/zimbabwe/3660739/Zimbabwes-cholera-victims-ten-times-more-likely-to-die.html

Berger, L. M. (2005). Income, family characteristics, and physical violence toward children. *Child Abuse & Neglect*, *29*(2), 107–133. doi:10.1016/j.chiabu.2004.02.006 PMID:15734178

Bernardi, M. (2009). *Educazione e libertà*. Milano: Rizzoli.

Bhana, D. (2016). Sex isnt better than love: Exploring South African Indian teenage male and female desires beyond danger. *Childhood*, *23*(3), 362–377. doi:10.1177/0907568216642828

Bhargava, D. (2009). *Child labour-a hindrance in development*. Retrieved 8 November 2016 from http://www.countercurrents.org/bhargava090709.htm

Bhargava, A., & Bigombe, B. (2003). Public policies and the orphans of AIDS in Africa. *British Medical Journal*, *326*(740), 1387–1389. doi:10.1136/bmj.326.7403.1387 PMID:12816831

Bianchi, A. M. (2012). Alla scoperta di ali e radici. Narrazioni di cittadinanza attiva. Metodologia Pedagogia dei Genitori. *Handicap & Scuola*, *27*(162), 3–14.

Bigombe, B., & Khadiagala, G. M. (n.d.). *Major trends affecting families in sub-Saharan Africa*. Retrieved from http://www.un.org/esa/socdev/family/Publications/mtbigombe.pdf

Biko, S. (2006). *I write what I like: A selection of his writing*. Johannesburg: Picador.

Bingham, K. S. (2011). *Helpleness to Hope: Cultural Transformations for the Maasai Girl-Child* (Unpublished doctoral dissertation). Liberty University. Retrieved 21 May 2016 from http://digitalcommons.liberty.edu/cgi/viewcontent.cgi?article=1490&context=doctoral

Birdsall, W. F. (2014). Development, Human Rights, and Human Capabilities: The Political Divide. *Journal of Human Rights*, *13*(1), 1–21. doi:10.1080/14754835.2013.824268

Birdthistle, I. J., Sian, F., Mwanasa, S., Auxillia, N., Gwiza, E., & Glynn, J. R. (2011). Child Sexual Abuse and Links to HIV and Orphanhood in Urban Zimbabwe. *Journal of Epidemiology and Community Health, 65*(12), 1075–1082. doi:10.1136/jech.2009.094359 PMID:20628080

Bissell, S. (2001). Young garment workers in Bangladesh: Raising the rights question. *Development, 44*(2), 75–80. doi:10.1057/palgrave.development.1110241

Black, M. (2005). *Child domestic workers: A handbook on good practice in programme interventions.* London: Anti-Slavery International.

Blagbrough, J. (2008). *They respect their animals more voices of child domestic workers.* London: Anti-Slavery International Thomas Clarkson House The Stableyard.

Blaise, M. (2010). Kiss and tell: Gendered narrative and childhood sexuality. *Australian Journal of Early Childhood, 35*(1), 1–9.

Blakemore, S., & Mills, K. (2014). Is Adolescence a Sensitive Period for Sociocultural Processing? *Annual Review of Psychology, 65*(1), 187–207. doi:10.1146/annurev-psych-010213-115202 PMID:24016274

Blank, M. J., Melville, A., & Shah, B. P. (2003). *Making the difference: Research and practice in community schools.* Retrieved from ERIC database. (ED499103)

Bonefeld, W. (2014). *Critical Theory and the Critique of political Economy.* London: Bloomsbury.

Borghi, L. (2000). *La città e la scuola.* Milano: Elèuthera.

Borman, G. D., & Overman, L. T. (2004). Academic resilience in mathematics among poor and minority students. *The Elementary School Journal, 104*(3), 177–195. doi:10.1086/499748

Bose, K. (2008). Gaps and remedies of early childhood care and education (ECCE) programs of Botswana. *Educational Research and Reviews, 3*(3), 77-82. Retrieved from http://www.academicjournals.org/article/article1379585818_Kabita.pdf

Botha, P.A & Brand, H. (2009). Development of a holistic wellness model for management in tertiary institutions. *S. A. Journal of Human Resources Management, 7*(1), 166-175.

Boulanger, S. (2008). A puppet on a string: The manipulation and nationalisation of the female body in the "female circumcision crisis" of colonial Kenya. *Wagadu, 6*, 61–74.

Bourdillon, M. (2010). Child domestic workers in Zimbabwe. In Working to be someone: Child focused research and practice with working children (pp. 55–65). London: Jessica Kingsley.

Bower, C. (2003). The Relationship between Child Abuse and Poverty. *Agenda (Durban, South Africa), 56*, 84–85.

Bowman, B. T., Donovan, M. S., & Burns, M. S. (Eds.). (2001). *Eager to learn: Educating our preschoolers.* Washington, DC: National Academy Press.

Boyd, D. (2014). *It's Complicated: The social lives of networked teens.* New Haven, CT: Yale.

Bradley, R., Henderson, K., & Monfore, D. A. (2004). A national perspective on children with emotional disorders. *Behavioral Disorders, 29*, 211–223.

Breckler, S. J. (2006). Psychology is translational science. *Science Directions, 37*(6), 22. Retrieved from http://www.apa.org/monitor/jun06/sd.aspx

Breidlid, A., Cheyeka, A. M., & Farag, A. I. (Eds.). (2015). *Perspectives on youth, HIV/AIDS and indigenous knowledges in Africa.* Boston: Sense Publishers. doi:10.1007/978-94-6300-196-0

Bronfenbrenner, U. (Ed.). (2004). The bioecological theory of human development. In U. Bronfenbrenner (Ed.), Making human beings human: Bioecological perspectives on human development (pp. 3-15). Thousand Oaks, CA: Sage.

Bronfenbrenner, U. (Ed.). (2004). The bioecological theory of human development. In U. Bronfenbrenner, (Ed.), Making human beings human: Bioecological perspectives on human development (pp. 3-15). Thousand Oaks, CA: Sage.

Bronfenbrenner, U. (1979). *The ecology of human development: Experiments by nature and design.* Cambridge, MA: Harvard University Press.

Bronfenbrenner, U. (2001). The bioecological theory of human development. In N. J. Smelser & P. B. Baltes (Eds.), *International encyclopaedia of the social and behavioral sciences* (Vol. 10, pp. 6963–6970). New York: Elsevier. doi:10.1016/B0-08-043076-7/00359-4

Bronfenbrenner, U., & Ceci, S. J. (1994). Nature-nurture reconceptualized in developmental perspective: A bioecological model. *Psychological Review*, *101*(4), 568–586. doi:10.1037/0033-295X.101.4.568 PMID:7984707

Brooks, J. E. (2006). Strengthening resilience in children and youths: Maximizing Opportunities through Schools. *Children & Schools*, *28*(2), 69–76. doi:10.1093/cs/28.2.69

Brown, G. (2012). *Child Labour & Educational Disadvantage – Breaking the Link, Building Opportunity. A Review by Gordon Brown.* London: The Office of the UN Special Envoy for Global Education.

Bub, K. L., McCartney, K., & Willett, J. B. (2007). Behavior problem trajectories and first-grade cognitive ability and achievement skills: A latent growth curve analysis. *Journal of Educational Psychology*, *99*(3), 653–670. doi:10.1037/0022-0663.99.3.653

Buckner, J. C., Bearslee, W. R., & Bassuk, E. L. (2004). Exposure to violence and low-income childrens mental health: Direct, moderated, and mediated relations. *The American Journal of Orthopsychiatry*, *74*(4), 413–423. doi:10.1037/0002-9432.74.4.413 PMID:15554803

Byrd-Clark, J. (2010). Making “wiggle room” in French as a second language/Français langue seconde: Reconfiguring identity, language, and policy. *Canadian Journal of Education*, *33*(2), 379–406.

Calkin, S. (2015). Feminism, interrupted? Gender and development in the era of Smart Economics.. *Progress in Development Studies*, *15*(4), 295–307. doi:10.1177/1464993415592737

Campbell, C., Skovdal, M., Mupambireyi, Z., & Gregson, S. (2010). Exploring Childrens Stigmatisation of AIDS-Affected Children in Zimbabwe through Drawings and Stories. *Social Science & Medicine*, *71*(5), 975–985. doi:10.1016/j.socscimed.2010.05.028 PMID:20591546

Carmody, B. (2004). *The evolution of education in Zambia.* Lusaka: Bookworld.

Caspi, A., McClay, J., Moffitt, T. E., Mill, J., Martin, J., Craig, I. W., & Poulton, R. (2002). Role of genotype in the cycle of violence in maltreated children. *Science*, *297*(5582), 851–854. doi:10.1126/science.1072290 PMID:12161658

Census Program. (2017, January 27). Retrieved from http://www12.statcan.gc.ca/census-recensement/index-eng.cfm

Central Statistical Office (CSO), Ministry of Health (MOH), and ICF International. (2014). *Zambia Demographic and Health Survey 2013-14.* Rockville, MD: Central Statistical Office, Ministry of Health, and ICF International.

Central Statistics Office. (2016). *Projected mid year population & projected eligible voter population.* Lusaka: CSO.

Centre for Services and Information on Disability (CSID) and the Daily Star. (2014). *End domestic child labour.* Retrieved from http://www.thedailystar.net/end-domestic-child-labour-57018

Chakona, L. (2012). *The Impact of the Fast Track Land Reform Programme on Women in Goromonzi District, Zimbabwe* (MA Thesis). Rhodes University.

Chen, M. E., Anderson, J. A., & Watkins, L. (2016). Parent perceptions of connectedness in a full service community school project. *Journal of Child and Family Studies*, (25): 7, 2268–2278. doi:10.1007/s10826-016-0398-5

Chikwanda, T. (2015). HIV and AIDS and teacher education in Zambia. In A. Breidlid, A. M. Cheyeka, & A. I. Farag (Eds.), *Perspectives on youth, HIV/AIDS and indigenous knowledges in Africa* (pp. 61–76). Boston: Sense Publishers. doi:10.1007/978-94-6300-196-0_5

Child Line. (2010). *An Analysis of Child Abuse Cases Reported to Child Line Zimbabwe in the Period December 31st, 2008 to January 1st, 2010*. Child Line Zimbabwe.

Chilisa, B. (2002). National policies on pregnancy in education systems in Sub-Saharan Africa: The case of Botswana. *Gender and Education, 14*(1), 21–35. doi:10.1080/09540250120098852

Chireshe, R., Chireshe, E., & Mudhovozi, P. (2009). Child Abuse: Psychosocial and Religious Intervention Strategies in Zimbabwe. *Journal of Psychology in Africa, 19*(2), 261–263.

Chiweshe, M. K. (2012a). *Farm Level Institutions in Emergent Communities in post-Fast Track Zimbabwe: Case of Mazowe District* (Unpublished PhD thesis). Rhodes University, South Africa.

Chiweshe, M. K. (2012b). *For Girls Only: Intersection of Age, Gender, Class and Race as a Source of Vulnerability for Adolescent Girls in Africa*. Addressing Inequalities: The Heart of the Post-2015 Development Agenda and the Future We Want for All, Global Thematic Consultation, UN. Retrieved May 3, 2015, from http://www.comminit.com/clickthru/58f0013972b7e97878b16db0b99c345a?node=9301387

Choate, L. H. (2012). Sexual trauma: An ecological approach to conceptualization and treatment. In L. L. Levers (Ed.), *Trauma counseling: Theories and interventions* (pp. 116–131). New York: Springer.

Chopra, M., & Rollins, N. (2008). Infant feeding in the time of HIV: Rapid assessment of infant feeding policy and programmes in four African countries scaling up prevention of mother to child transmission programmes. *Archives of Disease in Childhood, 93*(4), 288–291. doi:10.1136/adc.2006.096321 PMID:17686796

Choruma, T. (2006). *The Forgotten Tribe: People with Disabilities in Zimbabwe*. Progression Report.

Cicchetti, E., & Rogosch, F. (1997). *Predictors of Resilience in Maltreated and None maltreated Latino Children*. Academic Press.

Cicchetti, D., & Lynch, M. (1993). Toward an ecological/transactional model of community Violence and child maltreatment: Consequences for childrens development. *Psychiatry, 56*(1), 96–118. doi:10.1080/00332747.1993.11024624 PMID:8488217

Clacherty, G. (2003). *Poverty made this decision for me: Children in Musina: Their Experiences and Needs*. Save the Children UK.

Clements, D. H., & Sarama, J. (2009). *Learning and teaching early math: The learning trajectories approach*. New York: Routledge.

Cloward, K. (2015). Elites, Exit Options, and Social Barriers to Norm Change: The Complex Case of Female Genital Mutilation. *Studies in Comparative International Development, 50*, 378–407. doi:10.1007/s12116-015-9175-5

Cluver, L., & Gardner, F. (2007). The psychological well-being of children orphaned by Aids in Cape Town. *South Africa Journal, 7*(19), 5–8.

Clycq, N., Ward Nouwen, M. A., & Vandenbroucke, A. (2014). Meritocracy, deficit thinking, and the invisibility of the system: Discourses on educational success and failure. *British Educational Research Journal*, *40*(5), 796–819. doi:10.1002/berj.3109

Codello, F. (2005). *Vaso, creta o fiore? Né riempire, né plasmare ma educare*. Lugano: La Baronata.

Coletta, N. J., Balachander, J., & Liang, X. (1996). *The Condition of Young Children in Sub-Saharan Africa. The convergence of health, nutrition and early education*. World Bank Technical Paper 326, Africa Technical Department Series. World Bank.

Consortium on the School-Based Promotion of Social Competence. (1994). The school-based promotion of social competence: Theory, research, practice, and policy. In R. J. Haggerty, L. R. Sherrod, N. Gramezy, & M. Rutter (Eds.), *Stress, risk, and resilience in children and adolescents: Processes, mechanisms, and interventions* (pp. 268–316). Cambridge, UK: Cambridge University Press.

Conwill, W. L. (2003). Consultation and collaboration: An action research model for the full-service school. *Consulting Psychology Journal: Practice and Research*, *55*(4), 239–248. doi:10.1037/1061-4087.55.4.239

Cooper, M. (2014). *Cut Adrift: Families in Insecure Times*. University of California press.

Cornwall, A., Harrison, E., & Whitehead, A. (2007). Gender myths and feminist fables: The struggle for interpretive power in gender and development. *Development and Change*, *38*(1), 1–20. doi:10.1111/j.1467-7660.2007.00400.x

Coyne, C. J., & Coyne, R. L. (2014). The identity economics of female genital mutilation. *Journal of Developing Areas*, *48*(2), 137–152. doi:10.1353/jda.2014.0036

Creswell, J. W., Ebersohn, L., Ivankova, E. R. F., Jansen, J. D., Nieuwenhuis, J. P., Clark, V. L. P., & van der Westhuizen, C. (2011). *First Step in Research*. Pretoria: Van Schawk Publishers.

Crittenden, P. M. (1999). In H. Dubowitz (Ed.), *Neglected children: Research, practice, and policy* (pp. 47–68). Thousand Oaks, CA: Sage. doi:10.4135/9781452225586.n3

Cross, C., Woods, T. A., & Schweingruber, H. (2009). *Mathematics learning in early childhood: Paths toward excellence and equity*. Washington, DC: National Research.

Culham, A., & Nind, M. (2003). Deconstructing normalisation: Clearing the way for inclusion. *Journal of Intellectual & Developmental Disability*, *28*(1), 65–78. doi:10.1080/1366825031000086902

Cutland, M. (2012). Child abuse and its legislation: The global picture. *Archives of Disease in Childhood*, *97*(8), 679–684. doi:10.1136/archdischild-2012-301648 PMID:22563035

Daniel, M. (2005). Hidden wounds: Orphanhood, expediency and cultural silence in Botswana (PhD thesis). Norwich, UK: School of Development Studies, University of East Anglia. Retrieved from http://hdl.handle.net/1956/3294

Daniels, H., & Garner, P. (Eds.). (1999). *Inclusive education: supporting inclusion in education systems*. London: Kogan Page.

Davidov, J., Sigad, L. I., Lev-Wiesel, R., & Eisikovits, Z. (2016). Cross-disciplinary craftsmanship: The case of child abuse work. *Qualitative Social Work: Research and Practice*. doi:10.1177/1473325016641626

Davies, B. (2000). *A Body of Writing 1990-1999*. New York: Alta Mira Press.

Davis, K. (2012). Friendship 2.0: Adolescents experiences of belonging and self-disclosure online. *Journal of Adolescence*, *35*(6), 1527–1536. doi:10.1016/j.adolescence.2012.02.013 PMID:22475444

Dayıoğlu, M. (2013). *Impact of unpaid household services on the measurement of child labour. MICS Methodological papers. Paper No. 2, Statistics and Monitoring Section, Division of Policy and Strategy.* Ankara, Turkey: Department of Economics, Middle East Technical University.

De Giusti, G., & Kambhampati, U. S. (2015). Women's Work in Kenya: The Role of Social Institutions and Household Gender Attitudes. *Feminist Economics*, *22*(2), 87–113. doi:10.1080/13545701.2015.1115531

Decker, C. (2015). The elusive power of colonial prey: Sexualizing the schoolgirl in the Zanzibar Protectorate. *Africa Today*, *61*(4), 43–60. doi:10.2979/africatoday.61.4.43

Declaration of the Rights of the Child G.A. (1959). res. 1386 (XIV), 14 U.N. GAOR Supp. (No.16) at 19, U.N. Doc. A/4354.

Delap, E. (2001). Economic and cultural forces in the child labour debate: Evidence from urban Bangladesh. *The Journal of Development Studies*, *37*(4), 1–22. doi:10.1080/00220380412331322021

Denton, K., & West, J. (2002). *Children's reading and mathematics achievement in kindergarten and first grade*. Retrieved by 29 June 2011 from http://nces.ed.gov/pubsearch/pubsinfo.asp?pubid=2002125

Denzin, N. K., & Lincoln, Y. S. (2000). *Handbook of Qualitative Research*. London: Sage Publications.

Department of Education. (2001). *Education White Paper 6: Special needs education: Building and inclusive education and training system.* Pretoria: Government Printer.

DFE. (2014). *Cyber-bullying: Advice for Head Teachers and School Staff.* Available at: https://www.gov.uk/government/uploads/system/uploads/attachment_data/file/374850/Cyberbullying_Advice_for_Headteachers_and_School_Staff_121114.pdf

Diasio, N., & Vinel, V. (2010). Objets de soin, objets á soi. La fabrication d'un corps intime chez les enfants de 9 á 13 ans. In 9 émes journées de sociologie de l'enfance, Paris, France.

Diener, E. (2002). Subjective Well-Being: The Science of Happiness and Proposal for a National Index. *The American Psychologist*, *55*(1), 34–43. doi:10.1037/0003-066X.55.1.34 PMID:11392863

Dinerstein, A. (2014). Too bad for the facts: Confronting value with hope. *The South Atlantic Quarterly*, *113*(2), 367–378. doi:10.1215/00382876-2643675

Dingfelder, S. D. (2005, April). Fresh funding for translational research. *Monitor on Psychology*, *36*(4), 66. Retrieved from http://www.apa.org/monitor/apr05/funding.html

Donnerstein, E., Slaby, R. G., & Eron, L. D. (1994). The mass media and youth aggression. In L. D. Eron, J. H. Gentry, & P. Schlegel (Eds.), *Reason to hope: A psychosocial perspective on violence and youth* (pp. 219–250). Washington, DC: American Psychological Association. doi:10.1037/10164-010

Doyle, A., & Perlman, S. (2012). Trauma experienced in adolescence. In L. L. Levers (Ed.), *Trauma counseling: Theories and interventions* (pp. 146–160). New York: Springer.

Dryfoos, J. (2000). *Evaluation of community schools: Findings to date.* Retrieved from ERIC database. (ED450204)

Dryfoos, J. (2005). *Community schools in action: Lessons from a decade of practice.* Oxford University Press.

Dryfoos, J. G. (1994). *Full-Service Schools.* San Francisco: Jossey-Bass.

Dube, R. (2012). *Investigation into the experiences of undocumented child migrants from Zimbabwe to South Africa: A case study of experiences of irregular child migrants from Mberengwa* (Unpublished Masters Thesis). Women's University in Africa, Zimbabwe.

Dube, R. (2013). *She probably asked for it!" A Preliminary Study into Zimbabwean Societal Perceptions of Rape*. Harare: Research and Advocacy Unit.

Due, P., & Holstein, B. E. (2008). Bullying victimization among 13 to 15 year old school children: Results from two comparative studies in 66 countries and regions. *International Journal of Adolescent Medicine and Health, 20*(2), 209–222. doi:10.1515/IJAMH.2008.20.2.209 PMID:18714557

Dumontheil, I. (2015). Development of the Social Brain during Adolescence. *Psycologia Eucativa, 21*(2), 117–124. doi:10.1016/j.pse.2015.08.001

Dumontheil, I. (2016). Adolescent Brain Development. *Current Opinion in Behavioural Sciences, 10*(39), 39–44. doi:10.1016/j.cobeha.2016.04.012

Duncan, G. J., Claessens, A., Huston, A. C., Pagani, L. S., Engel, M., Sexton, H., & Duckworth, K. et al. (2007). School Readiness and Later Achievement. *Developmental Psychology, 43*(6), 1428–1446. doi:10.1037/0012-1649.43.6.1428 PMID:18020822

Dyson, A. (2001, March). *Varieties of Inclusion.* Paper presented at the conference VI Jornadas Cientificas de Investigacion sobre Personas con Discapacidad, Salamanca, Spain.

Ebersold, S., Schmitt, J. M., & Priestley, M. (2011). Inclusive Education For Young Disabled People in Europe: Trends, Issues, and Challenges. A synthesis of evidence from ANED country reports and additional sources. Academic Network of European Disability experts (ANED) – VT/2007/005. Human European Consultancy, University of Leeds.

Edleson, J. L. (1999). Childrens witnessing of adult domestic violence. *Journal of Interpersonal Violence, 14*(8), 839–870. doi:10.1177/088626099014008004

Edleson, J. L., Mbilinyi, L. F., Beeman, S. K., & Hageemeister, A. K. (2003). How children are involved in adult domestic violence: Results from a four city telephone survey. *Journal of Interpersonal Violence, 18*(1), 18–32. doi:10.1177/0886260502238538

Edmonds Eric, V. (2007). *Child Labour.* NBER Working Paper Series. Working Paper 12926. National Bureau of Economic Research. Retrieved 8 November 2016 from http://www.nber.org/papers/w12926

Egeland, B., Carlson, E., & Stroufe, L. (1993). Developmental Psychopathology: Vol. 5. *Resilience as a process*. Cambridge University Press.

Ekeke, C. E., & Ekeopara, C. A. (2010). God's divinities in African traditional religious ontology: A Conceptual and Philosophical Analysis. *American Journal of Social and Management Sciences., 1*(2), 209–218.

Elder, G. H. Jr. (1998). The life course as developmental theory. *Child Development, 69*(1), 1–12. doi:10.1111/j.1467-8624.1998.tb06128.x PMID:9499552

Engle, L.P., Castle, S., & Menon, P. (n.d.). Child development: Vulnerability and resilience. *Journal of Education, 4*(1), 621-635.

Enu, J., Agyman, O. K., & Nkum, D. (2015). Factors Influencing Students' Mathematics Performance in Some Selected Colleges of Education in Ghana. *International Journal of Education Learning and Development, 3*(3), 68–74.

Epstein, M. H., Nelson, J. R., Trout, A. L., & Mooney, P. (2005). Achievement and emotional disturbance. In M. H. Epstein, K. Kutash, & A. J. Duchnowski (Eds.), *Outcomes for children and youth with emotional and behavioral disorders and their families: Programs and evaluation best practice* (2nd ed.; pp. 451–477). Austin, TX: Pro-ed.

Essex, M. J., Kraemer, H. C., Armstrong, J. M., Boyce, W. T., Goldsmith, H. H., Klein, M. H., & Kupfer, D. J. et al. (2006, November 1). Exploring Risk Factors for the Emergence of Children's Mental Health Problems. *JAMA Psychiatry*, *63*(11), 1246–1256. doi:10.1001/archpsyc.63.11.1246 PMID:17088505

European Agency for Development in Special Needs Education. (2010). *Teacher Education for Inclusion: International Literature Review.* Odense, Denmark: European Agency for Development in Special Needs Education.

Falk, R. (2007). *World Economy and Development.* Retrieved October 13, 2016, from https://www.globalpolicy.org/component/content/article/211/44646.html

Fanelli, C. W., Musarandega, R., & Chawanda, L. (2007). Child Participation in Zimbabwe's National Action Plan for Orphans and Other Vulnerable Children: Progress, Challenges, and Possibilities. *Children, Youth and Environments*, *17*, 122–145.

Farrell, A. D., Meyer, A. L., & White, K. S. (2001). Evaluation of Responding in Peaceful and Positive Ways (RIPP); a school-based prevention program for reducing violence among urban adolescents. *Journal of Clinical Child Psychology*, *3*(4), 451–463. doi:10.1207/S15374424JCCP3004_02 PMID:11708233

Felitti, M. D., Vincent, J., Anda, M. D., Robert, F., Nordenberg, M. D., Williamson, M. S., & James, S. et al. (1998). Relationship of childhood abuse and household dysfunction to many of the leading causes of death in adults: The Adverse Childhood Experiences (ACE) Study. *American Journal of Preventive Medicine*, *14*(4), 245–258. doi:10.1016/S0749-3797(98)00017-8 PMID:9635069

Feng, J. Y., Jezewski, M. A., & Hsu, T. W. (2005). The meaning of child abuse for nurses in Taiwan. *Journal of Transcultural Nursing*, *16*(2), 142–149. doi:10.1177/1043659604273551 PMID:15764637

Feranil, I., Herstad, B., Jallow, W., & Mbuya-Brown, R. (2010). *Assessing Implementation of Botswana's Program for Orphans and Vulnerable Children.* Washington, DC: Futures Group, Health Policy Initiative, Task Order 1, for USAID. Retrieved from http://www.healthpolicyinitiative.com/Publications/Documents/1265_1_PIBA_Botswana_FINAL_acc.pdf

Ferguson, K. E. (1999). Patriarchy. In H. Tierney (Ed.), *Women's Studies Encyclopaedia.* Greenwood Publishing.

Feza, N. (2012). Can we afford to wait any longer? Young children in pre-school are ready to learn mathematics. *South African Journal of Childhood Education*, *2*(2), 58–63. doi:10.4102/sajce.v2i2.12

Feza, N. N. (2013). Inequities and lack of professionalisation of early childhood development practice hinder opportunities for mathematics stimulation and realisation of South African policy on quality education for all. *International Journal of Inclusive Education.* doi:10.1080/13603116.2013.855266

Feza, N. N. (2015). Teaching 5- and 6-Year-Olds to Count: Knowledge of South African Educators. *Early Childhood Education Journal*, *43*(5), 483–489. doi:10.1007/s10643-015-0736-z

Feza, N. N. (2016). Basic numeracy abilities of Xhosa Reception year students in South Africa: Language policy issues. *Issues in Educational Research*, *26*(4), 576–591.

Flores-Oebanda, C. (2006). *Addressing vulnerability and exploitation of child domestic workers: an open challenge to end a hidden shame.* Paper presented at the Expert Group Meeting "Elimination of all forms of discrimination and violence against the girl child", UNICEF Innocenti Research Centre, Florence, Italy.

Florian, L. (1998). Inclusive practice: what, why and how? In C. Tilstone, L. Florian, & R. Rose (Eds.), *Promoting inclusive practice*. London: Routledge.

Foster, G., Makufa, C., Drew, R., & Kralovec, E. (1997). Factors leading to the establishment of child-headed households: The case of Zimbabwe. *Health Transition Review*, *2*(7), 155–168.

Foster, G., & Williamson, J. (2000). A review of current literature of the impact of HIV/AIDS on children in sub-Saharan Africa. *AIDS (London, England)*, *14*(suppl. 3), S275–S284. PMID:11086871

Foucault, M. (1979). *Discipline and punish: The birth of the prison*. New York: Vintage Books.

Foucault, M. (1998). *The History of Sexuality: The Will to Knowledge*. London: Penguin.

Fraire, W. & Colapinto, L. (2012). *Genitori e figli... cercatori d'oro. La metodologia 'Pedagogia dei Genitori'*. Saluzzo: Fusta editore.

Fraser, N. (2013). How Feminism became Capitalism's Handmaiden and How to Reclaim It. *The Guardian*. Retrieved from www.theguardian.com/commentisfree/2013/oct/14/feminism-capitalist-handmaiden-neoliberal

French, L. (2010), Pamplin. Research. Child Labour. More complex than you think. *College of Business Magazine*. Retrieved 20 June 2016 from http://www.magazine.pamplin.vt.edu/spring10/childlabor.html

Fukuda-Parr, S. (2003). The Human Development Paradigm: Operationalizing Sens Ideas on Capabilities. *Feminist Economics*, *9*(2-3), 301–317. doi:10.1080/1354570022000077980

Fukuyama, F. (1992). *The end of history and the last man*. New York, NY: Penguin.

Fuller, J. M. (2013). *Spanish speakers in the USA*. Tonawanda, NY: Multilingual Matters.

Fuson, K. C., Clements, D. H., & Sarama, J. (2015). Making early math education work for all children. *Kappan*, *97*(3), 63–68.

Gale, T. (2000). Rethinking social justice in schools: How will we recognise it when we see it? *International Journal of Inclusive Education*, *4*(3), 253–269. doi:10.1080/136031100050059178

Gale, T., & Molla, T. (2015). Social justice intents in policy: An analysis of capability for and through education. *Journal of Education Policy*, *30*(6), 810–830. doi:10.1080/02680939.2014.987828

Galvan, A. (2014). Insights about adolescent behaviour: Plasticity and policy from neuroscience research. *Neuron*, *83*(2), 262–265. doi:10.1016/j.neuron.2014.06.027 PMID:25033176

Gamlin, J., Camacho, A. Z., Ong, M., & Hesketh, T. (2015). Is domestic work the worst form of child labour? The findings of a six-country study of the psychosocial effects of child domestic work. *Childrens Geographies*, *13*(2), 212–225. doi:10.1080/14733285.2013.829660

Garcia, A. F. (2015). *7 facts about child poverty you should know*. UNICEF Connect. Retrieved June 14, 2016, from https://blogs.unicef.org/blog/7-facts-about-child-poverty-you-should-know/

García, O. (2009). Emergent bilinguals and TESOL: Whats in a name? *TESOL Quarterly*, *43*(2), 322–326. doi:10.1002/j.1545-7249.2009.tb00172.x

García, O., & Sylvan, C. E. (2011). Pedagogies and practices in multilingual classrooms: Singularities in pluralities. *Modern Language Journal*, *95*(3), 385–400. doi:10.1111/j.1540-4781.2011.01208.x

Gardiner, B. (2015). *My Way on the Highway: why driving makes jerks of us all.* Available at: http://www.slate.com/articles/health_and_science/science/2015/05/the_psychology_of_road_rage_driving_makes_you_angry_anonymous_and_emotionally.html

Garmezy, N. (2015, January). Children in poverty: Resilience despite risk. *Psychiatry, 56*(1), 127–136. doi:10.1080/00332747.1993.11024627 PMID:8488208

Garmezy, N., & Masten, A. S. (1986). Stress, competence, and resilience: Common frontiers for therapist and psychopathologist. *Behavior Therapy, 17*(5), 500–521. doi:10.1016/S0005-7894(86)80091-0

George, S. (1990). *A Fate Worse Than Debt.* New York: Grove Weidenfeld.

Gil, D. G. (1975). Unravelling child abuse. *The American Journal of Orthopsychiatry, 45*(3), 346–356. doi:10.1111/j.1939-0025.1975.tb02545.x PMID:1146967

Ginsburg, K. R. (2014). *Building resilience in children and teens: Giving kids roots and wings* (3rd ed.). Washington, DC: American Academy of Pediatrics.

Ginsburg, K. R. (2015). *Raising kids to thrive: Balancing love with expectations and protection with trust.* Washington, DC: American Academy.

Girl Child Network. (2005). *Gravity of Girl Child Sexual Abuse in Zimbabwe: "Towards Creating a Culture of Prevention," 6–7.* Retrieved October 13, 2015, from, http://www.kubatana.net/docs/sexual/gcn_sexual_abuse_zim_050517.pdf

Global Education Partnership. Kenya. (n.d.). *Essays on child labour in Kenya written by young people.* Retrieved 21 May 2016 from http://www.iearn.org.au/clp/archive/write30.htm

Global Monitoring Report. (2015). *Development Goals in an Era of Demographic Change.* Retrieved December 12, 2016, from www.worldbank.org/gmr

Goldberg, D. T. (1993). *Racist culture.* Cambridge, UK: Blackwell.

Goldson, E. (1998). Children with disabilities and child maltreatment. *Child Abuse & Neglect, 22*, 663–667. PMID:9693844

Gonsoulin, S., & Read, N. W. (2011). Improving Educational Outcomes for Youth in the Juvenile Justice and Child Welfare Systems through Interagency Communication and Collaboration. Washington, DC: National Evaluation and Technical Assistance Center for Children and Youth Who are Neglected, Delinquent, or At-Risk (NDTAC).

González, J. M. (2011). Words were all we had: Reflections on becoming biliterate. In M. Reyes (Ed.), *Words were all we had: Becoming biliterate against the odds* (pp. 26–35). New York, NY: Teachers College Press.

Gore, J. (1993). *The Struggle for Pedagogies: Critical and Feminist Discourses as Regimes of Truth.* New York: Routledge.

Government of Zimbabwe & UNICEF. (2005). *Survey on Orphans and Other Vulnerable Children in Rural and Urban High Density Zimbabwe 2004/2005.* Harare: UNICEF.

Government of Zimbabwe. (2005). *Zimbabwe National Strategic Plan for the Education of Girls, Orphans, and other Vulnerable Children 2005-2010.* Author.

Graham-Bermann, S. A., & Seng, J. (2005). Violence exposure and traumatic stress symptoms as additional predictors of health problems in high-risk children. *The Journal of Pediatrics, 146*(3), 349–354. doi:10.1016/j.jpeds.2004.10.065 PMID:15756218

Gregson, S., Garnett, G. P., Nyamukapa, C. A., Hallet, T. B., Lewis, J. J. C., Mason, P. R., & Anderson, R. M. et al. (2002). HIV Decline Associated with Bahavior Change in Eastern Zimbabwe. *Science, 311*(5761), 664–666. doi:10.1126/science.1121054 PMID:16456081

Grier, B. C. (2006). *Invisible hands: Child labour and the state in colonial Zimbabwe*. Portsmouth, UK: Heinemann.

Grier, B. C. (2006). *Invisible Hands: Child labour and the State in Colonial Zimbabwe*. Portsmouth: Heinemann.

Griffin, K. W., Botvin, G. J., Nicholas, T. R., & Doyle, M. M. (2003). Effectiveness of a universal drug abuse prevention approach for youth at high risk for substance use initiation. *Preventive Medicine, 36*(1), 1–7. doi:10.1006/pmed.2002.1133 PMID:12473419

Griffiths, M. (2013). Social Networking Addiction: Emerging Themes and Issues. *Journal of Addiction Research & Therapy, 4*, 118. Available at http://www.omicsonline.org/social-networking-addiction-emerging-themes-and-issues-2155-6105.1000e118.php?aid=22152

Gruppo Pedagogia Libertaria. (2015). *Dalla parte dei bambini: Costruire una società diversa partendo dalla scuola*. Reggio Emilia: Pedagogia Libertaria ltd.

Gudyanga, E. (2014). Emerging Issues on Child Abuse: Voices of Student Teachers. *Education Journal, 3*, 146–152.

Guyer, A., Silk, J., & Nelson, E. (2016). The Neurobiology of the Emotional Adolescent. *Neuroscience Bio-Behaviour Review, 70*, 74–85. doi:10.1016/j.neubiorev.2016.07.037 PMID:27506384

Haddad, W., Colletta, N., Fisher, N., Lakin, M., & Rinaldi, R. (1990). *Final Report: World Conference on Education for All: Meeting Basic Learning Needs*. New York: The Inter-Agency Commission.

Haider, M. (2008). Recognising Complexity, Embracing Diversity Working Children in Bangladesh. *South Asia Research, 28*(1), 49–72. doi:10.1177/026272800702800103

Halcón, J. J. (2011). Obstinate Child. In M. Reyes (Ed.), *Words were all we had: Becoming biliterate against the odds* (pp. 85–95). New York, NY: Teachers College Press.

Hanmer, L., Pyatt, G., White, H., & Pouw, N. (1996). *Poverty in Sub-Saharan Africa. What can we learn from the World Bank's Poverty Assessments*. The Hague: Institute of Social Studies.

Harber, C. (1995). *Developing Democratic Education*. Derby: Education Now Books.

Harber, C. (1999). *Voices for Democracy: a North – South Dialogue on Education for Sustainable Democracy*. Derby: Education Now Books.

Harper, C., & Marcus, R. (2002). *Child poverty in Africa*. London: The Save the Children Fund.

Harré, R., & Van Langenhove, L. (Eds.). (1999). *Positioning theory: Moral contexts of international action*. Malden, MA: Blackwell Publishers Ltd.

Harris, E., & Wilkes, S. (2013). Partnerships for learning: Community support for youth success. Cambridge, MA: Harvard Family Research Project. Retrieved from www. hfrp. org

Harris, M. (2014). *The End of Absence: Reclaiming what we've lost in a world of constant connection*. New York: Penguin.

Harvey, D. (2009). *Social Justice and the City* (Revised ed.). Athens, GA: The University of Georgia Press.

Hatch, T. (1998). How community action contributes to achievement. *Educational Leadership, 55*(8), 16–19.

Hawk, S. (2004). Spiritual Wellness, Holistic Health, and the Practice of Health Education. *American Journal of Health.*, *35*(1), 11–16. doi:10.1080/19325037.2004.10603599

Hay, J., & Beyers, C. (2011). An Analysis of the South African Model of Inclusive Education with regard to Social Justice. *Africa Education Review*, *8*(2), 234–246. doi:10.1080/18146627.2011.603226

Heald, S. (2006). Abstain or die: The development of HIV/AIDS policy in Botswana. *Journal of Biosocial Science*, *38*(01), 29–41. doi:10.1017/S0021932005000933 PMID:16266444

Health Poverty Action. (2015). *Africa's billion dollar losses*. Retrieved October 13, 2016, from https://www.healthpovertyaction.org/speaking-out/honest-accounts/

Hettler, B. (1980). Wellness promotion on university campus. *Family & Community Health*, *3*(1), 77–95. doi:10.1097/00003727-198005000-00008 PMID:10246133

Higson-Smith, C., & Killian, B. J. (2000). Caring for Children in Fragmented Communities. In D. Donald, A. Dawes, & J. Louw (Eds.), *Addressing Childhood Adversity* (pp. 202–224). Cape Town: David Philip.

Hildyard, K. L., & Wolfe, D. A. (2002). Child neglect: Developmental issues and Outcomes. *Child Abuse & Neglect*, *26*(6), 679–695. doi:10.1016/S0145-2134(02)00341-1 PMID:12201162

Hodges, S., Hernandez, M., & Nesman, T. (2003). A developmental framework for collaboration in child-serving agencies. *Journal of Child and Family Studies*, *12*(3), 291–305. doi:10.1023/A:1023987710611

Hodkinson, A. & Devarakonda, C. (2011). Conceptions of Inclusion and Inclusive Education: A Critical Examination of the Perspectives and Practices of Teachers in England. *Educational Futures, 3*(1), 52-65.

Holden, G. W., & Ritchie, K. L. (1991). Linking extreme marital discord, child rearing, and child behavior problems: Evidence from battered women. *Child Development*, *62*(2), 311–327. doi:10.2307/1131005 PMID:2055124

Holden, S., & Otsuka, K. (2014). The roles of land tenure reforms and land markets in the context of population growth and land use intensification in Africa. *Food Policy*, *48*, 88–97. doi:10.1016/j.foodpol.2014.03.005

Holland, D., & Lave, J. (2009). Social practice theory and the historical production of persons. *Actio: An International Journal of Human Activity Theory*, *2*, 1–15.

Holloway, J. (2010). *Crack Capitalism*. New York: Pluto Press.

Holt, L. (2004). The voices of children: De-centring empowering research relations. *Childrens Geographies*, *2*(1), 13–27. doi:10.1080/1473328032000168732

Holt, S., Buckley, H., & Whelan, S. (2008). The impact of exposure to domestic violence on children and young people: A review of the literature. *Journal of Family Violence*, *13*(4), 345–363.

Hopewell, S., & Escamilla, K. (2013). Struggling reader or emerging, biliterate student? Reevaluating the criteria for labeling emergent bilingual students as low achieving. *Journal of Literacy Research*, *46*(1), 68–89. doi:10.1177/1086296X13504869

Hoppenbrouwer, E. M. (2011). *Introducing a child-centered numeracy play-center intervention in three rural preschools in Dennilton, South Africa* (Master's Thesis). University Utrecht.

Hornberger, N. H., & Link, H. (2012). Translanguaging in todays classrooms: A biliteracy lens. *Theory into Practice*, *51*(4), 239–247. doi:10.1080/00405841.2012.726051

Hossain, F. I. (2000). A view of Asia's hapless children: Save child workers. *The Independent*. Retrieved from http://independentbangladesh.com/news/aug/25/25082000pd.htm#1

Howard and Millard. (1997). *Hunger and Shame: Child Malnutrition and Poverty of Mount Kilimanjaro*. London: Routledge.

Human Rights Watch. (2007). *Thousands of Girls Face Abuse as Guinea Domestic Workers*. Guinea, Mali: Human Rights Watch.

Human Rights Watch. (2009). *Workers in the shadows abuse and exploitation of child domestic workers in Indonesia*. Jakarta: Human Rights Watch.

Humpage, L., & Fleras, A. (2001). Intersecting Discourses: Closing the Gaps, Social Justice and the Treaty of Waitangi. *Social Policy Journal of New Zealand*, *16*, 37–54.

Hutchinson, E., & Pournara, G. (2011). Preschool childrens mathematical understanding. *South African Journal of Childhood Education*, *1*(2), 92–111. doi:10.4102/sajce.v1i2.87

Ibhawoh, B. (2011). The Right to Development: The Politics and Polemics of Power and Resistance. *Human Rights Quarterly*, *33*(1), 76–104. doi:10.1353/hrq.2011.0001

ILO. (2016). *Child labour in Africa*. Retrieved January 13, 2017, from http://ilo.org/ipec/Regionsandcountries/Africa/lang--en/index.htm-title=IPEC-Africa-accessdate=17

Indabawa, A. S. (1997). Pupil's autonomy, cultural hegemony and education for democracy in an African society. In D. Bridges (Ed.), *Education, autonomy and democratic citizenship: Philosophy in a changing world*. London: Routledge.

Infoaut – Gruppo di discussion. (2016). *Per la ripresa di un movimento antagonista nelle scuole e nelle università*. Retrieved 1 October 2016, from: http://www.infoaut.org/index.php/blog/segnalazioni/item/16802-appunti-per-una-riflessione-collettiva-su-apparati-educativi-e-sistema-scolastico

International Labour Organisation. (n.d.a). *What is Child Labour?* Retrieved 6 April 2016 from http://www.ilo.org/ipec/facts/lang--en/index.htm

International Labour Organisation. (n.d.b). *Child Labour and Education for All*. Retrieved 21 May 2016 from http://www.ilo.org/ipec/Action/Education/ChildlabourandEducationforAll/lang--en/index.html

International Labour Organization. (2012). *Effective protection for domestic workers, a guide to designing labour laws*. Geneva: International Labour Organization.

International Labour Organization. (2016). *Child labour and domestic work*. Geneva: International Labour Organization.

Islam, E., Mahmud, K., & Naziza, R. (2014). The situation of Child Domestic Workers in Bangladesh. *Global Journal of Management and Business Research*, *13*(7), 24–34.

Islam, M. R. (2010). *A Child is in the home but imprisoned: a situation of domestic child workers in Dhaka City*. Dhaka: Bangladesh Shishi Adhikar Forum.

Islam, M. R. (2013). Brighter future of child domestic workers in Bangladesh: Government initiatives and challenges. *Elixir International Journal*, *60*, 16498–16503.

Islam, M. R., & Cojocaru, S. (2016). Migrant domestic workers in Asia: Transnational variations and policy concerns. *International Migration (Geneva, Switzerland)*, *54*(1), 48–63. doi:10.1111/imig.12201

Issues, G. (2015). *Causes of Poverty*. Retrieved October 13, 2016, from www.globalissues.org

Jacquemin, M. Y. (2004). Childrens domestic work in Abidjan, Côte dIvoire The Petites Bonnes have the Floor. *Childhood*, *11*(3), 383–397. doi:10.1177/0907568204044889

Jaggar, A. (2001). Is Globalization Good for Women? *Comparative Literature*, *53*(4), 298–300. doi:10.1215/-53-4-298

Jameel, S. N., Shah, S. A., & Gainaie, S. A. (2015). Perceived Social Support and Resilience among Orphans: A Systematic Review. *The International Journal of Indian Psychology.*, *3*(1), 1–6.

James, A. (2007). Giving voice to childrens voices: Practices and problems, pitfalls and potentials. *American Anthropologist*, *109*(2), 261–272. doi:10.1525/aa.2007.109.2.261

James, A. (2009). Agency. In J. Qvortrup, W. Corsaro, & M. S. Honig (Eds.), *Palgrave Handbook of Childhood Studies* (pp. 34–45). London: Palgrave MacMillan.

James, A., Jenks, C., & Prout, A. (1998). *Theorising childhood.* Cambridge, UK: Polity.

James, A., & Prout, A. (Eds.). (2015). *Constructing and reconstructing childhood.* Abingdon, UK: Routledge.

Jankey, O. M. (2013). Children, the forgotten victims of passion killings in Media reporting in Botswana between 2009 and 2013. In Thari ya Bana: Reflections on Children in Botswana 2013. Gaborone: UNICEF Press.

Jarger, A.G., Bensley, J. R., & Jarger. M. (2003). *Wellness from the Western and African Perspective: The Merging Point.* Academic Press.

Jarvis, P. (2006). Rough and Tumble Play: Lessons in Life. *Evolutionary Psychology*, *4*(1), 330–346. doi:10.1177/147470490600400128

Jarvis, P., Newman, S., & Swiniarski, L. (2014). On becoming social: The importance of collaborative free play in childhood. *International Journal of Play.*, *3*(1), 53–68. doi:10.1080/21594937.2013.863440

Jefferis, K. R., & Kelly, T. F. (1999). Botswana: Poverty Amid Plenty. *Oxford Development Studies*, *27*(2), 211–231. doi:10.1080/13600819908424174

Jenks, C. (1996). *Childhood.* Abingdon, UK: Routledge.

Jenks, C. (2009). Constructing childhood sociologically. In M. J. Kehily (Ed.), *An introduction to Childhood Studies.* Maidenhead, UK: Open University Press.

Jensen, K. B. (2007). Opportunities for agency and social participation among child domestic workers in Bangladesh. *Children, Youth and Environments*, *17*(1), 148–170.

Jha, M. M. (n.d.). *Barriers to Access and Success: Is Inclusive Education an Answer?* Retrieved August 10, 2016, from http://citeseerx.ist.psu.edu/viewdoc/download?doi=10.1.1.431.6785&rep=rep1&type=pdf

Johnson, L. J., Zorn, D., Yung Tam, B. K., Lamontagne, M., & Johnson, S. (2003). Stakeholders views of factors that impact successful interagency collaboration. *Council for Exceptional Children*, *69*(2), 195–209. doi:10.1177/001440290306900205

Jones, N., Moore, K., Villar-Marquez, E., & Broadbent, E. (2008). Painful lessons: The politics of preventing sexual violence and bullying at school. London: Overseas Development Institute (ODI).

Jones, L., Mitchell, K., & Finkellar, D. (2013). Online Harassment in Context: Trends from three youth internet surveys. *Psychology of Violence*, *3*, 53–69. doi:10.1037/a0030309

Jones, V. F., & Jones, L. S. (2015). *Comprehensive classroom management: Creating communities of support and solving problems* (11th ed.). New York: Pearson.

Jung, M., Kloosterman, P., & Macmullen, M. B. (2007). Young Children's Intuitions for Solving Problems in Mathematics, *Young children. NAEYC*, *2*(3), 50–57.

Kaiser Family Foundation. (2015). *The global HIV/AIDS epidemic.* Retrieved from http://kff.org/global-health-policy/fact-sheet/the-global-hivaids-epidemic/

Kambarami, M. (2006). *Femininity, Sexuality and Culture: Patriarchy and Female Subordination in Zimbabwe. In Understanding Human Sexuality Seminar Series*. Africa Regional Sexuality Resource Centre.

Kane, J. (2004). *Helping hands or shackled lives? Understanding child domestic labour and responses to it*. Geneva: ILO.

Kang, H-R. (2008). Transnational Women's Collectivities and Global Justice. *Journal of Social Philosophy*, *39*(3), 359-377.

Kanu, G. A. (2010). The Indispensability of the Basic Social Values in African Tradition: A philosophical appraisal. *African Health Sciences Journal*, *7*(5), 125–138.

Kaomba. (2013). *Role of Community Leaders and Impact of Culture in Eliminating Child Labour.* Retrieved 19 October 2016 http://www.eclt.org/wp-content/uploads/2013/07/Role_of_Community_Leaders_and_Impact_of_Culture_in_Eliminating_Child_Labour.pdf

Kapunda, S. M., & Moffat, B. D. (2010). *Corruption Control, Economic Growth and Poverty Reduction in SADC: The Case of Botswana and Tanzania*. Paper Presented at the SAUSSC Conference, Mafikeng.

Keddie, A. (2014). Identity Politics, Justice and the Schooling of Muslim Girls: Navigating the Tensions between Multiculturalism, Group Rights, and Feminism. *British Journal of Sociology of Education*, *35*(3), 353–370. doi:10.1080/01425692.2013.776930

Kelly, M. J. (2000). *What HIV/AIDS can do to education and what education can do to HIV/AIDS*. Lusaka: UNZA.

Kelly, M. J. (2010). *HIV/AIDS: A social Justice Perspective*. Nairobi: Paulines Publications.

Kelly, M. J., & Bain, B. (2005). *Education and HIV/AIDS in the Caribbean*. Paris: IAN Randle Publishers.

Kelly, P. (2001). Youth at risk: Processes of individualisation and responsibilisation in the risk society. *Discourse (Abingdon)*, *22*(1), 23–33. doi:10.1080/01596300120039731

Kerig, P. K. (1996). Assessing the links between marital conflict and child development: The conflicts and problem-solving scales. *Journal of Family Psychology*, *10*(4), 454–473. doi:10.1037/0893-3200.10.4.454

Khan, M., Kapoor, S., & Cooraswamy, R. (2000). Domestic violence against women and girls. *Innocenti Digest*, *6*, 1–30.

Khatlane, R. (n.d.). *Domestic Violence: How it Contributes to Sexual Exploitation of Children*. The National Consultative Conference against the Sexual Exploitation of Children.

Kim, E. M., Sheridan, S. M., Kwon, K., & Koziol, N. (2013). Parent beliefs and childrens social-behavioral functioning: The mediating role of parent-teacher relationships. *Journal of School Psychology*, *51*(2), 175–185. doi:10.1016/j.jsp.2013.01.003 PMID:23481083

Kjørholt, A. T. (2013). Childhood as social investment, rights and the valuing of education. *Children & Society*, *27*(4), 245–257. doi:10.1111/chso.12037

Korbin, J. E. (1991). Cross-cultural perspectives and research directions for the 21st century. *Child Abuse & Neglect*, *15*(Suppl. 1), 67–77. doi:10.1016/0145-2134(91)90010-B PMID:2032129

Kradin, R. L. (2012). When ancestral heritage is a source of discomfort: Culture, pre-object relatedness and self-alienation. *The Journal of Analytical Psychology*, *57*(2), 207–222. doi:10.1111/j.1468-5922.2011.01962.x PMID:22444356

Kridel, C. (2016). *An introduction to documentary research*. American Educational Research Association Website. Retrieved from http://www.aera.net/SIG013/ResearchConnections/IntroductiontoDocumentaryResearch/tabid/15485/Default.aspx

Krug, E. G., Dahlberg, L. L., Mercy, J. A., Zwi, A. B., & Lozano, R. L. (2002). *World Report on Violence and Health.* Geneva: World Health Organization.

Kymlicka, W. (1995). *Multicultural Citizenship: A Liberal Theory of Minority Rights.* Oxford, UK: Clarendon Press.

Lacey, L. A. (1970). *The life of W.E. B. Du Bois. Cheer the Lonesome Traveller.* New York: The Dial Press.

Lamb, B. (2014). *No justice for diplomatic abuse of domestic workers.* Retrieved from https://traffickingandlabor.wordpress.com/tag/domestic-workers/

Leach, F., & Machakanja, P. (2000). *Preliminary Investigation of the Abuse of Girls in Zimbabwean Junior Secondary Schools.* Education Research Paper 39, DFID.

Lee, A. (2015). *Foreign domestic workers more likely to develop mental health problems.* Retrieved from http://www.todayonline.com/singapore/foreign-domestic-workers-more-likely-develop-mental-health-problems

Lee, J., & Ginsburg, H. P. (2009). Early childhood teachers' misconceptions about mathematics education for young children in the United States. *Australian Journal of Early Childhood, 34*(4), 37–45.

Lee, J., & Md-Yunus, S. (2016). Investigating Childrens Abilities to Count and Make Quantitative Comparisons. *Early Childhood Education Journal, 44*(3), 255–262. doi:10.1007/s10643-015-0707-4

Lesetedi, G., & Ngcongco, N. (1995). A demographic and socio-economic profile of women and men in Botswana: A review of summary indicators of population composition and distribution, mortality, migration and economic ability. In 1991 Population and housing census dissemination seminar, (pp. 176-188). Gaborone, Botswana: Central Statistics Office.

Levers, L. L. (2012). An introduction to counseling survivors of trauma: Beginning to understand the context of trauma. In L. L. Levers (Ed.), *Trauma counseling: Theories and interventions* (pp. 1–22). New York: Springer.

Levitin, D. (2005). *The Organized Mind: How to better structure our time in the age of social media and constant distraction.* LSE Blog, British Politics, and Policy. Available at: http://blogs.lse.ac.uk/politicsandpolicy/the-organized-mind-how-to-better-structure-our-time-in-the-age-of-social-media-and-constant-distraction/

Livingstone, S., Olafsson, K., & Staksrud, E. (2013). Risky Social Networking Practices among underage users: Lessons for evidence-based policy. *Journal of Computer-Mediated Communication, 18*(3), 303–320. doi:10.1111/jcc4.12012

Loening-Voyse, H., & Wilson, M. (2001). *Approaches to caring for orphaned and vulnerable children: Essential elements for a quality service.* Institute for Urban Primary Health Care.

Lopes, J. A. (2007). Prevalence and comorbidity of emotional, behavioral, and learning problems: A study of 7th-grade students. *Education & Treatment of Children, 30*(4), 165–181. doi:10.1353/etc.2007.0027

Lynch, G. (2011). Kenyas new indigenes: Negotiating local identities in a global context. *Nations and Nationalism, 17*(1), 148–167. doi:10.1111/j.1469-8129.2010.00465.x

Lynch, M. F., & Levers, L. L. (2007). Ecological-transactional and motivational perspectives in counseling. In J. Gregoire & C. Jungers (Eds.), *Counselor's companion: Handbook for professional helpers* (pp. 586–605). New York: Earlbaum.

Lynch, P. J. (1994). Type A behavior, hostility, and cardiovascular function at rest and after playing video games in teenagers. *Psychosomatic Medicine, 2*(56), 152–152.

Lynch, P. J. (1999). Hostility, Type A behavior, and stress hormones at rest and after playing violent video games in teenagers. *Psychosomatic Medicine, 61*(1), 113. doi:10.1097/00006842-199901000-00157

Lyons-Ruth, K., & Jacobvitz, D. (1999). Attachment disorganization: Unresolved loss, relational violence, and lapses in behavioral and attentional strategies. *Psychosomatic Medicine*, *56*, 152.

Maasai Girls Education Fund. (n.d.). *The Life of the Maasai Woman.* Retrieved on 9 August 2016 from http://Maasaigirlseducation.org/the-need/the-life-of-a-Maasai-woman

MacPherson, S., & Midgely, J. (1987). *Comparative Social Policy and the Third World: Studies in International Social Policy and Welfare.* London: Palgrave Macmillan.

Mafumbate, R. (2011). *Academic performance of Child-Headed and Parent Headed Children: A Comparative Study, Masvingo Urban, Zimbabwe.* Leipzig: Lombard Academic Publishing.

Mafumbate, R., & Magano, D. M. (2016). The Ubuntu Principle amongst the Shona Speaking People in Promoting the Wellness of HIV and AIDS Orphaned Learners in Zimbabwe. *African Journal of Indigenous Knowledge Systems*, *15*(1), 28–45.

Mafumbathe, R. (2013). Sustainability of the role of extended families on orphan care in the era of HIV and AIDS in the Zimbabwean society. *Journal of Emerging Trends in Educational Research and Policy Studies*, *5*(1), 91–99.

Magwa, S., & Ingwani, V. (2014). Exploring Sexual Abuse of School Children in Families: A Case Study of Masvingo District, Zimbabwe. *The International Journal of Humanities & Social Studies*, *2*(9), 156–161.

Maiga, S. (2014). Gender and Indigenous Peoples' Rights. In Indigenous People in Africa: Contestations, Empowerment and Group Rights. African Institute of South Africa.

Maitra, B. (1996). Child abuse: A universal diagnostic category? The implication of culture in definition and assessment. *The International Journal of Social Psychiatry*, *42*(4), 287–304. doi:10.1177/002076409604200404 PMID:9023610

Makamure, E. (2010). *The Efficacy of the Family Support Trust, (FST) Post Rape Counselling for girl children aged 3 to 12 years in Harare Zimbabwe (Masters in Women's Law). Southern and Eastern African Regional Centre for Women's Law (SEARCWL)*, University of Zimbabwe.

Malema, N. (2006). *Challenges and adjustment strategies facing caregivers of children living with HIV in Gaborone: Implications for counselling* (Unpublished Master's Thesis). University of Botswana, Gaborone, Botswana.

Malinga, T., & Ntshwarang, P. N. (2011). Alternative care for children in Botswana: A reality or idealism? *Social Work and Society: International Online Journal*, *2*(9). Retrieved from http://www.socwork.net/sws/article/view/277/593

Manteuffel, B., Stephens, R. L., & Santiago, R. (2002). Overview of the national evaluation of the Comprehensive Community Mental Health Services for Children and Their Families Program and summary of current findings. *Childrens Services (Mahwah, N.J.)*, *5*(1), 3–20. doi:10.1207/S15326918CS0501_2

Manyanda, K. (2015). *Rehabilitation of Youths with Alcohol and Substance Use Disorders: Experiences from BOSASNET.* Paper presented at the Africa and middle east congress on addiction, Gaborone, Botswana.

Manzo, K. (2005). Exploiting West Africas Children: Trafficking, Slavery, and Uneven Development. *Area*, *37*(4), 393–401. doi:10.1111/j.1475-4762.2005.00644.x

Manzo, K. (2008). Imaging Humanitarianism: NGO Identity and the Iconography of Childhood. *Antipode*, *40*(4), 632–657. doi:10.1111/j.1467-8330.2008.00627.x

Martin, S. G. (2002). Children exposed to domestic violence: Psychological considerations for health care practitioners. *Holistic Nursing Practice*, *16*(3), 7–15. doi:10.1097/00004650-200204000-00005 PMID:11913229

Maruta, S. (2011). *Understanding the Impact of Domestic Violence on the Work or Organizations and Institutions in Ruwa*. Southern Institute of Peace Building and Development.

Marwick, A. (2012). The Public Domain: Surveillance in everyday life. *Surveillance & Society*, *9*(4), 378–393.

Mashiri, L. (2013). Conceptualisation of Gender Based Violence in Zimbabwe. *International Journal of Humanities and Social Science*, *3*(15), 94–103.

Mashumba, S., Musa, A., Mupeta, B., & Kinsani, M. (2004). *A Situation Analysis Study; reducing community Vulnerability to HIV/AIDS in Chipinge and Chiredzi Program Areas*. Harare: Plan Zimbabwe.

Mastein, A. S. (2014). *Ordinary magic: Resilience in development*. New York: Guilford Press.

Masten, A. S. (2006). Promoting resilience in development: A general framework for systems of care. In R. J. Flynn, P. M. Dudding, & J. G. Barber (Eds.), *Promoting resilience in child welfare* (pp. 3–17). Ottawa: University of Ottawa Press.

Mathambo, V., & Gibbs, A. (2009). Extended family childcare arrangements in a context of AIDS: Collapse or adaptation? *AIDS Care*, *21*(1), 22–27. doi:10.1080/09540120902942949 PMID:22380975

Maundeni, T. (2013). Early childhood care and education in Botswana: A necessity that is accessible to few children. *Creative Education, 4*(7A), 54-59. Retrieved from http://file.scirp.org/pdf/CE_2013071710353641.pdf

Maundeni, T. (2002). Wife Abuse Among a Sample of Divorced Women in Botswana A Research Note. *Violence Against Women*, *8*(2), 257–274. doi:10.1177/10778010222183035

Maundeni, T. (2010). Challenges Faced in the Implementation of Provisions of the United Nations Convention on the Rights of the Child (CRC) in Botswana. *Journal of Social Development in Africa*, *25*(1), 59–84. doi:10.4314/jsda.v25i1.54279

Maundeni, T., & Levers, L. L. (2006). Concerns about child subject research in Botswana: A call for establishing structures and guidelines that protect children. *African Sociological Review*, *9*(2), 153–167. doi:10.4314/asr.v9i2.23265

Maundeni, T., Levers, L. L., & Jacques, G. (Eds.). (2008). *Changing family systems: A global perspective*. Gaborone, Botswana: Bay Publishers.

Maundeni, T., & Mookodi, G. (2009). *Socio-cultural factors that place males at risk of HIV infection in Botswana: Implications for sexual and reproductive health strategies*. Academic Press.

Maundeni, T., Osei-Hwedie, B., McCauley, J., Kern, D. E., Kolodner, K., Dill, L., & Bass, E. B. et al. (1997). Clinical characteristics of women with a history of childhood abuse: Unhealed wounds. *Journal of the American Medical Association*, *277*(17), 1362–1368.

Maunganidze, L., & Tsamaase, M. (2014). Early childhood education in Botswana: A case of fragmented "fits". *International Education Studies, 7*(5), 1-7. Retrieved from http://files.eric.ed.gov/fulltext/EJ1069296.pdf

Mavhu, W., Berwick, J., Chirawu, P., Makamba, M., Copas, A., Dirawo, J., & Cowan, F. M. et al. (2013). Enhancing Psychosocial Support for HIV Positive Adolescents in Harare, Zimbabwe. *PLoS ONE*, *8*(7), e70254. doi:10.1371/journal.pone.0070254 PMID:23894625

Mbah, S., & Igariwey, I. E. (2001). *African Anarchism: The History of a Movement*. Tucson, AZ: Sharp Press.

Mbiti, J. S. (1969). *African Religions & Philosophy*. Durban: Heinemann Educational Books.

McCoyd, J. L. M., Walter, C. A., & Levers, L. L. (2012). Issues of loss and grief. In L. L. Levers (Ed.), *Trauma counseling: Theories and interventions* (pp. 77–97). New York: Springer.

McIntosh, J. E. (2003). Children living with domestic violence: Research foundations for early intervention. *Journal of Family Studies*, *9*(2), 219–234. doi:10.5172/jfs.9.2.219

McIvor, C. (2001). Do Not Look Down On Us. *Child Researchers Investigate Informal Settlements in Zimbabwe*, *42*, 3–4.

McLaren, P. (2000). *Che Guevara, Paulo Freire and the pedagogy of Revolution*. Lanham, MD: Rowman and Littlefield.

McMahon, C. (2015). Why do we 'like' Social Media? *The Psychologist*, *28*(9), 724–728.

Meijer, J. W. (2010). *Special Needs Education in Europe: Inclusive Policies and Practices*. Retrieved August 10, 2016, from http://www.inklusion-online.net/index.php/inklusion-online/article/view/136/136

Meinck, F., Cluver, L. D., Boyes, M. E., & Mhlongo, E. L. (2015). Risk and protective factors for physical and sexual abuse of children and adolescents in Africa a review and implications for practice. *Trauma, Violence & Abuse*, *16*(1), 81–107. doi:10.1177/1524838014523336 PMID:24648489

Merrill, L. L., Hervig, L. K., & Milner, J. S. (1996). Childhood parenting experiences, intimate partner conflict resolution, and adult risk for child physical abuse. *Child Abuse & Neglect*, *20*(11), 1049–1065. doi:10.1016/0145-2134(96)00094-4 PMID:8958455

Ministry of Education. (1996). *Educating our future*. Lusaka: Ministry of Education.

Ministry of Education. (2003). *HIV/AIDS guideline for educators*. Lusaka: Ministry of Education.

Ministry of Education. (2008). *Teaching in the window of hope: HIV/AIDS education for Zambian teachers*. Lusaka: Ministry of Education.

Ministry of Health (Republic of Kenya). (2007). *National Reproductive Health Policy: Enhancing Reproductive Health Status for All Kenyans*. Nairobi: Government of Kenya.

Ministry of Local Government. (2008). *National situational analysis on orphans and vulnerable children in Botswana*. Gaborone: Ministry of Local Government.

Mkabela, N. Q., & Lithuli, P. C. (1997). *Towards an African Philosophy of Education*. Durban: Kagiso Publishers.

Modie-Moroka. (2011). Infanticide, baby-dumping and abandonment in Botswana: implications for research, policy, and practice. In Thari ya Bana: Reflections on Children in Botswana 2013. Gaborone: UNICEF and University of Botswana.

Mogalakwe, M. (2006). The Use of Documentary Research Methods in Social Research. *African Sociological Review*, *10*(1), 221–230.

Mogwe, A. (1988). *A Go Itewa Ke Monna wa Gago ke Botshelo? A Preliminary Investigation into Battered Women in Botswana* (MPhil Dissertation). University of Cape Town.

Moletto, A., & Zucchi, R. (2011). Famiglia e cittadinanza attiva. *Handicap & Scuola*, *26*(158), 11–43.

Monash, R., & Boerma, J. T. (2004). Orphan -hood and Childcare patterns in sub-Saharan Africa: An analysis of national surveys from 40 countries. *AIDS Care*, *18*(2), 55–65. doi:10.1097/00002030-200406002-00007

Mookodi, G. (2004). Male violence against women in Botswana: A discussion of gendered uncertainties in a rapidly changing environment. *African Sociological Review/Revue Africaine de Sociologie*, *8*(1), 118-138.

Moore, K. (2000). Supporting Children in their Working Lives: Obstacles and Opportunities within the International Policy Context. *Journal of International Development*, *12*(4), 531–548. doi:10.1002/1099-1328(200005)12:4<531::AID-JID689>3.0.CO;2-J

Moskal, M. (2016). Language and cultural capital in school experience of Polish children in Scotland. *Race, Ethnicity and Education, 19*(1), 141–160. doi:10.1080/13613324.2014.911167

Moyo, D. (2010). *Dead Aid: Why aid is not working and how there is another way for Africa.* London: Penguin.

Mukamaambo, E., & Ntseane, P. (Eds.), *Male involvement in sexual and reproductive health: Prevention of violence and HIV and AIDS in Botswana.* Cape Town: Made Plain Communications.

Mulrow, D. C. (1994). Rationale for Systematic reviews. *British Journal of Medicine, 309*(6954), 597–599. doi:10.1136/bmj.309.6954.597 PMID:8086953

Munachonga, H. (2015). School and home sexuality discourse in selected girls' secondary schools in Lusaka. In A. Breidlid, A. M. Cheyeka, & A. I. Farag (Eds.), *Perspectives on youth, HIV/AIDS and indigenous knowledges in Africa* (pp. 77–96). Boston: Sense Publishers. doi:10.1007/978-94-6300-196-0_6

Munthali, J. (2001). *Education for All. Problems and Possibilities of Girls' schooling in Malawi* (Unpublished PhD Thesis). Edinburgh University

Muriithi, A. G. (2010). Education for All and Child Labour in Kenya: A conflict of capabilities?. *Procedia: Social and Behavioral Sciences, 2*(2), 4613–4621. doi:10.1016/j.sbspro.2010.03.739

Muronda, Y. (2009). *Social Security And The National Orphan Care Policy In Zimbabwe: Challenges From The Child Headed Household.* Academic Press.

Mutandwa, C. (2012). *How Can Criminal Justice Work Constructively With Shona Justice to Provide Effective Remedies to Child Sexual Abuse Victims?* The Danish Institute for Human Rights.

Muzi, M. (Ed.). (2009). *Pedagogia critica in Italia.* Bari: Carocci.

Mwanakatwe, J. M. (1968). *The Growth of education in Zambia since independence.* Lusaka: Oxford University Press.

Mwoma, T, & Pillay, J. (2015). Psychosocial support for orphans and vulnerable children in public primary schools in Soweto South Africa. *South Africa Journal of Education.*

Mwoma, T., & Pillay, J. (2016). Educational support for orphans and vulnerable children in public primary school: Challenges and interventions. *Issues in Educational Research, 26*(1), 82–97.

Nakamura, A. R., & Takano, T. (2008). Healthy lifestyle behaviour risks of being bullied, violence and injury. *Open Access Journal., 3*(2), 10–25.

Narayan, D., & Nyamwaya, D. (1996). *Learning from the poor: A participatory poverty assessment in Kenya. Environment Department working papers; no. 34. Participation series. Social Development papers; no. SDP 14.* Washington, DC: World Bank.

NASUWT. (2016). *Social Media Abuse Endemic in Schools.* Available at: https://www.nasuwt.org.uk/article-listing/social-media-abuse-endemic-in-schools-.html

National AIDS Council & Ministry of Health. (2015). *Global AIDS response progress reporting - Zambia country report: Monitoring the declaration of commitment on HIV and AIDS and the universal access.* UNGASS.

National Center for Mental Health in Schools (NCMHS) in the Department of Psychology at UCLA. (2016). *ESSA, equity of opportunity, and addressing barriers to learning.* Retrieved from ERIC database. (ED565303).

National Pro Bono Resource Centre. (2011). *What is social justice?* Retrieved July 15, 2016, from http://probonocentre.org.au/wp-content/uploads/2015/09/Occ_1_What-is-Social-Justice_FINAL.pdf

Ncube, W. (Ed.). (1998). Law, culture, tradition and children's rights in eastern and southern Africa. Aldershot, UK: Ashgate.

Newman, T. (2002). Promoting Resilience: A Review of effective Strategies for child Care Services. Prepared for Centre for Evidence-Based Social Services, University of Exeter.

Ngo, B. (2010). *Unresolved identities: Discourse, ambivalence, and urban immigrant students*. Albany, NY: State University of New York Press.

Ngwenya, M. C. (2014). *External and internal exclusion of black undergraduate students from impoverished township schools in historically advantaged universities in the Western Cape* (Unpublished Masters thesis). Stellenbosch University, Stellenbosch, South Africa.

Nhundu, T., & Shumba, A. (2001). The Nature and Frequency of Reported Cases of Teacher Perpetrated Child Sexual Abuse in Rural Primary Schools in Zimbabwe. *Child Abuse & Neglect*, *25*, 1517–1534.

Nieuwenhuis, J. (2010). Social justice in education revisited. *Education Inquiry*, *1*(4), 269–287. doi:10.3402/edui.v1i4.21946

Nsamenang, A. B. (2013). Dilemmas of rights-based approaches to child well-being in an African cultural context. In D. J. Johnson, . . . (Eds.), Vulnerable children: Global challenges in education, health, well-being, and child rights (pp. 13–25). New York: Springer. doi:10.1007/978-1-4614-6780-9_2

Nunes, T., Bryant, P., Evans, D., & Barros, R. (2015). Assessing quantitative reasoning in young children. *Mathematical Thinking and Learning*, *17*(2-3), 2–3, 178–196. doi:10.1080/10986065.2015.1016815

Nussbaum, M. C. (2003). Capabilities as Fundamental Entitlements: Sen and Social Justice. *Feminist Economics*, *9*(2-3), 33–59. doi:10.1080/1354570022000077926

Nyambedha, E., Wandibba, S., & Aagaard-Hansen, J. (2006). Changing Patterns of Orphan Care Due to the HIV Epidemic in Western Kenya. *Social Science & Medicine*, *5*(1), 301–311. PMID:12765710

Nyamukapa, C. A., & Gregson, S. (2005). Extended family and womens roles in safeguarding orphans education in AIDS-afflicted rural Zimbabwe. *Social Science & Medicine*, *60*(1), 2155–2167. doi:10.1016/j.socscimed.2004.10.005 PMID:15748665

Nyamukapa, C. A., Gregson, S., Wambe, M., Mushore, P., Lopman, B., Mupambireyi, Z., & Jukes, M. C. H. et al. (2010). Causes and Consequences of Psychological Distress among Orphans in Eastern Zimbabwe. *AIDS Care*, *22*(8), 988–996. doi:10.1080/09540121003615061 PMID:20552465

Nyaumwe, L. J., & Mkabela, Q. (2007). Revisiting the Traditional Cultural Framework of Ubuntuism: A Theoretical Perspective. *African Journal of Indigenous Knowledge*, *6*(2), 152–163.

Oduor-Ombaka, C. (2010). Girls in Transition: Negotiating, constructing and re-constructing girlhood after the Fall in rural Kenya. *Girlhood Studies*, *3*(2), 109–128. doi:10.3167/ghs.2010.030207

Ohnishi, M., Nakamura, K., Kizuki, M., Seino, K., Inose, T & Takano, T. (2008). *Caregivers' and non-caregivers' knowledge regarding HIV/AIDS and attitude towards HIV/AIDS and orphans in Nigeria*. Academic Press.

OKeefe, M. (1995). Predictors of child abuse in marital violent families. *Journal of Interpersonal Violence*, *10*(1), 3–25. doi:10.1177/088626095010001001

Okin, S. M. (1999). Is Multiculturalism Bad for Women? In S. M. Okin (Ed.), *Is Multiculturalism Bad for Women*. Princeton, NJ: Princeton University Press.

Okoye, U. O., & Tanyi, P. L. (n.d.). Perception of Child Labour in South Eastern Nigeria: A Study of Onitsha Metropolis. *International Journal of Research in Arts and Social Sciences, 1*, 425-440. Retrieved 25 October 2016 from http://academicexcellencesociety.com/perception_of_child_labour_in_south_eastern_nigeria.pdf

Okwany, A., Muhangi, A., & Mulongo, E. M. N. (2011). *The role of local knowledge and culture in child care in Africa: A sociological study of several ethnic groups in Kenya and Uganda*. Lewiston, NY: Edwin Mellen Press.

Oldfield, J., Hebron, J., & Humphrey, N. (2016). The role of school level protective factors in overcoming cumulative risk for behavior difficulties in children with special education needs and disabilities. *Psychology in the Schools*, 1–17. doi:10.1002/pits.21950

Oleke, C., Blystad, A., & Rekdal, O. (2007). Experiences of orphan care in Amach, Uganda: Assessing policy implications. *Journal of Social Aspects of HIV/AIDS, 4*(1), 1-12.

Ololtuaa Lekakeny John. (2012). *Effect of Child Labour on Access and Retention of Primary School Pupils in Mbita District, Homa Bay County*. Kenyatta University.

Olson, C. (2010). Childrens Motivations for Video Game Play in the Context of Normal Development. *Review of General Psychology, 13*(2), 180–187. doi:10.1037/a0018984

Oppenheimer, J. (2002). Considering Social Justice: A Review of David Millers Principles of Social Justice. *Social Justice Research, 15*(3), 295–311. doi:10.1023/A:1021066630225

Osofsky, J. D. (1995). The effect of exposure to violence on young children. *The American Psychologist, 50*(9), 782–788. doi:10.1037/0003-066X.50.9.782 PMID:7574189

OSullivan, D. (2012). Globalisation and the Politics of Indigeneity. *Globalizations, 9*(5), 637–650. doi:10.1080/14747731.2012.732424

Ottolini, D. (2012). *Unearthing the Invisible. Worst forms of Child Labour in Nairobi and Nyanza Provinces. A Baseline Survey Analytical Report*. Nairobi, Kenya: CESVI.

Ouane, A. (2008, November). *Creating education systems which offer opportunities lifelong learning*. Paper presented at UNESCO International Conference on Inclusive Education: The way of the future 48th session, Geneva, Switzerland.

Padare. (2014). *Walking in our Daughter's Shoes Evaluation Report*. Harare: Padare.

Parahoo, K. (2006). Nursing Research – Principles, Process and Issues (2nd ed.). Houndsmill, UK: Palgrave.

Parham, L. D., & Fazio, L. (2008). *Play in occupational therapy for children* (2nd ed.). St. Louis, MO: Elsevier.

Parke, R. D., & Collner, C. W. (1975). Child abuse: An interdisciplinary analysis. In M. E. Hetherinton (Ed.), *Review of Child Development Research* (Vol. 5). Chicago: University of Chicago Press.

Parliament of Zimbabwe. (2006). *Fact Sheet: Child Abuse in the Education Sector*. Harare: Parliament of Zimbabwe Research Department.

Parsons, E. R. (1994). Inner city children of trauma: Urban violence traumatic stress response syndrome (U-VTS) and therapists' responses. In J. Wilson & J. Lindy (Eds.), *Counter transference in the treatment of post-traumatic stress disorder* (pp. 151–178). New York: Guilford.

Pedagogia dei Genitori. (2016). Retrieved 5 October 2016, from: http://www.pedagogiadeigenitori.com/

Peleg, N. (2013). Reconceptualising the childs right to development: Children and the capability approach. *International Journal of Childrens Rights, 21*(3), 523–542. doi:10.1163/15718182-02103003

Pendlebury, S., & Enslin, P. (2004). Social justice and inclusion in education and politics: The South African case. *Journal of Education*, *34*, 31–50.

Perlman, S., & Doyle, A. (2012). Trauma experienced in early childhood. In L. L. Levers (Ed.), *Trauma counseling: Theories and interventions* (pp. 132–145). New York: Springer.

Peter, F. (2003). Gender and the Foundations of Social Choice: The Role of Situated Agency. *Feminist Economics*, *9*(2-3), 13–32. doi:10.1080/1354570022000078006

Petersen, A. C., Joseph, J., & Feit, M. (Eds.). (2014). *New directions in child abuse and neglect research*. National Academies Press.

Phorano, O., Nthomang, K., & Ntseane, D. (2005). Alcohol abuse, gender-based violence and HIV/AIDS in Botswana: establishing the link based on empirical evidence. *SAHARA-J: Journal of Social Aspects of HIV/AIDS*, *2*(1), 188-202.

Pipher, M. (1996). *Reviving Ophelia*. London: Vermillion.

Plan Zimbabwe. (2009). *Research Report on Child Abuse in Schools: A Baseline Study for the Learn Without Fear Campaign*. Harare: Plan International.

Pope, A. (1735). *Epistle to Dr. Arbuthnot*. Available at: https://www.poetryfoundation.org/resources/learning/core-poems/detail/44895

Population Council. (2009). *Adolescent Girls Programming and Capacity-Building Workshop*. Retrieved July 7, 2012, from, http://www.popcouncil.org/pdfs/PGY09_AdolWkshopNairobi08.pdf

Prizzon, A., & Mustapha, S. (2014). *Debt sustainability in HIPCs in a new age of choice*. Retrieved October 13, 2016, from: https://www.odi.org/publications/8476-debt-sustainability-hipcs-new-age-choice

Protocol on the Multi-Sectoral Management of Sexual Abuse and Violence in Zimbabwe. (2012). Zim Resources.

Prout, A. (2011). Taking a step away from modernity: Reconsidering the new sociology of childhood. *Global Studies of Childhood*, *1*(1), 4–14. doi:10.2304/gsch.2011.1.1.4

Prout, A., & James, A. (1990). A new paradigm for the sociology of childhood? Provenance, promise and problem. In A. James & A. Prout (Eds.), *Constructing and reconstructing childhood: Contemporary issues in the sociological study of childhood* (pp. 7–34). London: The Falmer Press.

Prout, A., & James, A. (2015). A new paradigm for the sociology of childhood? provenance, promise, and problems. In A. James & A. Prout (Eds.), *Constructing and reconstructing childhood*. Abingdon, UK: Routledge.

Provenzo, E. F., & Renaud, J. P. (Eds.). (2009). *Encyclopaedia of the Social and Cultural Foundations of Education*. SAGE Pub, Inc.

Punch, S. (2001). Multiple methods and research relations with children in rural Bolivia. In C. Dwyer & M. Limb (Eds.), *Qualitative methodologies for geographers*. London: Arnold.

Purewal, N. (2015). Interrogating the rights discourse on girls education: Neocolonialism, neoliberalism, and the Post-Beijing platform for action. *IDS Bulletin*, *46*(4), 47–53. doi:10.1111/1759-5436.12156

Rank, M. R., Hong-Sik, Y., & Hirschl, T. A. (2003). American Poverty as a Structural Failing: Evidence and Arguments. *Journal of Sociology and Social Welfare*, *30*(4), 3–29.

Rasing, T. (2003). *Love check: A game for children to prevent HIV/AIDS: Report of the game love check in Zambia*. WEB Foundation, Unpublished Report.

Rayner, T. (2012). Foucault and social media: life in a virtual panopticon. *Philosophy For Change*. Available at: https://philosophyforchange.wordpress.com/2012/06/21/foucault-and-social-media-life-in-a-virtual-panopticon/

Reale, D. (2008). *Away from Home. Protecting and Supporting Children on the Move*. London: Save the Children.

Reid, J. B., & Eddy, J. M. (1997). The prevention of antisocial behavior: Some considerations in the search for effective interventions. In D. M. Stoff, J. Breiling, & J. D. Maser (Eds.), *The Handbook of Antisocial Behavior* (pp. 343–356). New York: Wiley.

Reinke, W. M., Herman, K. C., Petras, H., & Ialongo, N. S. (2008). Empirically derived subtypes of child academic and behavior problems: Co-occurrence and distal outcomes. *Journal of Abnormal Child Psychology*, *36*(5), 759–770. doi:10.1007/s10802-007-9208-2 PMID:18205038

Republic of Kenya. (2001). *Kenya: Children's Act 8 of 2001*. Retrieved 21 May 2016 from http://www.chr.up.ac.za/undp/domestic/docs/legislation_03.pdf

Republic of Kenya. (2007). *Kenya Employment Act, 2007*. Retrieved on 4th August 2016 from http://www.lawnotes.in/Kenya_Employment_Act,_2007

Republic of Kenya. (2010). *Laws of Kenya. The Constitution of Kenya*. National Council for Law Reporting.

Republic of Kenya. (2014). *Education for All. The 2015 National Review*. Ministry of Education, Science and Technology.

Research and Advocacy Unit and Zimbabwe Association of Doctors for Human Rights. (2010). *No Hiding Place: Politically Motivated Rape of Women in Zimbabwe*. Retrieved May 1 2015, from, http://lexglobal.org/files/POLITICAL%20RAPE%20REPORT.pdf

Rete per l'Educazione Libertaria. (2016). Retrieved 2 October 2016, from: http://www.educazionelibertaria.org/

Reyes, I. (2006). Exploring connections between emergent biliteracy and bilingualism. *Journal of Early Childhood Literacy*, *6*(3), 267–292. doi:10.1177/1468798406069801

Rich, A. (2007). Notes towards a Politics of Location. In S. B. Freedman (Ed.), *The Essential Feminist Reader*. Modern Library.

Richter, L. (2013). Reported Physical and Sexual Abuse in Childhood and Adult HIV Risk Behaviour in Three African Countries: Findings from Project Accept (HPTN-043). *AIDS and Behavior*. doi:10.1007/s10461-013-0439-7 PMID:23474641

Richter, L., Manegold, J., & Pather, R. (2004). *Family and Community Interventions for Children Affected by AIDS*. Cape Town: HSRC Publishers.

Riddell, S. (2009). Social justice, equality and inclusion in Scottish education. *Discourse (Berkeley, Calif.)*, *30*(3), 283–297.

Ridley, M. (2003). *Nature via Nurture: Genes, experience, and what makes us human*. New York, NY: HarperCollins.

Rikowski, G. (2002). Fuel for the living fire: labour-power! In A. Dinerstein & M. Neary (Eds.), *The labour debate*. Aldershot, UK: Ashgate Publishing Company.

Ringrose, J., Harvey, L., Gill, R., & Livingstone, S. (2013). Teen Girls, Sexual Double Standards and Sexting: Gendered value in digital image exchange. *Feminist Theory*, *14*(3), 305–323. doi:10.1177/1464700113499853

Ritvo, E. (2012). Facebook and your Brain. *Psychology Today*. Available at: https://www.psychologytoday.com/blog/vitality/201205/facebook-and-your-brain

Rivera-Batiz, F. L. (1999). *Democracy, governance and economic growth: Theory and evidence.* New York: Columbia University.

Rodney, W. (1981). *How Europe Underdeveloped Africa.* New York: Howard University Press.

Rones, M., & Hoagwood, K. (2000). School-based mental health services: A research review. *Clinical Child and Family Psychology Review, 3*(4), 223–241. doi:10.1023/A:1026425104386 PMID:11225738

Rossetti, S. (2001). *Children in School: A Safe Place?* Gaborone, Botswana: UNESCO.

Rossouw, D. (2003). *Intellectual tools skills for the learners.* Pretoria: Van Schaik.

Ross, S. (1996). Risk of physical abuse to children of spouse abusing parents. *Child Abuse & Neglect, 20*(7), 589–598. doi:10.1016/0145-2134(96)00046-4 PMID:8832115

Rowntree, S. (1901). *Poverty: A Study of Town Life.* London: Macmillan.

Ruairc, G. M., Ottesen, E., & Prece, R. (2013). *Leadership for Inclusive Education Values, Vision, and Voices.* Rotterdam: Sense Publishers. doi:10.1007/978-94-6209-134-4

Runyan, A. S., & Marchand, M. H. (2011). *Gender and Global Restructuring: Sightings, Sites, and Resistances.* Routledge.

Rutter, M. (1985). Resilience in the face of adversity: Protective factors and resistance to psychiatric disorders. *The British Journal of Psychiatry, 147*(6), 598–611. doi:10.1192/bjp.147.6.598 PMID:3830321

Sabates, R. (2008). The Impact of Lifelong Learning on Poverty Reduction. IFLL Public Value Paper 1. Latimer Trend.

Sachikonye, L. (2004). Land Reform and Farm Workers. In D. Harold-Barry (Ed.), *Zimbabwe: The Past is the Future.* Harare: Weaver Press.

Sadler, F. H. (2009). Help! They Still Don't Understand Counting A Feature Article. *Teaching Exceptional Children Plus, 6*(1), 1-12. Retrieved 14 November 2016 from http://www.files.eric.ed.gov/fulltext/EJ875422.pdf

Safaids. (2009a). *Zimbabwean stories of "Best Practice" in Mitigating the HIV Crisis through a Cultural and Gender Perspective.* Harare: Safaids.

Safaids. (2009b). *Children to the Fore!: An Easy-to-Use Training Handbook That Promotes Child Rights And Cultural Issues in the Face of HIV in Southern Africa.* Harare: Safaids.

Safaids. (2011). *Best Practices on Challenging Gender Dynamics in Cultural Context.* Harare: Safaids.

Safman, R. M. (2004). Assessing the impact of orphanhood on Thai children affected by AIDS and their caregivers. *AIDS Care, 16*(1), 11–19. doi:10.1080/09540120310001633930 PMID:14660140

Salih, M. M. A. (2001). *African Democracies and African Politics.* New York: Pluto Press.

Salmon, C. (2005). Child labor in Bangladesh are children the last economic resource of the household? *Journal of Developing Societies, 21*(1-2), 33–54. doi:10.1177/0169796X05053066

Sarama, J., & Clements, D. H. (2008). Mathematics in early childhood. In Contemporary perspectives in mathematics in early childhood education (pp. 67-94). Information Age Publishing.

Sarama, J., & Clements, D. H. (2015). Scaling up early mathematics interventions: transitioning with trajectories and technologies. In Mathematics and Transition School, Early Mathematics Learning and Development (pp. 153-169). doi:10.1007/978-981-287-215-9_10

Saunders, B. E. (2003). Understanding children exposed to violence: Towards an integration of overlapping fields. *Journal of Interpersonal Violence, 18*(4), 356–376. doi:10.1177/0886260502250840

Save the Children Norway, Childline and Streets Ahead. (2009). *The Nature and Prevalence of Violence and Sexual Abuse among Boys Living and Working on the Streets of Harare.* Harare: Childline.

Save the Children Sweden-Denmark. (2010). *Living inside room outside law A study on child domestic worker and the role of government and civil society.* Dhaka: Save the Children Sweden-Denmark.

Save the Children UK. (2007). *Children Crossing Borders: Report on Unaccompanied Minors who have Travelled to South Africa.* Johannesburg: Save the Children UK.

Save the Children. (2002). *Schools for All: Including disabled children in education.* Retrieved June 30, 2016, from www.savethechildren.org.uk/development

Save the Children. (2007). *Children Crossing Borders.* Johannesburg: Save the Children UK.

Save the Children. (2008a). *Our Broken Dream: Child Migration in Southern Africa.* Johannesburg: Save the Children UK.

Save the Children. (2008b). *Save the Children Expands Assistance to Children Hurt by Zimbabwe Hunger Crisis.* Save the Children Organisation. Retrieved May 3 2015, from, http://www.savethechildren.org/newsroom/2008/zimbabwe-hungercrisis.html?print=t

Save the Children. (2010). *Child Carers: Child Led Research with Children who are Carers.* Pretoria: Save the Children Southern Africa.

Sayed, Y., Subrahmanian, R., Soudien, C., & Carrim, N. (2007). *Education Exclusion and Inclusion: Policy and Implementation in South Africa and India.* London: DFID Publications.

Schalk, L., Saalbachb, H., Grabnerc, R. H., & Stern, E. (2016). Relational Quantitative Reasoning in Kindergarten Predicts Mathematical Achievement in Third Grade. *Journal of Numerical Cognition, 2*(2), 77–90. doi:10.5964/jnc.v2i2.29

Schraad-Tischler, D. (2011). Social Justice in the OECD – How Do the Member States Compare? Gütersloh, Germany: Bertelsmann Stiftung.

Scott, J. (1990). *A Matter of Record, Documentary Sources in Social Research.* Cambridge, UK: Polity Press.

Seboni, N., Maundeni, T., & Rapinyana, O. (2015). An Analysis of Responses to Orphaned and Vulnerable Children (OVC) in Botswana. In M. Lombe (Ed.), *Children and AIDS.* Ashgate Publishing Ltd.

Seedet, M., Duncan, N., & Lazarus, S. (2001). *Community Psychology Theory, Method and Practice.* London: Unisa Press.

Seloilwe, E. S., & Thupayagale-Tshweneagae, G. (2009). Sexual Abuse and Violence Among Adolescent Girls in Botswana: A Mental Health Perspective. *Issues in Mental Health Nursing, 30*(7), 456–459. doi:10.1080/01612840903039367 PMID:19544130

Sen, A. (1990). Gender and Cooperative Conflict. In I. Tinker (Ed.), Persistent Inequalities, (pp. 123-49). New York: Clarendon Press.

Sen, A. (1999). *Development as Freedom.* New York: Knopf.

Sen, A. (2005). Human Rights and Capabilities. *Journal of Human Development, 6*(2), 151–166. doi:10.1080/14649880500120491

Sensoy, O., & DiAngelo, R. (2009). Developing social justice literacy: An open letter to our faculty colleagues. *Phi Delta Kappan, 90*(5), 350. doi:10.1177/003172170909000508

Shizha, E., & Charema, J. (2008). *Counseling Indigenous Shona People in Zimbabwe: Traditional Practices* versus Western Eurocentric Perspectives. *Journal of Psychology and Counseling*, *4*(5), 59–67.

Shumba, A. (2001). 'Who Guards the Guards in Schools?' A Study of Reported Cases of Child Abuse by Teachers in Zimbabwean Secondary Schools Sex Education. *Sexuality, Society and Learning*, *1*(1), 77–86.

Shumba, A. (2008). Emotional Abuse in the Classroom. *Journal of Emotional Abuse*, *4*(3-4), 139–149. doi:10.1300/J135v04n03_09

Shurgin OKeeffe, G., & Clarke Pearson, K. (2011). Clinical Report- The Impact of Social Media on Children, Adolescents and Families. *Paediatrics*, *127*(4), 800–804. doi:10.1542/peds.2011-0054

Sibanda, M. (2011). *Married too Soon: Child Marriage in Zimbabwe*. Retrieved June 3 2015, from, http://www.researchandadvocacyunit.org/index.php?view=download&alias=294-child-marriages-in-zimbabwe-printers-version-final&category_slug=womens-programme-1&option=com_docman&Itemid=115

Siddiqi, F., & Patrinos, H. A. (1995). *Child Labour: Issues, Causes and Interventions*. World Bank.

Sirin, S. R. (2005). Socioeconomic status and academic achievement: A meta-analytic review of the research. *Educational Research Journal*, *75*(3), 417–453.

Skalli, L. H. (2015). The Girl Factor and the (In)security of coloniality: A view from the The Middle East. Alternatives: *Global, Local. Political*, *40*(2), 174–187.

Snelson, P. (1974). *Educational development in northern Rhodesia 1883 – 1945*. Lusaka: Kenneth Kaunda Foundation.

Soro, A. (2007). Living Together: African Community-Based Values in Toni Morrison's Song of Solomon. *Nouvelle Serie*, *9*(2), 1–10.

Spaull, N. (2011). *Primary school performance in Botswana, Mozambique, Namibia and South Africa*. Paris: Southern and Eastern African Consortium for Monitoring Educational Quality (SACMEQ) Working Paper no.8.

Spaull, N., & Kotze, J. (2015). Starting behind and staying behind in South Africa: The case of insurmountable learning deficits in mathematics. *International Journal of Educational Development*, *41*, 12–24. doi:10.1016/j.ijedudev.2015.01.002

Spies Shapiro, L., & Margolin, G. (2014). Growing up Wired: Social networking sites and adolescent psychosocial development. *Clinical and Family Psychology Review*, *17*(1), 1–18. doi:10.1007/s10567-013-0135-1 PMID:23645343

Stofile, S. Y. (2008). *Factors affecting the implementation of inclusive education policy: A case study in one province in South Africa* (Unpublished doctoral dissertation). University of the Western Cape, Cape Town, South Africa.

Stoler, A. L. (2006). Tense and tender ties: the politics of comparison in North American history and (post)colonial studies. In A. L. Stoler (Ed.), *Haunted by empire: Geographies of Intimacy in North American history*. London: Duke University Press. doi:10.1215/9780822387992-002

Strauss, Gelles, & Smith. (1990). Physical Violence in American Families. New Brunswick, NJ: Transaction Publishers.

Stroul, B. A., & Blau, G. M. (2010). Defining the system of care concept and philosophy: To update or not to update? *Evaluation and Program Planning*, *33*(1), 59–62. doi:10.1016/j.evalprogplan.2009.06.003 PMID:19836078

Stroul, B., & Friedman, R. M. (1986). *A system of care for children and youth with severe emotional disturbances* (Rev. ed.). Washington, DC: Georgetown University Child Development Center, CASSP Technical Assistance Center.

Sugai, G., & Horner, R. H. (2002). Introduction to a special series on positive behavior support in schools. *Journal of Emotional and Behavioral Disorders*, *10*(3), 130–136. doi:10.1177/10634266020100030101

Summers, C. (2002). *Colonial Lessons: African's education in Southern Rhodesia, 1918-1940*. Cape Town: David Phillip Publishers.

Sutton, M. (2005). The Globalization of Multicultural Education. *Indiana Journal of Global Legal Studies*, *12*(1), 97–108. doi:10.2979/GLS.2005.12.1.97

Swart, E., & Pettipher, R. (2005). A framework for understanding inclusion. In E. Landsberg, D. Kruger, & N. Nel (Eds.), Addressing barriers to learning (pp. 3-23). Pretoria: Van Schaik.

Switzer, H. (2010). Disruptive Discourses: Kenyan Maasai Schoolgirls make themselves. *Girlhood Studies*, *3*(1), 137–155. doi:10.3167/ghs.2010.030109

Switzer, H. (2013). (Post)Feminist development fables: The Girl Effect and the production of sexual subjects. *Feminist Theory*, *14*(3), 345–360. doi:10.1177/1464700113499855

Sylvain, R. (2010). At the intersections: San women and the rights of indigenous people in Africa. *International Journal of Human Rights*, *15*(1), 90.

Synodi, M. (2010). *Early Childhood Special Education Update*. Retrieved July 30, 2016, from http://www.sde.ct.gov/sde/lib/sde/PDF/DEPS/Early/preschoolSE/B5Spring10.pdf

Tafa, E. M. (2002). Corporal punishment: The brutal face of Botswanas authoritarian schools. *Educational Review*, *54*(1), 17–26. doi:10.1080/00131910120110848

Tagle, R. (2005). Full service community schools: Cause and outcome of public engagement. *New Directions for Youth Development*, *2005*(107), 45–54. doi:10.1002/yd.128 PMID:16315516

Tajima, E. A. (2000). The relative importance of wife abuse as a risk factor for violence against children. *Child Abuse & Neglect*, *24*(11), 1383–1398. doi:10.1016/S0145-2134(00)00194-0 PMID:11128172

Tapper, D., & Kleinman, P., & Nakashian. (1997, July). An Interagency Collaboration Strategy for Linking Schools with Social and Criminal Justice Services. *Social Work in Education*, *19*(3), 176–188.

Tatar, M., & Myers, J. E. (2010). Wellness of children in Israel and the United States: A preliminary examination of culture and well-being. *Journal of Psychological Being.*, *23*(1), 17–33.

Terzi, T. (2010). *Justice and Equality in Education: A Capability Perspective on Disability and Special Educational Needs*. New York: Continuum International Publishing Group.

Thamuku, M., & Daniel, M. (2013). Exploring responses to transformative group therapy for orphaned children in the context of mass orphaning in Botswana. *Death Studies*, *37*(5), 413–447. doi:10.1080/07481187.2012.654594 PMID:24517564

The International Forum for Social Development. (2006). *Social Justice in an Open World: The Role of the United Nations*. New York: United Nations Publication.

The United Nations and Human Rights. (1995). *1945-1995, Department of Public Information*. New York: United Nations.

Thula, M. (2015). *Rehabilitation of youths who abuse drugs and substances: Lessons from Sbrana Hospital*. Paper presented at the Africa and middle east congress on addiction, Gaborone, Botswana.

Thumi, K. C., & Horsefield, G. E. (2004). *Traditional African values, guide to effective community-based health care*. Presented at the International Conf. AIDS.

Tirussew, T. (2005). *Disability in Ethiopia: Issues, Insights, and Implications*. Addis Ababa: Addis Ababa University Printing Press.

Tischler, S. (2008). *Tiempo y Emancipación – M. Bajtín y W. Benjamin en la Selva Lacandona*. Guatemala: F&G Editores.

Together for Girls: Sexual Violence Fact Sheet. (2012). Retrieved May 1 2015, from, http://www.togetherforgirls.org/docs/Together%20for%20Girls%20Sexual%20Violence%20Fact%20Sheet%20July%202012.pdf

Toth, S. L. & Cicchetti, D. (2004, December). Child maltreatment and its impact on psychosocial child development. In *Encyclopedia on Early Childhood Development.* Mt. Hope Family Center & University of Rochester.

Tourse, R. W. C., & Sulick, J. (1999). The collaborative alliance: Supporting vulnerable children in school. In R. Tourse & J. F. Mooney (Eds.), *Collaborative practice: School and human service partnerships* (pp. 59–78). Westport, CT: Praeger.

Trasatti, F. (2004). *Lessico minimo di pedagogia libertaria.* Milano: Elèuthera.

Trussell, R. P. (2008). Promoting school-wide mental health. *International Journal of Special Education, 23*(3), 149–155.

Tshabalala, T., & Khosa, M. T. (2014). Awareness of Various Forms of Child Abuse: Pupils' Attributions – A Case Study of Gomadoda Cluster. *Asian Journal of Social Sciences and Management Studies, 1*(1), 23–28.

Turkel, S. (2011). *Alone Together: Why we expect more from technology and less from each other*. New York: Basic Books.

Tyrell, P., & Jurgens, B. (1983). *African Heritage*. London: Macmillan Press.

U. S. Department of Education. (1998). *Twentieth annual report to congress on the implementation of the Individuals with Disabilities Education Act*. Washington, DC: Author.

U. S. Department of Education. (2001). *Twenty-third annual report to Congress on the Implementation of the Individuals with Disabilities Education Act*. Washington, DC: Author.

UK Council for Child Internet Safety. (2016). *Online Safety in Schools and Colleges.* Available at: https://www.gov.uk/government/uploads/system/uploads/attachment_data/file/562876/Guidance_for_School_Governors_-_Question_list.pdf

UK Council for Child Internet Safety. (2016). *Sexting in Schools*. Available at: https://www.gov.uk/government/uploads/system/uploads/attachment_data/file/551575/6.2439_KG_NCA_Sexting_in_Schools_WEB__1_.PDF

Underwood, M., Rosen, L., More, D., Erenreich, S., & Gentsch, J. (2012). The Blackberry Project: Capturing the messaging of adolescent text. *Developmental Psychology, 48*(2), 295–302. doi:10.1037/a0025914 PMID:22004337

UNESCO. (1994). *The Salamanca Statement and Framework for action on Special Needs Education*. Paris: UNESCO.

UNESCO. (2007). *UNESCO's strategy for responding to HIV and AIDS*. Paris: IIEP.

UNESCO. (2008). Inclusive Education: The Way of the Future. *International Conference on Education: 48th Session in Geneva*. Paris: UNESCO.

UNESCO. (2009). *Policy Guidelines on Inclusion in Education*. Paris: UNESCO.

UNESCO. (2013/14). *Education for All: Global monitoring report*. UNESCO.

UNESCO. (2015). *Poverty*. Retrieved October 13, 2016, from: http://www.unesco.org

UNFPA. (2005). *Child Marriage Factsheet: State of World Population*. New York: UNFPA.

UNICEF & Zimbabwe National Statistics Agency. (2011). *National Baseline Survey on Life Experiences of Adolescents Report*. Harare: ZimStat.

UNICEF. (1989). *A Summary of the United Nations Convention on the Rights of the Child*. Available at: http://www.unicef.org/crc/files/Rights_overview.pdf

UNICEF. (2005). *Africa's orphaned generations*. New York: UNICEF.

UNICEF. (2006). *Situation analysis of child domestic workers in Dhaka City*. Dhaka: UNICEF Bangladesh.

UNICEF. (2008). *Economic Meltdown Worsens Child Abuse in Zimbabwe*. Harare: UNICEF.

UNICEF. (2010). *Status of Women's and Children's Rights in Zimbabwe, 2005 – 2010: A Call for Reducing Disparities and Improving Equity*. Retrieved September 11 2015, from, http://reliefweb.int/sites/reliefweb.int/files/resources/ADAAAF5498C907248525785700717288-Full_Report.pdf

UNICEF. (2011). *The situation analysis of children and their families in Botswana*. Botswana: UNICEF.

UNICEF. (2012). *Child maltreatment, prevalence, incidence, and consequences in the East Asia and Pacific Region*. New York: UNICEF.

UNICEF. (2016). *Child poverty and social protection*. Retrieved October 13, 2016, from: https://www.unicef.org/socialpolicy/index_childpoverty.html

UNICEF. (2016). *The State of the World's Children 2016*. Retrieved April 6, 2016, from http://www.unicef.org/protection/57929_child_labour.html

UNICEF. (n.d.). *Basic education and gender equality. Child Labour and Exploitation*. Retrieved 21 May 2016 from http://www.unicef.org/education/index_focus_exploitation.html

United Nations Children's Fund. (2011). *UNICEF Botswana: Annual report 2011*. Retrieved from http://www.unicef.org/botswana/BCO__Annual_Report_2011.pdf

United Nations Children's Fund. (2012). *UNICEF Botswana: Annual report 2011*. Gaborone, Botswana: Author. Retrieved from http://www.unicef.org/botswana/BCO__Annual_Report_2011.pdf

United Nations Children's Fund. (n.d.). *UNICEF Botswana: Annual report 2015*. Retrieved from http://www.unicef.org/about/annualreport/files/Botswana_2015_COAR.pdf

United Nations Human Rights Office of the High Commissioner. (1989, November). *Convention on the rights of the child*. Retrieved from http://www.ohchr.org/EN/ProfessionalInterest/Pages/CRC.aspx

United Nations Resources for Speakers on Global Issues. (n.d.). *Child Labour. International Conventions of Child Labour*. Retrieved 21 May 2016 from http://www.un.org/en/globalissues/briefingpapers/childlabour/intlconvs.shtml

United Nations. (1976). *International Covenant on Civil and Political Rights*. Available at: http://www.ohchr.org/en/professionalinterest/pages/ccpr.aspx

United Nations. (2011). *Report of the Special Rapporteur on the promotion and protection of the right to freedom of opinion and expression*. Available at: http://www2.ohchr.org/english/bodies/hrcouncil/docs/17session/A.HRC.17.27_en.pdfAccessed

United Nations. (n.d.). *Child labour. Overview. What is Child Labour?* Retrieved April 6, 2016, from http://www.un.org/en/globalissues/briefingpapers/childlabour/

USAID. (2003). *Unsafe schools: A literature review of school-related gender-based violence in developing countries*. Washington, DC: Wellesley Centers for Research on Women & DTS/USAID.

Van Den Berg, E. (2006). *Factors influencing the capacity of Extended Families to provide psychological support to AIDS orphans*. Academic Press.

Van der Berg, S. (2008). How effective are poor schools? Poverty and educational outcomes in South Africa. *Studies in Educational Evaluation*, *34*(3), 145–154. doi:10.1016/j.stueduc.2008.07.005

van Dijck, J. (2013). You have one identity: Performing the self on Facebook and Linked-in. *Media Culture & Society*, *35*(2), 199–215. doi:10.1177/0163443712468605

Varia, N., & Becker, J. (2012). *A landmark victory for domestic workers: New convention establishes first global labor standards for millions of women and girls*. New York: Human Rights Watch.

Venkat, H., & Spaull, N. (2015). What do we know about primary teachers mathematical content knowledge in South Africa? An analysis of SACMEQ, 2007. *International Journal of Educational Development*, *41*, 121–130. doi:10.1016/j.ijedudev.2015.02.002

Viner, K. (2016). How Technology Disrupted the Truth. *The Guardian Long Read*. Available at: https://www.theguardian.com/media/2016/jul/12/how-technology-disrupted-the-truth

Violi, P. (1992). Gender, subjectivity and language. In G. Bock & S. James (Eds.), *Beyond Equality and Difference: Citizenship, Feminist Politics and Female Subjectivity*. Routledge.

Visser, M., Juan, A., & Feza, N. N. (2015). Home and school resources as predictors of mathematics performance in South Africa. *South African Journal of Education*, *35*(1), 1–10. doi:10.15700/201503062354

Vitaro, F., Brendgen, M., Larose, S., & Trembaly, R. E. (2005). Kindergarten Disruptive Behaviors, Protective Factors, and Educational Achievement by Early Adulthood. *Journal of Educational Psychology*, *97*(4), 617–629. doi:10.1037/0022-0663.97.4.617

Voléry, I. (2016). Sexualization and the transition from childhood to adulthood in France: From age-related child development control to the construction of civilizational divides. *Childhood*, *23*(1), 140–153. doi:10.1177/0907568215576525

Wagner, A. (2012). Is Internet Access a Human Right? *UK Human Rights Blog*. Available at: https://ukhumanrightsblog.com/2012/01/11/is-internet-access-a-human-right/

Wagner, S., & Walters, J. (1982). A Longitudinal Analysis of Early Number Concepts: From Numbers and Numbers. In Action and Thought, (pp. 137-161). New York: Academic Press.

Walker, H. M., Ramsey, E., & Gresham, F. M. (2004). *Antisocial behavior in schools: Evidence-based practices* (2nd ed.). Belmont, CA: Wadsworth.

Wall, J. (2008). Human rights in light of childhood. *International Journal of Childrens Rights*, *16*(4), 523–543. doi:10.1163/157181808X312122

Wang, T. Q., Cornell, H., & Anderson, J. A. (2016). *IPS Kaleidoscope Program Evaluation Report: 2007- 2015*. Indianapolis Public Schools. Bloomington, IN: Families, Communities, and Schools.

Wang, A. H., Shen, F., & Byrnes, J. P. (2013). Does the opportunity–propensity framework predict the early mathematics skills of low-income pre-kindergarten children? *Contemporary Educational Psychology*, *38*(3), 259–270. doi:10.1016/j.cedpsych.2013.04.004

Wang, L., Lee, X., & Li, N. (2014). Socio-economic status and mathematics achievement in China: A review. *ZDM Mathematics Education*, *46*(7), 1051–1060. doi:10.1007/s11858-014-0617-8

Wang, M. C., Haertel, G. D., & Walberg, H. J. (1998). *Educational resilience (Publication Series No. 11)*. Philadelphia: National Research Center on Education in the Inner Cities.

Webbink, E., Smits, J. & de Jong, E. (2013). Social Indicators Research. *International and Interdisciplinary Journal for Quality-of-Life Measurement, 110*(2), 819-836. doi:10.1007/s11205-011-9960-0

Webster-Stratton, C. (1990). Stress: A potential disruptor of parent perceptions and family interactions. *Journal of Clinical Child Psychology, 19*(4), 302–312. doi:10.1207/s15374424jccp1904_2

Webster-Stratton, C., & Hammond, M. (1998). Conduct problems and level of social competence in Head Start children: Prevalence, pervasiveness, and associated risk factors. *Clinical Child Psychology and Family Psychology Review, 1*(2), 101–124. doi:10.1023/A:1021835728803 PMID:11324301

Werner, E. (1989). High-risk children in young adulthood: A longitudinal study from birth to 32 years. *The American Journal of Orthopsychiatry, 59*(1), 72–81. doi:10.1111/j.1939-0025.1989.tb01636.x PMID:2467566

Werner, E. E., & Smith, R. S. (2001). *Journey from childhood to midlife: Risk, resilience, and recovery.* New York: Cornell University Press.

Westwood, P. (2013). *Inclusive and Adaptive Teaching: Meeting the Challenge of Diversity in the Classroom.* Oxon, UK: Rutledge.

WHO. (2015). *Global Health Observatory (GHO) data: Under-five mortality.* Retrieved October 13, 2016, from: http://www.who.int/gho/child_health/mortality/mortality_under_five_text/en/

Wible, B. (2004). *Making Schools Safe for Girls: Combating Gender-based Violence in Benin.* Washington, DC: US Academy for Educational Development.

Widom, C. S., & Hiller-Sturmhofel, S. (2001). Alcohol abuse as a risk factor for and consequence of child abuse. *Alcohol Research & Health, 25*(1), 52–52. PMID:11496967

Wilson-Oyelaran, E. B. (1989). The ecological model and the study of child abuse in Nigeria. *Child Abuse & Neglect, 13*(3), 379–387. doi:10.1016/0145-2134(89)90078-1 PMID:2776046

Wiredu, K. (1990). Are there cultural universals? Quest: An African International. *The Journal of Philosophy, 4*(2), 5–19.

Wise, J. (2016). Anxiety in teenage girls rises sharply between 2006 and 2016. *BMJ (Clinical Research Ed.), 354*, 4649.

Wissow, L. S. (1995). Child abuse and neglect. *The New England Journal of Medicine, 332*(21), 1425–1431. doi:10.1056/NEJM199505253322107 PMID:7723800

Wolf, L., Bazargan, N., Kilford, E., Dumontheil, I., & Blakemore, S. J. (2015). The audience effect in adolescence depends on whos looking over your shoulder. *Journal of Adolescence, 43*, 5–14. doi:10.1016/j.adolescence.2015.05.003 PMID:26043167

Wong, B., & Donohue, M. (2002). *The social dimensions of learning disabilities.* Lawrence Erlbaum.

Woodhead, M. (2009). Childhood studies: past, present and future. In M. J. Kehily (Ed.), *An introduction to Childhood Studies.* Maidenhead, UK: Open University Press.

Work in Freedom. (2016). *Child Labour in Africa.* Retrieved January 13, 2017, from: http://www.ilo.org/wcmsp5/groups/public/---ed_norm/---declaration/documents/publication/wcms_decl_fs_37_en.pdf

World Bank. (1998). *Status Report on Poverty. Gender, Growth and Poverty Reduction in Sub-Saharan Africa, discussion draft for SPA.* World Bank.

World Bank. (2002). *Education and HIV/AIDS: A window of hope.* Washington, DC: World Bank.

World Bank. (2014). *Sub-Saharan Africa: Poverty headcount ratio.* Washington, DC: World Bank.

World Health Organization (WHO). (2010). *Child maltreatment*. Geneva: WHO. Retrieved from http://www.who.int/mediacentre/factsheets/fs150/en/index.html

Wright, R. J., Martland, J., & Stafford, A. K. (2000). *Early numeracy: Assessment for teaching and intervention*. London: Chapman.

Wyness, M. (2012). *Childhood and society* (2nd ed.). London: Palgrave MacMillan. doi:10.1007/978-0-230-35725-9

Zavalloni, G. (2008). *La pedagogia della lumaca*. Bologna: EMI.

ZEC. (2004). *A pastoral letter from the catholic bishops of Zambia on education: Empowerment through education*. Mission Press.

Zerhouni, E. A. (2005). US biomedical research: Basic, translational, and clinical sciences. *Journal of the American Medical Association*, *294*(11), 1352–1358. doi:10.1001/jama.294.11.1352 PMID:16174693

Zhao, L., Fang, X., Zhao, J., Yang, H., & Bonita, S. (2007). Care arrangement, grief, and psychological problems among children orphaned by AIDS in China. *AIDS Care*, *19*(9), 1075–1082. doi:10.1080/09540120701335220 PMID:18058390

Zimbabwe National Statistics Agency (ZIMSTAT) & ICF International. (2012). *Zimbabwe Demographic and Health Survey 2010-11*. Calverton, MD: ZIMSTAT and ICF International Inc.

Zimbabwe National Statistics Agency. (2011). *Child Labour Survey*. Harare: ZimStat.

Zimbabwe Youth Council. (2014). *Harmful Cultural and Social Practices Affecting Children: Our Collective Responsibility*. Harare: ZYC.

About the Contributors

Icarbord Tshabangu, PhD, is a graduate of Manchester Metropolitan University, UK and lectures at the Institute of Childhood and Education at Leeds Trinity University, UK. He has previously worked as a Senior Lecturer and Coordinator of Educational Foundations and Management programmes, teaching postgraduate and undergraduate courses at the University of Arusha, Tanzania and at the University of Namibia, Namibia. He was also associated with the University of Liverpool Online as Honorary Senior Lecturer. He has served as internal and external examiner at both undergraduate and postgraduate levels and continues to be research supervisor. His teaching and research interests are largely on children's rights, democratic citizenship and qualitative methodologies. He is coordinator for Global Citizenship and Diaspora Network (GLOCIDIN) and Non-Executive Director for Community Development and Services Alliances (CODESA), UK.

***

Jeffrey Alvin Anderson is a tenured professor of special education in the School of Education at Indiana University-Bloomington, where he is the principal investigator of Project FoCuS (Families, Communities, and Schools): "Supporting partnerships among schools, families, and communities through collaboration, engagement, and research". Author of 40 peer-reviewed publications, his research interests broadly examine the role and impact of interagency collaboration and family engagement in public schools. Preventing mental illness and improving educational and social outcomes, especially for young people with emotional and behavioral challenges, are core goals of his work.

Stefano Ba, PhD, who has a dual national academic background (taught doctorate from University of Perugia, Italy and PhD from University of Manchester, Great Britain) who researches family life, children and job insecurity. He is a sociologist who has grounding in Critical Theory and recently published in *Capital and Class*. He also contributed to the following peer-reviewed journals: *Sociological Research Online*, *Community Work and Family* and *Quaderni di Teoria Sociale* [social theory notebooks]. A chapter on 'Families in Insecure Jobs' is forthcoming in an edited book from Routledge.

Kristina Bixler is a second-year PhD student in Special Education with a minor in Educational Leadership at Indiana University Bloomington. Her research interests focus on special education policy and teacher education.

Joseph Chita obtained a Master in International Education and Development from Oslo and Akershus University College of Applied Sciences - Oslo in 2010 and Master of Education in Religious Studies from the University of Zambia - Lusaka in 2011. He joined the University of Zambia as lecturer in the Department of Religious Studies in 2011. His research interests are in religion and education, religion and society, and comparative education. Some of his publications have cut across the aforementioned areas of interest.

Manase Chiweshe, PhD, is a Senior Lecturer in the Institute of Lifelong Learning and Development Studies at Chinhoyi University of Technology and winner of the 2015 Gerti Hessling Award for the best paper in African studies. Dr Chiweshe's work revolves around the sociology of everyday life in African spaces with special focus on promoting African ways of knowing. He has interest in agrarian studies, livelihoods, football, gender, feminist theory and youth studies.

Nosisi Feza has obtained her PhD in Mathematics Education from the State University of New York at Buffalo, New York as a Fulbright scholar. In 2008 she was a recipient of the inaugural Leroy and Margaret H. Callahan award for a promising researcher. Her PhD dissertation titled: Being a sheep in a "cattle's kraal" does not make you a cow: Black students' thought processes in measurement activity, this work won her an Emerging Diversity Scholar Award from the National Center for Institutional Diversity in Michigan in 2009. She turned her dissertation into a book title: My culture my learning capital my tool for thought. N Tutelea (Ed). LAP LAMBERT Academic Publishing, Germany. Her first collaboration was on her final year of PhD when she initiated a mathematics education project between the University of KwaZulu-Natal/ State University of New York at Buffalo from June- 2009 to December 2011 Training African female teachers for FET mathematics in South Africa funded by USAid. The aim of this project was to empower female teachers of UKZN. During the last four years she worked for the Human Sciences Research Council (HSRC) as a Senior Research Specialist conducting mathematics education research informing policies. She has secured a number of grants while at HSRC. Within her month appointment at UNISA she already secured a three year grant from NRF amounting to R320 000. Nosisi has lectured mathematics education at Nelson Mandela Metropolitan University for twelve years where she obtained her Masters in Mathematics Education and published papers on her Masters work. She is currently a Head of the Institute of Science and Technology Education at the University of South Africa. Her publications are on students of African descendants thinking processes in mathematics. Recently her publications focused on early childhood mathematics stimulation and teacher development. Most of her work will be found in her website https://sites.google.com/site/nosisifeza/classroom-news.

Velisiwe Gasa is a Professor and Head of Graduate Studies and Research in the College of Education, University of South Africa, Pretoria. She has published a number of scholarly works in accredited and peer-reviewed journals, peer-reviewed book chapters and peer-reviewed conference proceedings. She has presented a number of papers in national and international conferences. She serves on the editorial boards of a number of academic journals and has been, internationally as well as nationally, involved in a sustained peer review of journal articles, book chapters, and conference proceedings. She also serves in a number of faculty and university committees. Her research areas include learners' aggressive behaviour; socio-economic barriers to learning; inclusive leadership and school inclusivity; youth involvement in risk behaviours; alternative parenting; and incarcerated students.

Elizabeth Goulette, Ph.D. (The State University of New York at Buffalo, USA), is a Lecturer of Foreign Language Education at Georgia State University (USA) where she supervises world language teacher candidates. She also teaches Spanish and Foreign Language Education courses. Her research focuses on preparing teachers to meet the needs of culturally and linguistically diverse students in their classrooms.

M. Rezaul Islam received his MSW and PhD from the University of Nottingham, England in 2005 and 2009 respectively. He is a Professor in Social Work at the Institute of Social Welfare & Research, University of Dhaka. He is actively involved in social work education and professional development of Social Work in Bangladesh. His main research area focuses on poverty, social exclusion and social justice. His research covers a wide range of areas such as climate change and disasters, displaced people, International labour migration, NGOs and community development, and child welfare, which are embedded by human rights approach and inspired by people who are vulnerable and affected by structural causes of poverty, unemployment and inequalities.

Odireleng Jankey (Ph.D., MSW) is a senior lecturer in the Department of Social Work at the University of Botswana. She graduated from the University of Utah, USA with a PhD in Social Work. She is currently based in Botswana and teaching courses in the clinical stream at the University of Botswana. She has participated in several research studies including; coping strategies of informal caregivers in Botswana, children as victims of violence, parenting of adolescence, counseling of students, evaluation of disability programmes in Botswana, linking alcohol abuse, gender-based violence and HIV/AIDS in Botswana, assessing the magnitude of disability, teenage pregnancy as well as substance use and abuse, and the evaluation of District multi-sectoral AIDS Committee (DMSAC). She has published fairly extensively on issues pertaining to social protection, care giving, health, and gender based violence. She has experience with working with NGO's, FBO's and communities. She is currently the board chairperson of Kagisano Women's Shelter.

Pam Jarvis (PhD) is a Chartered Psychologist and Historian. Her key research focus is the creation of developmentally-informed policy for children, young people and families, and she has a range of publications in this area. She is a Senior Lecturer at Leeds Trinity University and an advisor to the UK Save Childhood Movement and Too Much, Too Soon Campaign. She is also a regular blogger in the UK edition of the Huffington Post.

Serena Koissaba is a PhD student in the department of Education Policy, Organization and Leadership at the University of Illinois at Urbana-Champaign. She writes and presents widely at conferences on comparative and international education and transnational feminism topics.

Lisa Lopez Levers, Ph.D., LPCC-S, LPC, CRC, NCC, is the Rev. Francis Philben Endowed Chair in African Studies and a Professor of Counselor Education and Supervision in the Department of Counseling, Psychology, and Special Education; School of Education; Duquesne University. She is in her 28th year of university teaching. Prior to entering the academy, she worked in community mental health for 15 years, counseling extensively with child, adolescent, and adult survivors of trauma. Professor Levers has published books, scholarly chapters in textbooks, and articles in peer-reviewed journals regarding issues of relevance to African culture, trauma and disaster, and the counseling profession in general. She recently edited a textbook, Trauma Counseling: Theories and Interventions. She has been awarded numerous grants and was a Fulbright Scholar at the University of Botswana, 2003-2004. Professor Levers first traveled to Africa in 1993. She has worked extensively throughout the southern, eastern, and central regions of Africa. Her current scholarly project involves the HIV/AIDS pandemic in sub-Saharan Africa, especially cultural implications and psychosocial effects; indigenous knowledge; roles of indigenous healers and local authorities in constructing culturally appropriate interventions; the impact of trauma on childhood and adolescent development; adult sequelae associated with early childhood trauma; designing and developing culturally sensitive community-based services for vulnerable children; psychosocial issues of disability; and, building culturally relevant systems of training for helping professionals. She works with marginalized communities in developing culturally sensitive systems of care, creating better access to health/mental health services, designing responses to community trauma, and building community resilience.

Racheal Mafumbate is a PhD holder in Career and Life Orientation Skills-Psychology with the University of Johannesburg, South Africa and a Masters in Educational Psychology. She has worked at the Zimbabwe Open University as Regional Program Co-coordinator/ Counsellor for 8 years. She has also been the National Program Leader - Counselling, for 5 years until end of January 2015 when she joined the University of South Africa. She writes and publishes on 'Ubuntu' and Wellness of orphans, wellness of juvenile offender learners, Indigenous African Knowledge, empowerment of children at risk and also on Guidance and Counselling for Empowerment. Currently she works as a Research Fellow in the Department of Psychology of Education at the University of South Africa. She has published a book, book chapters and articles in accredited journals.

Tapologo Maundeni is a Professor in the Department of Social Work at the University of Botswana. She holds a Masters in Social Work from the University of Wisconsin Madison, and a PhD from the University of Glasgow. She also chairs the research sub-committee of the University of Botswana's Gender Policy and Programme Committee (GPPC) as well as the Committee that reviews the University of Botswana's Sexual Harassment Policy. Professor Maundeni serves as a reviewer of manuscripts submitted for publication in various internationally renowned journals. Previous positions include Head of the Social Work Department at the University of Botswana, External Examiner for the University of Witwatersrand, the Executive Secretary for OSSREA – Botswana Chapter and a member of the National Children's Council. She also served as a consultant for international and national organizations such as UNICEF, UNESCO, as well as DIFD. Her areas of specialization include: human rights, child and family welfare, sexual and reproductive health issues, gender and development, as well as HIV and AIDS. She has published extensively on these issues.

Josephine Munthali, PhD, is a woman educationalist from both the western and Africa traditions. She played a significant role in setting up the Child Support Project which is a registered Charity in Scotland and supported disadvantaged children in Malawi. Furthermore, she raised the profile of Malawi through the Scotland Malawi Partnership Network and the Scottish Executive International Aid Fund for Malawi. She advocated for the right to education and poverty alleviation, for orphans and vulnerable children, to high profiled political leaders and policy makers internationally including the G8 Leaders spouses. She has over 10 years of experience in international development with a track record in strategic planning, organisational management and providing technical support and coordinating gender responsive programmes and research in Africa. She keeps track on recent trends particularly in girls' education through research and publications and presentations at international conferences.

Index

T

U

V

W

Y

Z

www.ingramcontent.com/pod-product-compliance
Lightning Source LLC
LaVergne TN
LVHW062145300926
849161LV00010B/2634
* 9 7 8 1 5 2 2 5 2 5 7 8 3 *